ELEMENTS OF SPACEMAKING

ELEMENTS OF SPACEMAKING

Yatin Pandya | **Vastu-Shilpa Foundation**
for Studies and Research in Environmental Design

Mapin Publishing

Reprinted in 2023 by
Mapin Publishing Pvt. Ltd
706 Kaivanna, Panchvati, Ellisbridge
Ahmedabad 380006 INDIA
T: +91 79 40 228 228 • F: +91 79 40 228 201
E: mapin@mapinpub.com • www.mapinpub.com

Research & Text: Yatin Pandya

Research associates & text support: Kishori Dalwadi, Dilip Karpoor, Ashka Naik

Assistance: Sharvey Dhongde, Sajid M. Saiyed, Munjal Bhatt, Rujuta Bhatt, Ranish Trivedi, Joseph Varughese

Sketches: Ashka Naik, Sujan Shrestha, Prachi Modi, Smitha G., Surat Mantoo

This research is done at and with the support of Vastu-Shilpa Foundation for Studies and Research in Enviroment Design, Ahmedabad.

Vastu-Shilpa Foundation for Studies and Research in Environmental Design
'Sangath', Thaltej Road,
Ahmedabad 380 054

ISBN: 978-81-89995-74-4

Edited by: Diana Romany / Mapin Editorial
Revised format edited by: Neha Manke / Mapin Editorial
Designed by: Gopal Limbad / Mapin Design Studio
Printed at Thomson Press (India) Ltd.

Contents

List of Illustrations

MISCELLANEOUS EXAMPLES

Preface

The dimension of space along with the dimension of time, constitutes the basis for conception and perception of the world as we experience it. The abstract notion of space is however physically perceivable in objects around us through the senses of sight, sound, touch, smell and taste. The three dimensions of length, breadth and height along with the fourth dimension of time give us a tangible framework to understand physical reality through relative comparisons and judgements of its component parts.

The notions of space are made physically manifest in architecture through the different elements that constitute the basic identifiable parts of the man made built environment. These elements are broadly classifiable as roof, walls, doors, windows, column, stairs and floors.

Each of these elements possess attributes inherent to their morphological construct which endow them with particular spatial properties, providing potential for their use and design in architectural compositions. They thus influence space and its experience, thereby orchestrating the perception of the built environment. For this, the elements rely almost entirely on their basic inherent spatial properties to which the additional overlays of stylisation, construction, rendering and treatment only add value.

Good architecture is a balanced composition of these elements and results from premeditated decisions in a synthesis of these parts to make a harmonised whole. Understanding the fundamental spatial and perceptual attributes of the elements in the 'space making kit' and their potentials for articulation and expression is critical to effective designing of space. Details like style, material, technique and construction become ancillary to the primary understanding of spatial attributes which remain universal and anthropocentric- relying solely on human perception and devoid of any contextual, cultural or regional conditioning.

This document examines the inherent qualities of these basic 'space-making' elements and analyses their characteristics to highlight their implicit influences in the design of space. This is a fundamental understanding of spatial elements and their nature- the primary attributes of the elements of space-making.

The document traces the linguistic origin of the terms/words associated with the elements through history as a basis to understand the most fundamental concepts, attributes or association the element possess and purpose for which they were developed.

It presents their basic anatomy for an understanding of the critical components of each element and associated terminology.

-Yatin Pandya

FLOOR

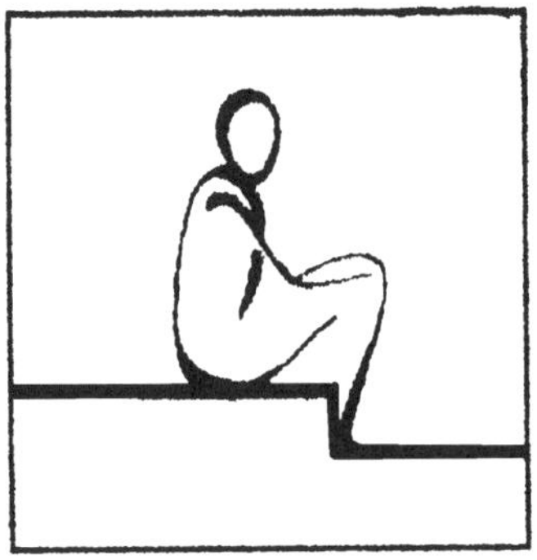

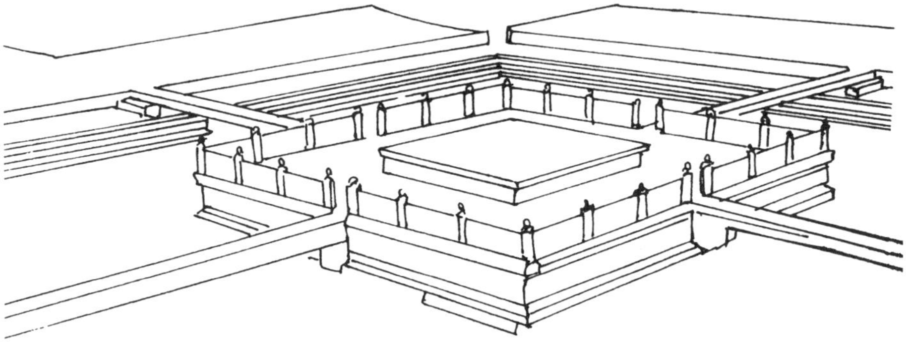

Anup Talao, Fatehpur Sikri

The floor is essentially a horizontal plane, providing a firm datum, a resting plane for all objects in that space. As the base plane, the floor is a single entity with references only to gravity, the 'downward' force. Where levels are involved, the relative positions of other base planes get perceived as 'above' or 'below' the reference plane. Originating from an Old High German word *fluor* meaning meadow, it refers to both plane and the ground. The Latin equivalent *planus* refers to it as levels while the Greek word *planasthai* means "to wander". The floor in modern German is referred to as *flur* or *fem* meaning field or plain. The floor assumes connotations to firmness, stability and repose—the physical substrate datum for buildings to and repose. The Sanskrit word for floor is *bhutal*, where *bhu* refers to the earth or ground. It also means, 'to exist', and *tal* refers to the bottom or base surface. Floor essentialy deliniates territory.

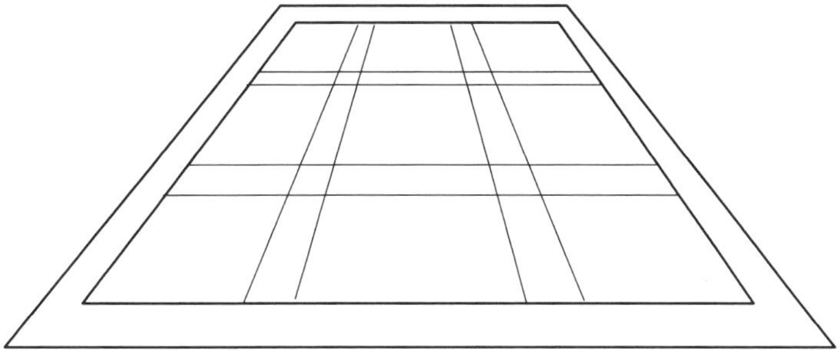

Typological Variations

Typology with respect to form................................

Unmodulated
Flat, level floors with no change or modulation form a single datum for all objects on it relating to the ground in the same manner.

Modulated
These floors take on different forms, undulating, sloped or rough, with a variation of levels within itself, define subspaces and each relates differently.

Typology with respect to material treatment................................

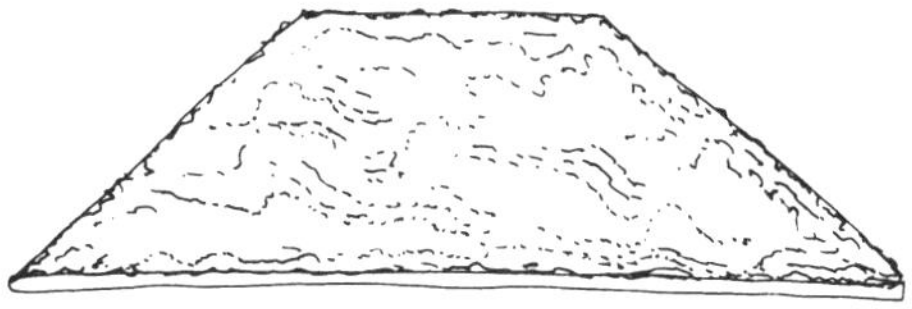

Natural
Floors with vegetation cover, soil, natural stone, sand, water, snow etc. denote natural ground with nature at the helm of its formation. Such treatments are used to create extensions to the vista provided by the constructed floor-space.

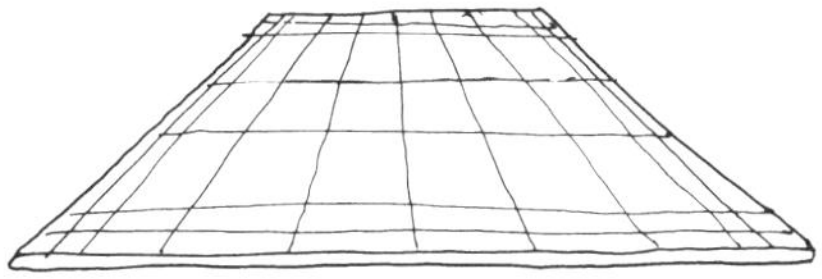

Man-made
Articulation, expression and design interventions to enhance the performance of floors through demarcation of extent, treatment against weathering, aiding circulation etc., involve the treatment of natural floors in a predetermined manner. These constitute constructed floors, which could use dressed stone, timber, ceramic, glass, concrete etc. as the surface finish.

Ever since human race started locomotion on two feet, maintaining the balance of the body became a criterion. A horizontal surface provides the most secure and stable surface for the human habitation. It is due to this reason that most of human development happened in the plains. Demarcation of domain was another aspect kept in mind for creation of captive, cleared out areas for private usage. Further definition came through the creation of level as plinth from the ground plane. The floor also passed through the characterization that every dwelling passes through after habitation.

Mythology, in most cultures, refers to a time when the world was completely covered with water—a flat plate or a swirling sphere. The land emerged from this primordial ocean, generating life, as we know it. Allusion to this is seen in the metaphorical depictions in churches of the early Christian era as well as Greek temples, where wave patterns in the flooring and marble veins are used to simulate ripples, translating such fantasy on to the floor.

Several Egyptian temples have the lower parts of walls painted with aquatic plants and the floors are embellished with zigzag line patterns denoting water. In some Indian temples too, at the external junctions of walls and floor, bands of decoration are found showing rippling waters, aquatic plants and grotesque monsters from the Netherworld—a reiteration of the connotation the floor had to an element emerging from the sea.

The land emerging from the primordial ocean, represented by the patterns of wave and grotesque figures

Aquatic creatures symbolic of the sea

'Symbolic Place', Bird-shaped altar for a fine sacrifice, Kerala

Imitation of water, temples of Greek and churches of Italy

Bhima on the ghats, Banaras

Modulating the surface in a natural way by scooping the surface

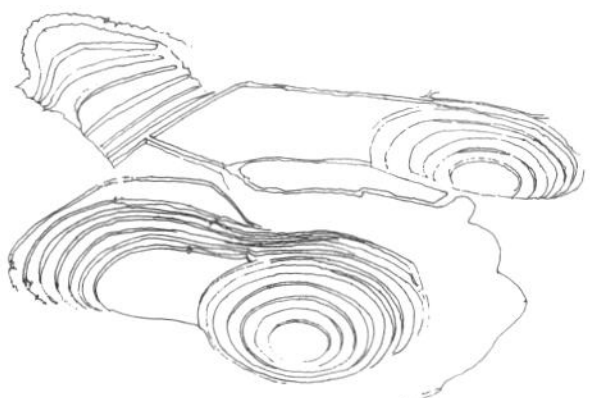

A Moray, Maras, Peru

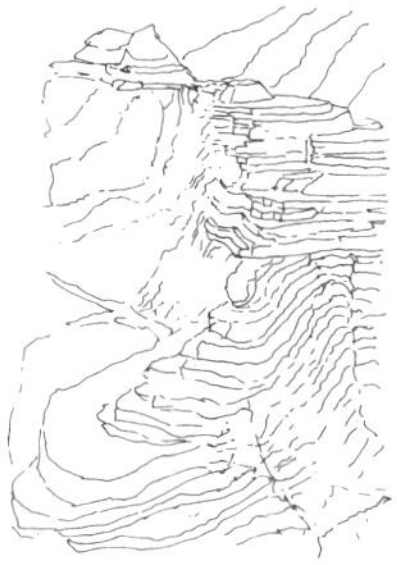

Rice fields, Philippines

Golden Temple, Amritsar

Different patterns guiding movement

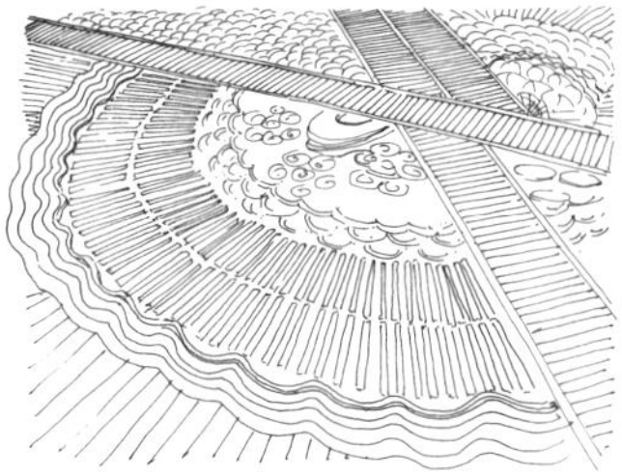

Kurakuen Garden, Japan

Shalimar Garden, Kashmir

HORIZONTALITY

As a treated surface created to provide a comfortable datum, the floor forms the base plane for any composition upon it. As flatness and horizontality are inherent attributes of the floor, they become an omnipresent reference, throughout the level, stretching the entire extent of the space. Minor undulations in the ground are taken care of by adjusting the level of the plinth ground plane to make it absolutely horizontal.

The floor distinctly defined in two dimensional plane as in X-axis and Z-axis............................

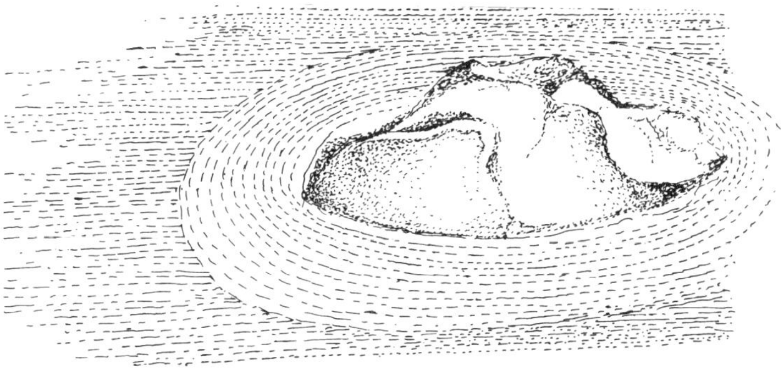

Floor distinctly emphasizing the horizontality, The Zen Garden, China

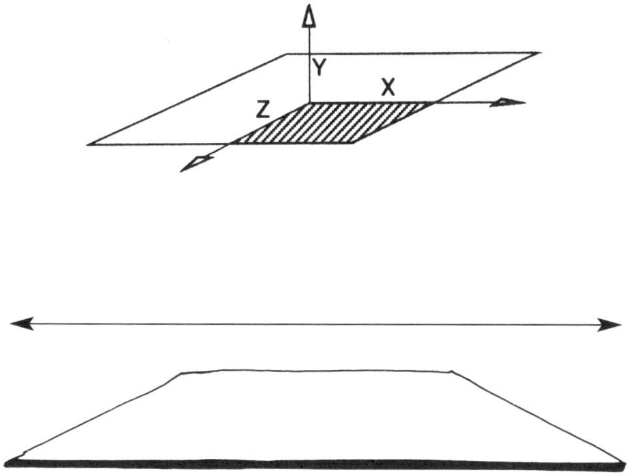

Outstretching floor plane acquiring its own vista

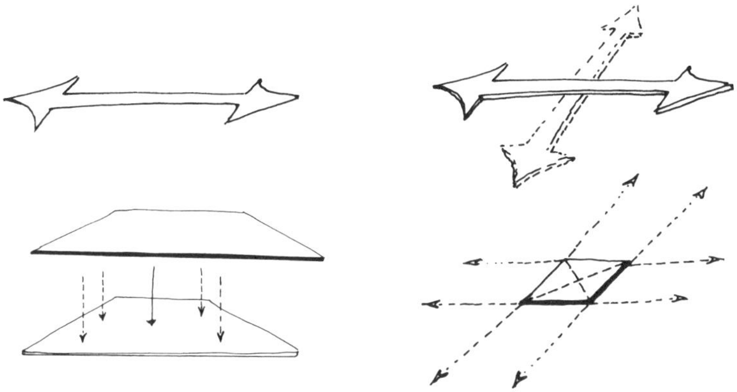

Multi-directional evolution accentuating in horizontal plane

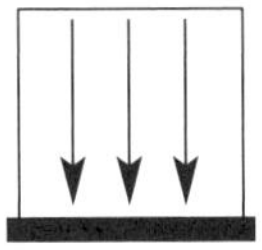

SUPPORT AND STABILITY

The horizontal ground plane, offering the perfect foil to gravity, induces into any object a state of repose—a state of equilibrium, where the object is at total rest. The floor, therefore, not only physically supports the composition, but it also brings about a semblance of balance. The floor has a much more pragmatic meaning, where one must be able to move around on it or place objects. It emphasizes our conception of the ground as something firm and immovable, conveying the feeling of solid footing. Gravity confers upon it a role linked to the idea of support. It is therefore, less manipulatable. It largely remains horizontal and flat in order to assure versatility and the possibility of movement, which gives the floor a stabilizing character, unifying different parts of space.

Floor volunteers to a sense of balance by maintaining the state of equilibrium

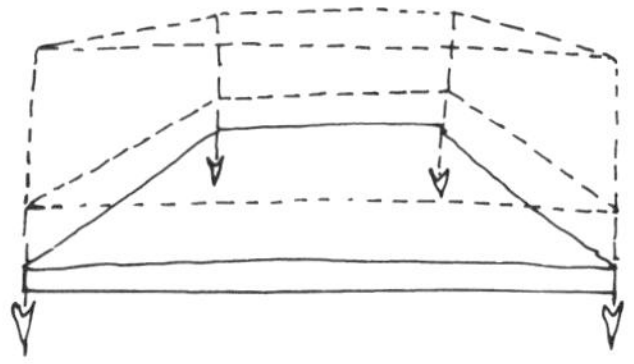

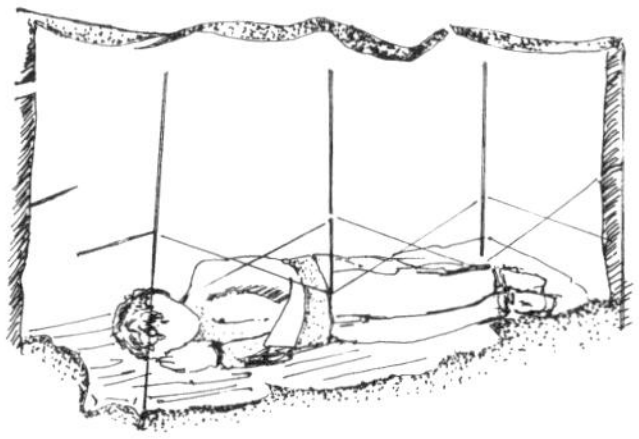

Gol Gumbaj, Bijapur

Floor giving gravity control for solid footing and a stabilized plane for movement

Cantilevered planes over the floor, Fallingwater, Pennsylvania

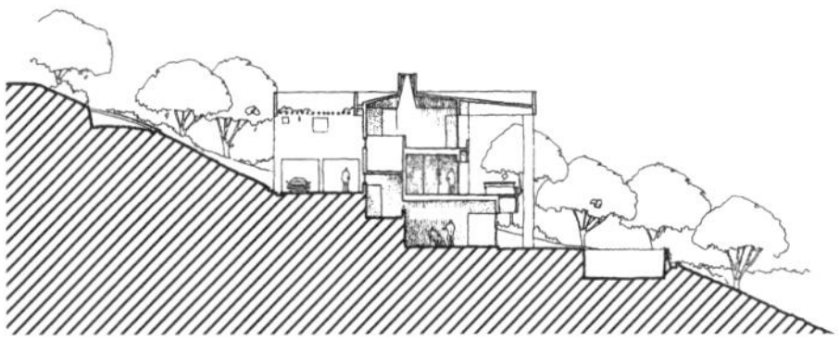

Bukit Cahaya, Kuala Lumpur, Malaysia

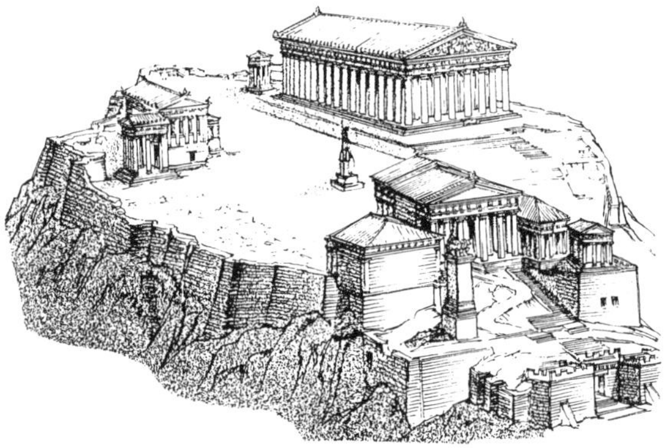

Acropolis of Athens, Greece

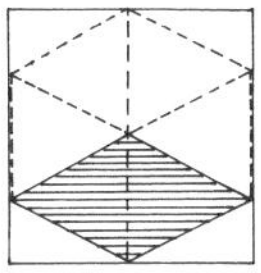

FLOOR FOR DEFINITION OF SPACE

A perceptible change in the flooring strongly delineates and demarcates a difference in the zone. Flooring materials are perceived differently through their colour, textural rendering, finishes, grain structure, base material etc. For example, naturally occurring materials like stone, mud and grass register differently, each defining its own extent and boundary. This property helps articulate and define the boundaries of space by merely expressing their extent in a graphical manner on a two dimensional footprint. Apart from floor finish even its modulation as elevations and depressions help in creating subspaces through their mutual references, wherein each level registers itself as a distinct space. Accessories such as rugs, dhurries, carpets etc. when placed on an otherwise level floor, become an extension of it and help in delineating that much space for a different function through a change in texture.

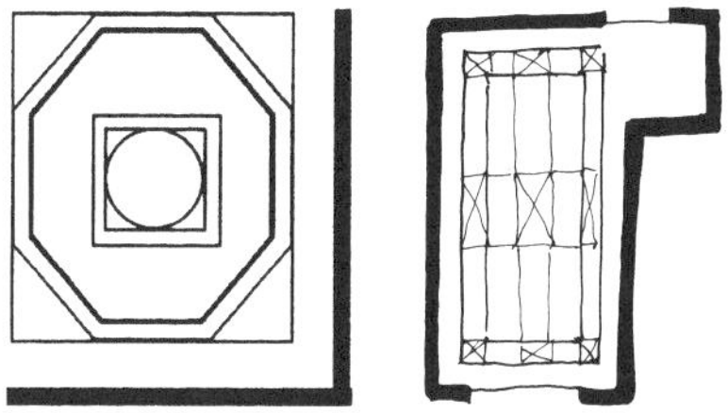

Floor defining the zones within a space

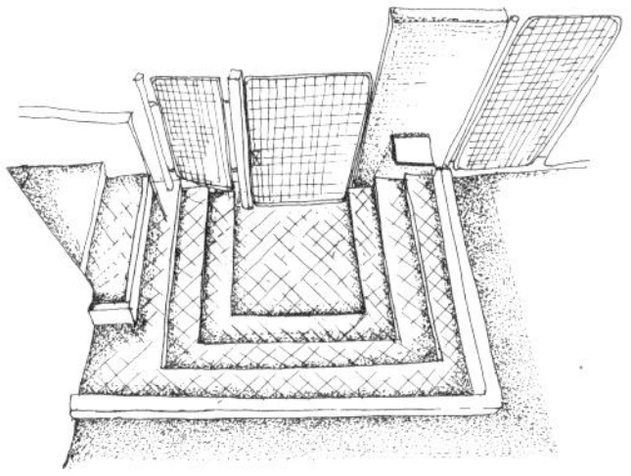

Glazed texture finish defining the entry, house in Tokyo

Spaces made conspicuous by various expressions...

Carved marble flooring, Lotus Fountain, Red Fort, Delhi

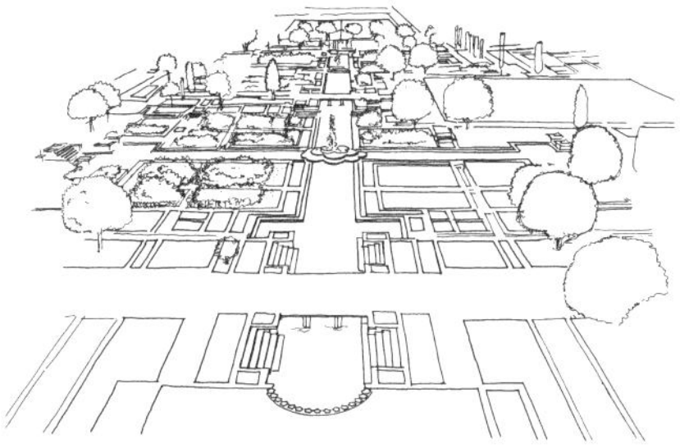

Mughal Gardens, Rashtrapati Bhavan, New Delhi

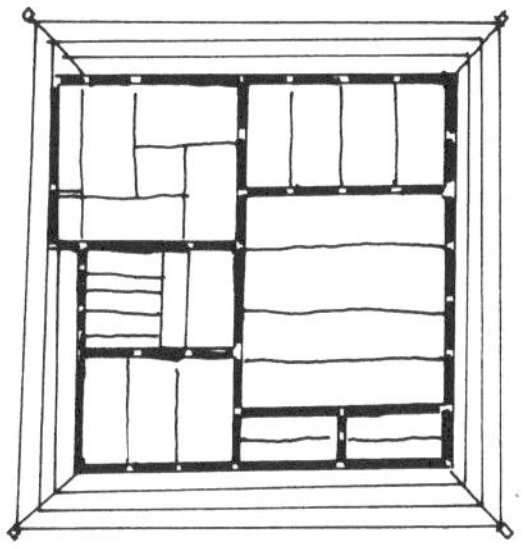

Plan,Togudo, Kyoto

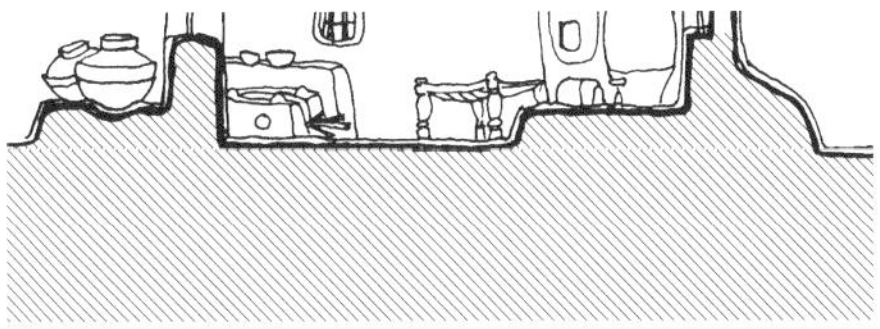

Plane modulated to satisfy different utilitarian functions within the unit, part section of Bhunga house, Kutch

DATUM AND REFERENCE

Due to its flatness floor automatically provides a reference to all the elements that come above it or below it. Within itself it again provides a visual reference plane for the various components of a composition. This aspect of common reference makes it the datum, the unifying base factor in the organization of space, which binds the individual parts through its omnipresence. This aspect is often explored through the plinth element upon which objects/buildings sit. The plinth ties up the independent structures through the contiguity of horizontal planes.

Floor as a horizontal plane.............................

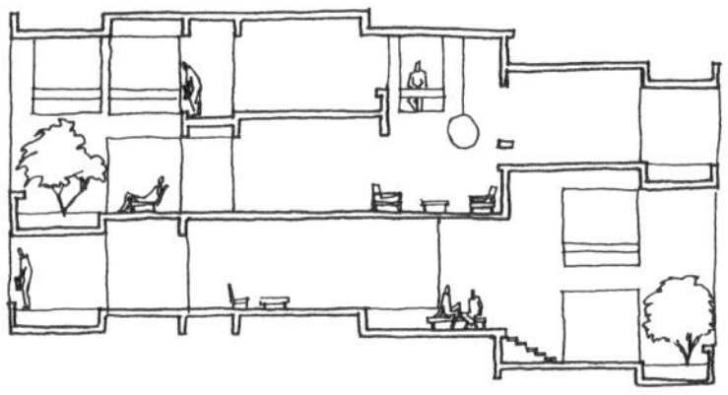

Section of split levels
Kanchanjunga Flats, Mumbai

Floor becomes an ultimate reference node, ensembling the spaces together enhanced in different ways

Floor emerging from beneath

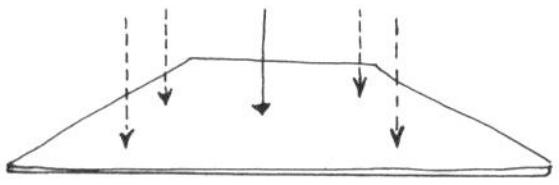

Nehru Pavilion, New Delhi

Kundi—an underground watertank

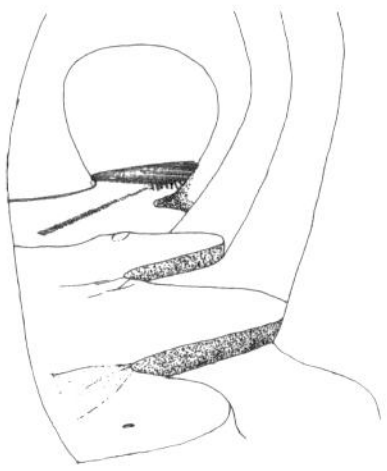

Amdavad ni Gufa, Ahmedabad

Floor as plinth...

Plinth connecting independent structure,
Bhunga cluster plan, Kutch

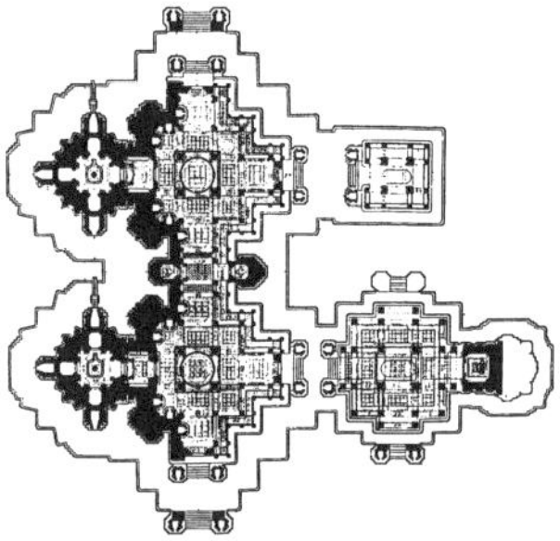

Plinth connecting two temples
Hoysaleswara Temple, Halebeed

Panch Mahal, Fatehpur Sikri

Tholos at Delphi, Greece

FLOORING AS MOVEMENT GUIDE

The floor being the datum upon which all movement of both persons and goods takes place, it can be effectively used to accentuate movement patterns. This can be achieved by creation of guiding lines through articulations in shapes, levels, or surface differentiation by explorations in different materials, colours or even textures. Floor patterns are often used to punctuate pauses, emphasise movement directions or plainly to generate a 'place' through continuous texture.

By variations in level and surface of the horizontal plane, movement pattern is generated

Daitokuji Temple, Kyoto

Katsura Palace, Kyoto

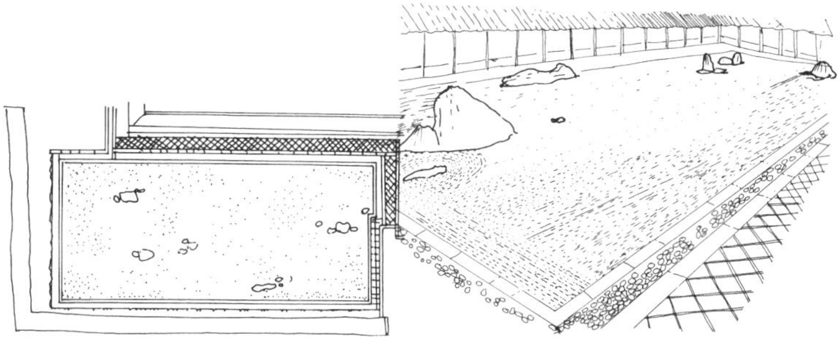

Ryoanji Temple Garden, Kyoto

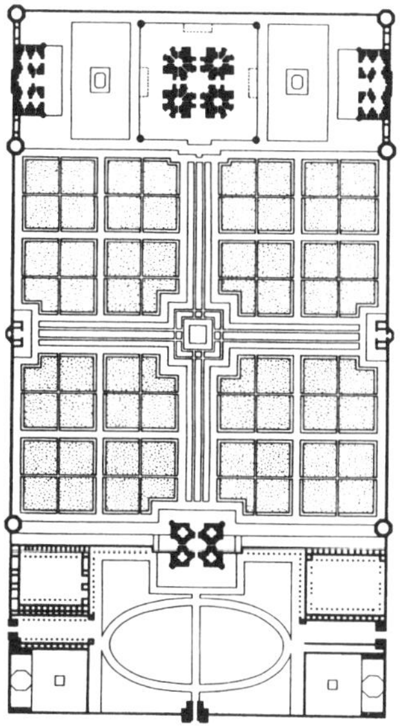

Plan, Mughal Gardens,Taj Mahal, Agra

Mughal Garden, Red Fort, Delhi

Piazza Ducale, Vigevano

FLOOR TO EXPRESS THRESHOLD

Floor as platform or plinth, upon the ground surface, defines space. As prelude to the next spatial sequence, it signifies a threshold and offers a transition from ambiguous surrounding to contained volumes. The threshold is also sometimes hinted at through raising the floor plane by a small interval and again lowering it. The act of crossing this raised level induces a sense of crossover between spaces in an otherwise uniformly treated floor space. The aspect of space definition and demarcation through pattern also helps signify the floor as a prelude to the threshold to different realms. In such cases where the movement path is perpendicular to the entry into the next space, the flooring takes a pattern, which differentiates it and demarcates the spot, upon reaching where the next entry sequence is revealed.

A transition into different realms is distinctly identified in the floor

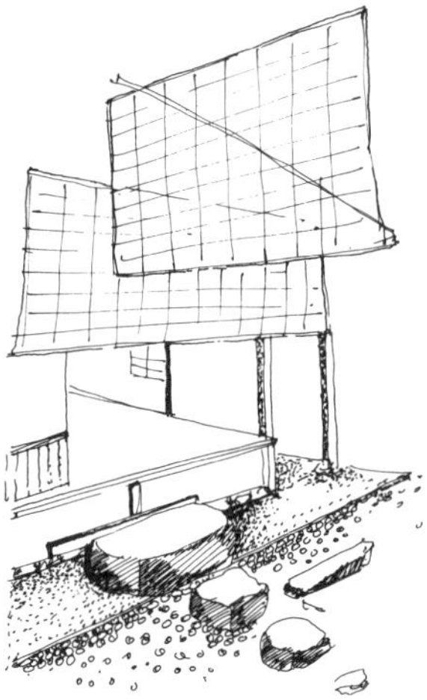

Stones approaching the entrance defining the threshold of a house, Kyoto

Traditional Tatami flooring in the interior of a house, Kyoto

Texture and level change denote threshold

Series of flat stepping-stones in a house, Osaka

Elevated floor defining threshold, Franceworth House, Illinois

Bhunga houses, Kutch

FLOOR FOR COMMUNICATION

As the horizontal base plane, floors are walked over and this horizontality makes them pragmatic. The basic functional needs demand constant visual reference to this plane underfoot. This provides the floor with a high potential for superimposing motifs, signs and symbols as they surely and effectively get registered. Thus, floors can effectively communicate metaphysical messages while retaining its practical nature. Rangoli done by women in India on floor plane near entrance, patterns and motifs inlaid in floor are commonly exercised forms of floor renderings for auspicious purposes.

Water channels carved out decoratively, serving the dual purpose of supplying water and of an aesthetic expression

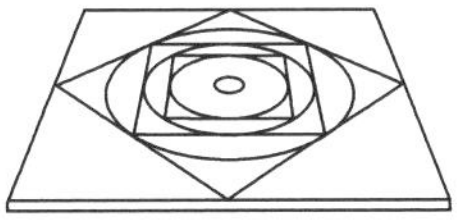

Rangoli

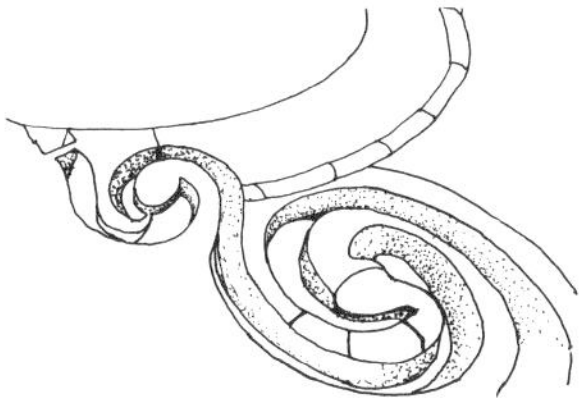

Water channel at Jahaz Mahal, Mandu

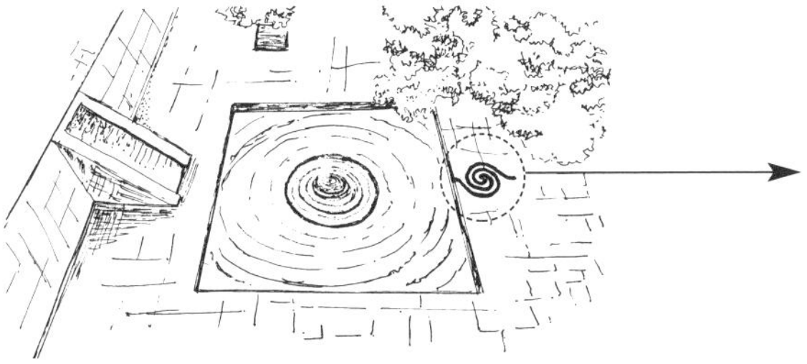

Nilkantha Temple, Mandu

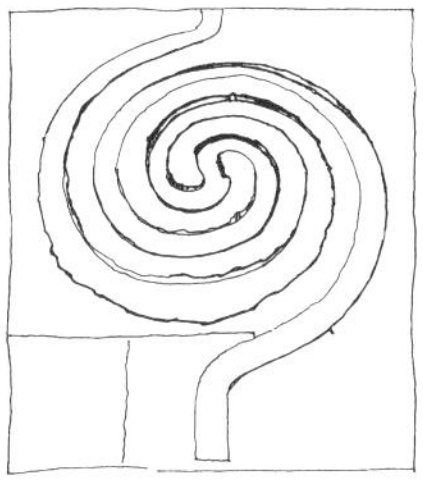

Detail of the water channel

Superimposing motifs, signs and symbols to welcome and to reflect individual identification

The maze at Chartres Cathedral, France

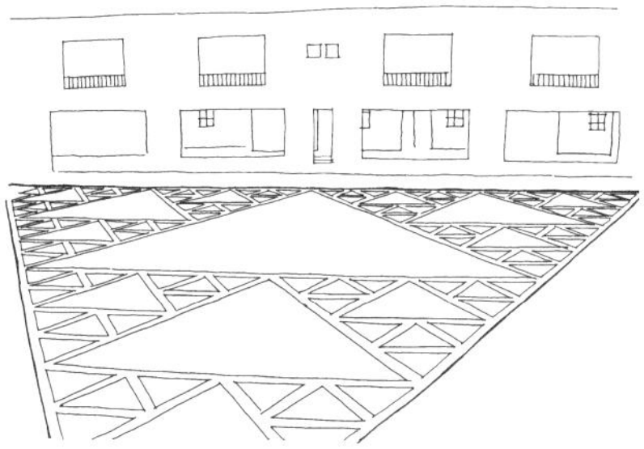

IUCAA, Pune

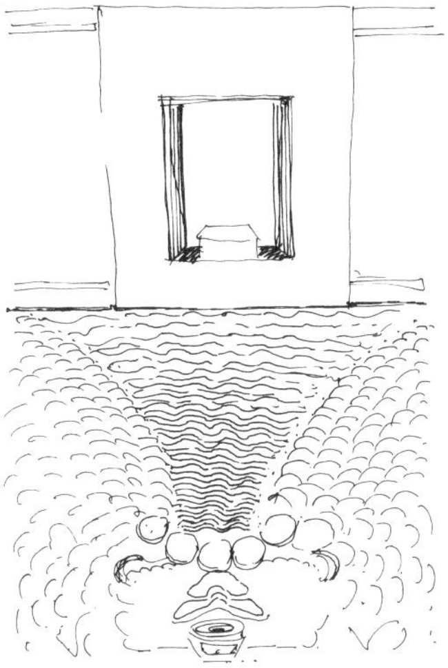

Motifs of dragon depicted in garden pavement in a house, Kurakuen, Japan

SANGATH, AHMEDABAD

Sangath, architect Balkrishna Doshi's studio, was built in 1979-80. The entire ensemble has an organicity and contiguity through the modulation of the landscape. The exterior landscape slowly merges up with the vaults creating a harmonious earth form. The entire journey from the entry to the campus to the entry into the structure is a phantasmagoria of nuances and hints. The flooring plays a vital role in giving directionality and inducing notions. Patterns, textures and semiotics are used extensively to demarcate movement flow. Placement position and typology of the vegetation adds to the attribute of floors in creating a harmonious continuity.

Floor modulating to create spaces subspaces

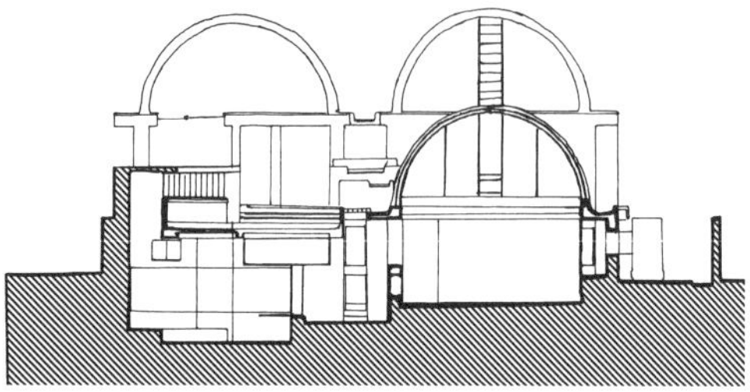

The entire building is partially sunk in the ground, becoming the referential floor plane enhancing the definition of space. The eye level from within meets the ground outside

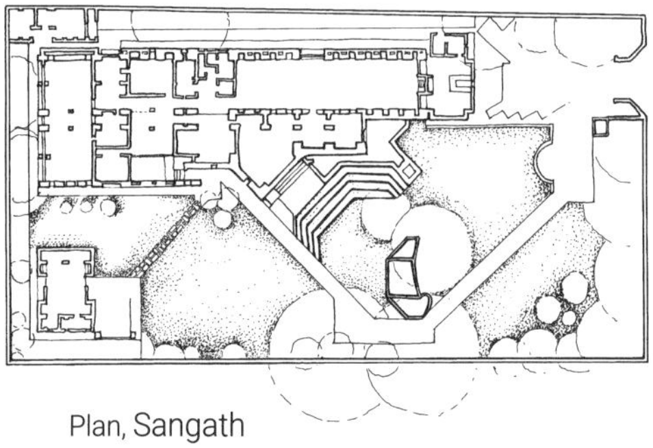

Plan, Sangath

Floor streching out horizontally

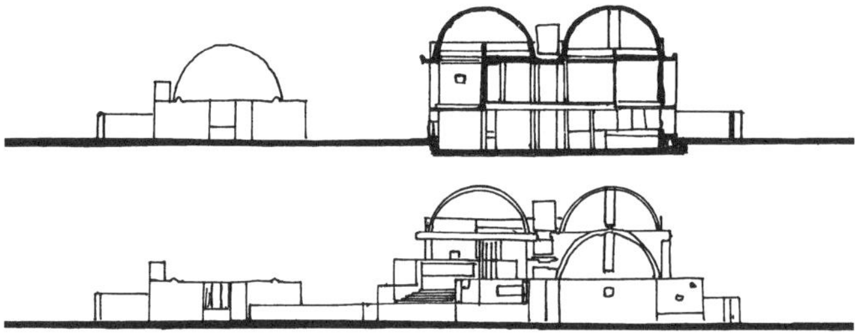

Floor as datum and reference

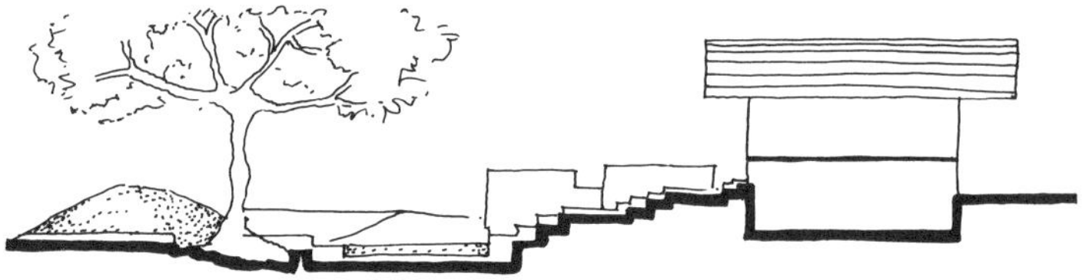

Modulation of floor plane creating diverse functional spaces like amphitheatres, mounds, ponds etc.

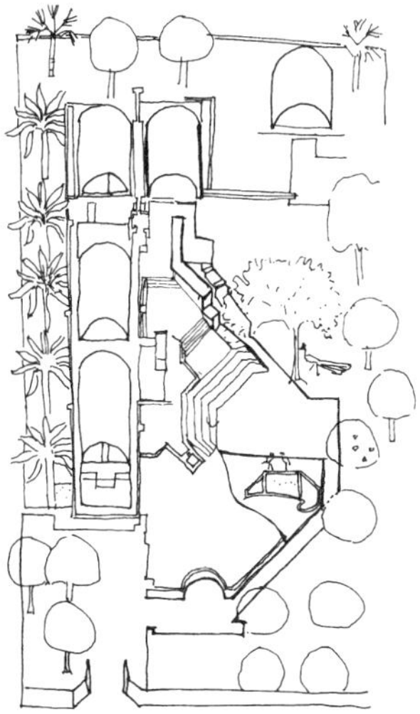

Floor looses its passiveness of just being a horizontal plane by creating various referential points and contributing to the overall context of spacemaking

Floor as defining sequence of pause and movement

Floor is a composition of myriad textures and materiality in accord to the natural habitat surrounding it

Floor as an element connecting and binding landscape with the built space

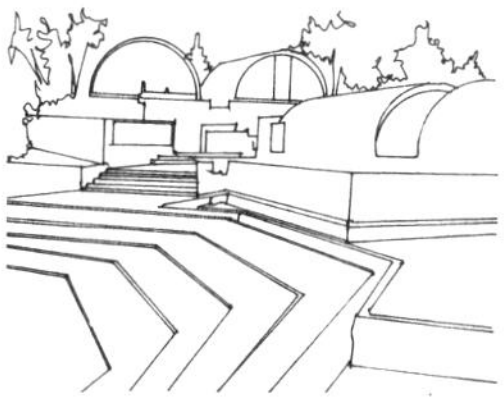

Gradual ascending of the floor planes create a series of levels formalizing the space for gathering, becoming an amphitheatre

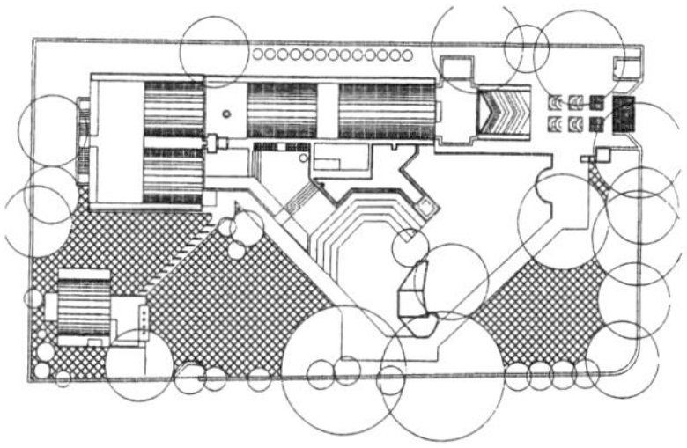

The flooring pattern in the exterior landscaping becomes a guiding element and defines a clear movement axis throughout the site

Floor as a communicator

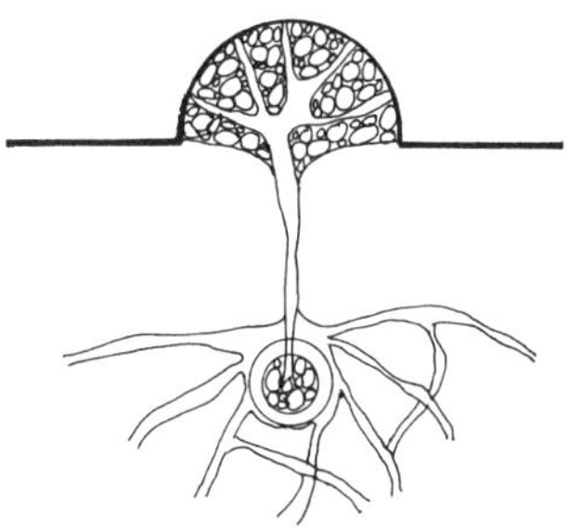

Floor as a communicative element with natural iconography

ROYAL COMPLEX OF FATEHPUR SIKRI

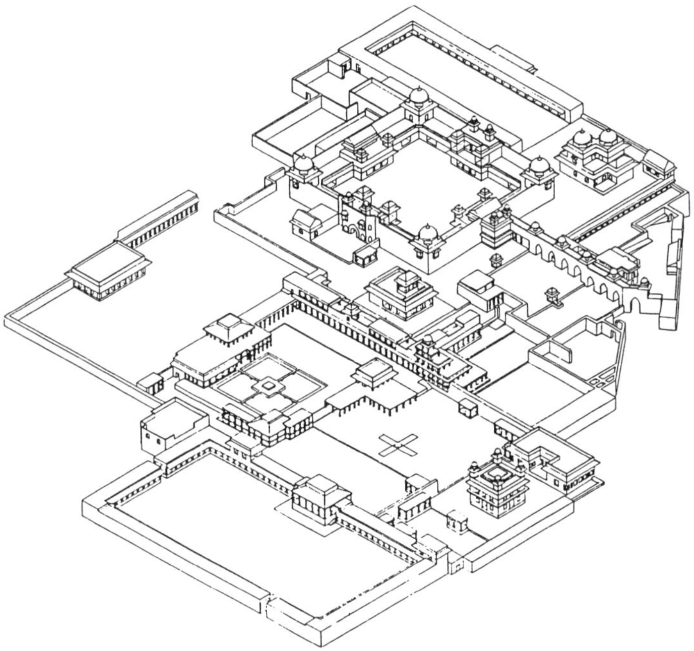

Floor plane for one level becomes a roof for the one below, expanding horizontally as it approaches the ground plane

Mughal emperor Akbar conceived and built this royal complex between 1571 and 1585. It was built upon a hill but the top was flattened out to create this horizontally spread out citadel. Spaces were demarcated through level differences and plane punctured walls. The labyrinthine structure is woven together only through the contiguity of the floor plane. The floor plane and the structures are symbiotic and each accentuates the other mutually. The roofs created by the built masses generate floors for a different level. The Panch Mahal structure with its open colonnaded frame structure collects the space vertically, unifying individual parts making it a pivotal reference point upon which the emperor would sit. Other modulations such as depressions and plinths help in creating sub-identities within the spaces.

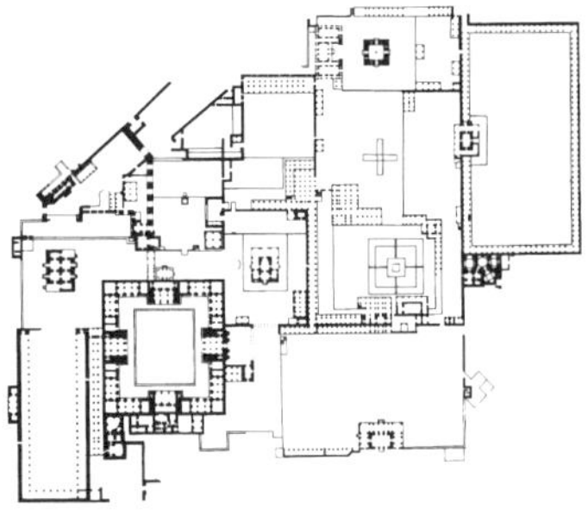

Plan

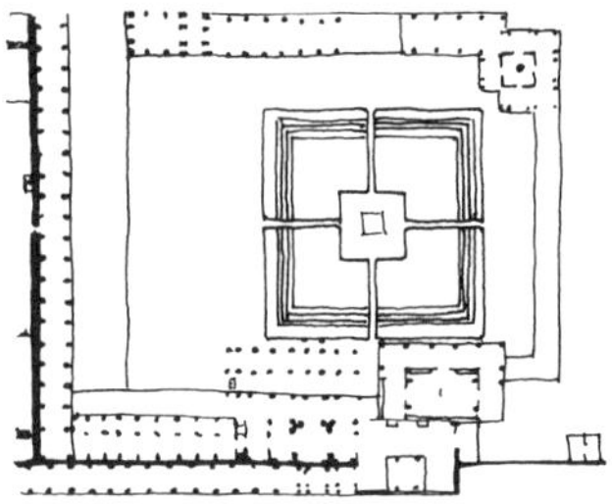

Part plan-Anoop Talao (pool)

Floor as a datum and reference

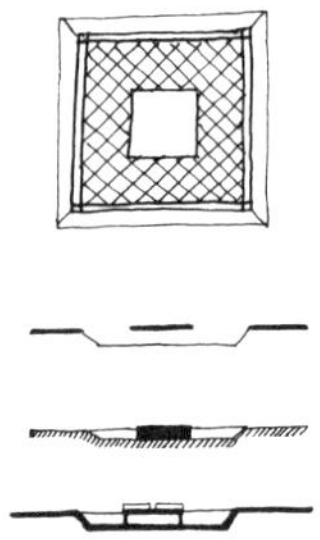

Floor defining the movement guide

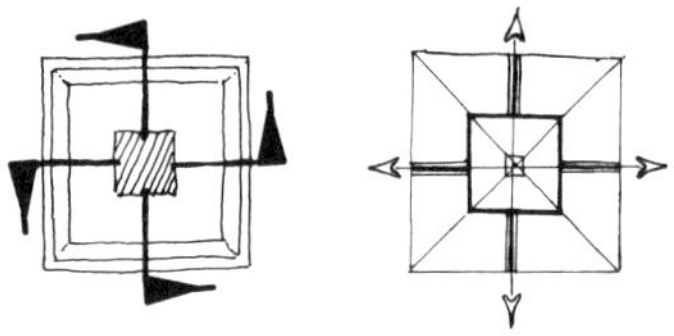

Detached floor becomes the focus creating a strong movement pattern around

Floor as a communicator

Floor symbolizes the royal game of *Chaupat*

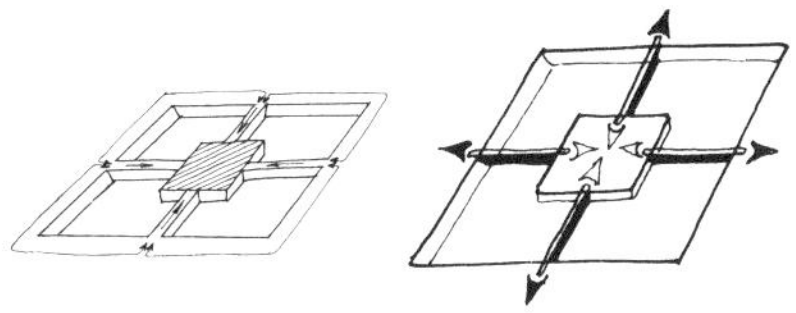

The independence of the detached floor asserts the multidirectional relationship with the surrounding spaces

Floor as a space-definer

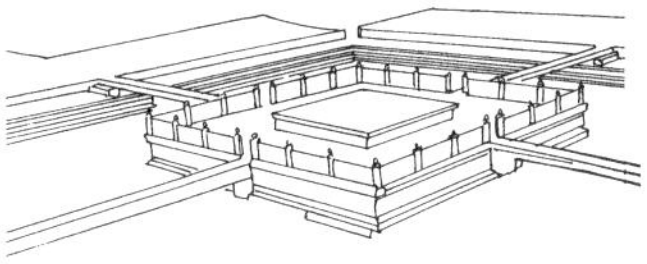

Level difference becomes an attribute of demarcation

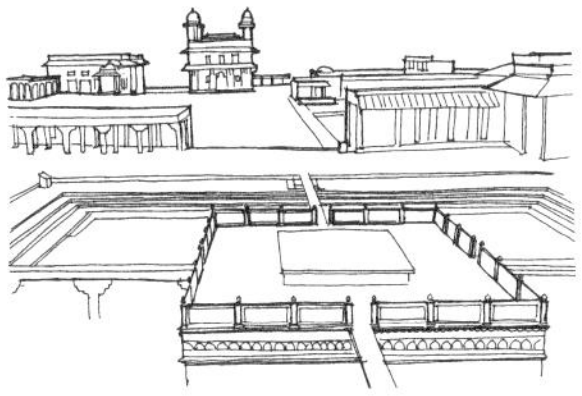

Water gains a spatial definition by its natural quality and becomes a conspicuous element

The plinth becomes a receiving plane to the building

Floor defining spaces at different levels

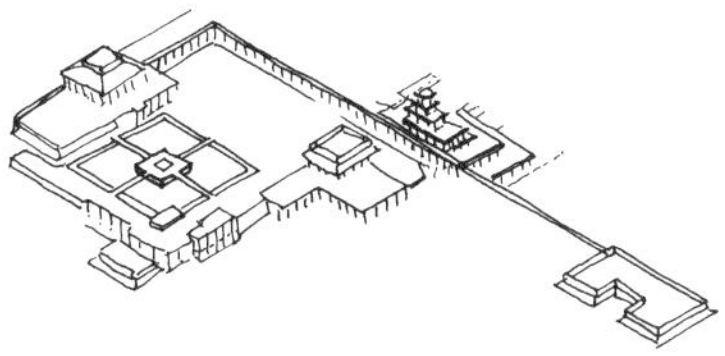

The spaces are derived by the planar relationships on different levels

Floors as horizontal planes

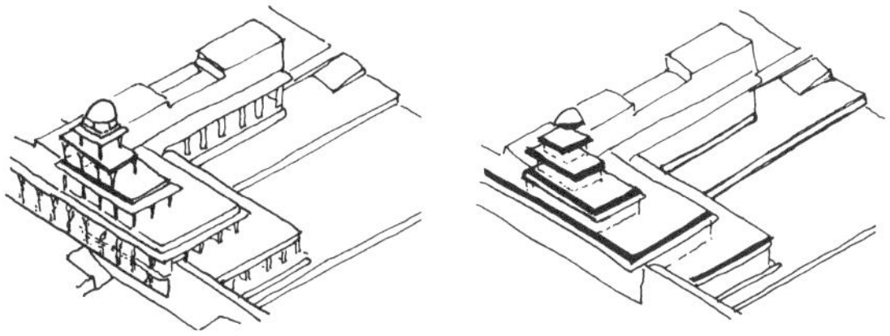

Strong physical links are established with extending floor planes to the detached planes creating axial concentric movement

Floors as layers

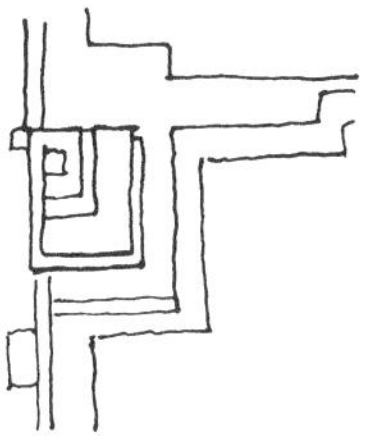

Floor as a plinth, receiving buiding in totality

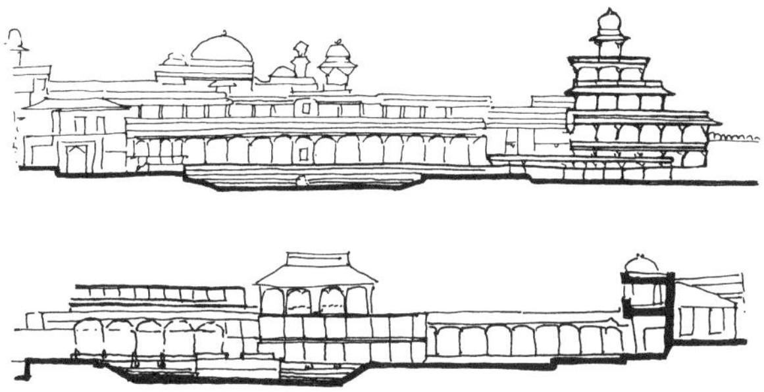

Floor planes establish a hierarchy of spaces in the vertical axis

Floor decreasing in its expanse as it is layered on top of the other creating semicovered and open spaces

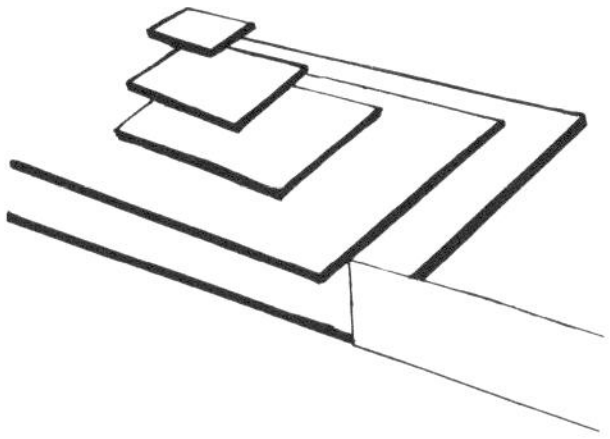

The sequential layering of planes reflect a growth of built mass

Floor as a datum and reference

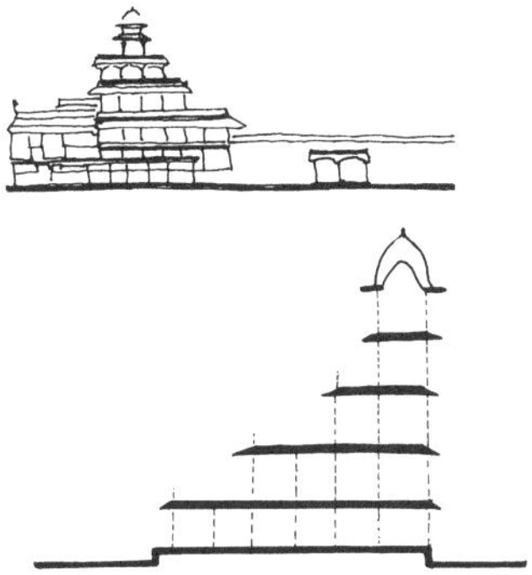

Part section, Panch Mahal

FALLINGWATER, PENNSYLVANIA

Architect Frank Lloyd Wright designed Fallingwater or Kaufmann Residence at Pennsylvania in 1936-39. Terraces working as extended balcony planes emphasize strong horizontality here. The siting of the structure is upon the bedrock. The usage of the same rocks for the flooring inside increases the feeling of connectivity to the surroundings. The openings on all the sides allow the floors to spread out and intersperse with the greenery around. At the central hearth, an original piece of rock pierces through the flooring emphasizing itself. A stairway as plain horizontal levels descends into the calm and flat plunge pool as if the surface of the water were another floor to descend into. Other terraces and modulations create a hierarchy of semi-covered and open spaces.

Floor as planes

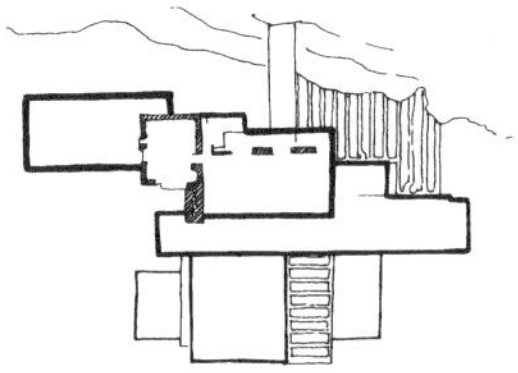

Plan

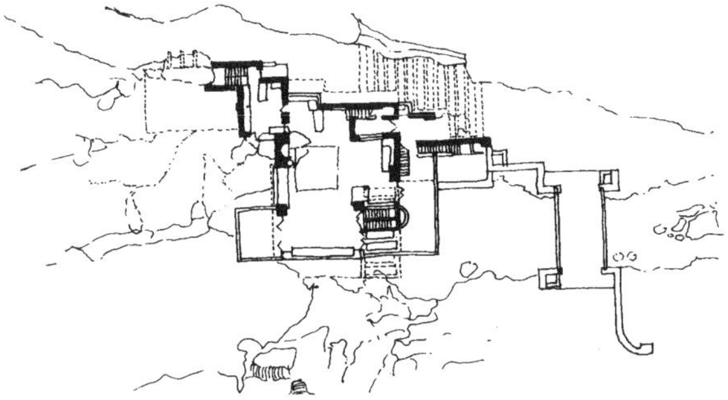

Site plan-built to the unbuilt

The stratification of planes collaborates the nature's order of evolution

Entire space conceived in the landscape as an integrate part of the environment

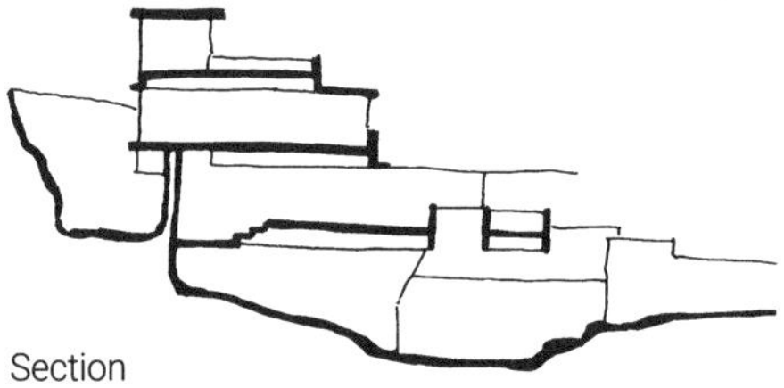

Section

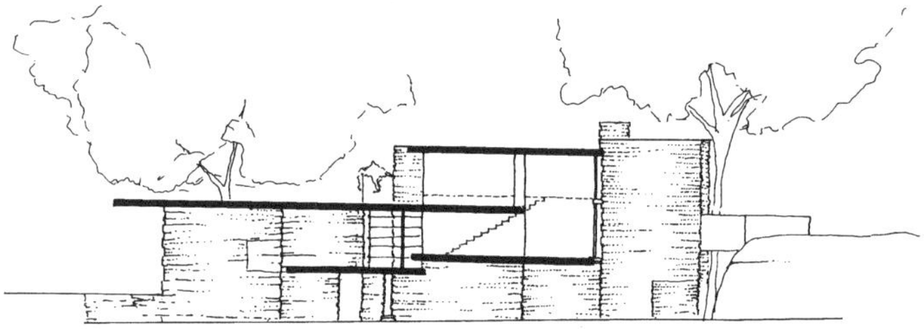

The subtle formalization of floor complements the contextual starkness and purity of the landscape

The floor planes become extensions of the landscape elements creating a homogeneity with the environment

Floor becomes an element communicating its coherence with nature..

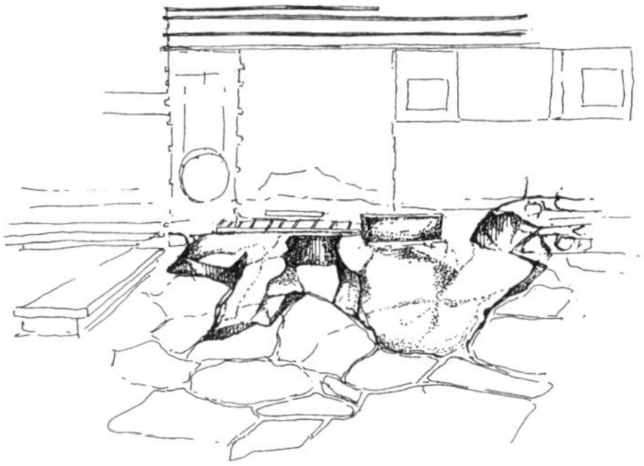

The treatments of floor reflect continuity between inside and outside by dissolving the strong boundaries of these two realms

Floor as a datum and reference

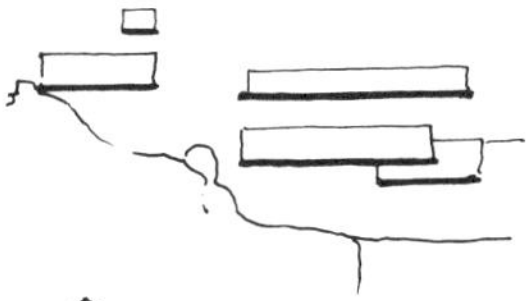

Floor enhancing the all pervasive natural richness of water and stone

Floor as a movement guide

Floor defining spaces of myriad characteristics

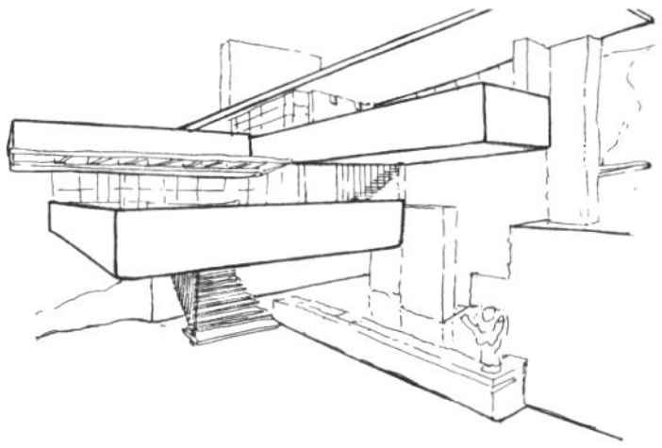

Floors with their ambiguous spatial roles define spaces above and below their expanse

The demarcations of spaces occur with the juxtaposition of floor planes

Sense of unity is achieved by the relationship of planes and their reciprocal actions to the natural plane of reference

HOUSES AT JAISALMER, RAJASTHAN

Climatically, Jaisalmer is a hot and dry region. The houses here are, thus, articulated to suit such a climate. The dwelling units themselves occupy a small footprint and are mostly used as storage and for spending the afternoon hours. The daytime is hot but the evenings and nights are pleasant. Most of the activities during these times are carried out collectively outside the house on the plinth. The raised floor plinth plays a vital role of defining the extent of a cluster or a house in different ways. The threshold here is defined by a raised level and decoration of the entrance by rangoli (ritualistic patterns created by coloured powder pigments). The cooking place within the unit is molded out of the floor itself, thus it again superimposes its pragmatic meaning of communication with utilitarian idea. The short dwelling units have a flat roof which form utilitarian level for the upper floor. The courtyard and its modulations within the dwellings generate a hierarchy within the same cluster.

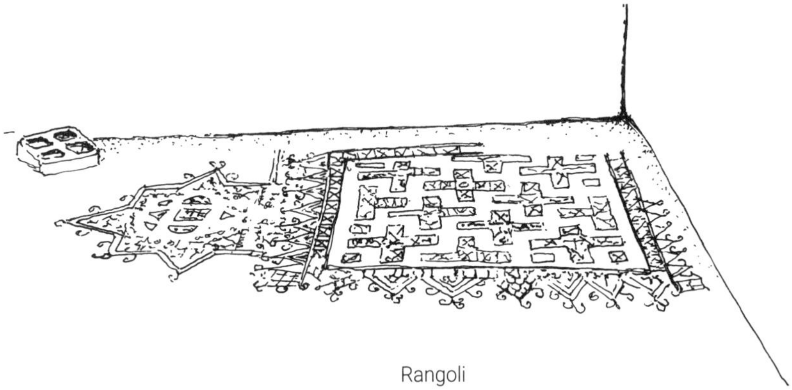

Rangoli

Floor as datum and reference

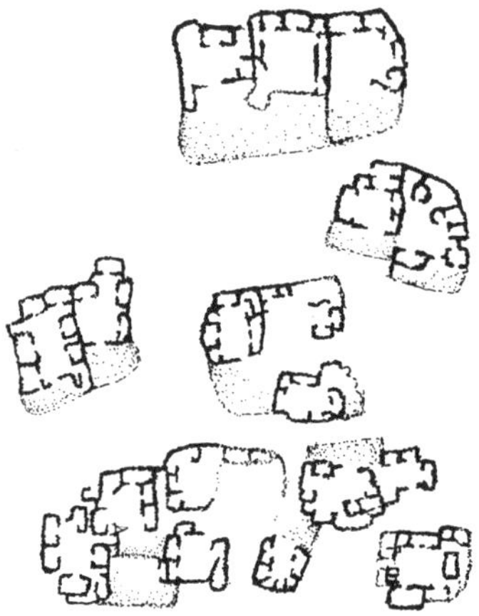

Part cluster plan

Floor connecting spaces and receiving the built space

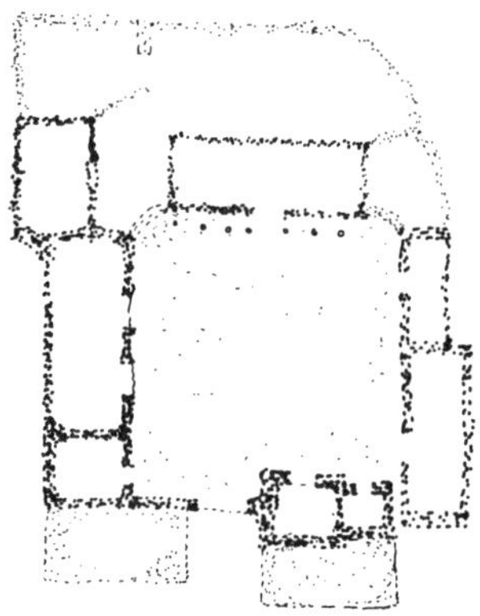

Unit plan- floor demarcating the levels of privacy within the unit, by raised plinth

Floor for support and stability

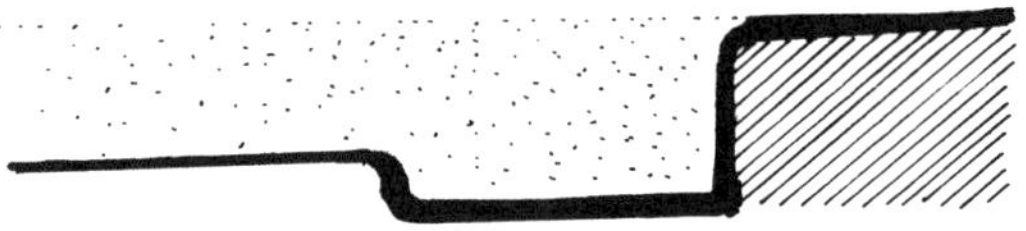

Units are totally submerged in the ground, where terraces become the ground itself, thus protecting the unit from high wind flow

Floor modulating for different fuctions

Terraces, courtyards and ground level become coherent within the same plane notionally

Floorforcommunication

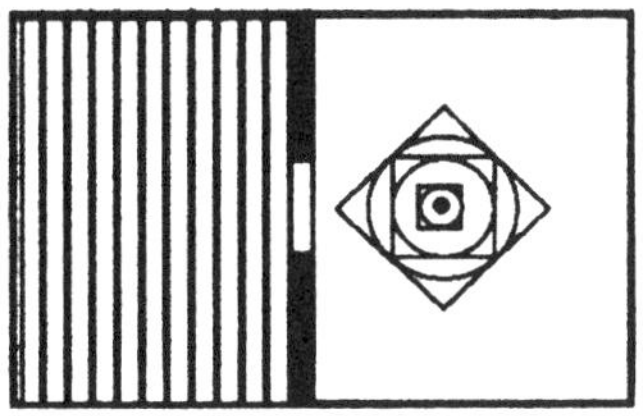

Rangoli on the floor as an expression of threshold, making the entrance identifiable and inviting, from the alien and homogenous space outside

Personal identification is achieved through personalized decorations of shapes, symbols and motifs

Floor defining space

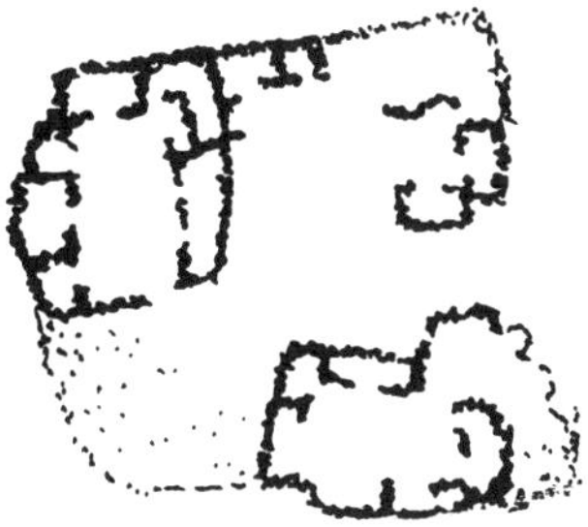

The auspicious space, demarcated by motifs on floor

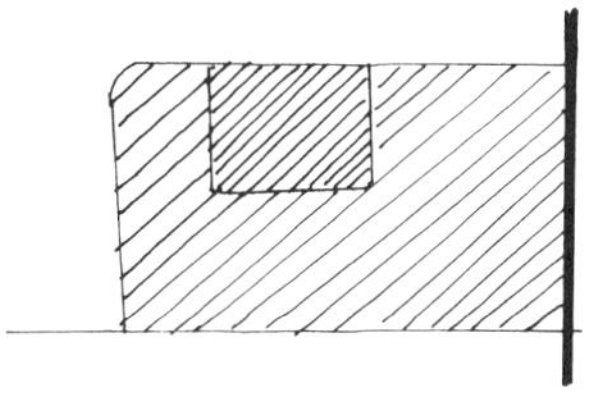

Space elevated from the floor thus serving the utilitarian need

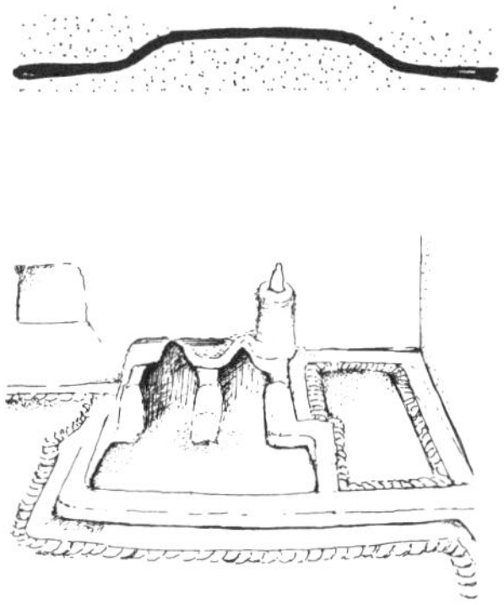

Kitchen space, a platform modulated smoothly out of the mud floor itself

- The floor must convey a notion of support, stability, firmness and repose.

- The floor fundamentally defines territories. The interface between datum plane, the plinth and the surrounding ground can dictate the relationship of superstructure with ground which is pragmatic as one has to move on it. Hence slightest modulation to it, by way of slope or level change can register effectively. This feature can be exploited to achieve desired impact. Elevated floor or the floors distnct from the circulation zones afford dignity and sanctity.

- The floor receives visual attention as one has to walk on it. Hence, it can be overlaid with visual clues (pattern, texture etc.) for impact and communication.

- Being the element connecting the superstructure to the ground/earth, the floor becomes a platform for the perception of all that is conceived above and around it. It should thus provide a base and foreground to all the other elements.

- Floors can effectively double up as surfaces to sit on or conduct activities. Appropriate floor levels, their rendering and softness can conveniently accommodate such opportunities.

- As floor is one of the few architectural elements that surely involves perception through touch, textural rendering, material variations and its gradient can be creatively exploited to enhance the experience and the perception of space.

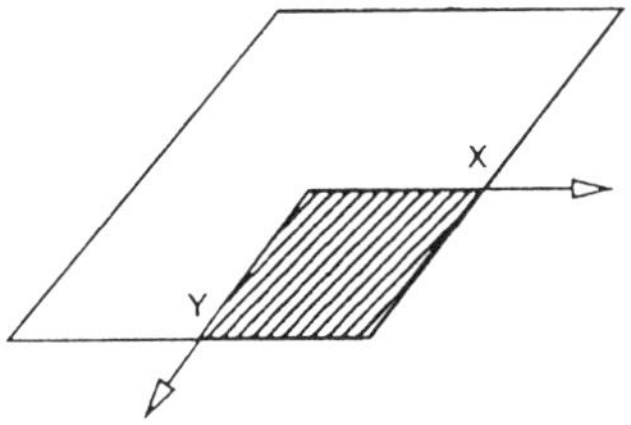

Floor as a reference on X and Y axes

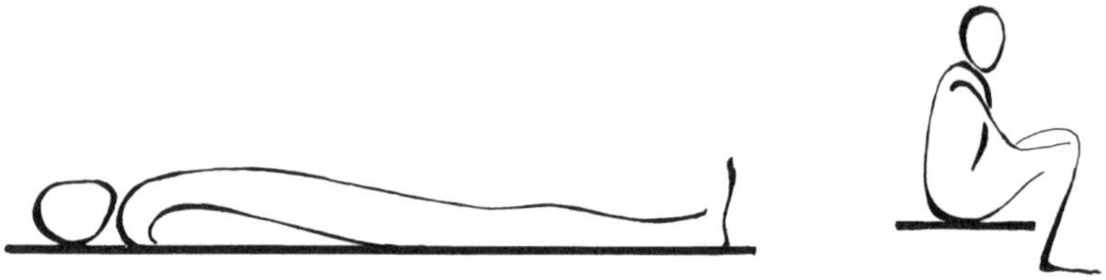

Floor having support and stability in its very conceptual translation

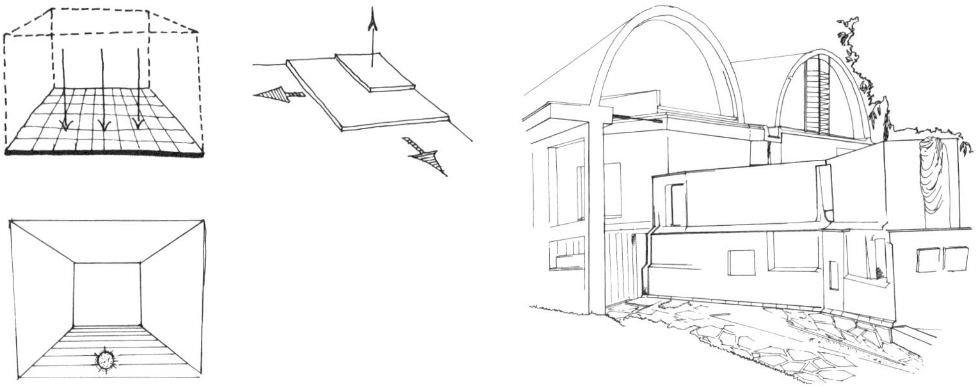

Floor as datum to all elements

Floor modulation defining different zones of circulation

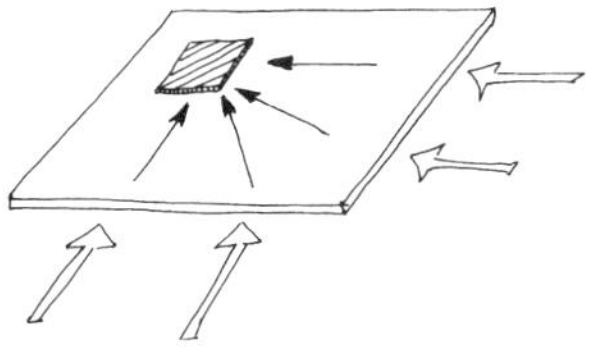

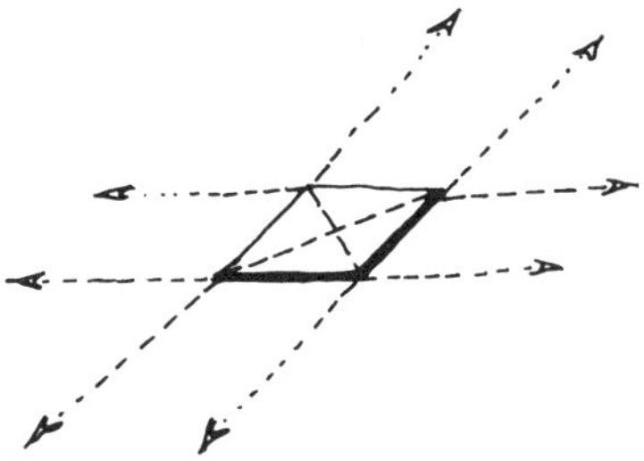

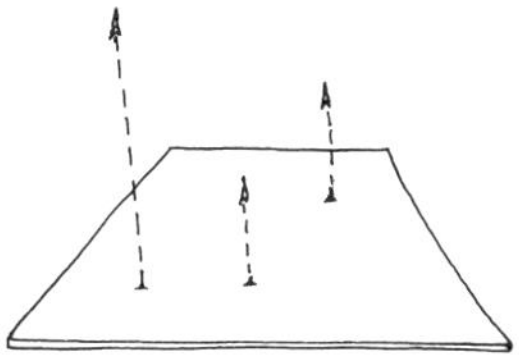

Floor as superstructure to the ground/earth

Floor as backdrop for other elements

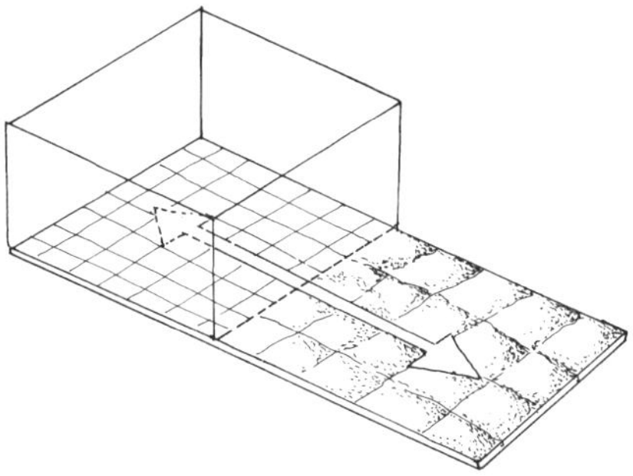

Floor for communication through textural variation

Floor adding to dignity and
sanctity of the space

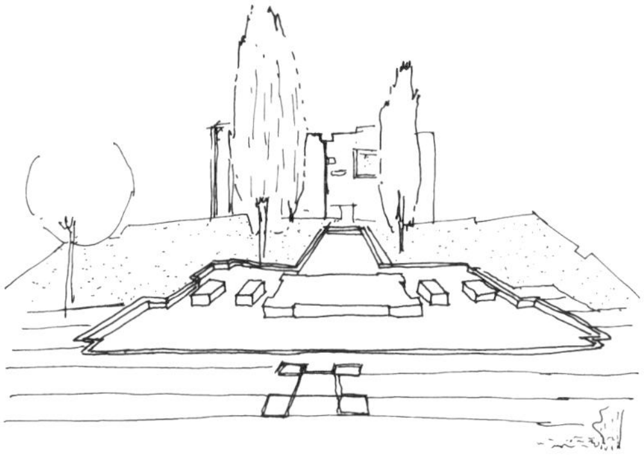

Floor modulating to make a visual impact

I

COLUMN

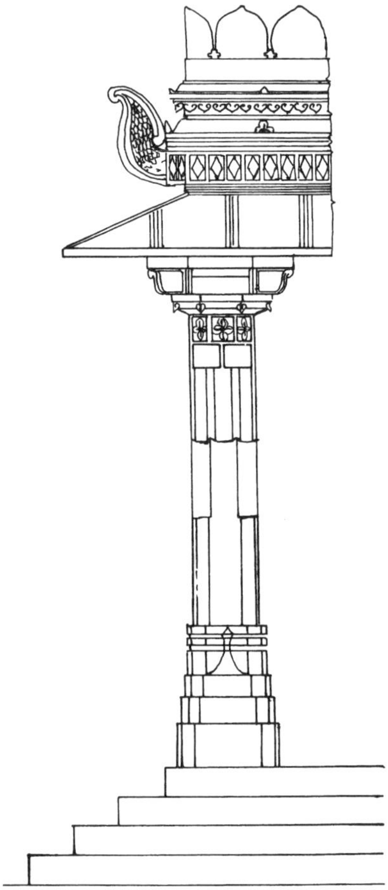

Column detail at Sarkhej Roza, Ahmedabad

A column is essentially a slender, vertical supporting element, loaded from the top and transferring the load axially to the base. It is free-standing except for the structure above it and the anchorage at the base. The term 'column' is derived from Middle English. In old French it is stated as *columpne*. In Latin it is *columna* which means pillar. Latin *columna* was a collateral form of *columen*, *culmen* as elevated object or pillar. A similar word *celsus* is a parallel of 'high' or 'lofty'. The Sanskrit equivalent for the word column is *stambh*.

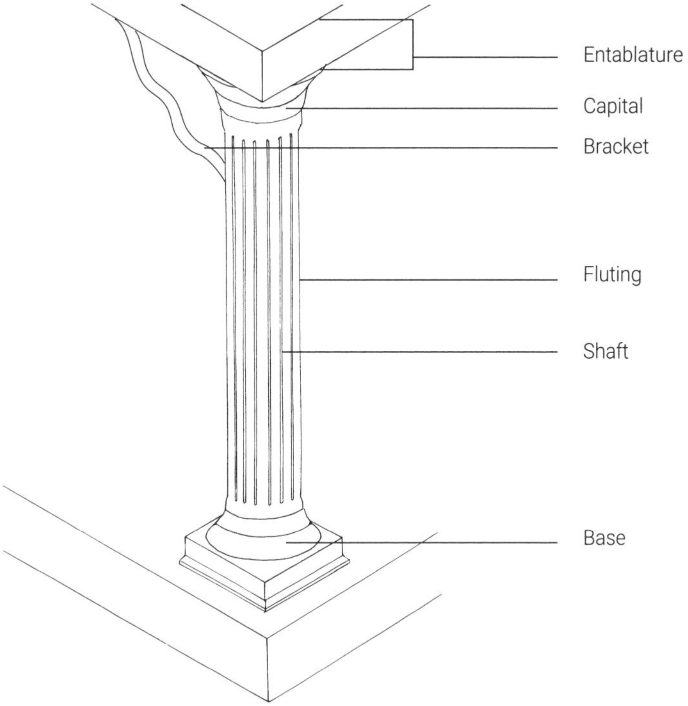

Typological Variations

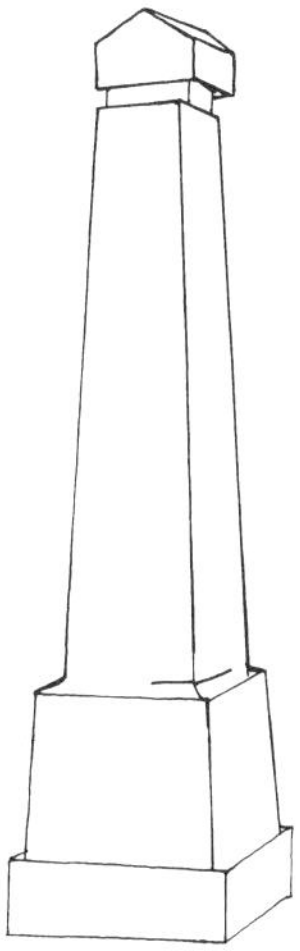

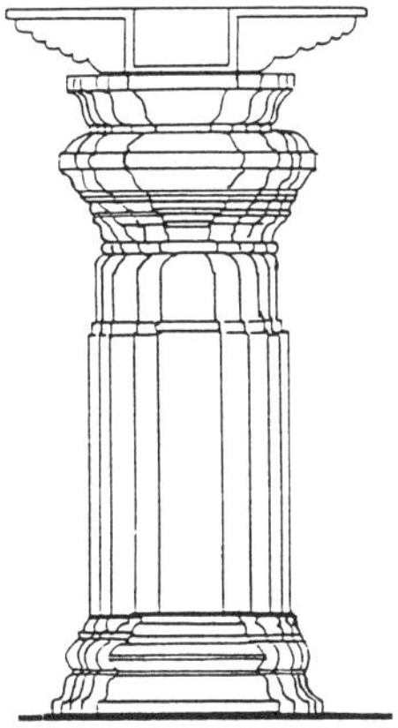

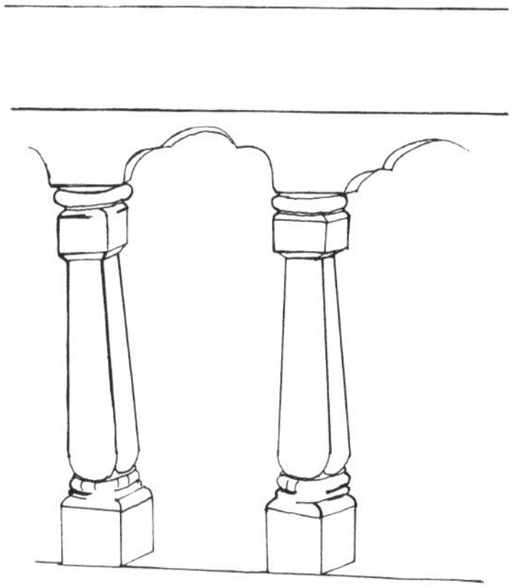

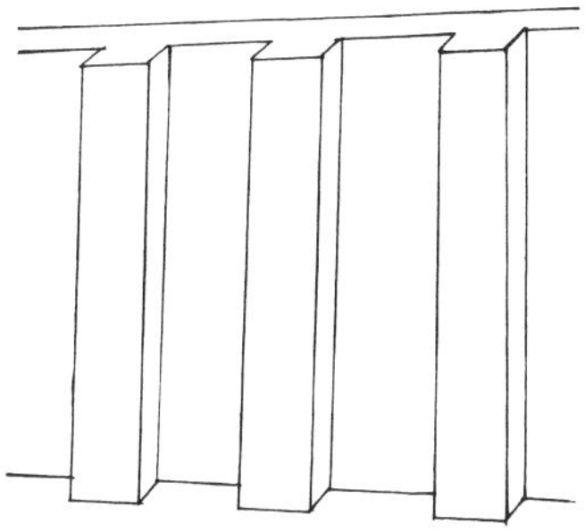

Obelisk
A free-standing non-structural column marking the focus of space, radiating aura around it.

Column
Free-standing linear vertical thick shaft as structural element.

Pier
Free-standing vertical structural element with length more than four times width.

Pilaster
Vertical structural element attached to wall yet protruding out as stiffener and recognizable linear form.

During the ages when the earth was considered as a flat plate floating on a sea of water with the sky as another solid plane, the mountains, due to their inaccessible heights and formability, were supposed to be the points on earth on which the sky rested, the *axis mundi*—the primary support. The supporting element was seen as an epitome of strength and thereby its importance finds roots here. This notional proximity to the celestial beings led to the practice of sages and wise men going up the mountains for penance. These expressions of strength, support, celestial connection and verticality were manifested as the column—the man-made equivalent in the built environment. The column, thus, initially reflected the qualities of its direct references in nature representing the same features—trees, mountains etc.

In early rock-cut architecture, where the emphasis was upon 'void-making', the column took embellishment, decoration and inscription (historical records)—a visual element more than anything else.

Myths/Values—Associations

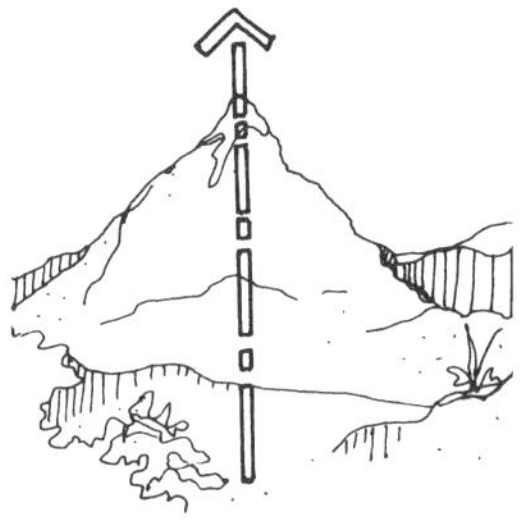

The axis mundi

Tree trunk as column

Egyptain column depicted as palm trees at the Great Temple of Amun Karnak

Detail

Connection between Man and God, Columns of Sun, Peru

Detail

Column depicted as the charioteer of the God, also expressing the strengh, support and security, Vitthal Temple, Hampi

The carved out support

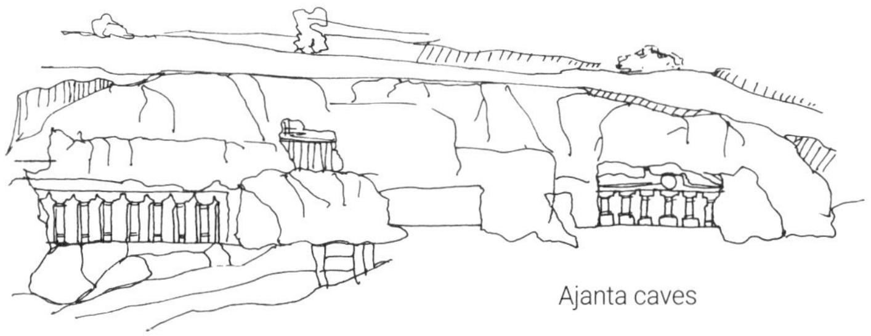

Ajanta caves

Wooden column as primary element of support

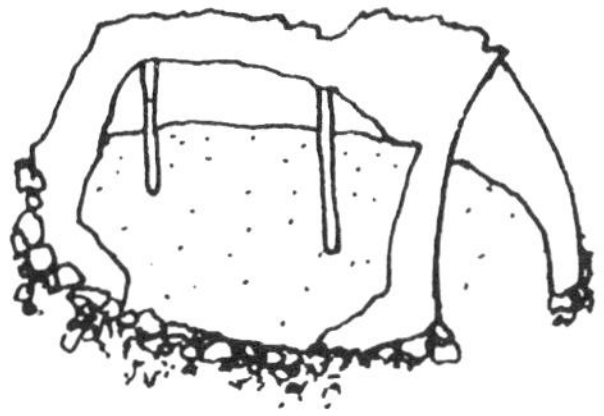

Terra Amata, Nice, France

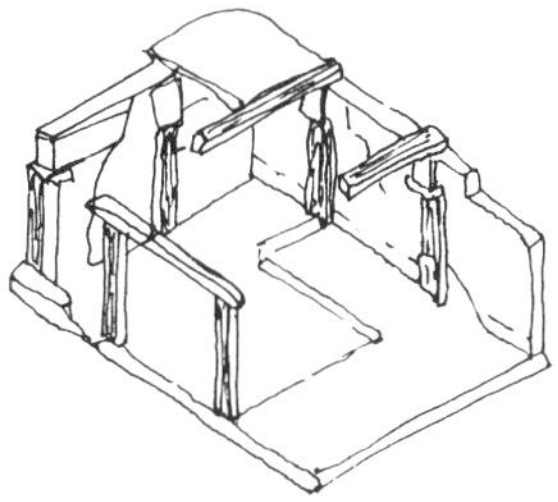

Wooden columns

With built-up architecture, the column took on significant structural responsibilities, the notion of "support" became primary, though plastic treatment and decoration still continued to add value to its functionality. From the early hacked timber columns in mud houses to the decorated stone ones used later for permanence and monumentality, columns derived aesthetic expression from nature, especially as manifestations of the tree. The proportions of the column varied and evolved gradually with different materials as their properties were discovered, taking on decorative and symbolic dimensions possible in that medium. Changing technology and new materials played a key role in reducing the girth of columns and increasing their height, allowing them to take on soaring proportions and skeletal expressions. Egyptian columns were large, circular and adorned with hieroglyphics. The Greeks formulated 'orders' for columns. Arrangement of columns supporting the entablature defined the columnar facades forming the decorative shell of Greek temples.

Columns emphasizing monumentality with symbolic inscriptions

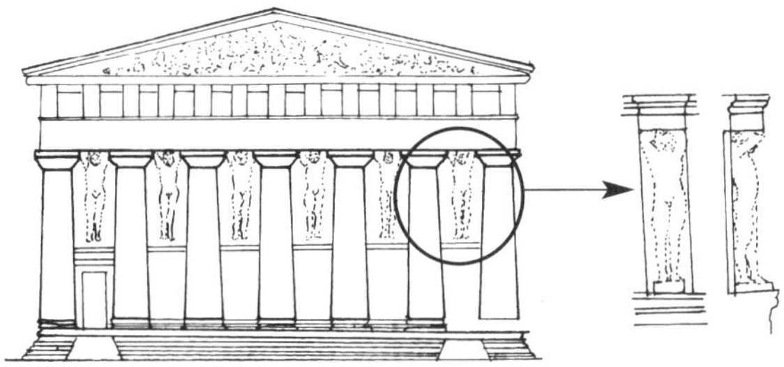

Egyptian columns depicted as human figures
Temple of Neptune, Paestum

Greek Temple with Trabeated System

Doric Ionic Corinthian

In the Roman era, the columns supported arches, thus, increasing the inter-columnar distance. This allowed greater freedom in spatial experimentation. Columns were used not only as primary support but also as decorated piers and pilasters.

With changing technology during the Gothic period, masonry was reduced to minimum. Columns became slender and supported a ribbed roof, emphasing height and spaciousness.

During the Renaissance period, though there was no structural innovation, columns were the elements to take on heavy decoration.

The Industrial Revolution brought out new materials, technology and thereby new building types. Large column-less spaces were sought after. Steel and R.C.C. (reinforced cement concrete) opened up immense possibilities of spanning structurally reducing column spacing and girth. The applied decoration resulted in the material finish and structural form itself becoming elements of expression.

Columns acquiring forms of piers and pilasters, giving freedom to spatial explorations

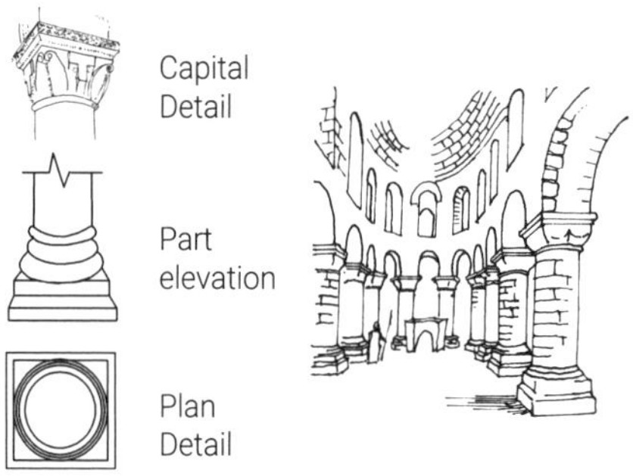

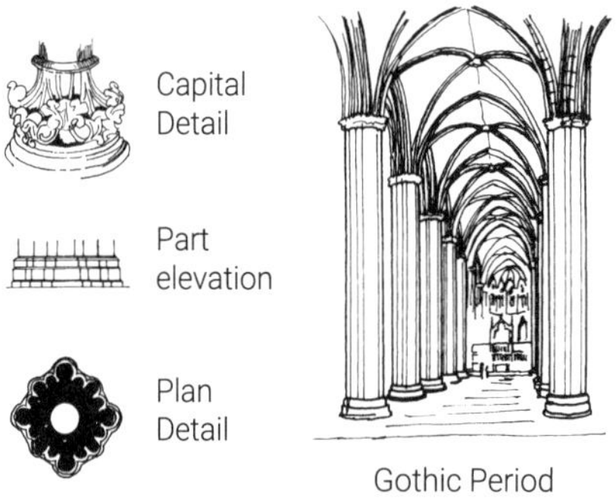

Gothic Period

Column with elaborate decorations

Renaissance Period

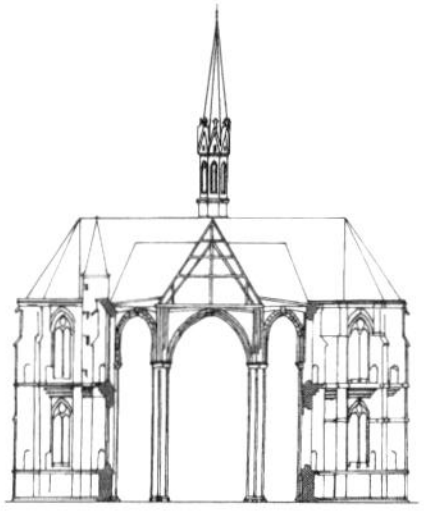

St. Elizabeth Church, Marburg, Germany

A new formal language emerging out of modern technology with introduction of steel and R. C. C. column

Bibliotheque St. Genevieve, Paris

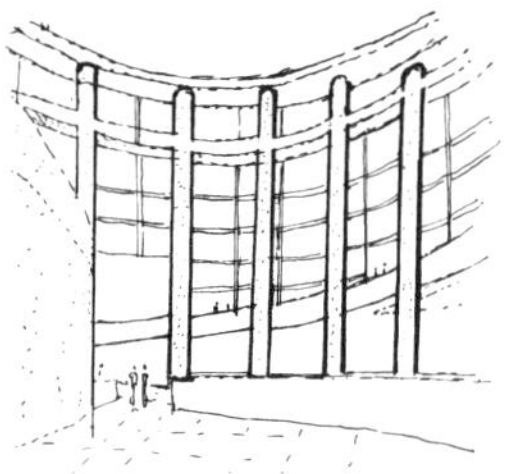

Raika Headquarters, Osaka

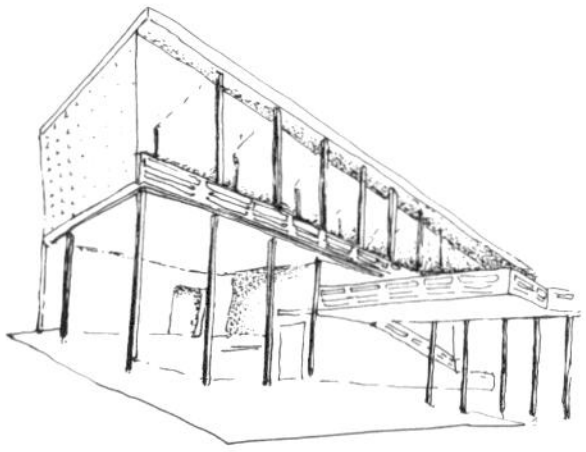

Japanese Pavillion, Paris Exposition, Paris

Colonia Guell Chruch, Barcelona

EUROPEAN ORDERS

Greek Doric | Greek Ionic | Greek Corinthian | Roman Tuscan | Roman Composite

Greek Doric: Simple, baseless columns, they have spreading capitals and a patterned frieze above the slightly convex profile. The height was initially not more than four times the diameter at the base, which later became 51/2 to 5 3/4 the diameter.

Greek Ionic: It has a base. The shaft is fluted while the capital is elaborately carved in spiral floral hoops on either side. The height is nine to ten times their lower diameter. The structure seems lighter and more elegant than the Doric.

Greek Corinthian: Shaped as an upturned bell, its capital is deeper than Ionic and finished with intricately detailed floral carving. Its advantage over the Ionic order was that the corner columns could be viewed from any side as opposed to only front in case of the Ionic order. The height of the capital is about 11/3 diameter.

Roman Tuscan: It resembles the Greek Doric in all respects but it has very plain entablature. The height is seven times the diameter of base. The diameter at capital is 3/4th the diameter at the base.

Roman Composite: It combines the prominent volutes of the Ionic with the acanthus of the Corinthian. Its capital becomes highly decorative, while the shaft is either fluted or plain.

INDIAN ORDERS

Indic
Has a faceted shaft.

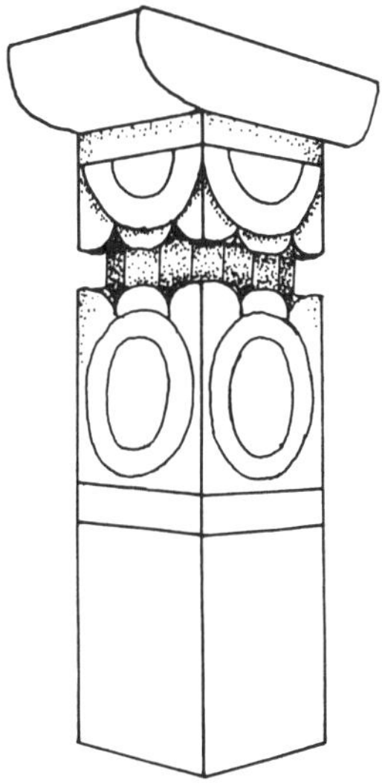

Meso-Indic
Has primary facet on one end of shaft and secondary facet on the rest of the column.

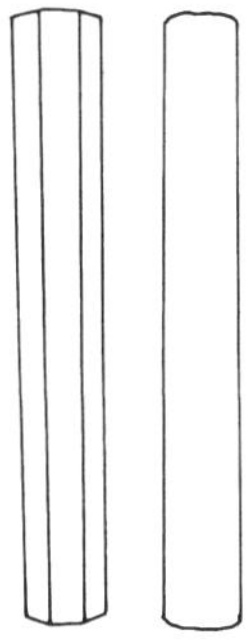

Neo-indic
Has primary facets at both ends.

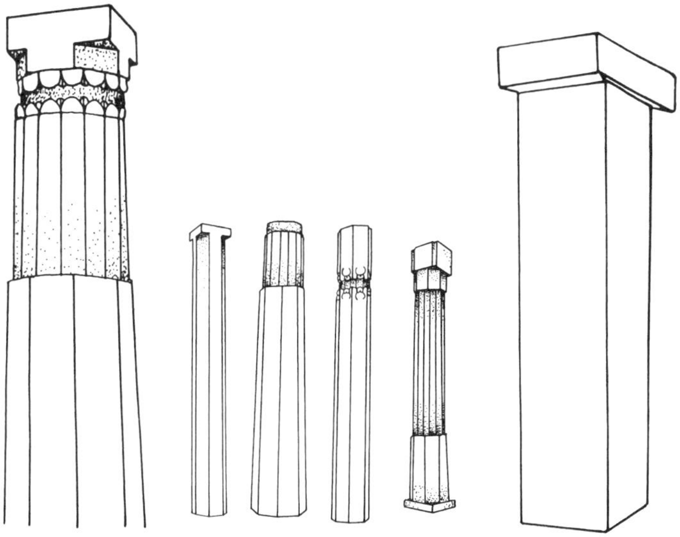

Deutro-indic
Has shaft with abacus and base.

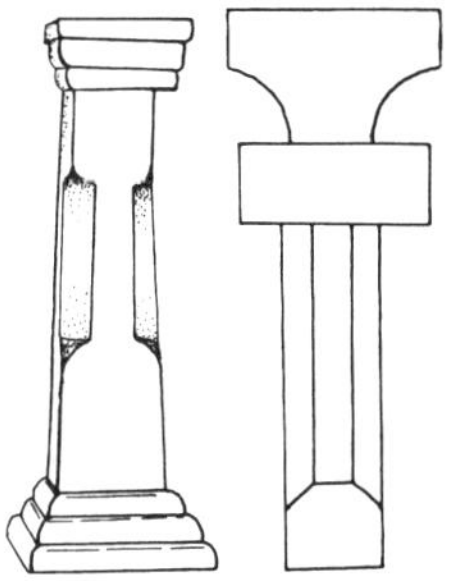

Indo Persepolitan

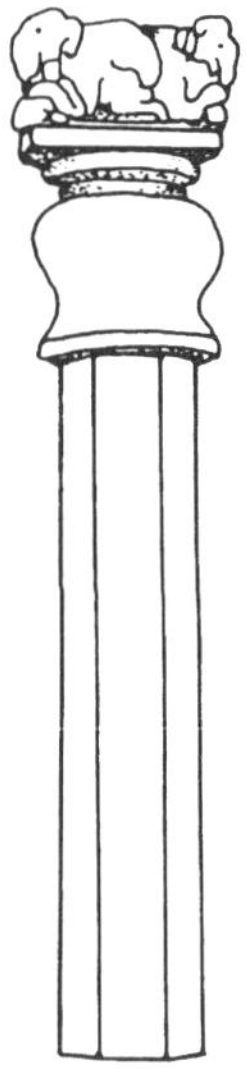

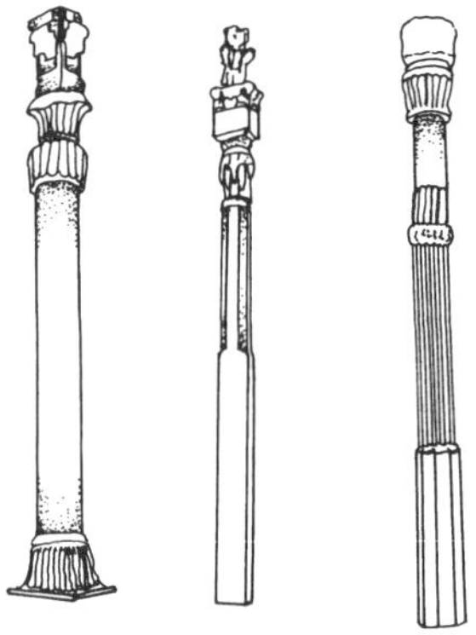

The capital is bell shaped with dropping corolla of petals surmounted by fillet-like sphere.

Proto Gangetic

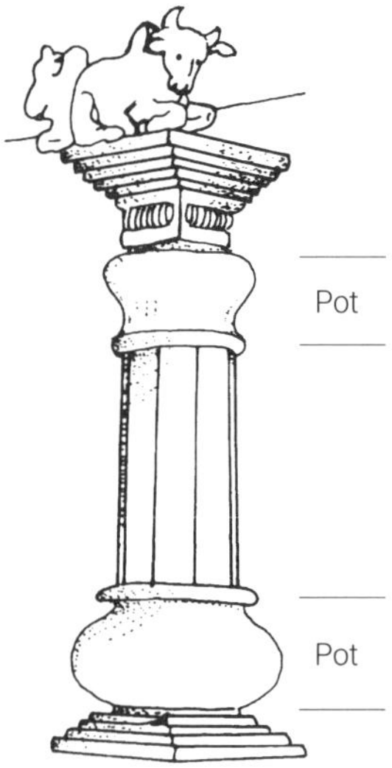

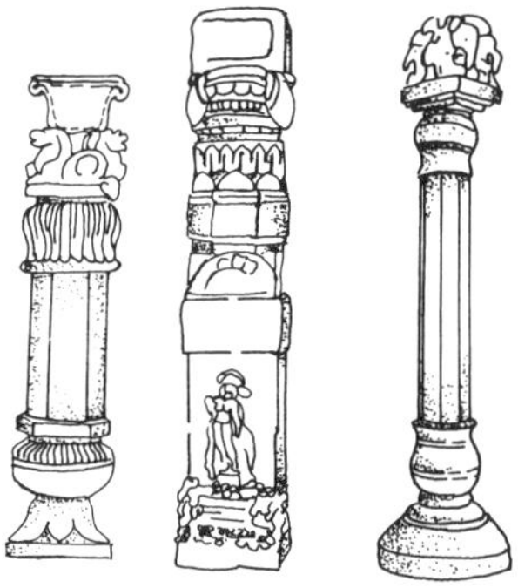

Shaft terminates in the mouth of pots at both ends.

Gangetic

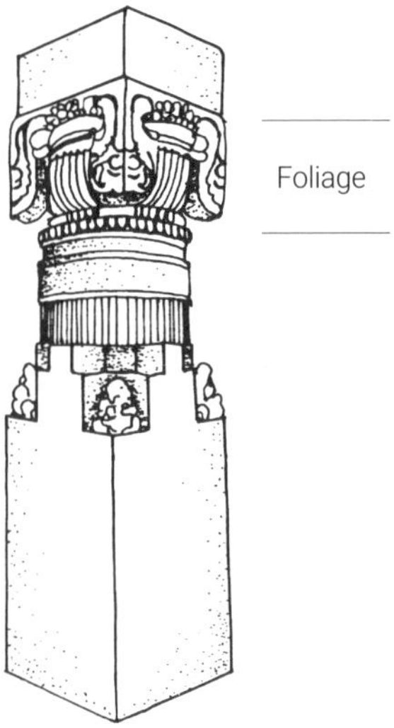

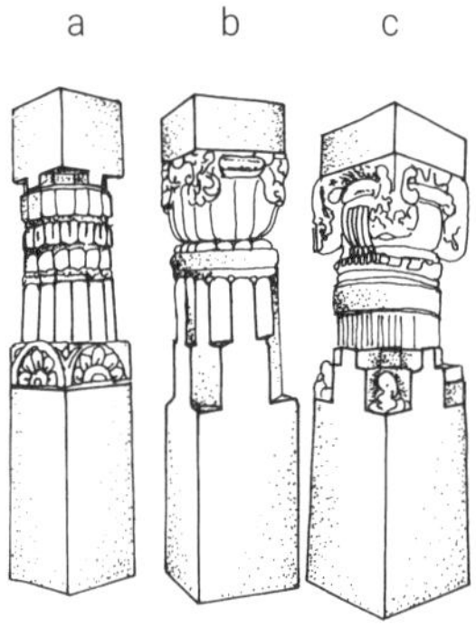

Order of bell, with the pot at top.

a. Only pot as capital
b. Pot and foliage as capital
c. Pot, foliage and flowers as capital

Deccani

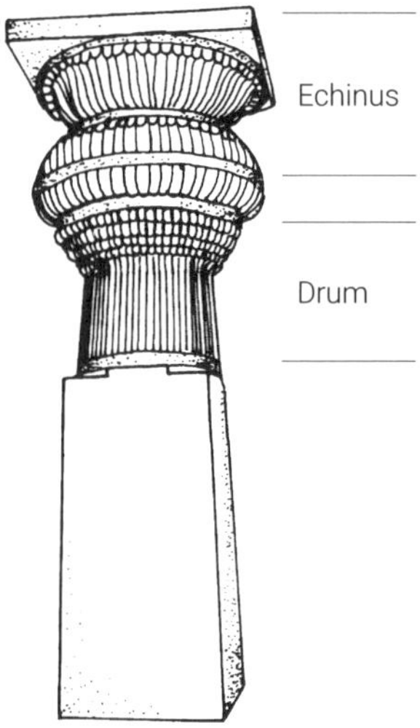

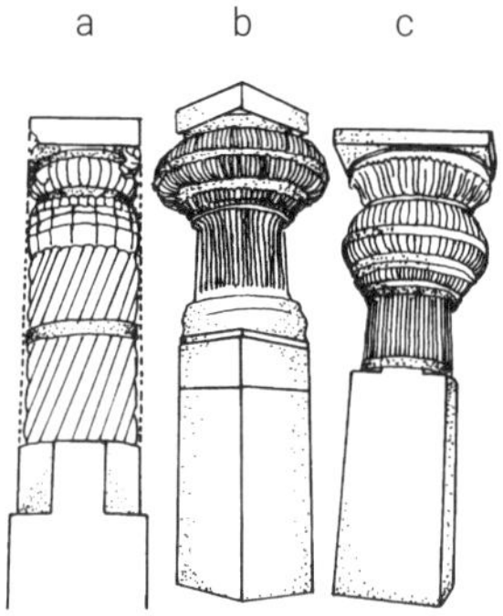

Order of sphere

a. Sphere as capital
b. Capital over drum with straightened entasis.
c. Capital over inverted bell drum surmounted by inverted echinus.

CENTRALITY

A column—due to negligible girth as compared to its height—marks a locus, a position in space. It, being omnidirectional, therefore takes on the properties of a point, seemingly not occupying space but radiating aura all around it. It assumes a central position. Due to this, other elements which form a part of the ensemble gravitate towards the column, making it automatically referential, a notional centre, which commands space around it .The size of the column is determined from the area commanded by it.

Commanding space with its off-centre placement within the piazza or complex

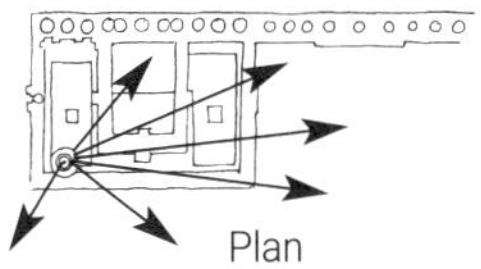

Plan

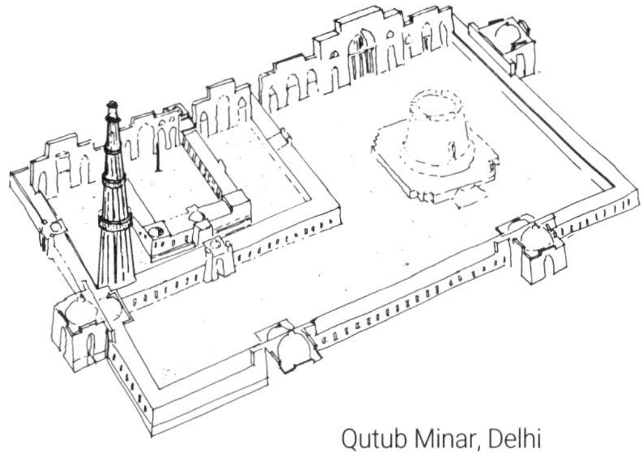

Qutub Minar, Delhi

Commanding space with its placement in the centre within the piazza or complex..

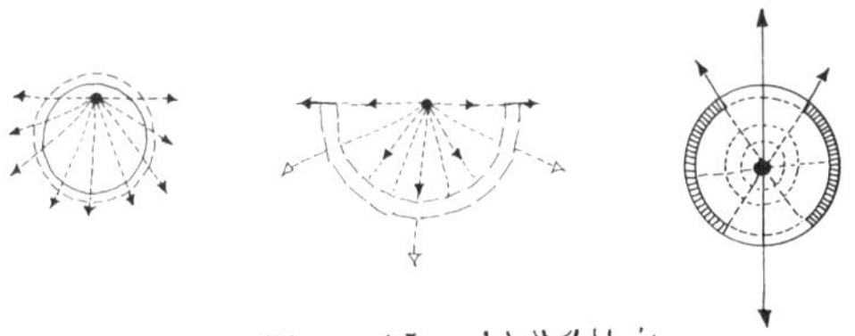

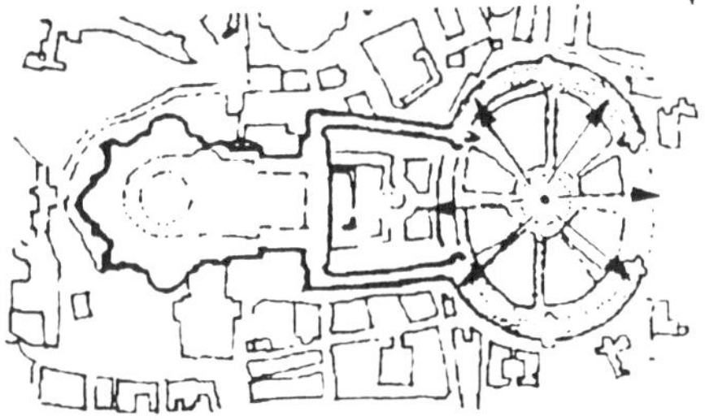

Plan

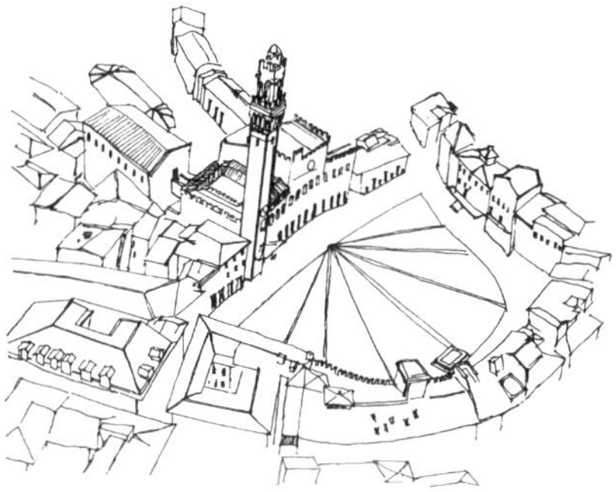

Palazzo Pubblico, Siena

St. Peter's Bascilica, Vatican City

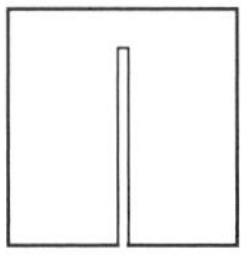

VERTICALITY

In principle, a point extruded upwards, the column assumes verticality and guides vision upwards from the horizontal plane (ground), lending it an upward thrust and imparting dynamism to the space. The verticality induced through this element balances the horizontal spread of ground-based tiers of construction aiding visual composition of space, and becoming loci imparting graphic qualities.

Columns together adding visual composition to the space

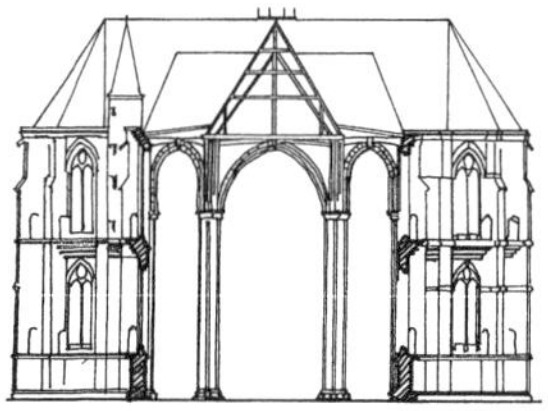

St. Elizabeth Church, Marburg

Street view of Ahmedabad

Eiffel Tower, Paris

Extruding movement in upward direction..

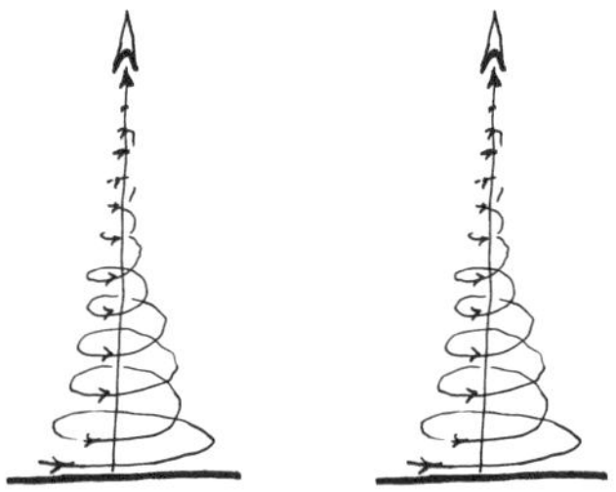

Shodhan House, Ahmedabad

Penetrating forcibly upwards with its dynamism..................................

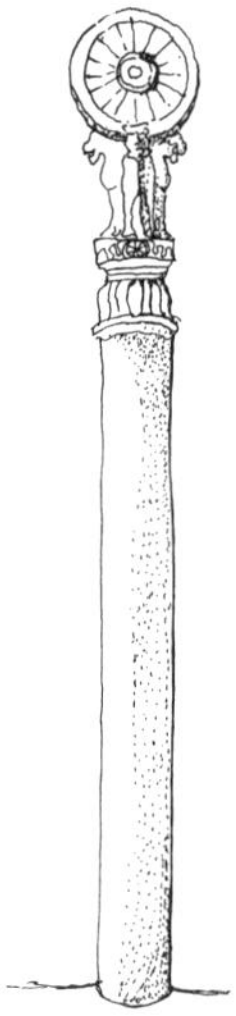

Ashok Stambh, Sarnath

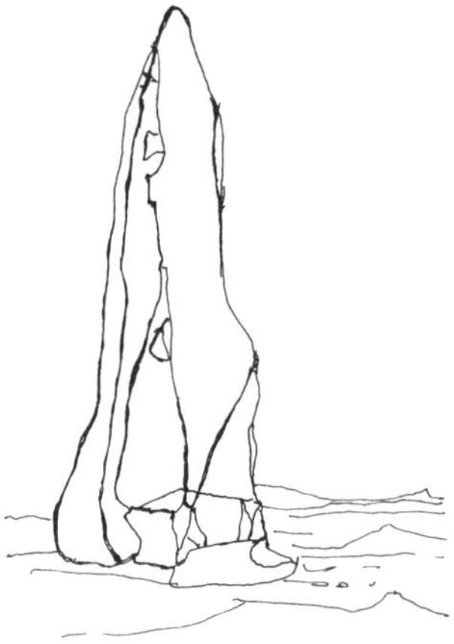

A Menhir

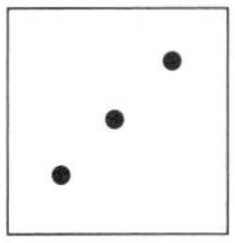

DIRECTIONALITY

As with points generating a line, columns placed linearly guide direction. They establish, thereby, an imaginary plane with consistently perforated visual features, perceptually and spatially taking on directive qualities and guide the eye and movement along the line of repetition. A single column is omnidirectional. However, a linear repetition of the columns begins imparting directions. Two columns placed nearby emphasise the direction perpendicular to the line joining the columns. More than two columns become a line emphasising direction along the procession of columns.

Single Column—Omnidirectional

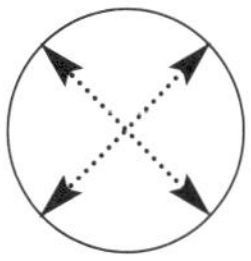

Qutub Minar, Delhi

Diwan-e-Khas, Fatehpur Sikri

Two Columns—Imparting direction perpendicular to columns

Piazza St. Marco, Venice

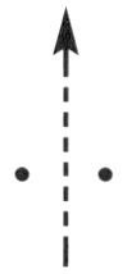

Jami Masjid, Champaner

Multiple Columns—Emphasizing direction along the row and column

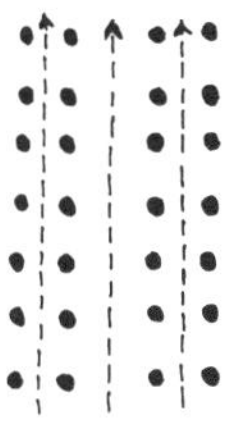

Chruch of St. Lorenzo, Florence, Italy

Rameshwaram temple, Madurai

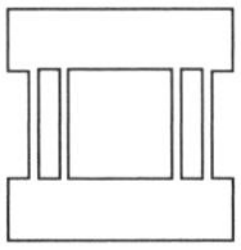

RHYTHM

Linear repetition of columns with changing distances gives rise to a rhythm, a sense of continuity and consistency determined by their spacing and frequency of occurrence. The invisible plane established between two columns with penetrability perpendicular to the plane of connection is modulated.

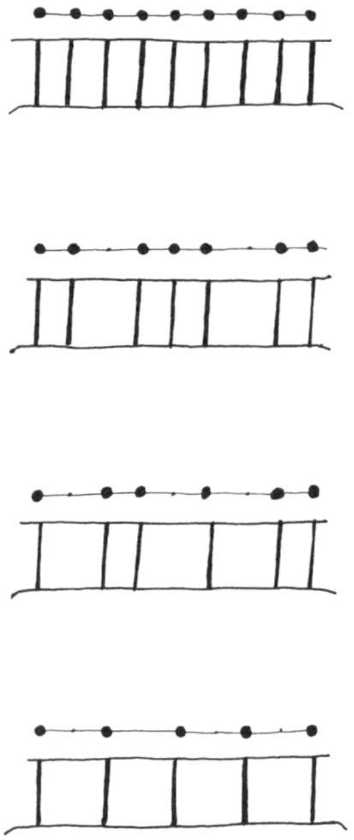

Columns stipulating rhythm through their placements..

Palais Garnier, Paris

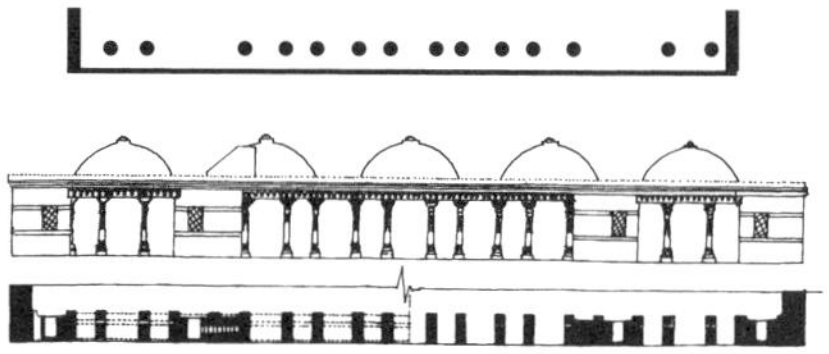

Sakar Khan's Mosque, Ahmedabad

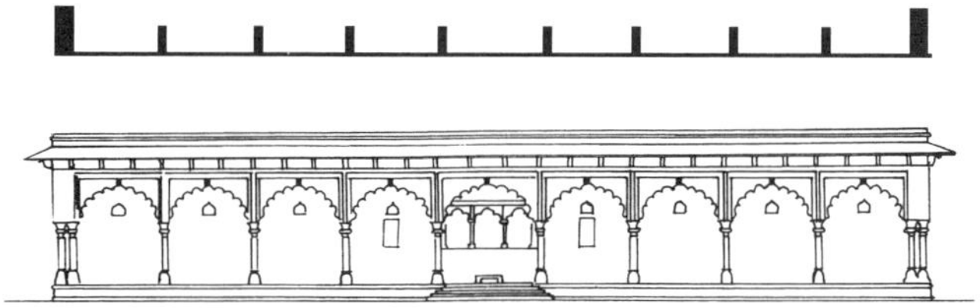

Diwan-E-Am, Fatehpur Sikri

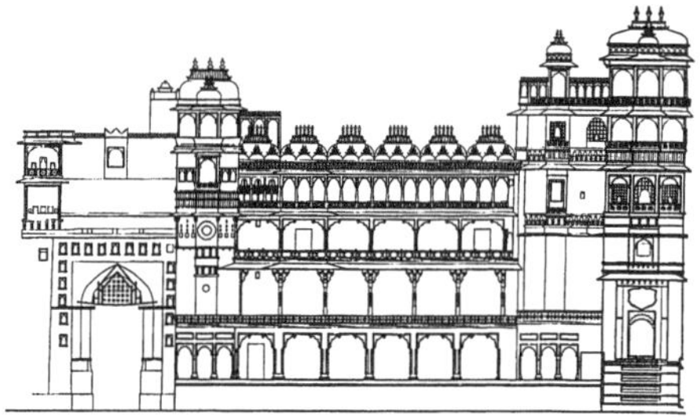

City Palace, Udaipur

Rani Sipri's Mosque, Ahmedabad

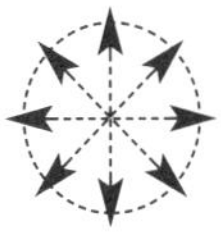

COLUMN AS FOCUS OF SPACE

A free-standing column, as a point in space, commands centrality and as a graphical element adds vitality to the composition. The column, as an obelisk, acts as the focus in spatial ensembles, ordering the various parts with reference to it. In such ensembles, the area commanded by the column determines its proportions.

Column creating focus, as a point in sapce

The Jaipur Column, Delhi

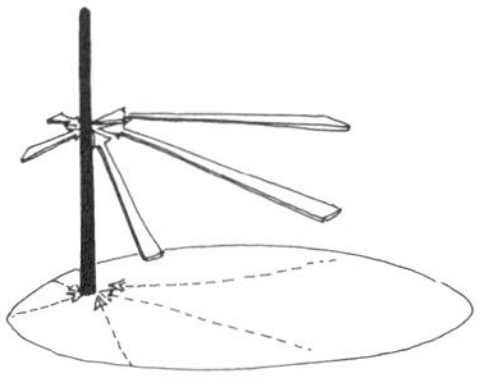

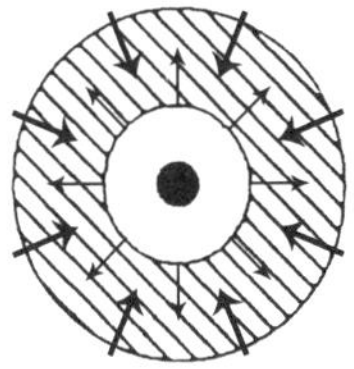

Loh Stambh, New Delhi

Dhwajastambha, Kailashnath Temple, Ellora Caves

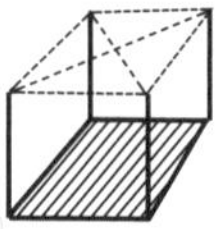

COLUMN FOR SPACE DEFINITION

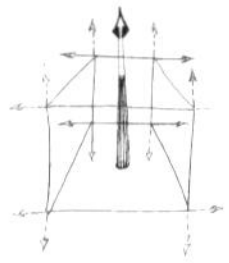

DEFINITION OF VOLUME
Three or more columns that are not placed along the same line enclose space by acting as the vertices of an invisible polygon holding it together. Such a definition creates a notional enclosure with roof while retaining the advantages of an open space.

Palace of Emperor Charles V, Granada, Spain

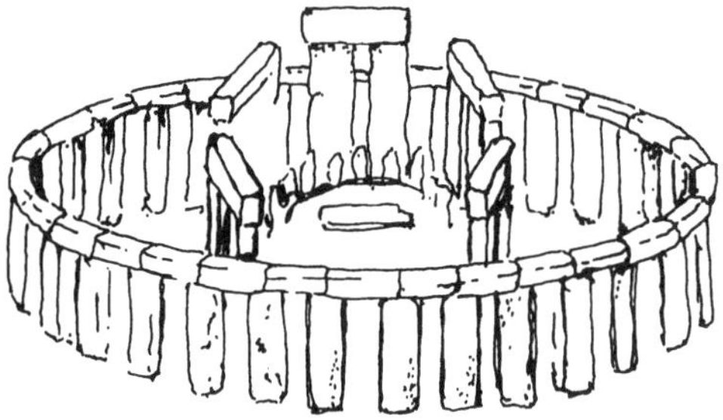

The Stonehenge, Wiltshire, Great Britain

Taj Mahal, Agra,

Pavillion at Sarkhej Roza, Ahmedabad

COLUMN FOR SPACE DEFINITION

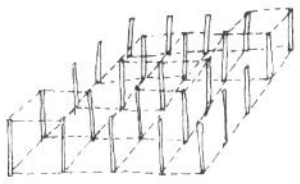

SUB DIVISION OF SPACE
In a composite arrangement, columns not only subdivide the main volume into many smaller ones but, at the same time, also help in the proper definition of sub volumes.

Rudabai Stepwell, Adalaj

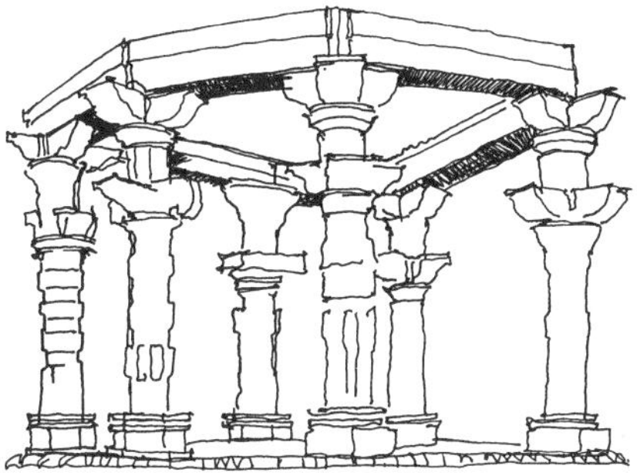

Someshwara Temple, Kiradu

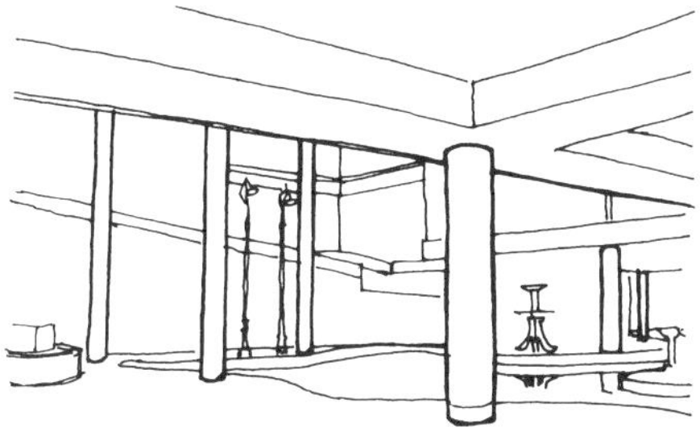

Sanskar Kendra, Ahmedabad

Amdavad ni Gufa, Ahmedabad

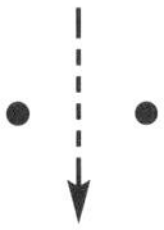

COLUMN AS MOVEMENT GUIDE

A series of columns when placed along a line creates an imaginary plane binding them, through Gestalt's principles, setting up strong perspectives and, thus, establishing direction, inviting movement along them. This aspect is critical for the spatial attribute of 'directionality'.

Free-standing column

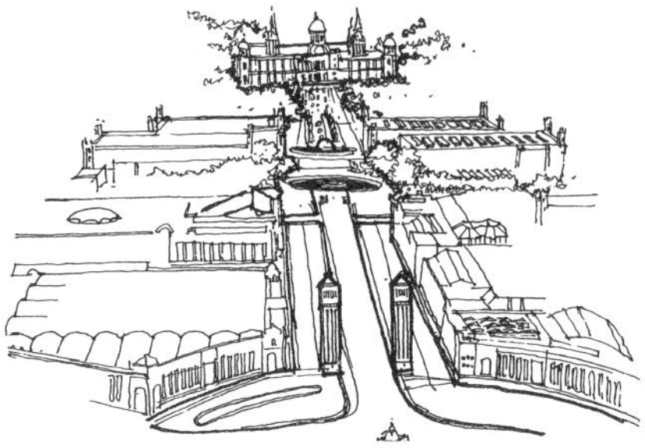

Column as a plan creating a movement

St. Peter's Bascilica, Vatican City

Column as a plan attributing a sense of direction to the space

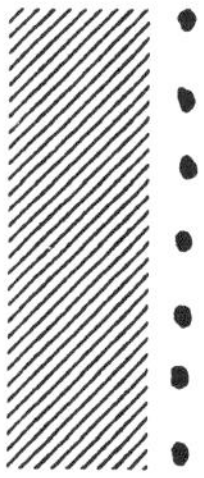

Indian Institute of Management, Bangalore

Column enveloping space creating an enclosure

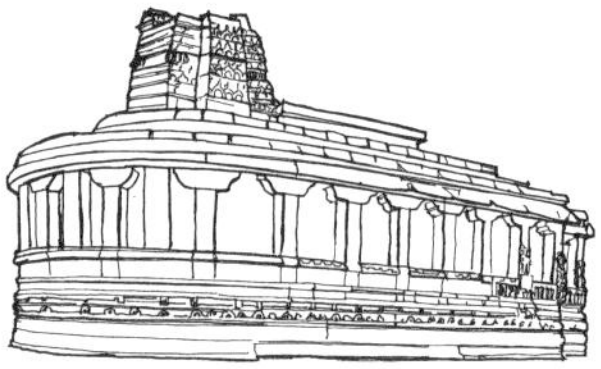

Durga Temple, Aihole

COLUMN AS MODULATOR OF FACADE

Columns, when exposed as an elevational element, even as fins, sun-breakers etc., scale, compose and modulate the facade due to their rhythm, verticality as well as sculptural quality.

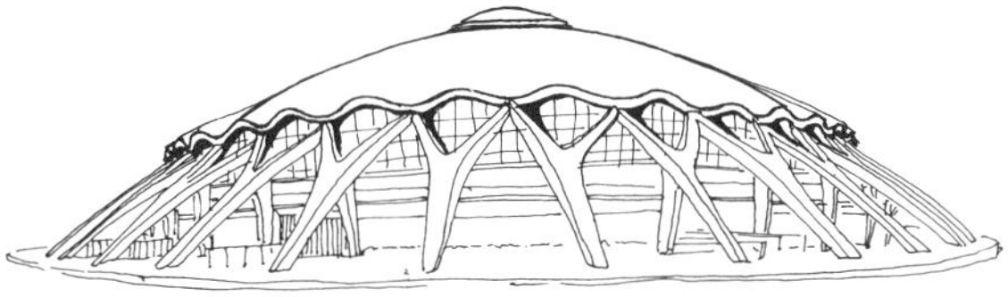

Palazzetto dello Sport, Rome

Ana Sagar Pavilion, Ajmer

Lion Guard, Mahabalipuram

LIC Building, New Delhi

Caryatids at Erechtheion, Athens

Royal Cresent, Bath

DIWAN-E-KHAS, FATEHPUR SIKRI

Column as an image-maker

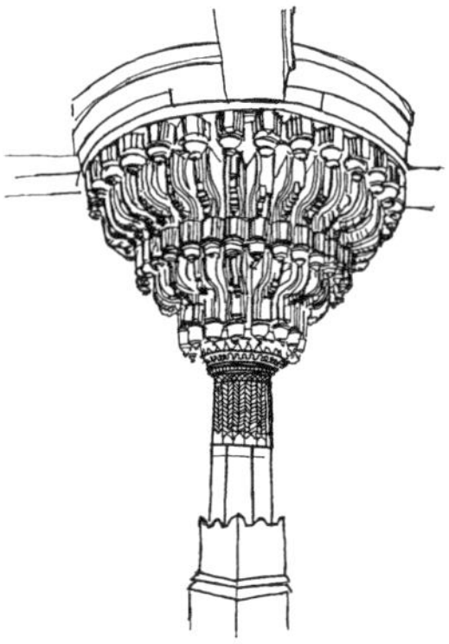

In the central axis of the space, with the elaborate intricacy, imparts uniqueness and becomes an image maker

Section

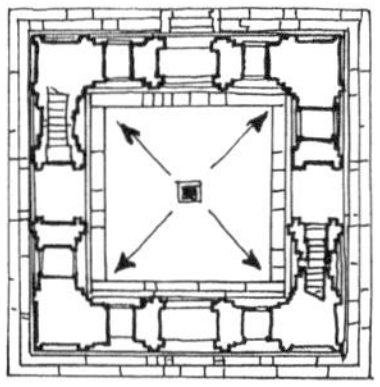

Plan

Column accentuating centrality.....................

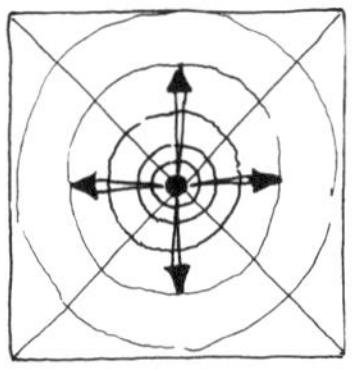

Column commanding the space with its extravagant scale and structure

Column as a focus of space..........................

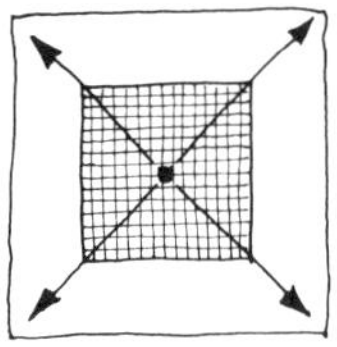

Centrally located column gives multidirectionality to the space

The complex was built between 1571 and 1585 built to commemorate the birth of Akbar's son and heir Jehangir. The Diwan-e-Khas, a special audience hall located in the royal precincts of Fatehpur Sikri, epitomizes the symbolic qualities of the column.

At the centre of a square hall of modest proportions, a single freestanding column mushrooms outward through brackets and supports the seat of the emperor at the upper level, which is linked by bridges to the four corners where the emperor's advisors used to sit.

1. The column as a free-standing element, a point ordering space around it, radiating aura.
2. The single column, symbolizing the axis mundi—the cosmic axis, supporting the seat of the emperor—the embodiment of celestial power on earth.
3. Intricate decoration and fine plastic treatment of the column capital as brackets accentuates its focal value and visual impact.
4. Due to its free-standing nature, form and visual quality, the column becomes the principal architectural feature of the space, imparting uniqueness to the structure- the" image maker". The visually unstable column defies the sense of repose, vitalising the space with a dynamic sculptural quality.

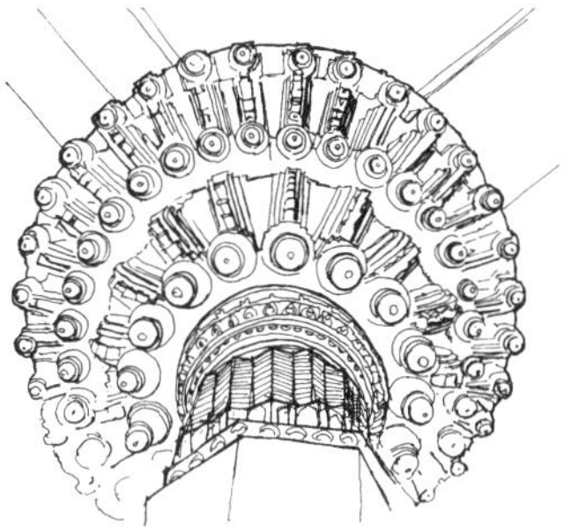

The column capital symbolizes its integration with nature by the carvings and depictions of motifs

Column as an axis mundi

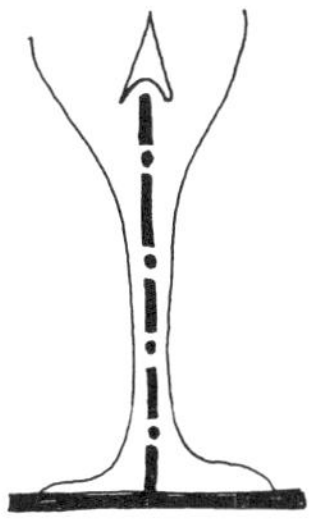

Column as an element enhancing verticality

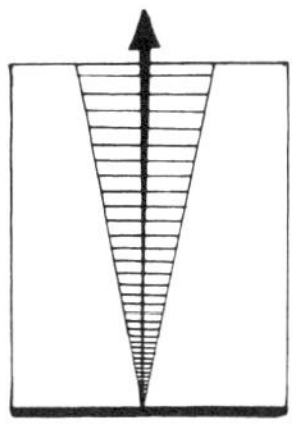

Column as an element supporting the structure

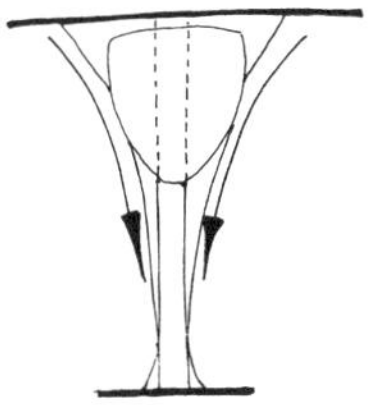

Column as a creator of space

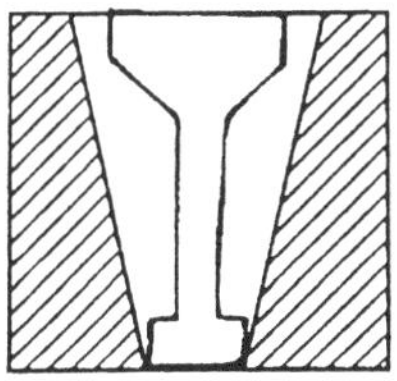

Visually column appears inverted.

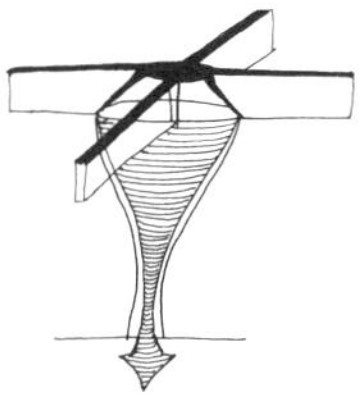

Column becomes an independent and pivotal element in the spatial configuration

Capital performing multiple functions of a structural element, platform and seat

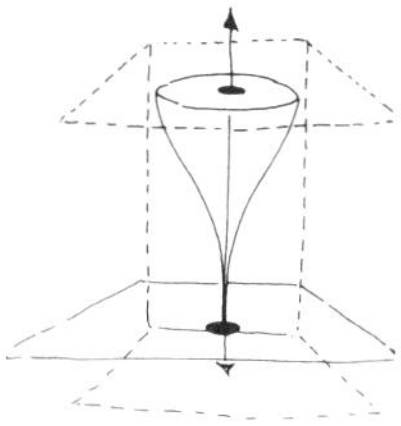

The formal identity creates a physical link between two horizontal planes

Column defining and dividing space around it

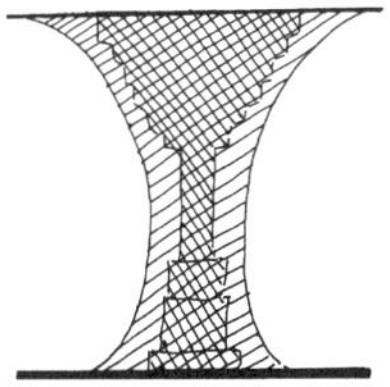

Its growth pattern denotes lateral evolution

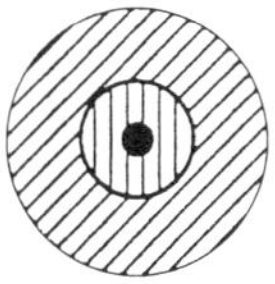

With growth in vertical axis it expands horizontally, becoming an element scaling the space around

Column as a movement guide

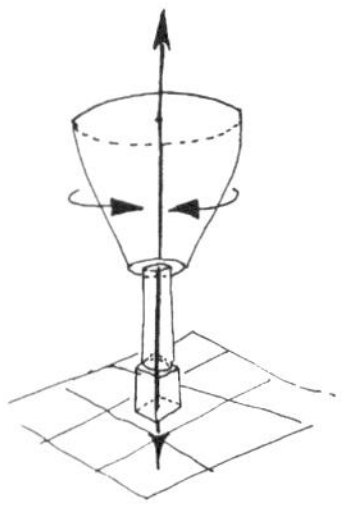

Column defines rotational movement around its axis

POL-HOUSE, AHMEDABAD

Pols, typical of mediaeval urban centres in Gujarat, are the residential precincts. The urbanized form of Ahmedabad within the fortified camp was founded in 1411. The residences in the pols confirm to long linear contiguous plots, internal courts with wooden structure and masonry walls.

Columns, here, play a vital role in defining the central space in addition to becoming the visible structural element. Its role varies from being a supporting element to that of space definer, facade rhythm modulator and also as defining the volume within. The carved work on the column further enhances, beautifies and lends unique character to the structure.

Column as a modulator of facade

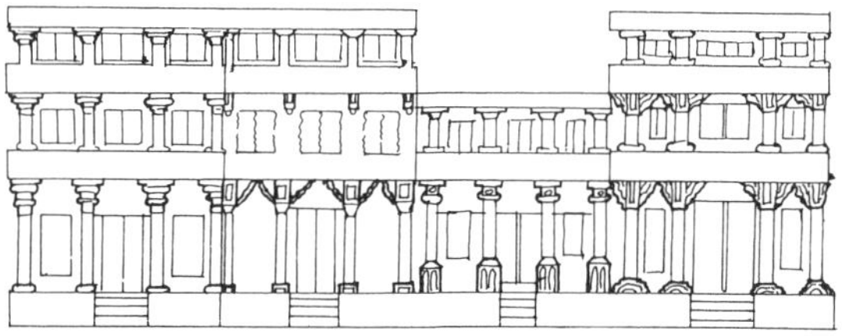

Columns with their multiplicity of scale and form become a modulator of facade

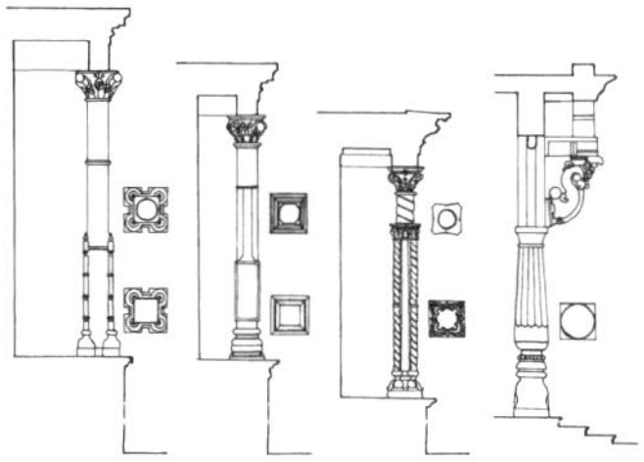

Typical column variations as in a pol house

Columns spatially define the directionality

Columns defining entry point

Columns on the facade humanize the vertically enhanced scale by breaking the volume

Columns enclosing space, defining the volume

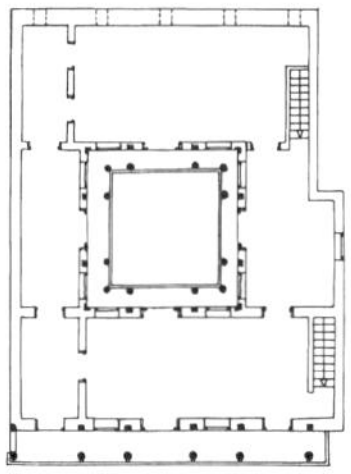

Plan at ground level

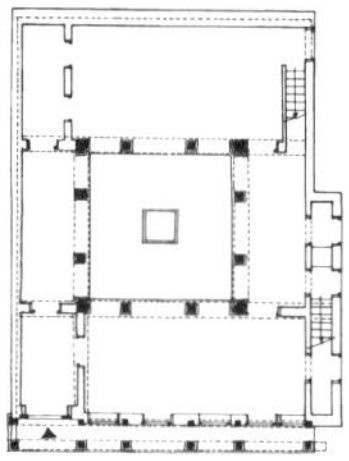

Plan at first floor level

Columns as a creator of subspaces

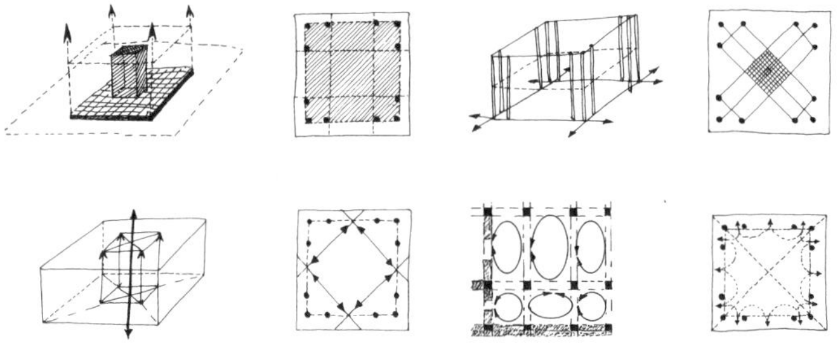

Columns in the courtyard and in the interior zones create spaces by rhythmic, peripheral presence, generating various movements and spatial patterns

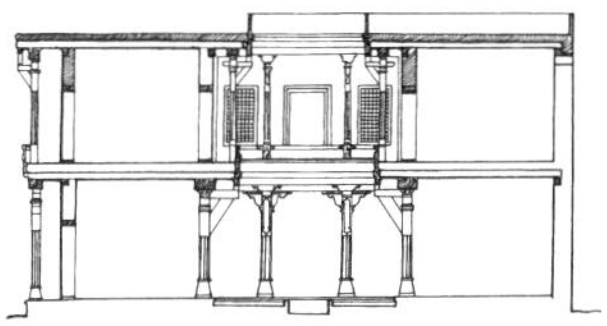

Section

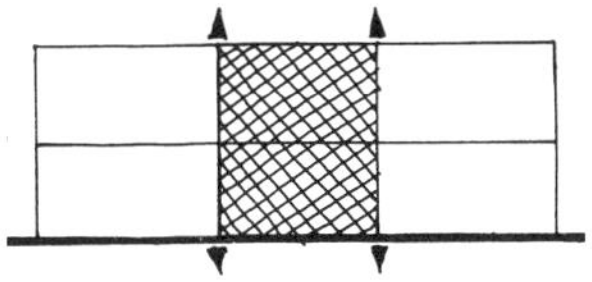

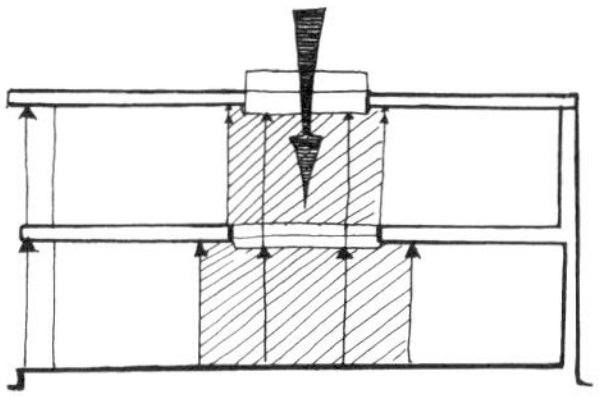

In the larger volume of the house, columns define centrally located subspace, which becomes the pivot to other functional zones

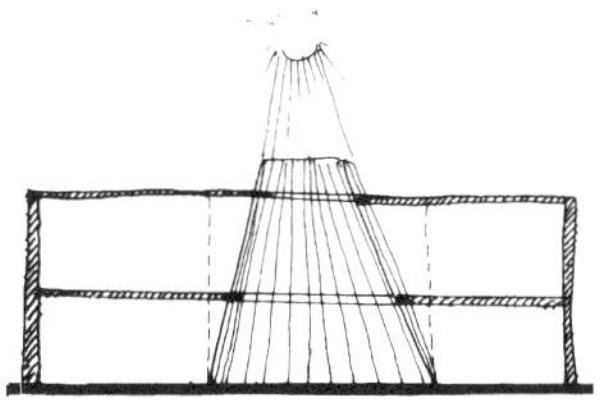

Centrally created shaft interacts efficaciously with the external climate

Columns generating rhythm..........................

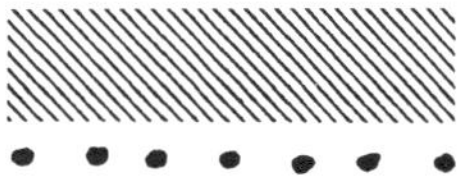

Plane created by columns on the facade generates space, termed as verandah

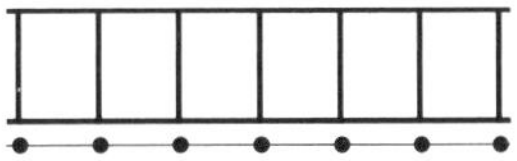

Plane created by columns defining the facade, attributing uniqueness to each dwellining unit

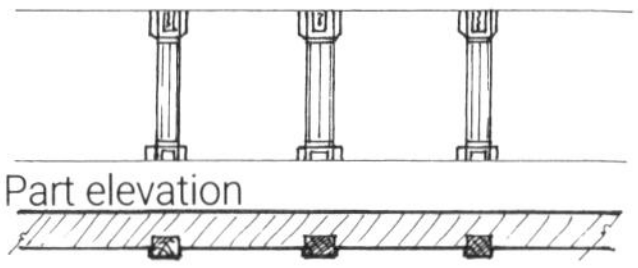

Rhythm is derived by the inter columniation on the facade

Column with its embellishments...

Column as an element giving a vertical volume to the otherwise small space of the entrance

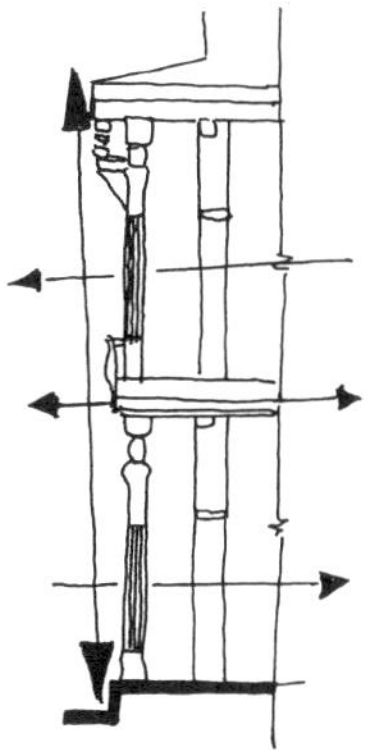

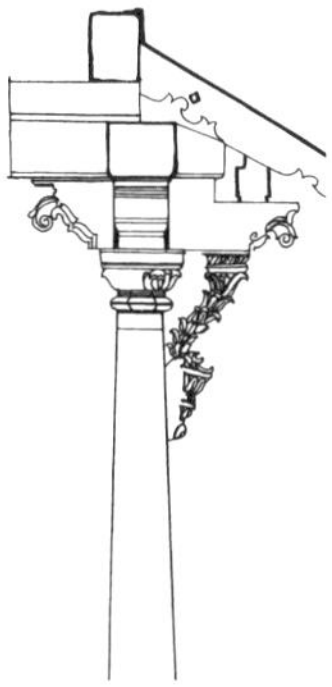

The verticality and the spatial order on the facade establishes a strong link between inside out

Carved out wooden bracket bearing motifs from nature and often religion

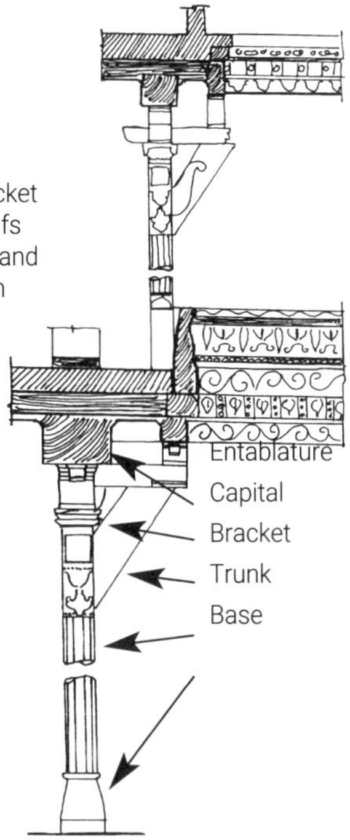

Column reflecting the intricate craftsmanship

JOHNSON WAX HEADQUARTERS, WISCONSIN

Architect Frank Lloyd Wright designed the Johnson Waxworks Building built in 1936-39. The mushroom columns here were defined as 'dendiform'—tree shaped, and divided into four segments: base, stem, calyx and petal. The base of the column was defined as crow's foot. The core is made up of a hollow steel section. The calyx takes the load of a hollow pad called petal. The stem, calyx and petals are reinforced with mesh and bars. Due to the floating nature of the roof above, these columns successfully provided the necessary structural support, at the same time affording a free flow of undivided democratic workspace.

Column as an image-maker

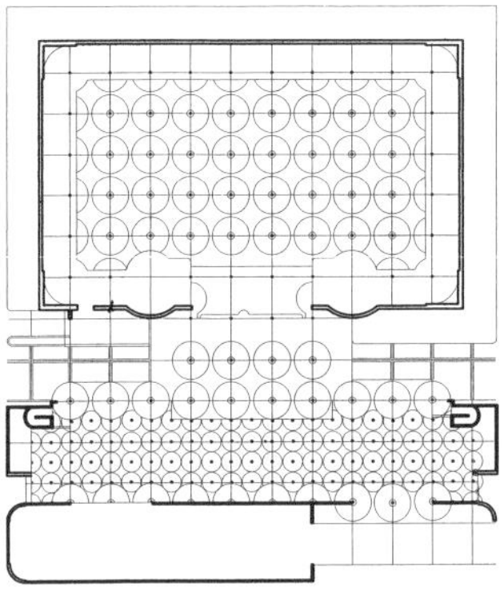

The structural language enhances the penetrability of light and together with the column grid, conjures a sense of unified whole

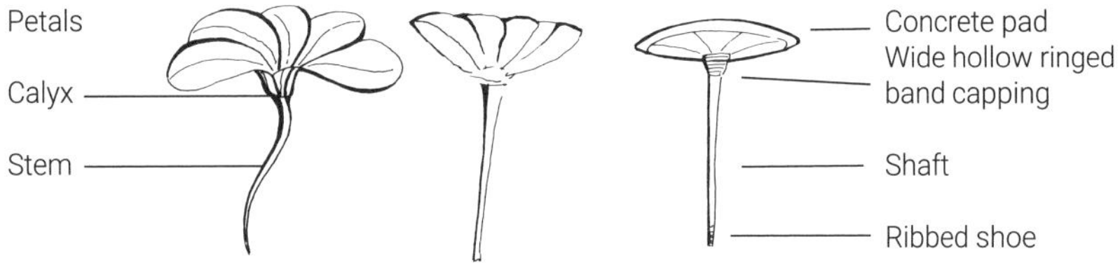

Designed as a lotus, columns create a jungle of concrete trees

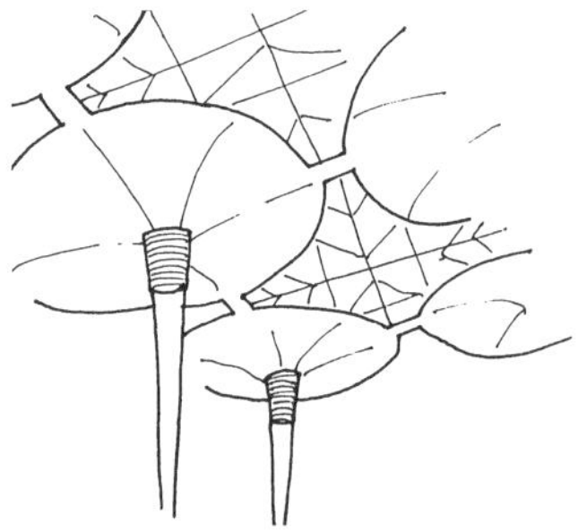

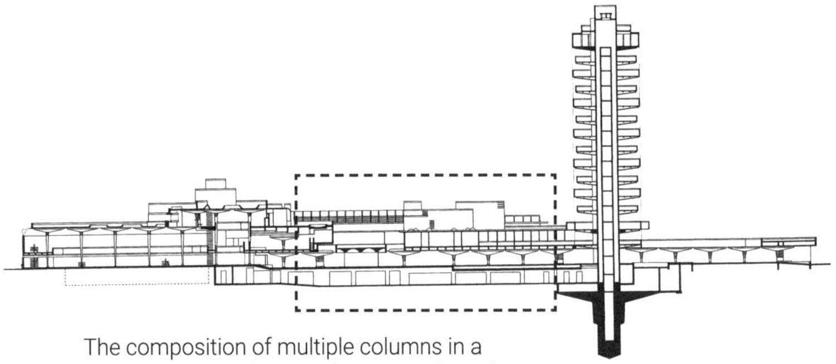

The composition of multiple columns in a geometrical grid attributes a human scale to the otherwise large space

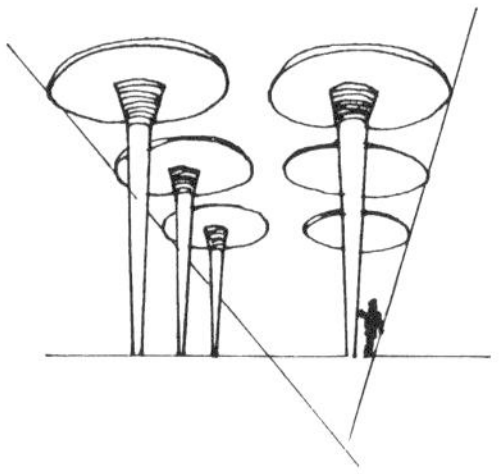

The imposed network of columns creates play of visual frames, and adds disciplined order to the overall schema

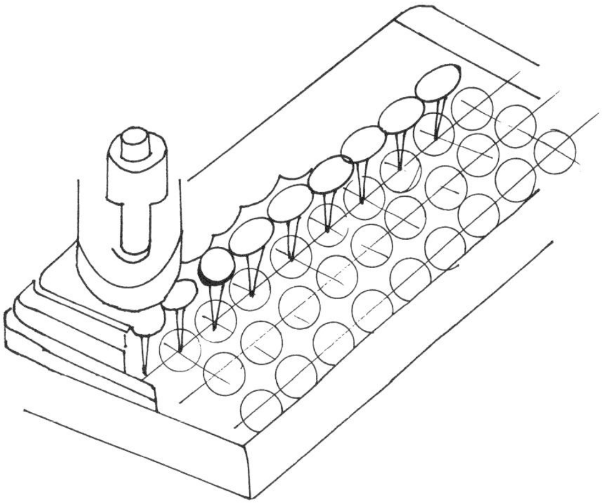

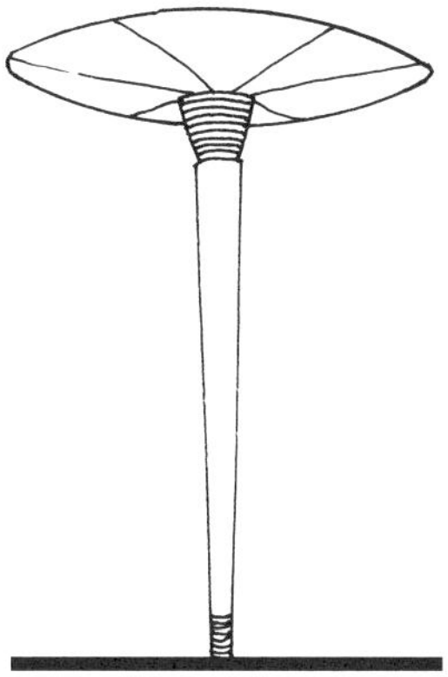

Columns in large space creating significantly individual sub-units harmonize the overall volume by strong presence in their form and position

Expression of Verticality

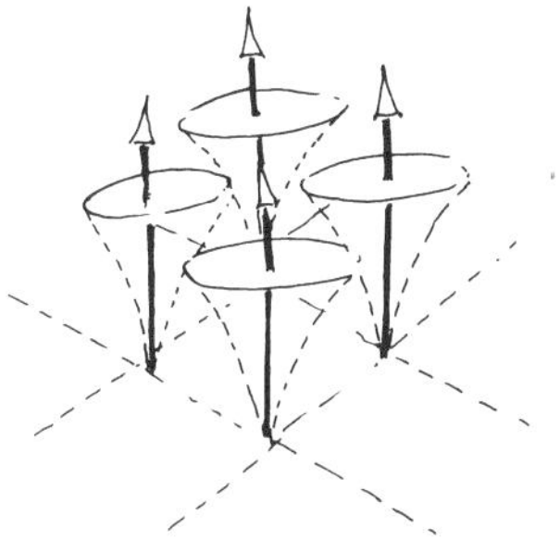

Columns enclose volume and also create a shelter as they form a space below them

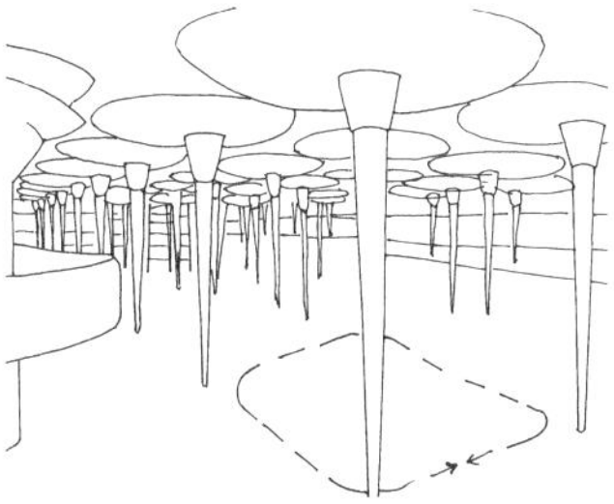

Each column acts as a central pivotal shelter for the space enveloping it

Column with its intercolumniation creates a rhythm, which becomes an imposed grid

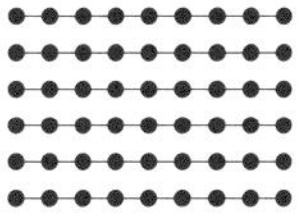

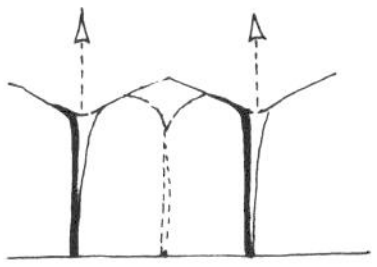

The structure of column modulates the overall volume and imposes a definite visual characteristic to the entire space

Each column governing certain space around its axis , creating a focused zone with its pivotal presence

Column as a focus of space

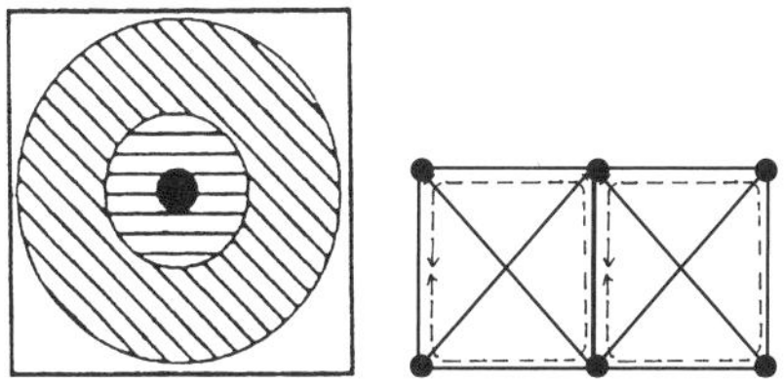

Column defining spaces and subspaces

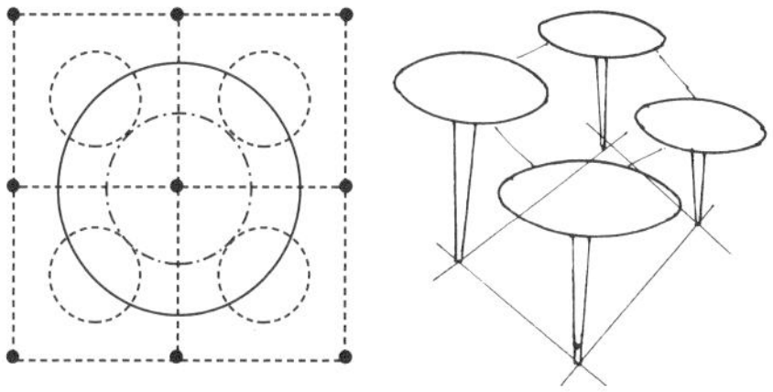

Many subspaces created by individual columns get unified into a large colossal volume

ST. PETER'S SQUARE, VATICAN CITY

Masterbuilder Gian Lorenzo Bernini designed the piazza colonnade of St. Peter's Basilica, built in 1656-57. It is a vast oval piazza circumvented by Doric colonnades, branching out in two hemi-cycles. A central obelisk dominates the space around the oval open space. This strongly emphasizes a centrality by becoming a locus determining the spatial roles of the all the builtform surrounding it through its radiating aura. A relatively low colonnade around it permits wide visibility, giving an impression of forest of verticals. Repetition of column generates a rhythm through frequency and consistency.

Columns as modulator of facade

Column as an image-maker..

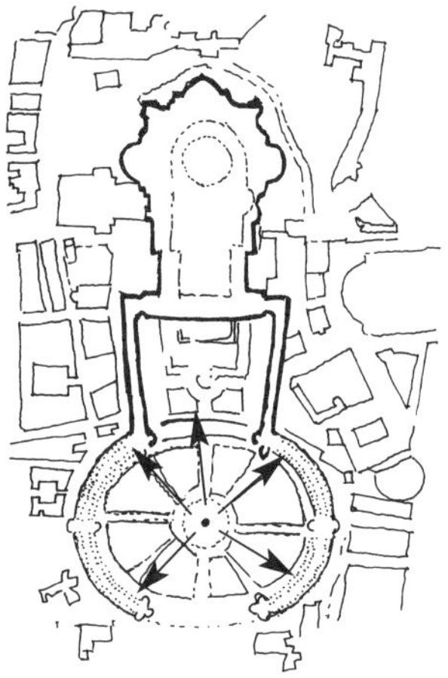

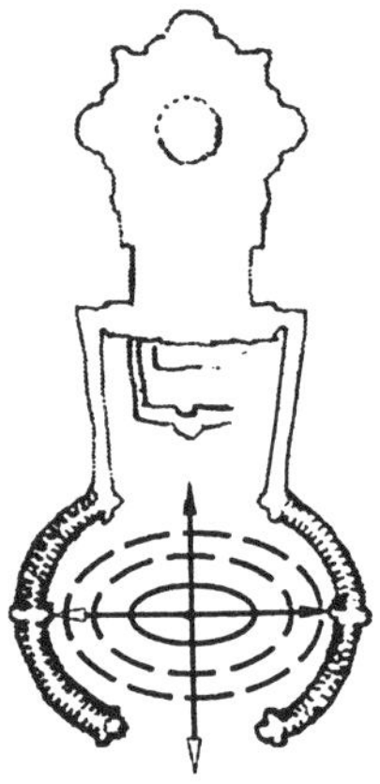

Plan

The central axis with its conspicuous presence attributes a strong image to the entire open vista

Column emphasizing centrality and verticality

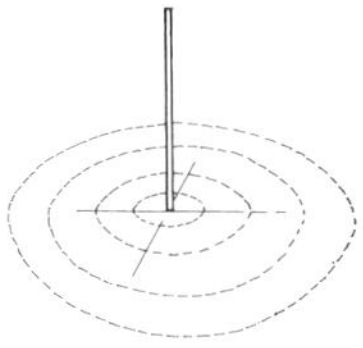

Obelisk with its verticality, commands the space in totality

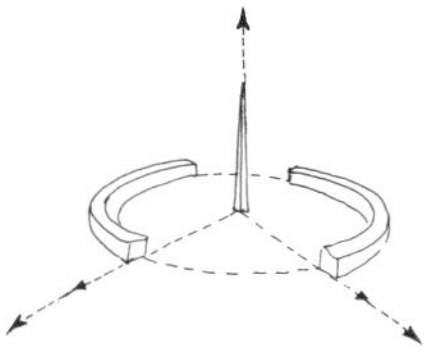

Obelisk with its centrality focuses the main cathedral

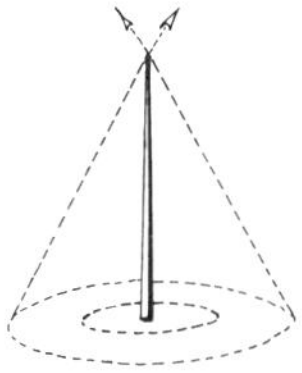

Obelisk with its axial presence generates an aura

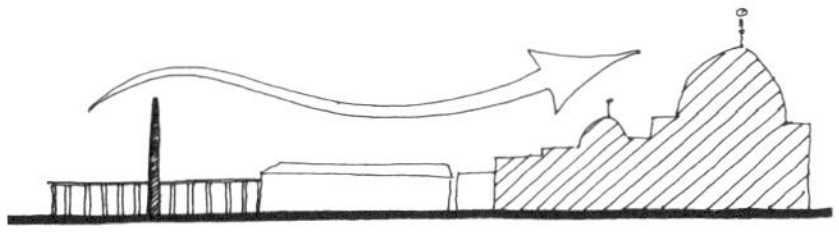

Obelisk governs the perception to the cathedral, becoming the landmark of the arena

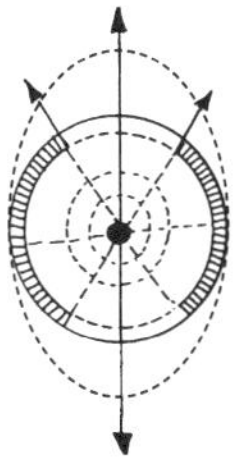

Axis defines the central zone as an interactive space with staging multiple acitivities

Columns attributes in forming rhythm

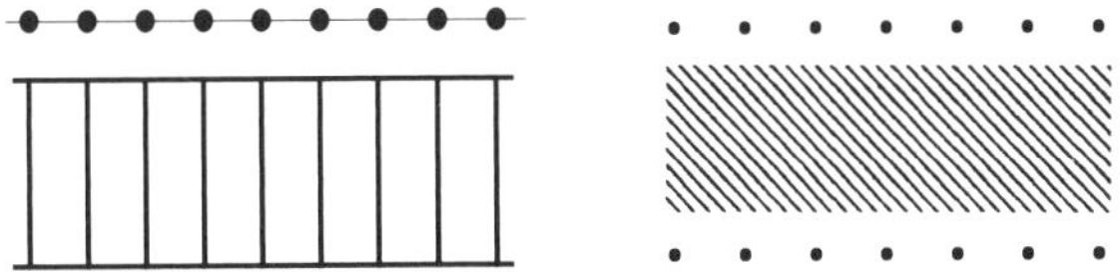

With constant rhythm and proportions, collonades together acquire planar quality

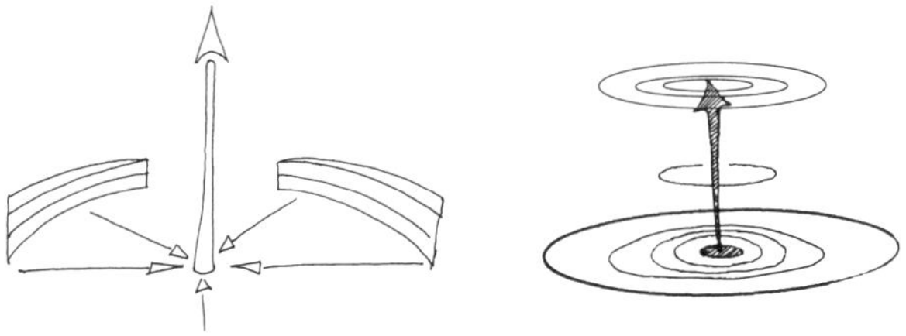

Collonades around the obelisk by creation of planes, giving a sense of definition and enclosure to the large open space, containg space within

Columns as movement guide

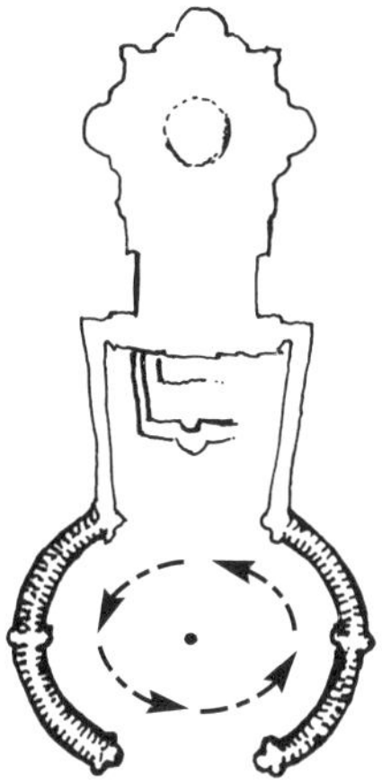

Collonades defining movement path

Collonades with a strong sense of direction, creating a concentrated and focused path of movement

• A column consists of three energy zones: the capital, the shaft (trunk) and the base. These should be articulated in such way that they juxtapose aesthetics and functions most naturally.

The capital, the junction of column shaft and the beam/lintel is generally expressed as an enlarged arm or girth at the top conveying a sense of holding the roof/lintel and relieving its weight to the trunk.

The girth of the trunk should feel reassuring, corresponding to the visual weight it supports, or can be used vice-versa to generate a tension in the space.

The base functions as a firm anchor that supports as well as absorbs the entire load.

• A freestanding column commands volume all around it. As far as possible column should be located independently to be received well by the surrounding components and retain its own identity and expression.

• Rhythm is the most potent attribute of the column, achieved through repetition. This can be exploited most creatively to introduce subspaces and impart dynamic perception while in movement. Any change in the established rhythm gets perceived as marking a node—a notional pause along the visual/ physical movement.Change in the rhythm can be offered through its spacing, the form of column or even the textural renderings, materials etc.

• Non-planar placement of columns defines volume, which can subtly sub-scale larger spaces, yet maintaining visual continuity and perception of the entire volume.

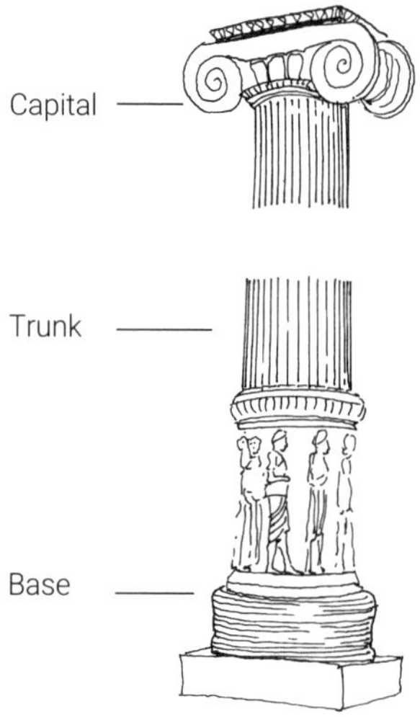

Energy Section

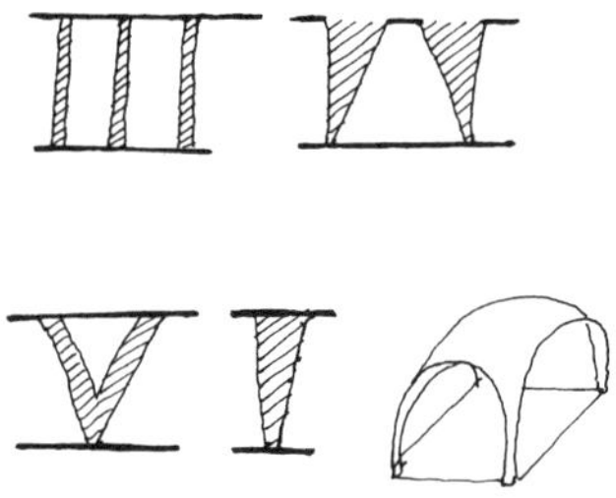
Various forms of column in accordance of transformation of load

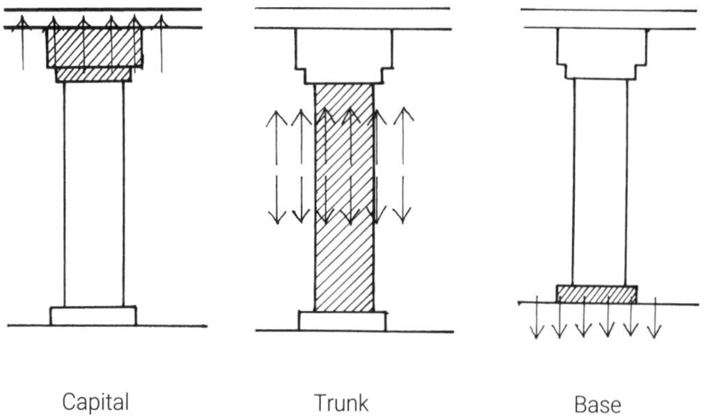

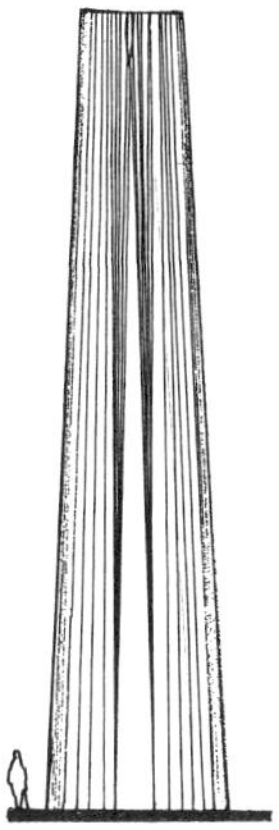

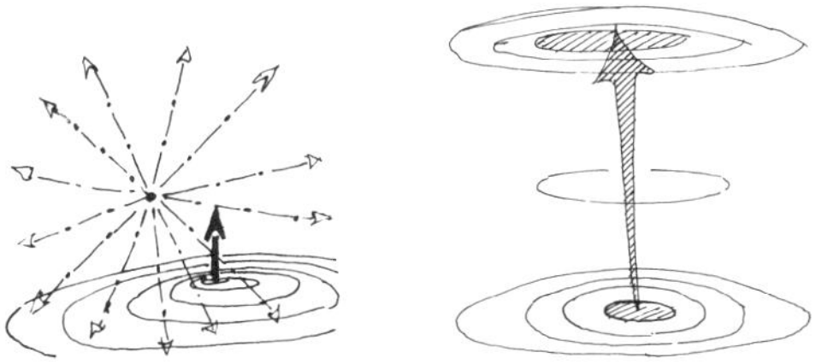

Column with an aura around enhances verticality around the space

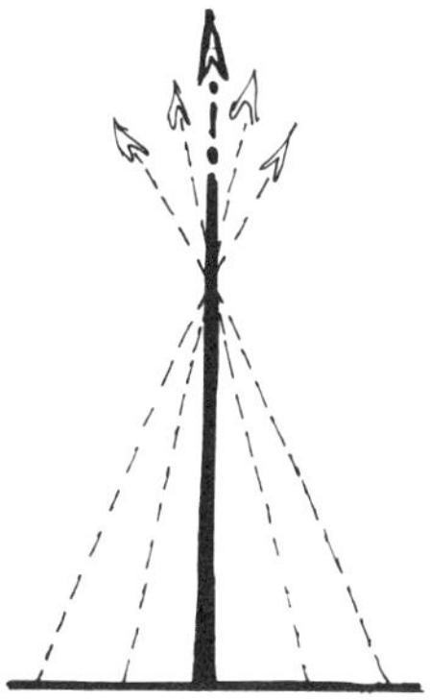

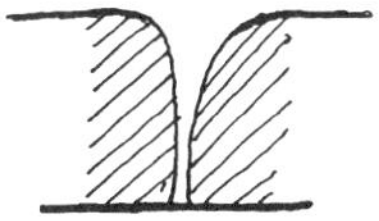

Column commanding over the space

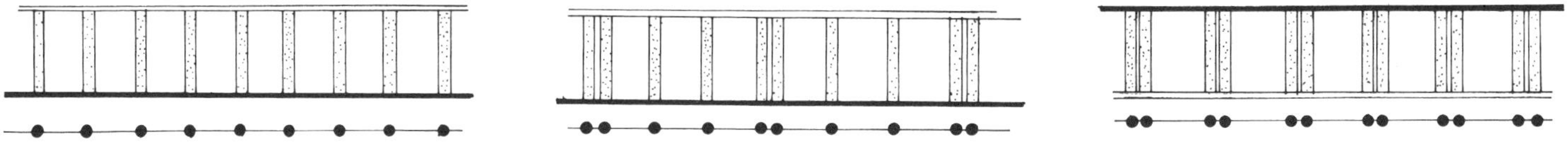

Diverse patterns created by various rythms formed by multiple columns introduced together

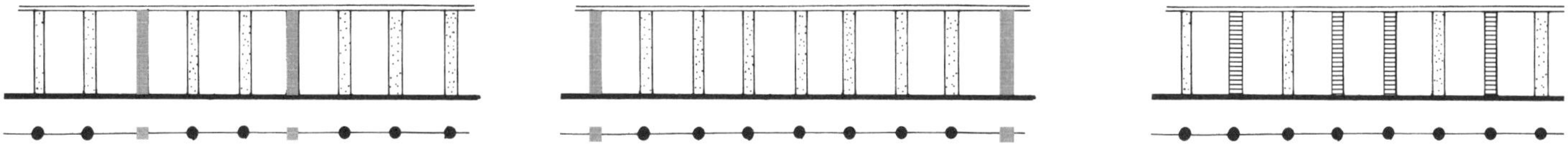

Diverse patterns created by various rythms formed by combination of columns varying in form or texture

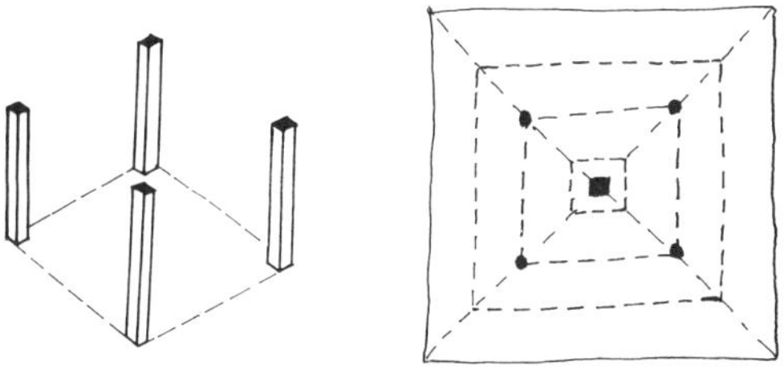

Placement of column forming subspaces within

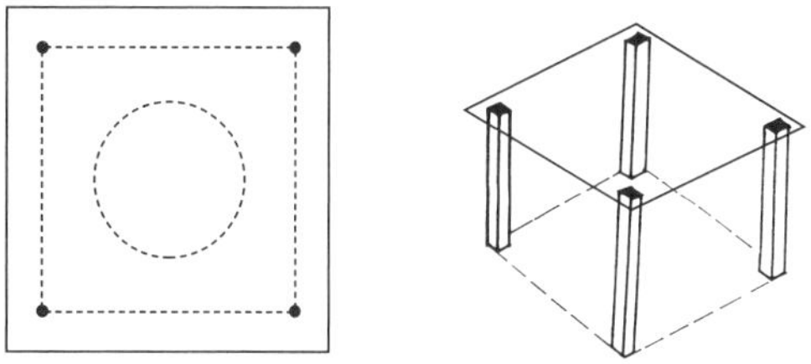

Columns help to define the space within, by suggesting an imaginary zone or boundary connecting them

WALL

Interior of a bhunga, Kutch

The wall is a vertical plane, which defines an enclosure. One of its prime purposes through time, even before the column, is that of taking structural load of the roof. Here masonry walls assume thickness dictated by material strength and the weight exerted by the structures above.

The word wall has its origin in Latin *vallum* meaning rampart, which can be further defined as an embankment of earth, stone, or other material constructed for defensive purposes. As *vallus* it is referred to as 'stake'. In Old English, it is also defined as a natural rampart, hill or cliff. The Sanskrit equivalent for the wall is *bhitti* which originates from the term *bhit* meaning to separate. Thus, primary obligation of the wall is to support, defend, barricade and separate spaces.

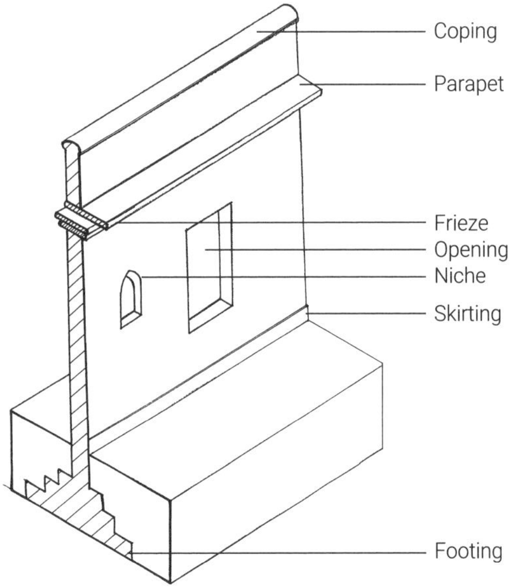

Typological Variations

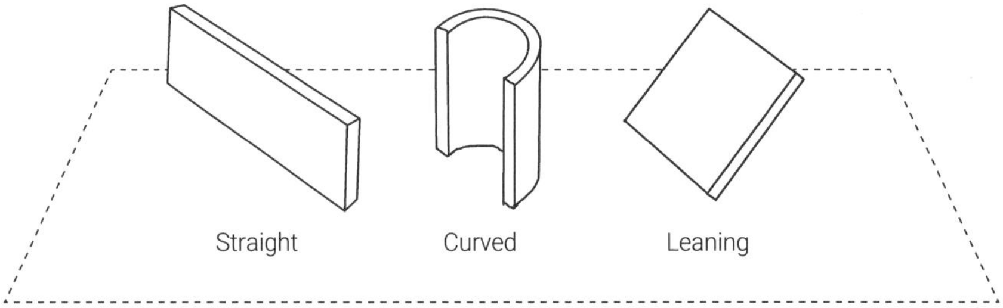

Shapes and inherent potentials

Wall as protective barrier—Individual dwellings

Walls form the main protective enclosure of a builtform from within and a defensive barrier from outside. They are also the visual plane surfaces, which may be punctured, if needed, to permit light, air, view and entry inside the building. Walls manifest themselves mainly as variations of solid and void spaces in a plane. Apart from becoming an envelope to spaces, walls also play the structural role of transmitting the roof-load to the ground. Accordingly, developments and variations in wall structures can be traced through history with regard to their structural significance, construction material and opening sizes. In prehistoric cave dwellings, the living spaces were scooped out of living rock providing inherently the vertical surfaces. Only when man began to build independent / freestanding structures, did the problem of constructing walls arise. In these earlier forms of buildings, walls were generally circular in plan, lapped at the top by a contiguous roof. With civilization and technological development, masonry structures evolved to resolve corners. This is when rectilinear load-bearing masonry walls carrying roof loads came to being.

Cave dwelling

Bushmen skerm

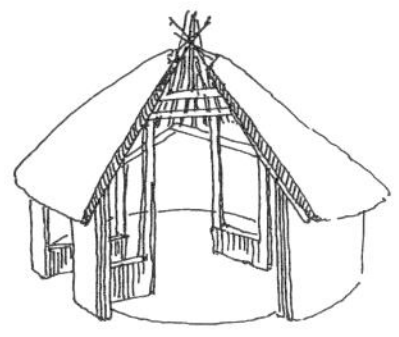

Pan-p'o dwelling

Tepees

Mesakin Quisare cluster dwelling, Sudan

Ludiya dwellling

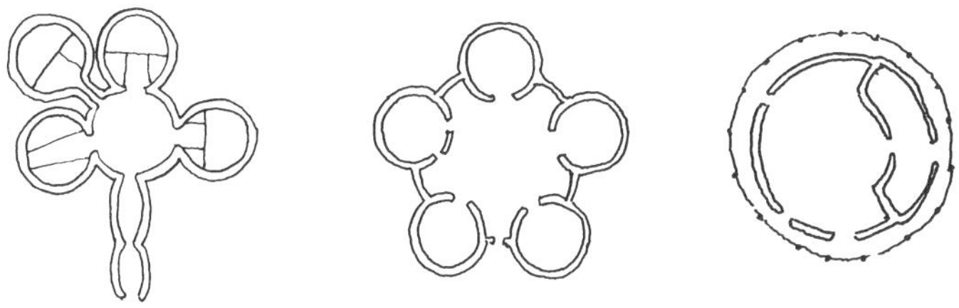

Walls circular in plan, gradually developing into spatial clusters of individual dwelling units

Wall as protective barrier—Collective dwellings

Arles, medieval city
within the amphitheatre

Taos Pueblo, New Mexico

Tower dwelling, Detwang (near Rothernburg)

The wall also served as a good protective element against external forces of climate and barbaric attacks. Thick walls with bastions and ramparts around the entire settlement became the norm in middle ages where defense was the main criteria of design.

The walls in domestic architecture being thick, provided an opportunity for carving out small portions in them which were used for storage or seating. But due to their structural requirements the opening sizes were restricted. Smaller windows and fewer openings placed sufficiently apart characterized these walls. Such walls became too heavy for multiple storeyed structures. To overcome these problems, reinforcement in the form of timber posts were introduced. This helped to reduce wall thickness and facilitate larger openings.

The introduction of arches in the Roman era allowed for larger punctures in the wall plane. Gothic and Renaissance saw it reach its peak with planes as arcade having more voids than solid. Finally with the development of frame structure, in steel or reinforced cement concrete, walls were completely relieved of all limitation of structure. Becoming thin and transparent, as they had in many ways also lost their protective expectations, the walls remained merely as partitions or curtains providing physical enclosure. They could however be used with great flexibility of form; shape and layout achieving varied spatial experiences.

The, once strong, massive ramparts, walls have come of age to become fragile, thin curtains, in steel and glass, demarcating and subdividing space and creating varied spatial experiences due to their flexibility of form and independence of structure. Its behaviour now resembles that of a fabric, flowing and enclosing freely, without any restrictions of form or function to generate sculptural qualities in the builtform.

Rectilinear load-bearing masonry walls carrying roof loads came into existence as civilization and technological development occured evolving into masonry structure resovling corners

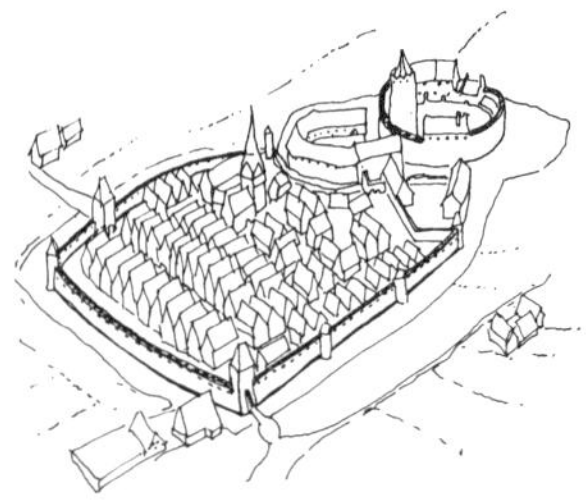

Budingen, German medieval city

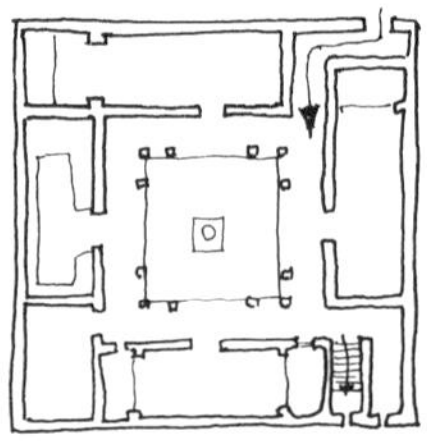

Moorish dars

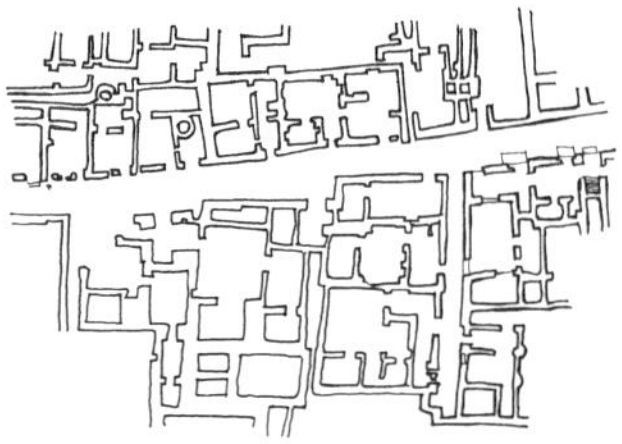

Mohenjo-Daro: Third Street area

Temple of Edfu, showing the first pylon

Roman wall system (thick walls with arches)

Timber framed building, Salisbury

Walls to form street facade

Introduction of arches and larger openings in Roman era

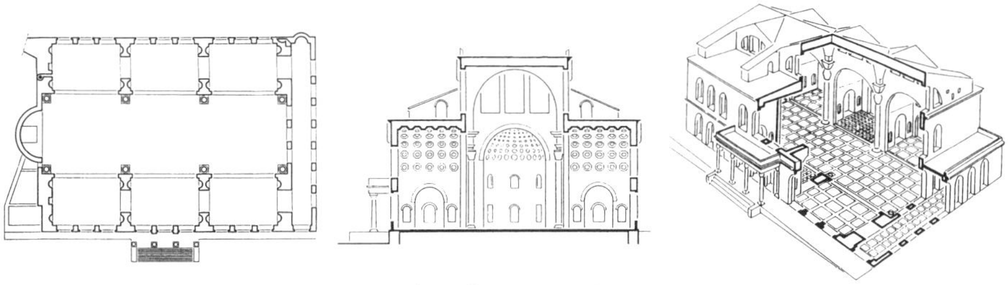

Basilica of Maxentius, Rome

Flying buttresses at Notre Dame Cathedral, Paris

In Gothic and Renaissance wall with its changing planar quality in form of arcades with more void than solid

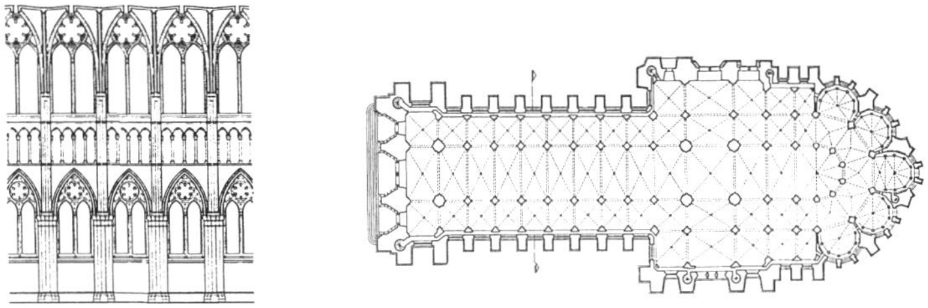

Reims Cathedral (Gothic period)

Palazzo della Cancelleria, Rome (Renaissance period)

Wall as fragile and thin planes of steel and glass with the industrialization and discovery of new building materials and techniques

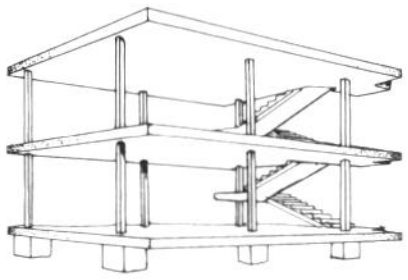

Domino House Project

The Glass House at New Canaan, Connecticut

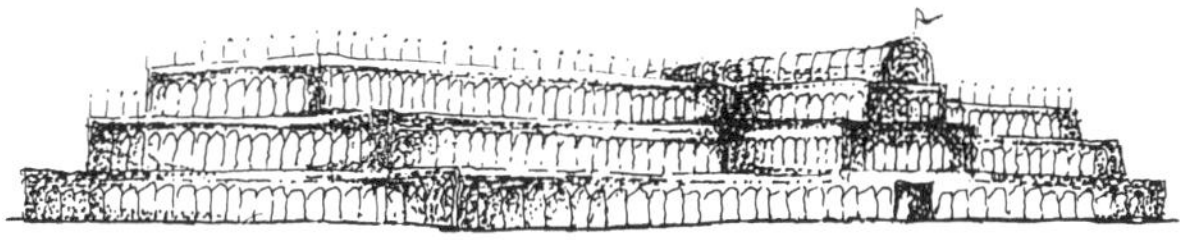

The Crystal Palace, London

Freedom of formal language and independence from structural constraints with the technological progress

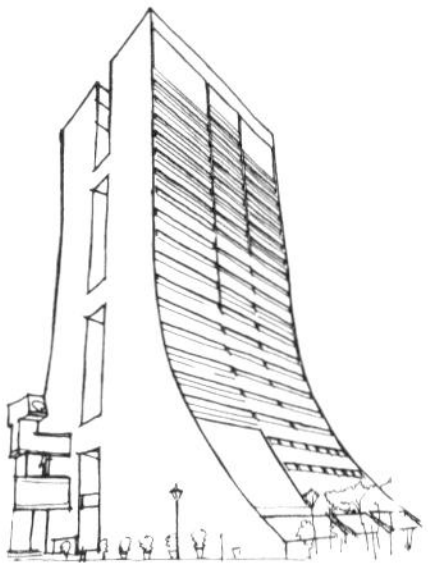

Civic centre, New Delhi

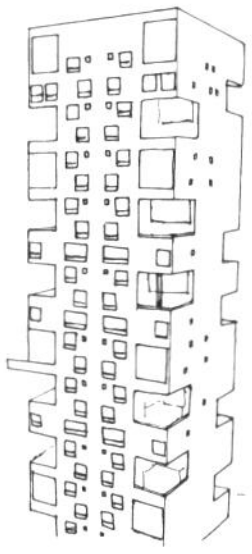

Kanchanjunga flats, Bombay

Einstein Tower, Postdam

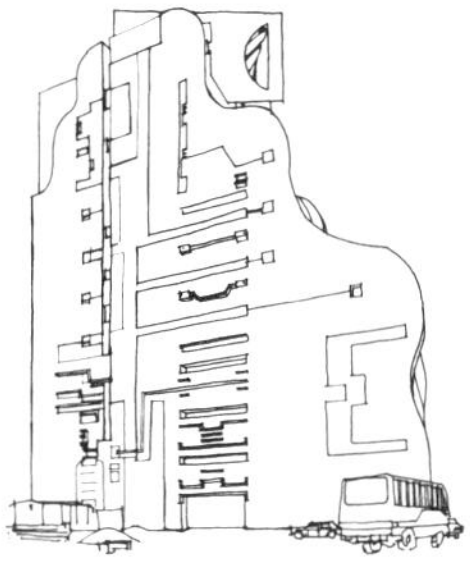

Nation Tower, Bangkok

VERTICALITY

Wall is essentially an extrusion of a line in the Z axis to generate a vertical plane. Thus, its primary definition is more through its modulation in the vertical dimension than the horizontal. Verticality, if not necessarily perpendicularity, from the ground plane is thus, an inherent aspect of a wall plane. With this attribute, walls naturally emerge as baffles or barriers. The unity or convergence of two or more wall planes also remains primary to creating a sense of enclosure and volume.

Wall creating space with the verticality and enclosing volumes with its compositional language

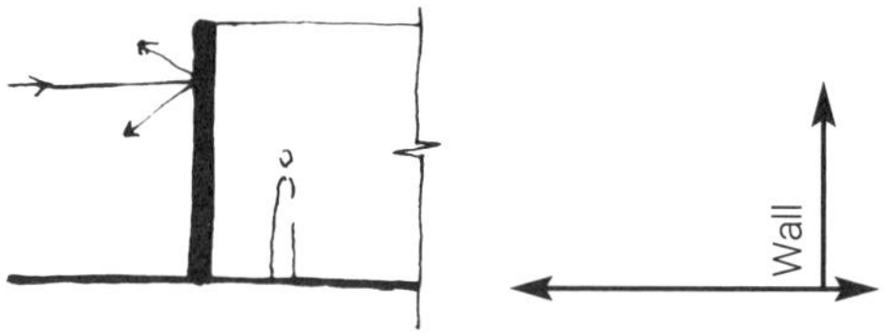

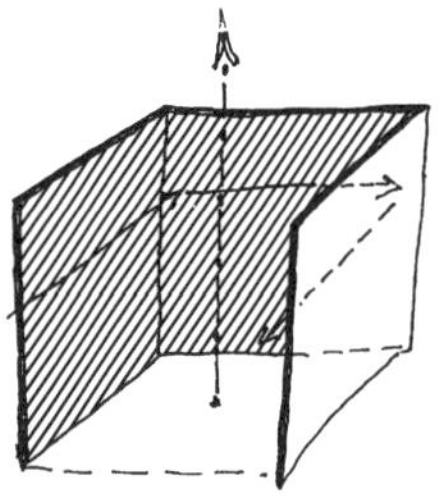

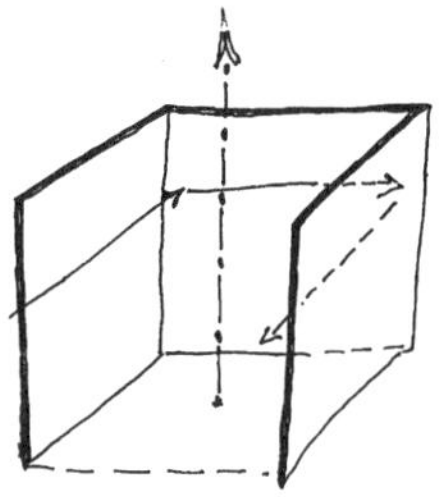

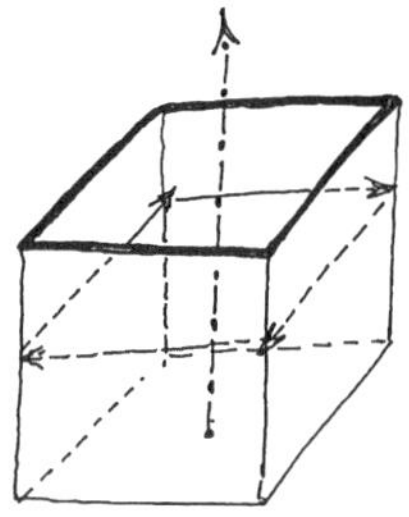

Wall with planar compositions creating openings, subspaces and movement zones

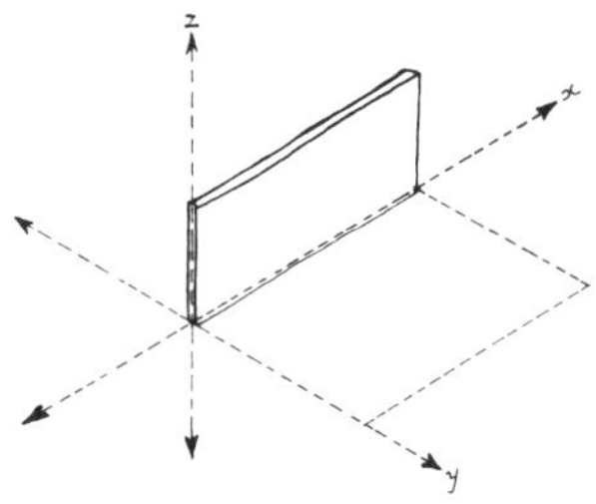

Wall as an extrusion of a line in Z Axis

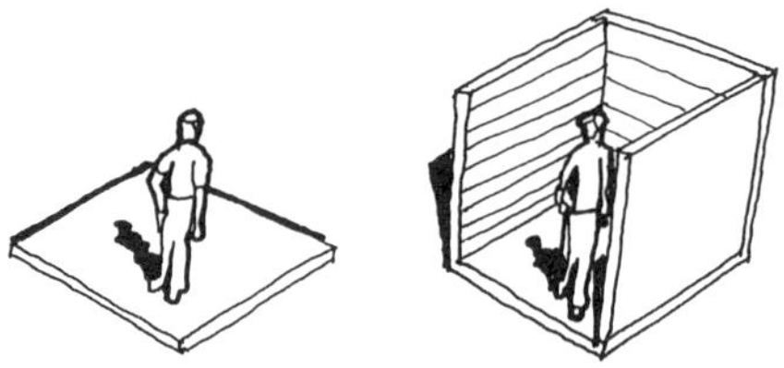

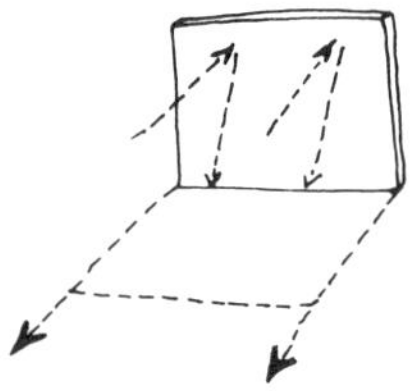

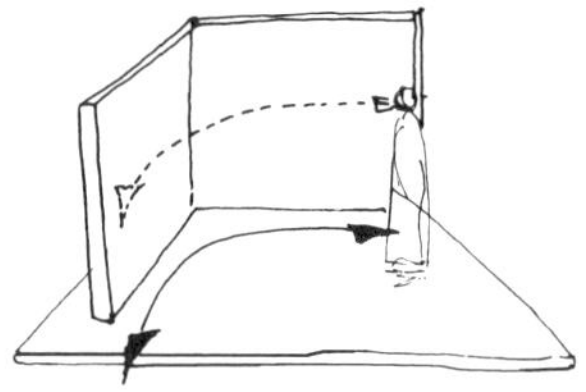

Wall defining space with the planar organization

PLANARITY

From the initial usage of fabric as infill between support struts by the nomads, the wall as a vertical surface has come a long way but it has still not lost, even through the ages, its essence of planarity. After having gone though the ages where more structural responsibility was expected of the wall, it has once again freed itself of all determinants to express as a planar fabric free to explore sculptural forms as fabric. The height and length of the wall, defining the planarity, with respect to its position in space endow it with varied characteristics. The thickness of the wall does not matter as much in terms of sensory perception and is more of a defence or structural requirement. This aspect of planarity provides the opportunity for surface articulation to be the common rendering upon the wall.

Wall demarcating spaces with its planarity..

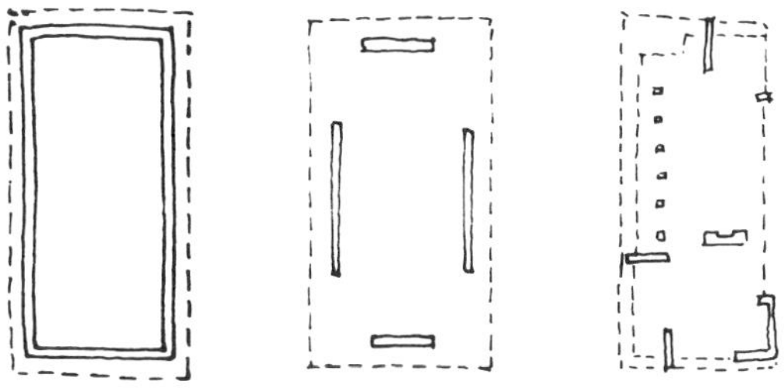

Wall as a plane expanding in Z and X axis

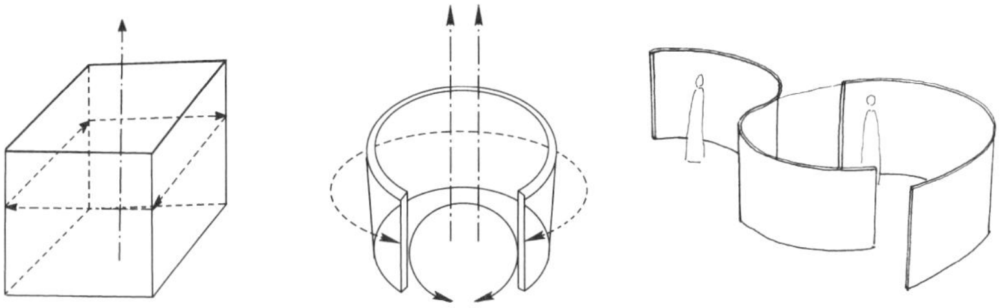

Wall creating volumes with its planarity

The propensity of wall to create planes with the surface configuration attributes strong spatial language to the element.......................................

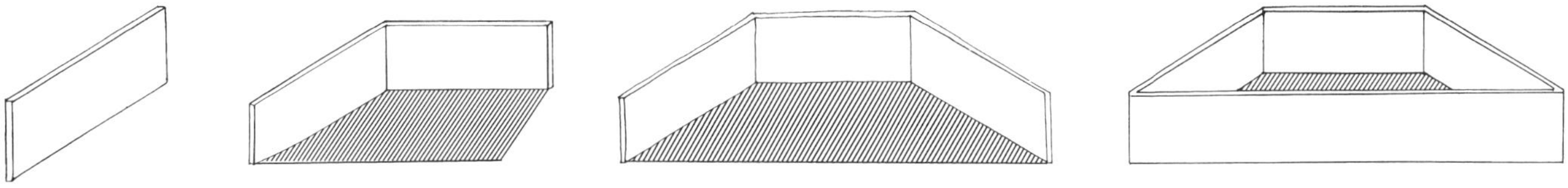

Wall acts as a barrier and delimits the space it creates

WALL FOR DEMARCATING TERRITORY

The wall, as a vertical plane, defines and delineates extent of the horizontal surface. With opacity, it becomes a termination of realms. The points of entry and egress become the thresholds of these realms, initiating notions of transition, an interstitial space between two absolute domains. This is accentuated through the superimposition of semiotics—notional meanings, over vertical spatial ensembles leading to ready perception and added import. The wall, being the physical separator of spaces, takes on these notional connotations as surface decoration, embellishment and articulation. This demarcation of realms with different qualitative and spatial attributes, through diverse encoded symbolism, displays gestalt. Private and public nature, accessibility and political rights, sacred and profane-determined by hierarchies of sanctity, protected and exposed are suggested by treatment, degrees of enclosure and quality of light, scale, etc.

Wall as an element defining extent..

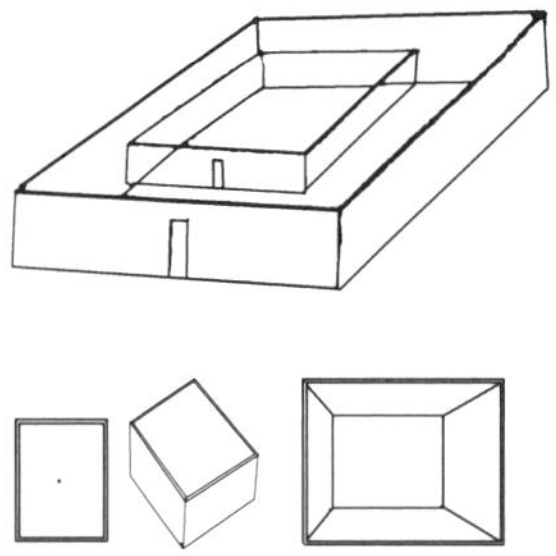

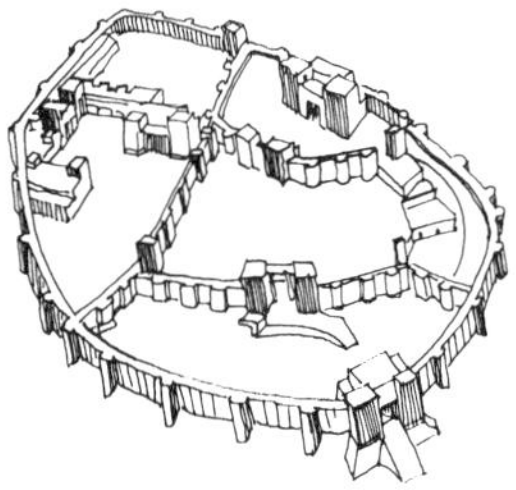

Citadel, Zincirli

In the religious complex, wall acquires a meaning as it distinguishes sacred from profane

Chapel of Notre Dame du Haut, Ronchamp

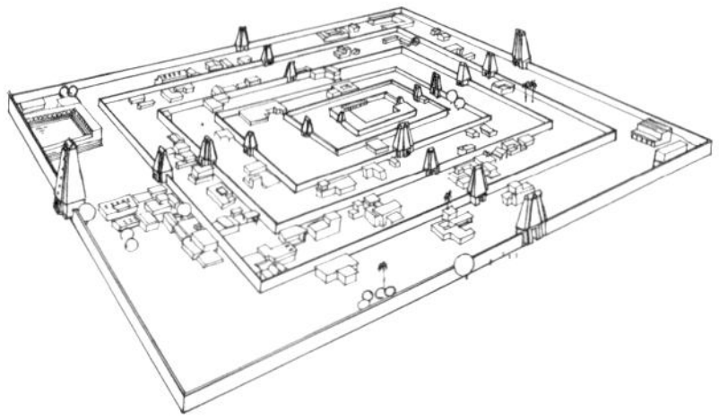

Temple complex, Srirangam

At domestic scale, wall becomes an element demarcating public realm from the private, with its placement and spatial organization

Mud wall, Rajasthan

At public scale, wall signifies various levels of accessibility and political territories

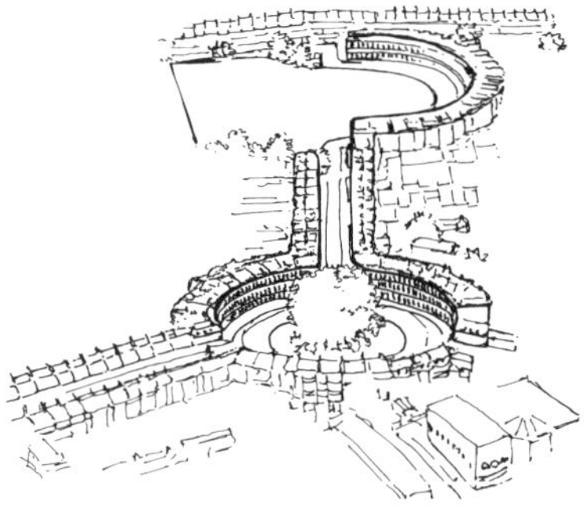

Circus and Royal Crescent at Bath, Avon

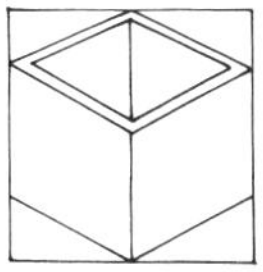

WALL FOR ENCLOSING VOLUME

The inherent verticality of the wall makes it command volume and the attribute of planarity helps contain this in. A singular wall plane can dominate the entire volume facing the visual axis in-between the perceiver along the entire extent of the wall plane. Two angularly placed wall planes can contain volume through their physical or implied corners, while more than two wall planes bind the volume within them. While containing the space within it also evokes notions associated with within and without.

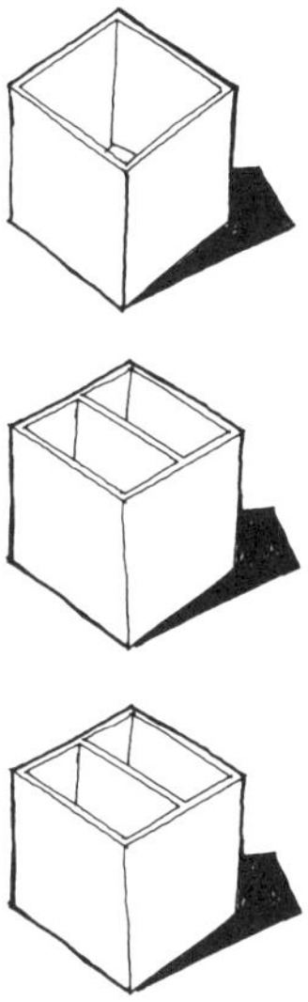

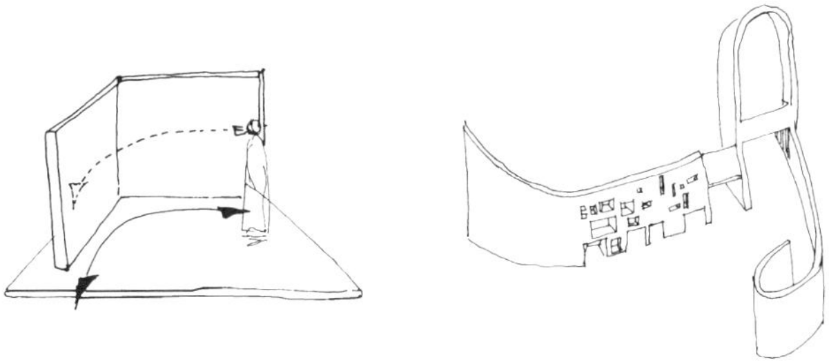

Chapel of Notre Dame du Haut, Ronchamp

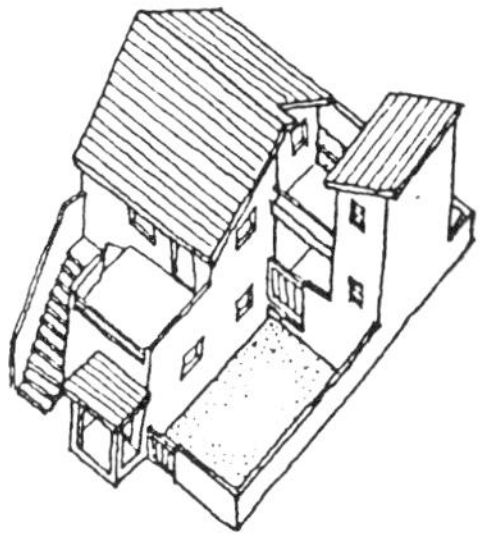

Belapur Housing, New Bombay, Maharashtra

The uniquely characterized form of the wall attributes a distinct sensual quality to the space within

Conservatory, Chatsworth, Derbyshire

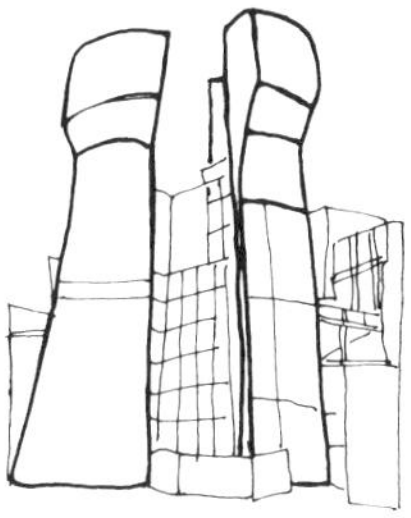

Wexner Center, Ohio

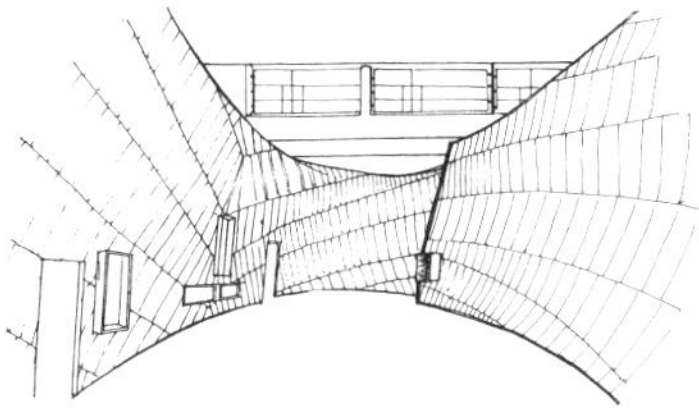

Ahmedabad Textile Mill Owners' Association House, Ahmedabad

Wall creating a sense of inside/outside, by containing spaces through its contiguity

Ahmedabad pol, Ahmedabad

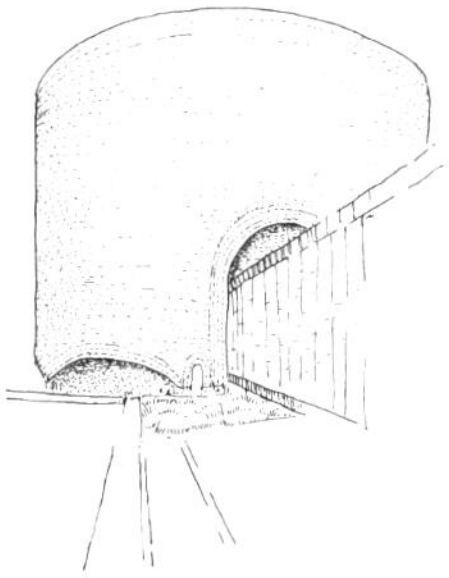

MIT Chapel, Massachusetts

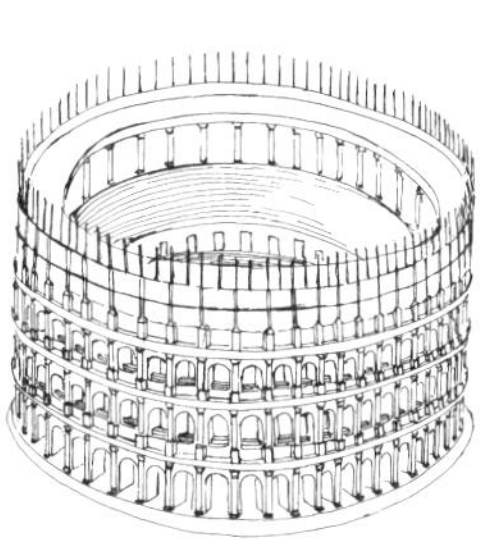

Colosseum, Rome

WALL FOR SUBDIVISION OF SPACE

Based on the different kinds of activity patterns, uses and requirements, large spaces need to be subdivided into smaller pockets, performing specific roles. As physical, visual, notional barriers, depending on the material and construction, walls subdivide and modulate space into smaller or larger, contiguous or discretely perceptible subspaces. These trigger ideas of privacy, microcosm and concentricity. The division creates adjunct spaces with the intention of making discernable parts within the whole. Just as the wall along with the roof defines notion of "indoors" or "outdoors" between built and open space and segregates the interiors from the exteriors, the interior walls of a structure differentiate and demarcate subspaces or rooms within it, thereby forming the thresholds within.

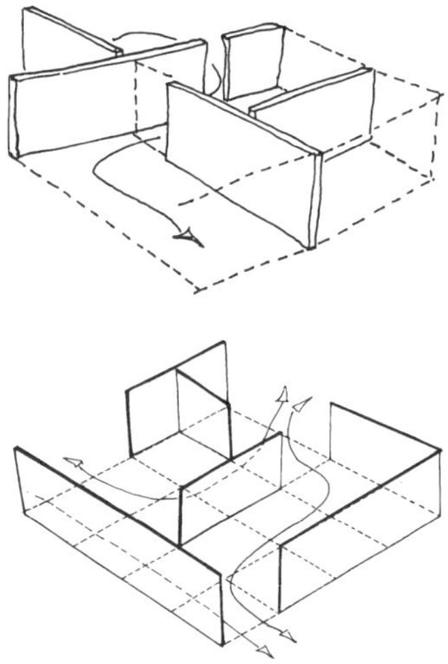

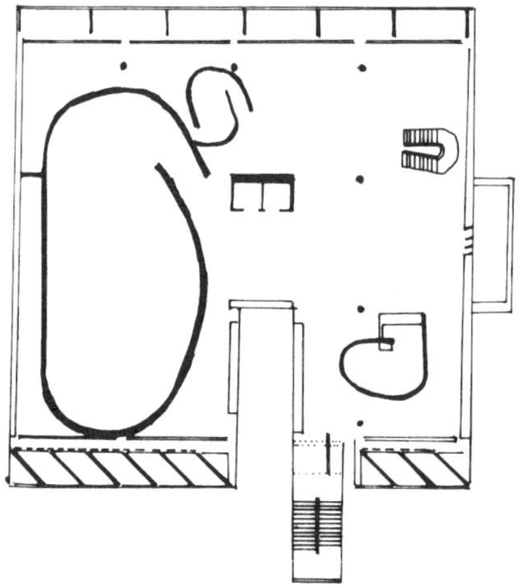

Ahmedabad Textile Mill Owners' Association House, Ahmedabad

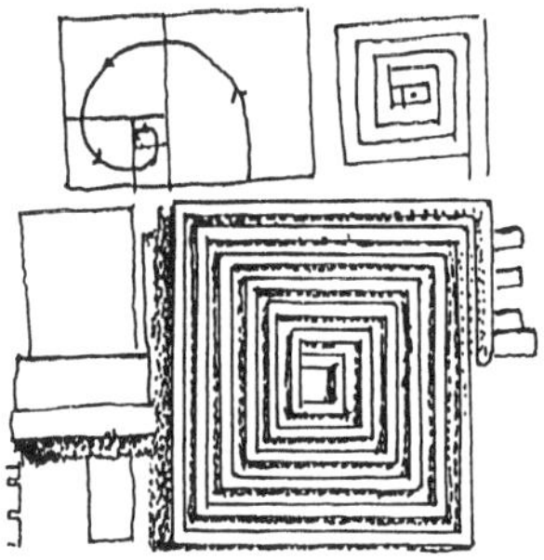

Museum of Endless Growth, Algeria

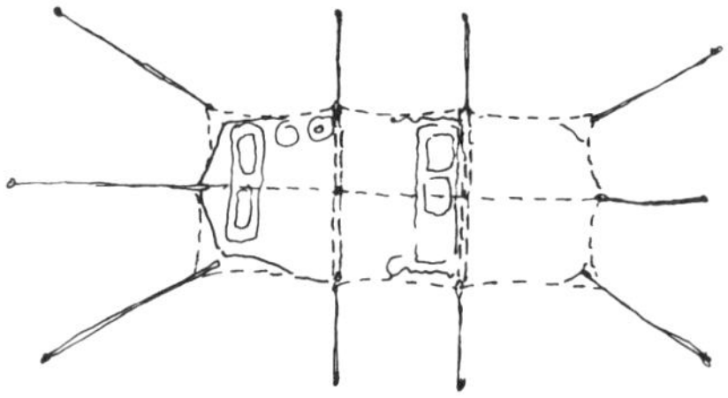

Bedouin Tent, North Africa

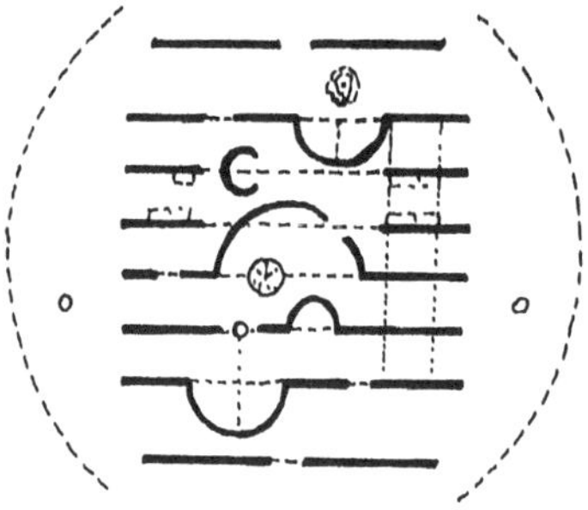

Arnhem Pavilion, Netherland

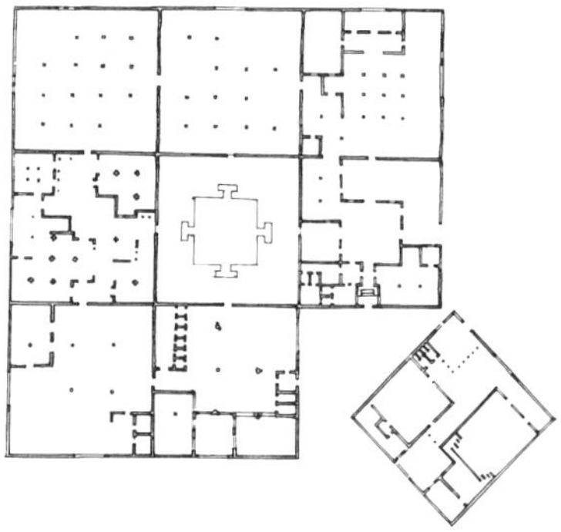

Jawahar Kala Kendra, Jaipur

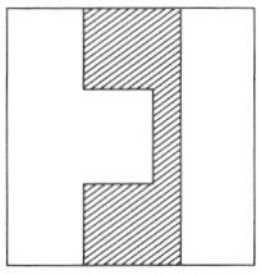

WALL AS DISPLAY AND STORAGE ELEMENT

Though walls convey the idea of planes, their construction technique and material used requires them to possess some thickness. In masonry walls, plasticized earth or rock cut architecture, especially, the wall begins to assume mass due to various other requirements of load-bearing combined with the structural capacities of the material, defence etc. This depth affords the provision of small niches, alcoves, and shelves within the wall, which could be used for various kinds of storage, as well as display. In some cases the niches open out on the external side creating a seating space interacting with the exteriors. The requirements for storage are also met with by creating alcoves through folding walls.

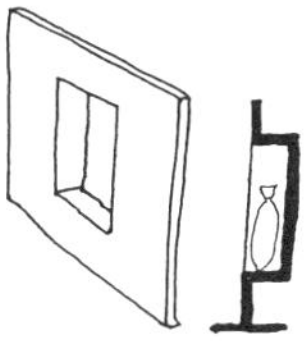

Wall as alcolve

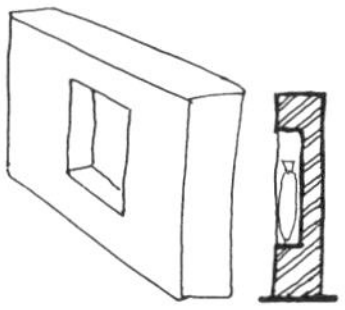

Wall as niche

Wall as a display element

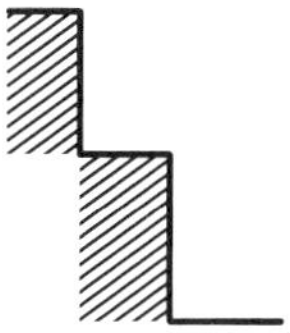

Wall terminating to form storage area

Gokhla-a niche

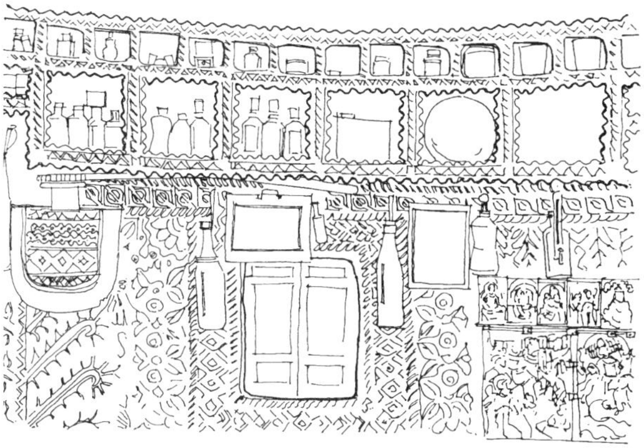

Interior wall of Kutch house

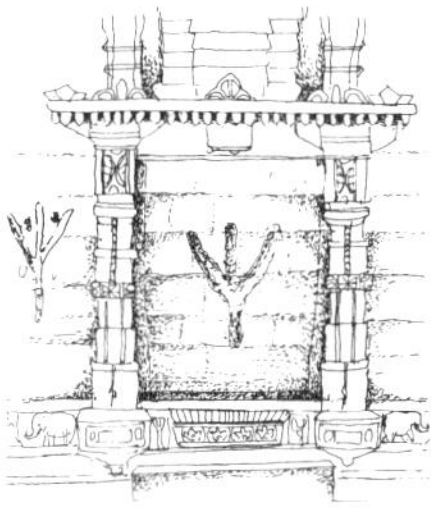

Wall baring religious motifs

Mayur Chowk in City Palace, Udaipur

Jaoul House, France

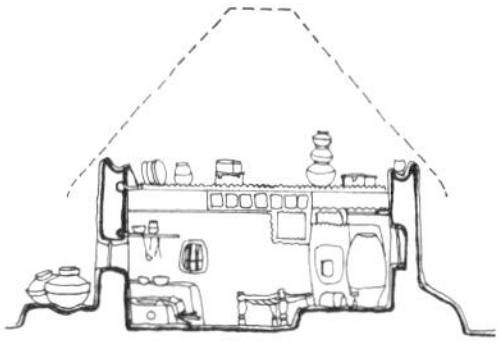

Interiors of Bhunga house, Kutch

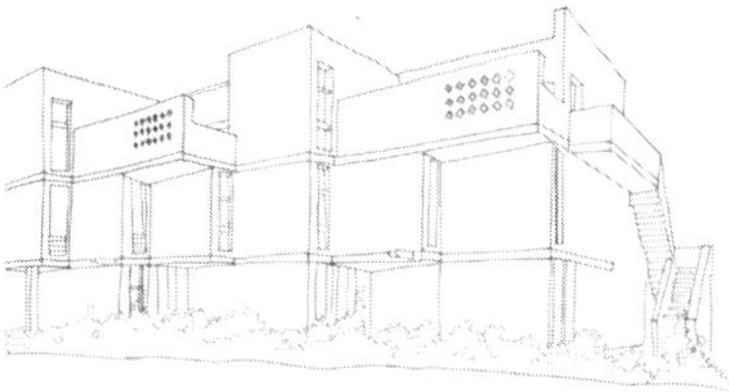

Asian Games village

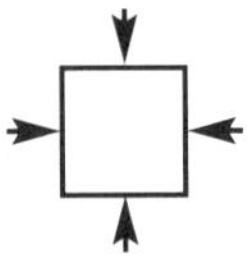

WALL AS PROTECTIVE BARRIER

As planes possessing height, walls entrap space when they close in on themselves. This, combined with the property of being a physical barrier bestows upon it the responsibility of protection—of a controlled microcosm within a vast macrocosm—physically, notionally, climatically etc. The primary realization of man, who, through evolution, possessed remarkable mental capacities, but comparatively negligible physical prowess to even survive in the wilderness sought to protect himself extraneously by seeking shelter or building it. This aspect of protective barrier was applied profusely for individual as well as collective defense in the medieval period. Ramparts for settlements and the entirely fortified cities are unique architectural resolutions of walls for their purpose.

Wall as an individual and collective defence barrier

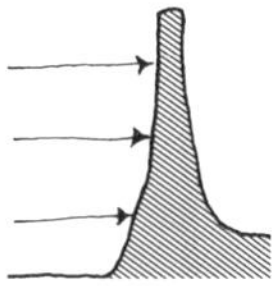

Wall as an individual and collective defence barrier

Entrance of Sam house, Jaisalmer

Fort wall of Jaisalmer, Rajasthan

Gwalior Fort, Madhya Pradesh

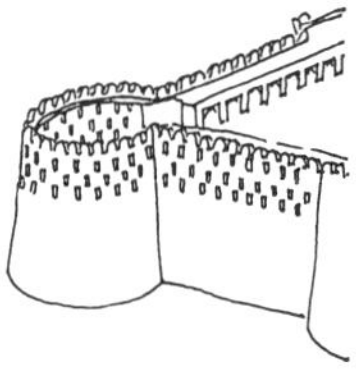

Bastion Wall

Anthill Mosque, Central Africa

Taos Pueblo, New Mexico

Sayyid Usman's Mosque, Ahmedabad

Hogan dwelling of Navajo people, South-West USA

Structure and form of the wall serves the purpose of defense

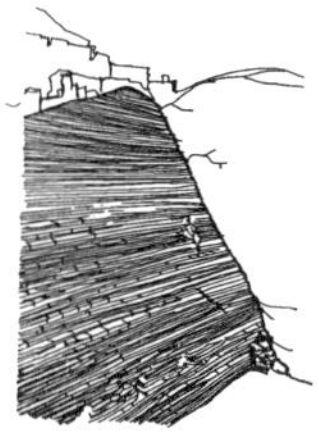

Ramparts

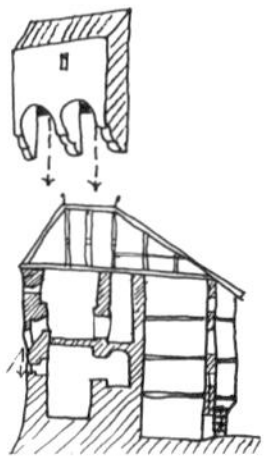

Bastion with loopholes and machicoulis

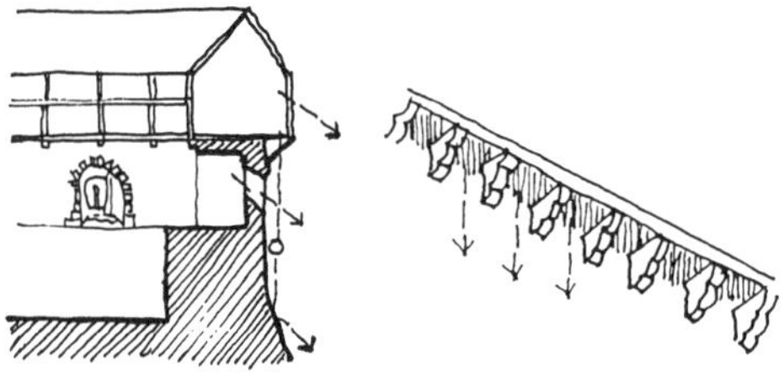

Wall walle or 'chemin-de-ronde'

WALL AS MOVEMENT GUIDE

Being a physical barrier, the wall does not allow penetration through it. Combined with its planarity through stretched planes, it guides movement along its length. Also, due to other aspects of the wall, such as visual composition and graphics, degree of opacity, texture, scale and proximity with other elements, the wall generates physical patterns of movement. Also with spatial notions of constriction and release, synonymous with the sense of movement and arrival, it implies route and place respectively. Through baffles, it induces the element of surprise in the journey.

Walls modulated to form movement guide..

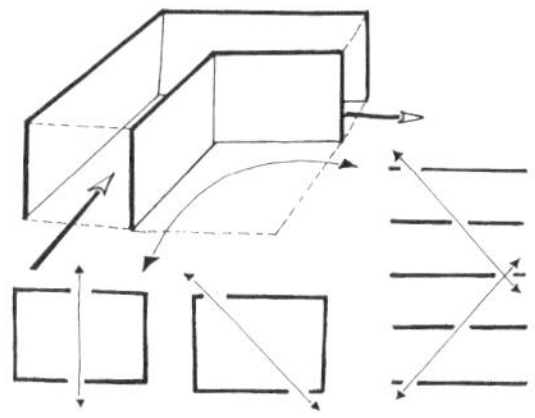
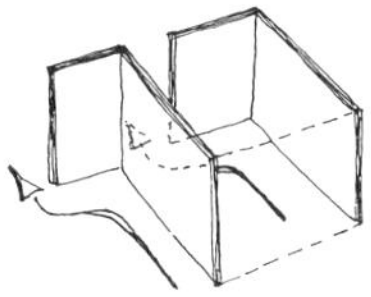
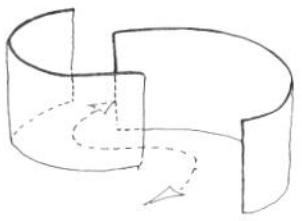
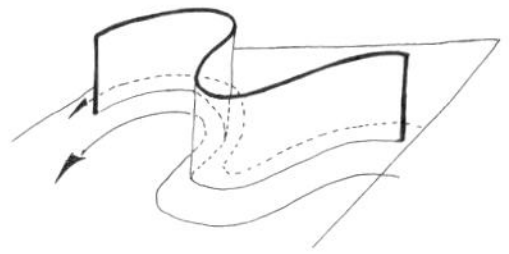

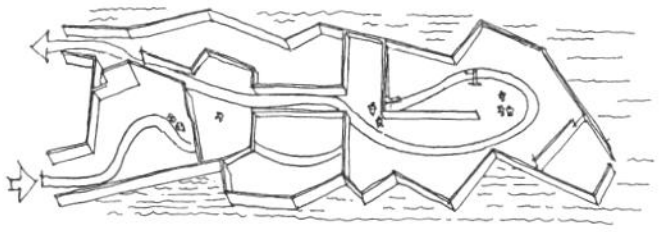

Hindustan Lever Pavilion, New Delhi

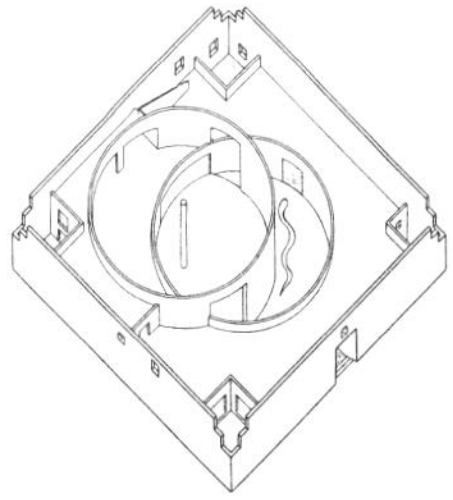

Documentation-space of Jawahar Kala Kendra, Jaipur

Massing of the wall defines the movement zone...

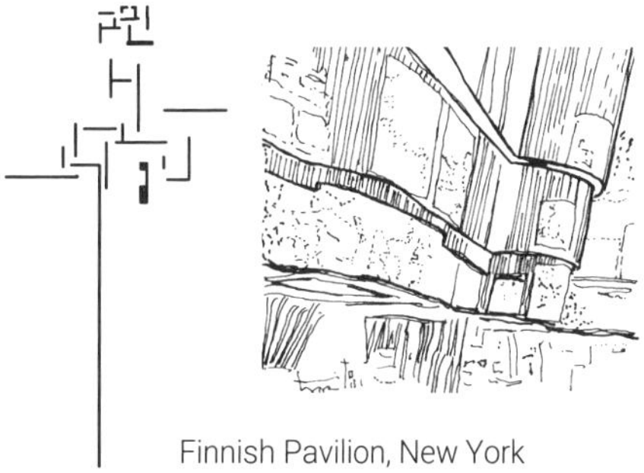

Finnish Pavilion, New York

Cidade-de-Goa, Goa

Indian Institute of Management, Ahmedabad

Udaipur City Palace, Udaipur

Pol street, Ahmedabad

WALL AS FORM GIVER AND FACADE MODULATOR

The wall plane-as the external envelope of interior space, perpendicular to the line of sight becomes the single most conspicuous element forming the facade of any structure. It faces competition only from the roof to complete the image of the building. The profile, proportion, placement, articulation, degree and kind of openings and material of the wall plane impart character to the building and define the external edge. It moulds the facade of the structure also by taking on surface embellishment, applied decoration and cladding.

National Dairy Development Board, New Delhi

Bank of China, Hong Kong

University of Jodhpur, Rajasthan

Casa Mila, Barcelona

Kunsthaus, Vienna

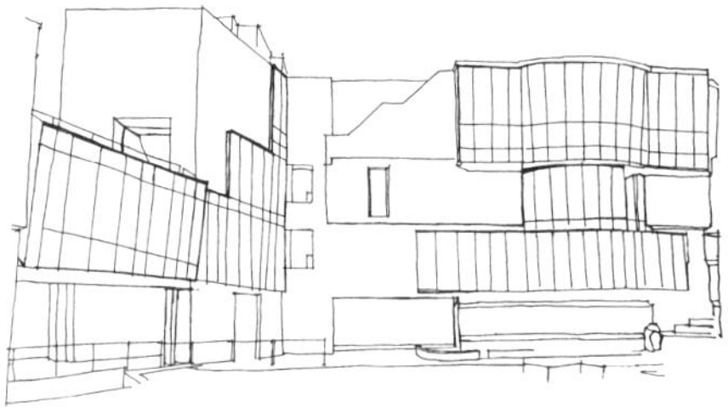

NIFT, New Delhi

Church of St. Carlo alle Quattro Fontane

Habitat Expo'67, Canada

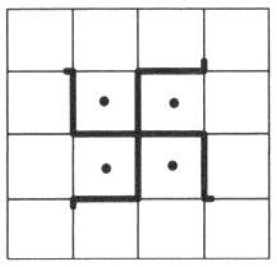

WALL AS COMMUNICATOR AND ENCODER OF MESSAGES

As a vertical plane, most evident in the cone of vision, walls as barriers become the most potent communication elements capable of encoding messages.

Visual messages through set of motifs, symbols and decorations articulated on wall surfaces instill meaning, more notional than physical. The transparency or opacity, the directness or indirectness, the solidity or delicacy, the impairing or inviting scales of the walls are also other forms of communication. Wall also engages itself in suggesting invitation or restriction.

Bhunga, Kutch

Airavateswarar Temple, Darasuram, Tamil Nadu

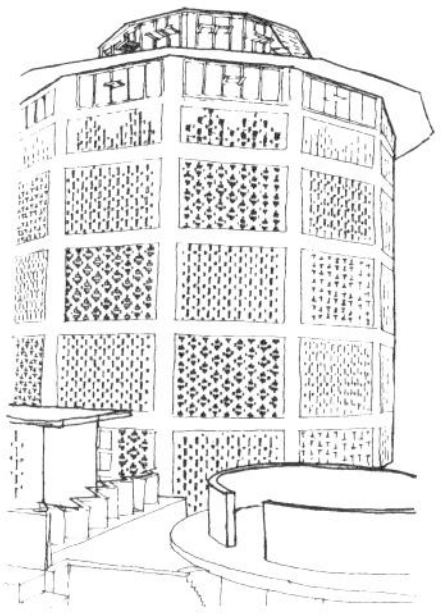

Centre for Development Studies, Thiruvananthapuram

Street facade, Jaipur

Wall with its visual legibility as a vertical plane becomes a conspicuous element for communication

Wall bearing folk art in the form of paintings and symbols

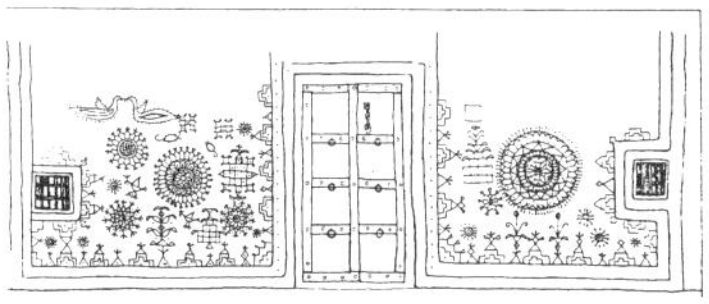

Bhunga House, Kutch

Shekhawat Haveli, Shekhawat

Wall communicating through mythological and religious motifs, in the form of relief

Airavateswarar Temple, Darasuram, Tamil Nadu

Temple Plinth

UDAIPUR PALACE,RAJASTHAN

The City Palace, Udaipur, dates from the period after 1567, undergoing accretive development.

The wall here, possessing great height, dwarfs the human scale and functions as a protective barrier and makes up the imposing facade of the builtform when seen over the expanse of the lake. The smaller bastions and articulations help in proportioning and scaling the mass.

The overall form is further enhanced engulfing the volume within.

With its sheer verticality, it becomes the most potent communication element capable of encoding messages while guiding movement along it to the entry. Internally, the walls delineate territories creating varied zones and different ambiences.

Wall modulating the facade

Walls articulating forms and conjuring masses throughout the palace complex

Wall attributing verticality

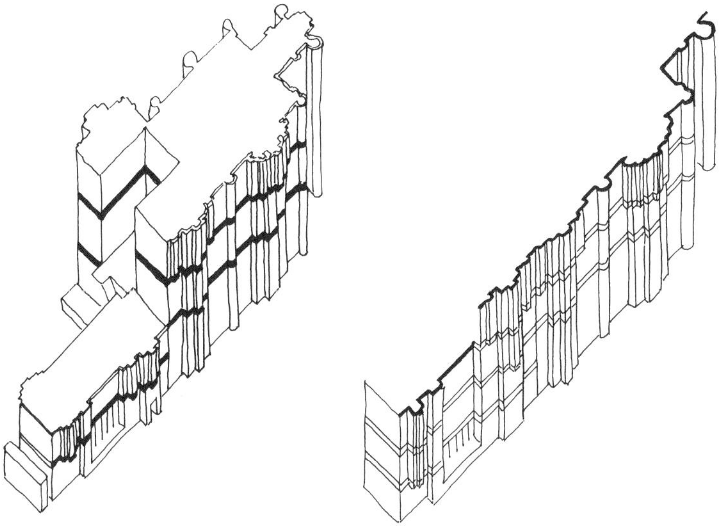

Forming the envelope for the interior spaces, the exterior wall becomes the most discernible element asserting the massive and majestic palace complex

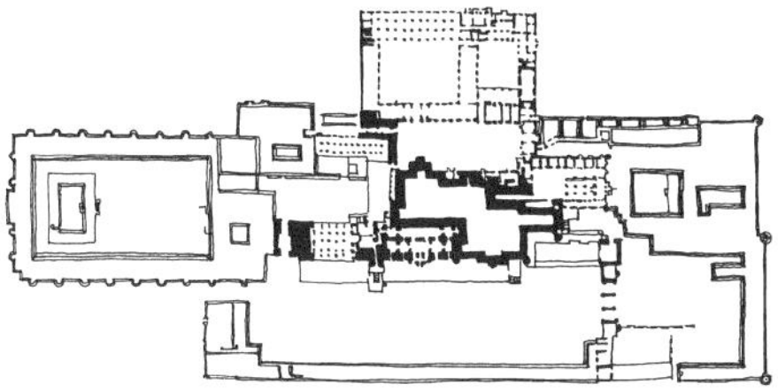

Wall enclosing volume

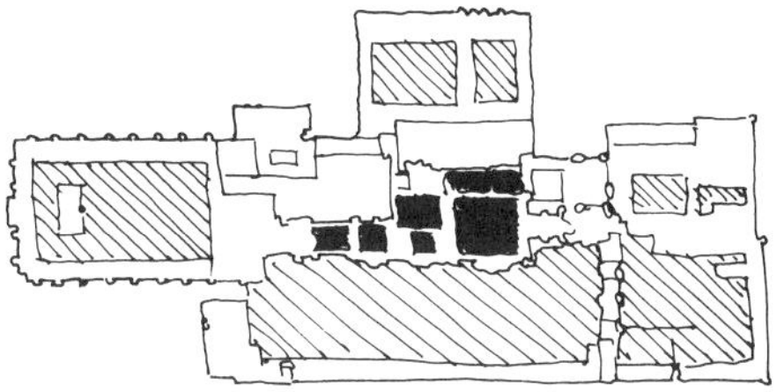

Wall as a protective barrier

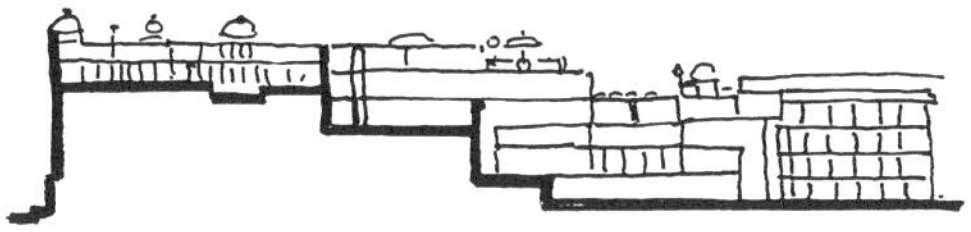

Wall becomes a plane with thickness, portrays strength and creates a sense of security

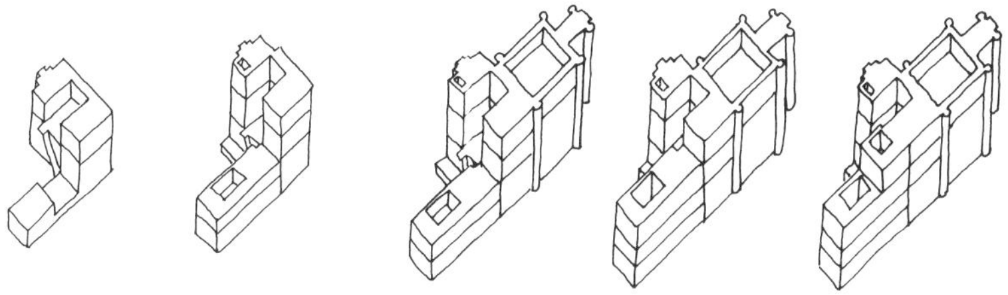

Evolution of the complex by vertical layering and additions of courtyard and terraces created by composition of mass, wherein the mass is a result of the organization of walls.

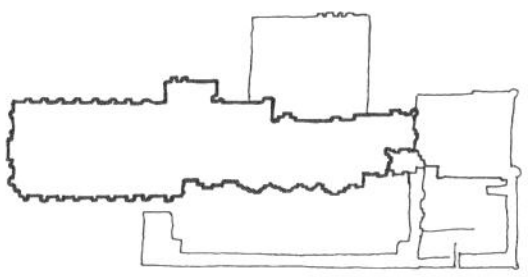

Cascading of the wall at the periphery

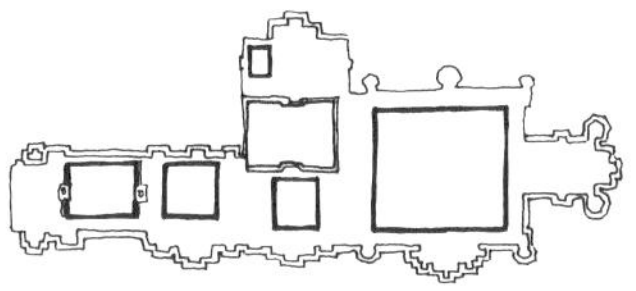

Wall forming the facade by articulating openings and attributing rhythm to the facade

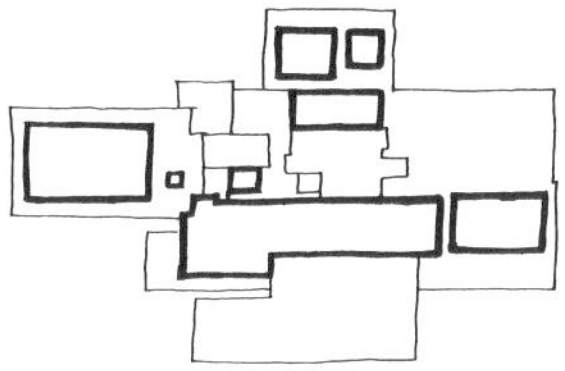

Walls enclosing the volume to define spaces, reciprocating the activity pattern within

Walls creating enclosed subspaces and courtyards by subdividing and defining movement paths

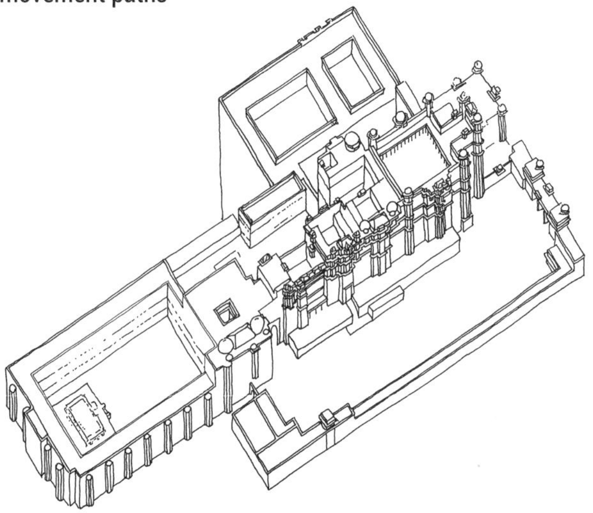

Wall as an identifiable element demarcating areas of different attributes and hierarchy

Wall demarcating zones and spatial clusters in the complex

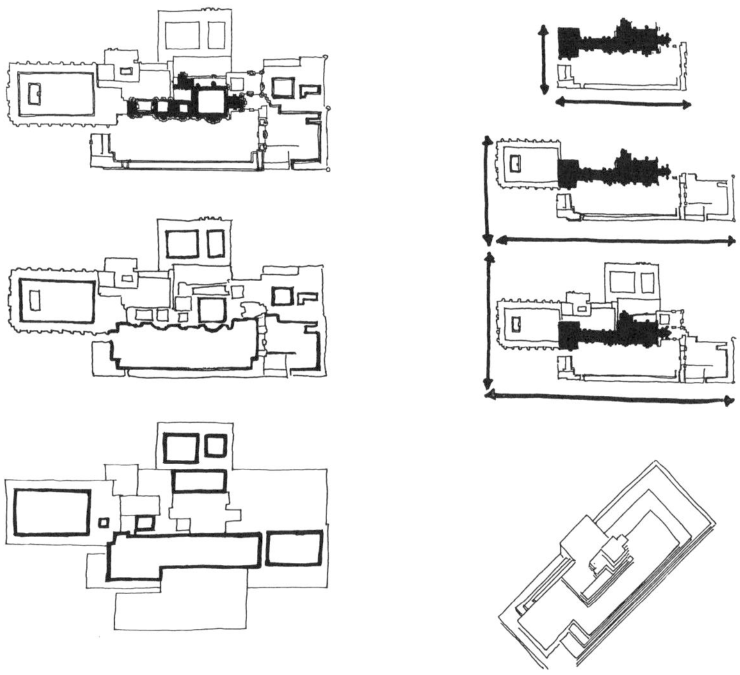

Wall performing a dual function of subdivision and definition

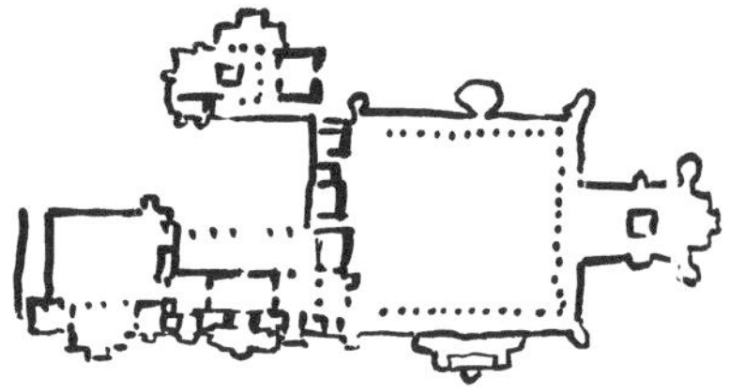

Plan

Enclosure of the entire volume predominantly occurs by the external configuration of walls

Multilayered organization of the palace complex reflects a strong growth patterns

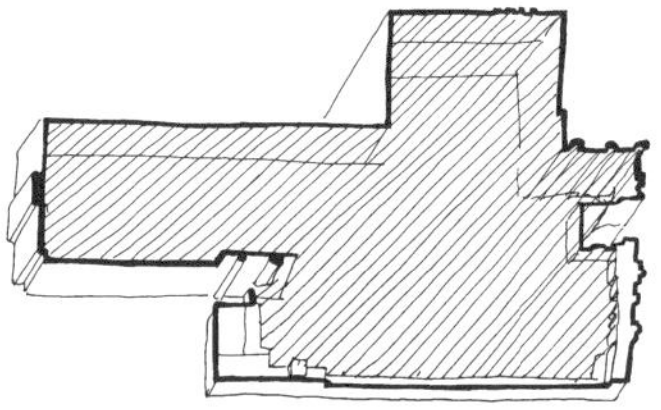

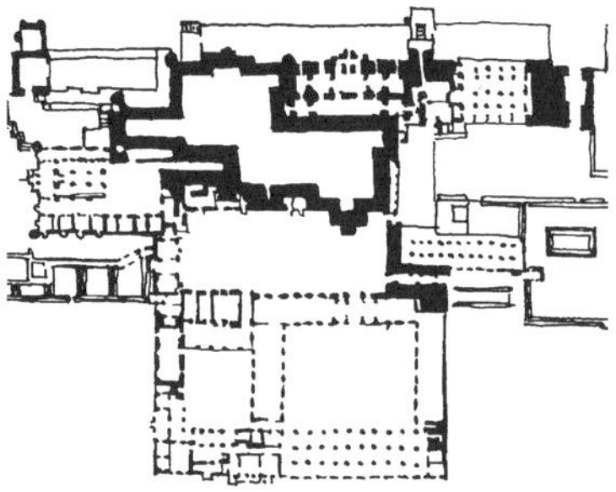

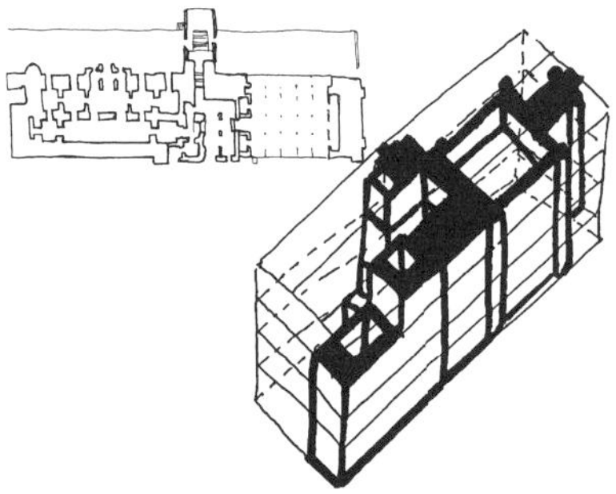

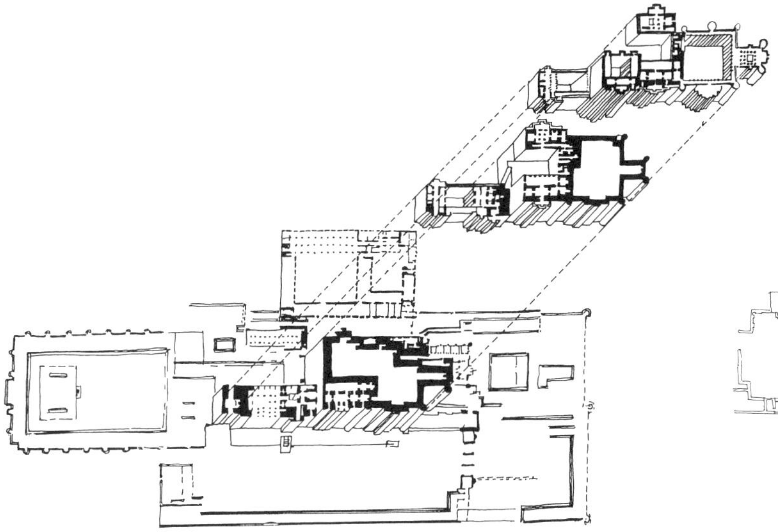

Palace complex with the floors and the geometry of walls in a detailed view

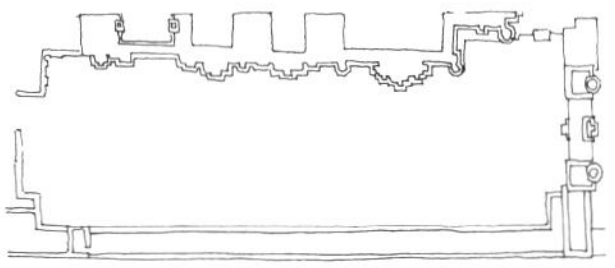

In Mayur Chowk the walls encase the volume and create frames focusing the embellishments.

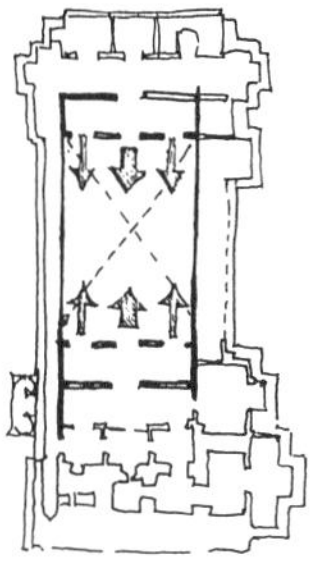

Interactive courtyards enhance the inside–outside communication

Wall as an element for display, communication and encoding messages

Wall is an interactive element with paintings, engravings, reliefs and religious motifs narrating mythological stories and historical events.

BHUNGA HOUSE, KUTCH

Bhungas—the typical traditional dwellings of Kutch, a hot and dry desert region, are characterized by thick circular adobe wall enclosures with small openings and a conical thatched roof.

Decorations and ornamentation on the wall with clay and mirror murals give a distinct identity to each unit within the homogenous clusters. With minimum openings it encloses a volume in itself and functions as a protective barrier against the climatic forces. The walls are also creatively used to accommodate built-in niches and extended plinths for storage.

Walls demarcating the territory

Village plan—territories defined by wall-composition

View of the Bhunga

Wall as an element defining zones and subspaces

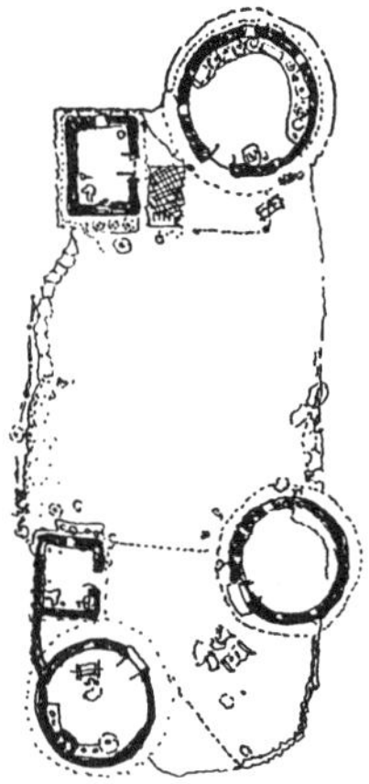

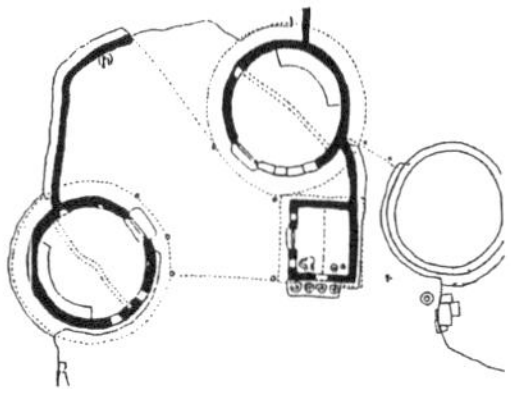

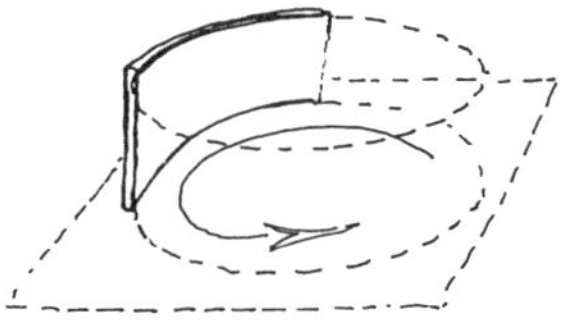

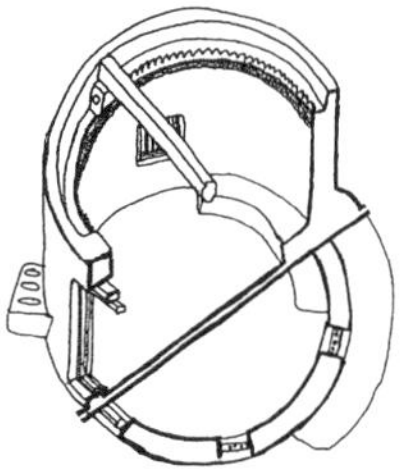

Wall as an encloser of volume

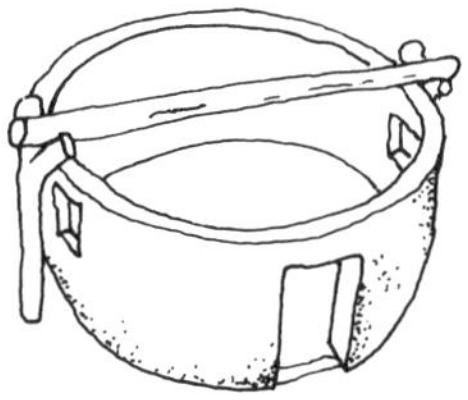

Articulation of wall creating homogenouos structure

Wall attributing verticality along z axis

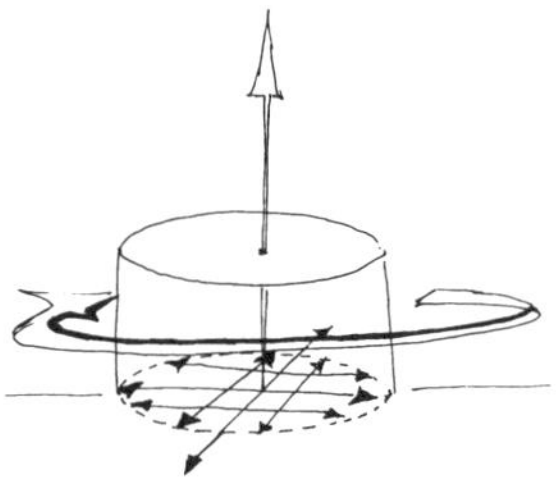

Wall demarcating the extent of the space within

Wall as an element communicating personalization and social identity

Plan

Wall finish with cow-dung with unique surface texture created by the dwellers themselves

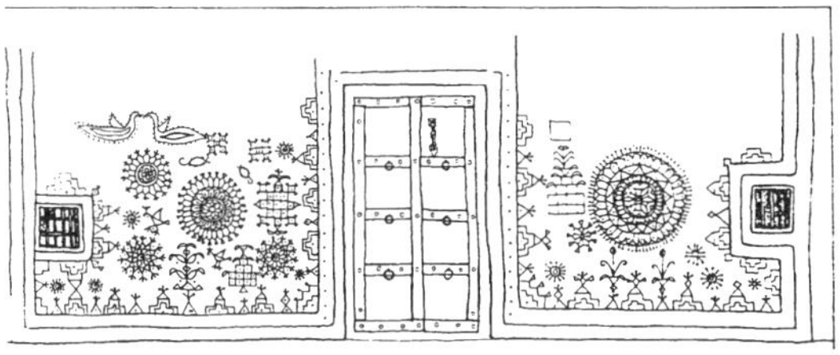

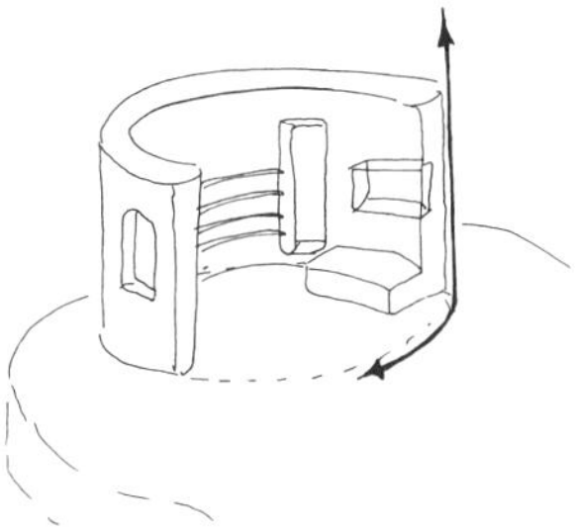

Wall as movement guide within the cluster

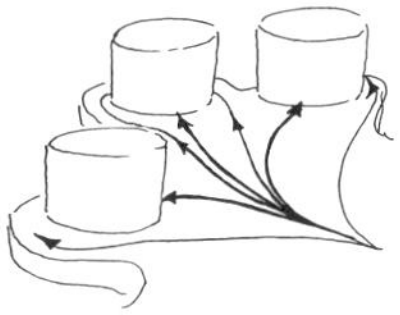

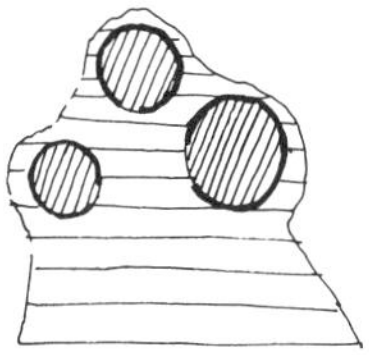

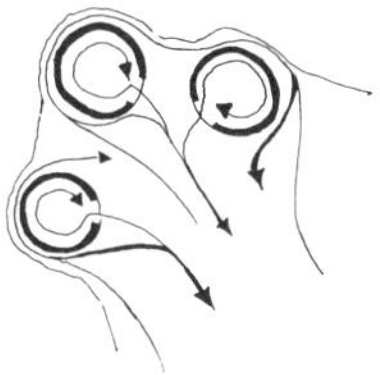

Articulation of interior wall for storage and display

Articulation of interior wall for storage and display

Elaborate embellishment of the wall encoding cultural symbols and images

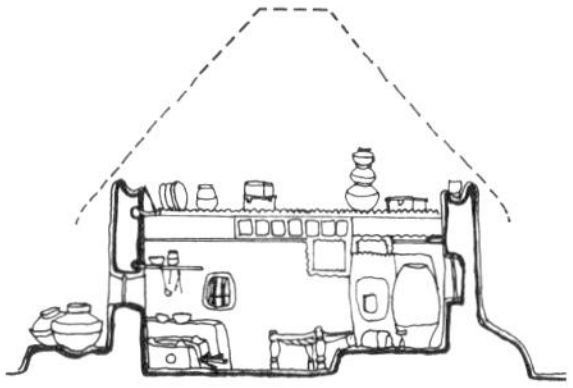

Wall as a modulator of form

Elevational facade

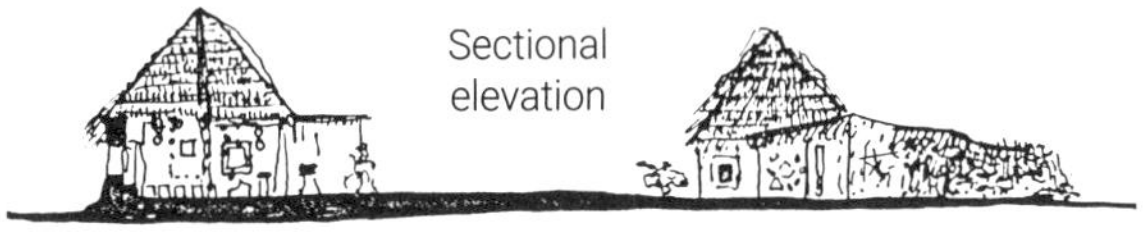

Sectional elevation

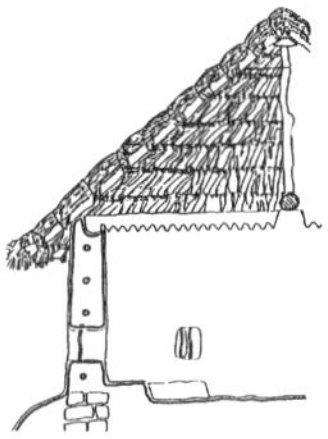

Wall as a protective barrier

VIETNAM MEMORIAL, WASHINGTON

The Vietnam Memorial, built in 1982, by architect Maya Ying Lin, is located in the Smithsonian Mall. It is a memorial to mark the martyrdom of American soldiers in the Vietnam War. The Vietnam Memorial is inspired by the development of the 1960s minimalist design attitude. Essentially an L-shaped wall structure wedging into the ground and designed as a landscape element, it creates a great deal of spatial, notional and experiential richness.

Lin's scheme is a vast earth-mound wedging inwards as a triangular plane, sectioned by a granite wall in the shape of a long sloping pyramid. The two walls establish the axes of power, as one of the walls suggests the connection with Washington Memorial, connoting its involvement in its existence. The shiny granite provides a surface on which to inscribe the list of names of martyrs in the war. With this symbolism, it evokes emotional reactions as well. A combination of the Acropolis and the Wailing Wall, the meeting of geometry and of amorphousness, it manifests an impossibility of representing the 'lessons' to be drawn from the national tragedy.

Siting of the wall on the landscape defining direction with strong axial position

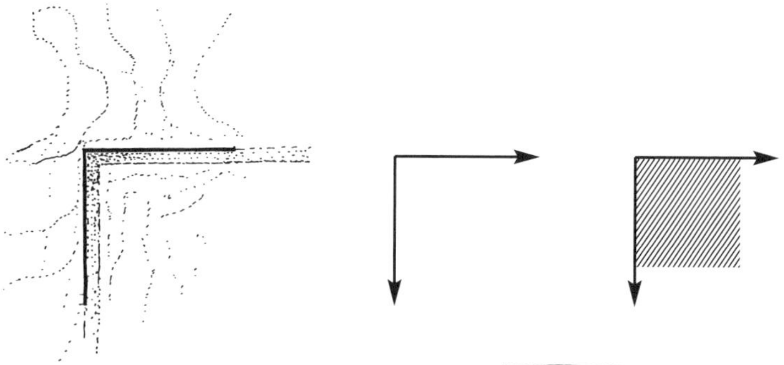

Terrain gives wall the form

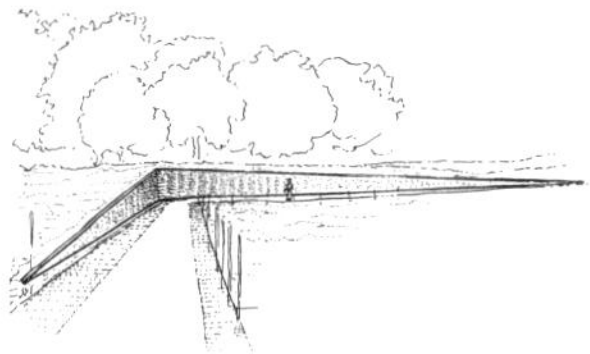

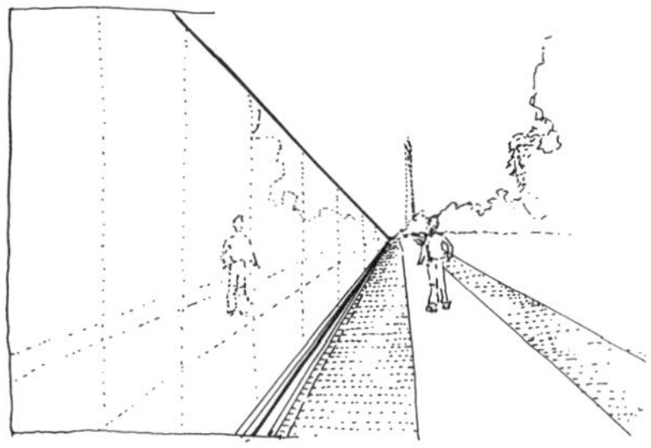

The wall acquires a strong directionality and creates a movement path with a definite focal point.

With the form and siting, wall becomes an element of focus acquiring a sculptural quality

Walls begin to enclose space as one approaches the point of junction

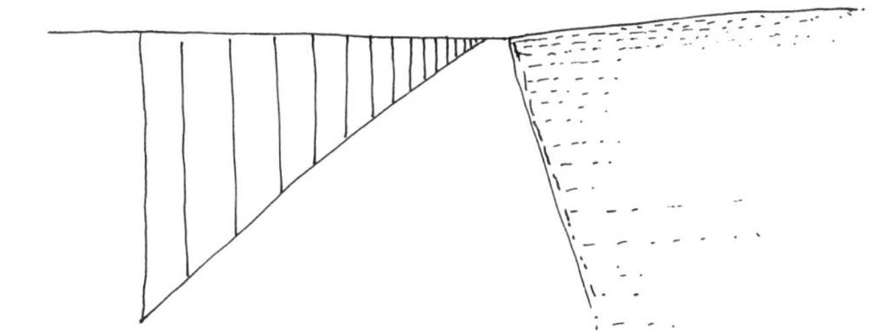

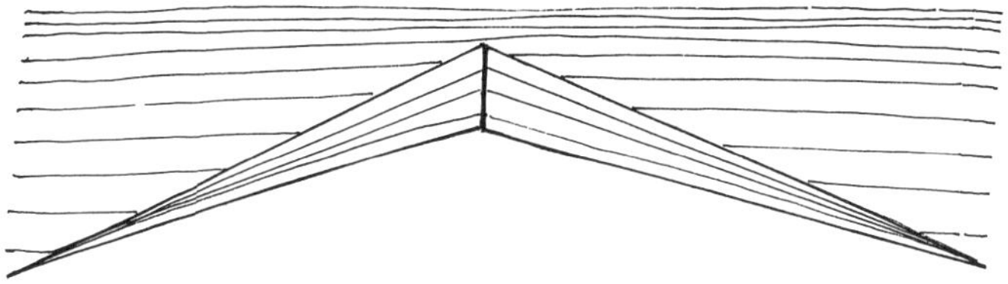

Wall as a communicator and encoder of messages with textural renderings

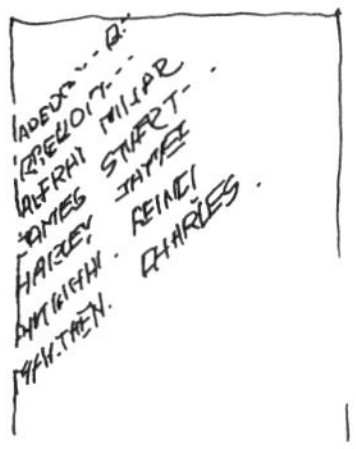

Wall becomes an element of reminiscence, communicating the tragic story of war, bearing names of each and every soldier who lost life in Vietnam.

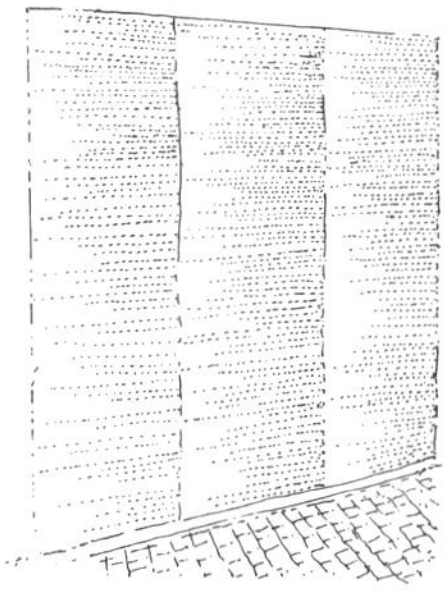

The wall becomes a collective grave and tomb-stone of the martyrs.

Vertical growth of the wall, from point to a plane

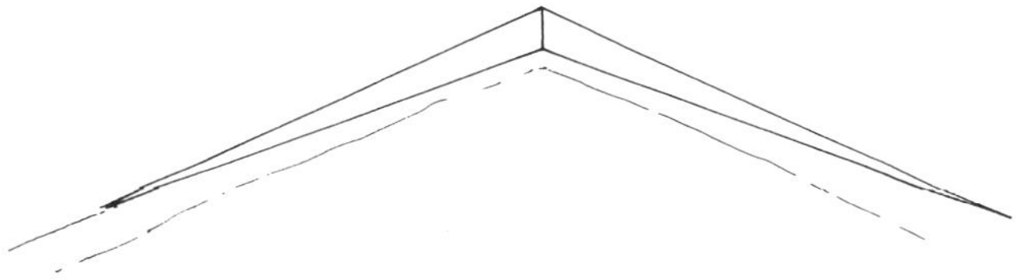

With this composition these the walls confirm a space within

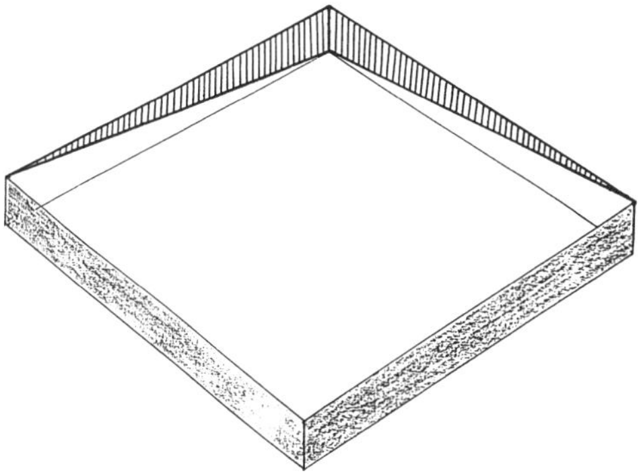

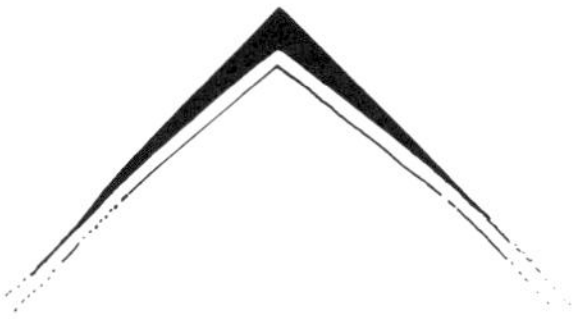

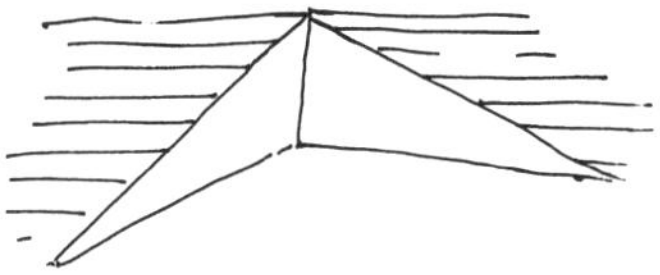

BARCELONA PAVILION, BARCELONA

Architect Mies Van der Rohe designed the Barcelona Pavilion built in 1926. The plan suggests the usage of wall as the primary component in design. The wall functions as freestanding screen walls, forming buffers of spaces within the unit by thus enclosing spaces and subspaces.

The wall, due to its height, guides the movement along its length. At the sculpture pool, the walls around it create a focus along the enclosed vertical axis and guide vision towards the pool and the wall behind frames a mural respectively of natural and textural renderings. Walls are also placed effectively to reflect and compose vignettes.

Wall as an element demarcating spaces and functional zones.

Sequential introductions of vertical planes creating spaces and movements

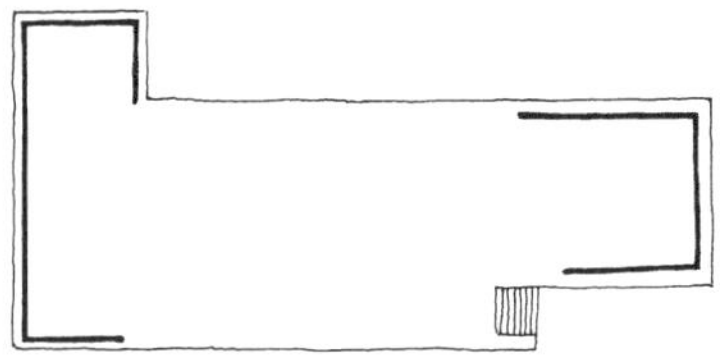

The peripheral walls define the territory of the entire building.

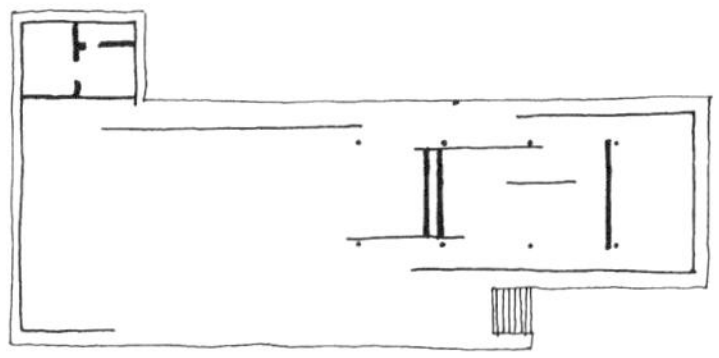

Monodirectionality is perceived due to parallel walls

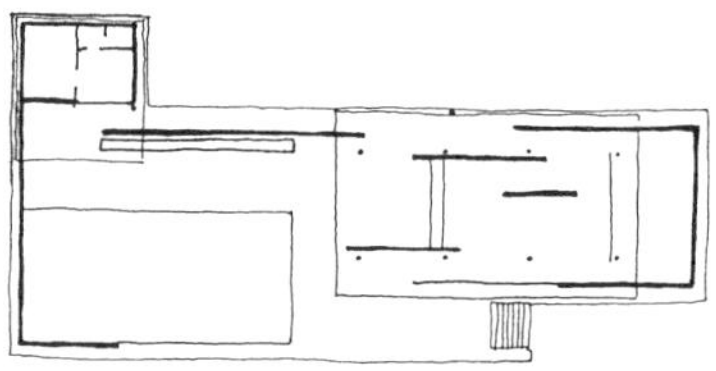

Spaces get formed with the inception of walls perpendicular to the existing ones

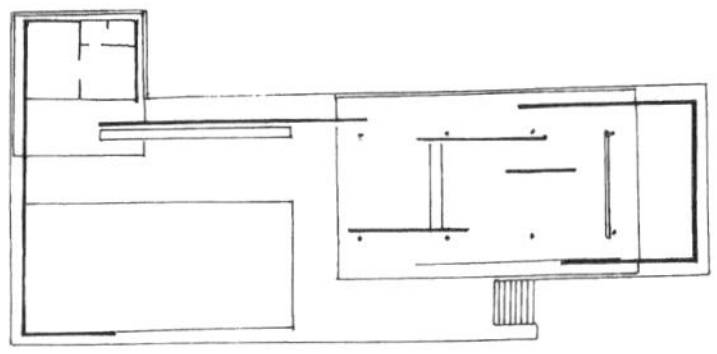

More complex composition with pause points, visual frames and subspaces get derived

Wall creating a pattern of movement path

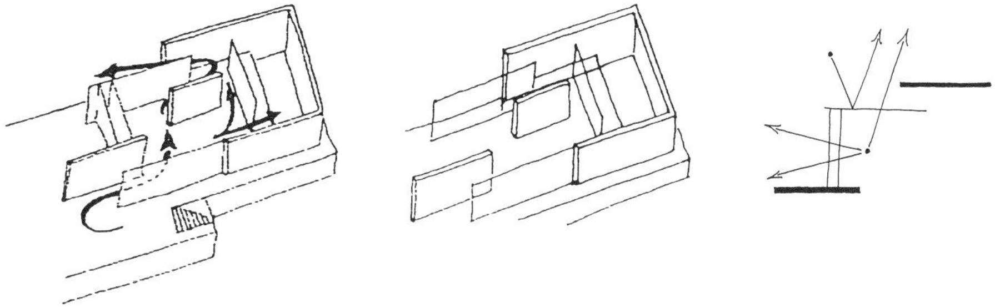

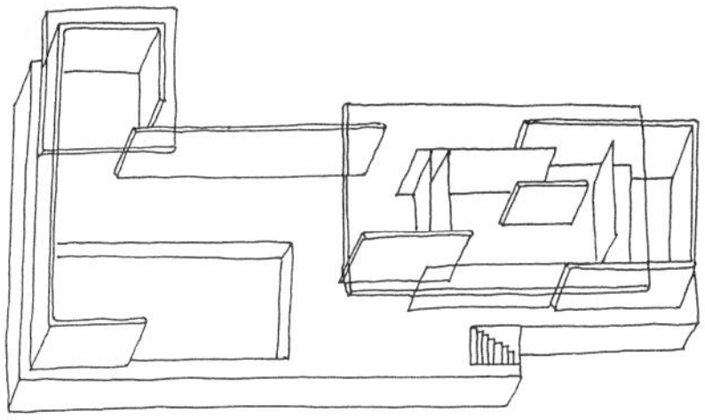

Relationships between the walls invigorate various actions in the space, by creating series of openings and guiding the movement to subsequent space as an interactive spatial link

Axonometric view of the pavilion

The configuration of wall-planes makes spaces, enclosing volumes

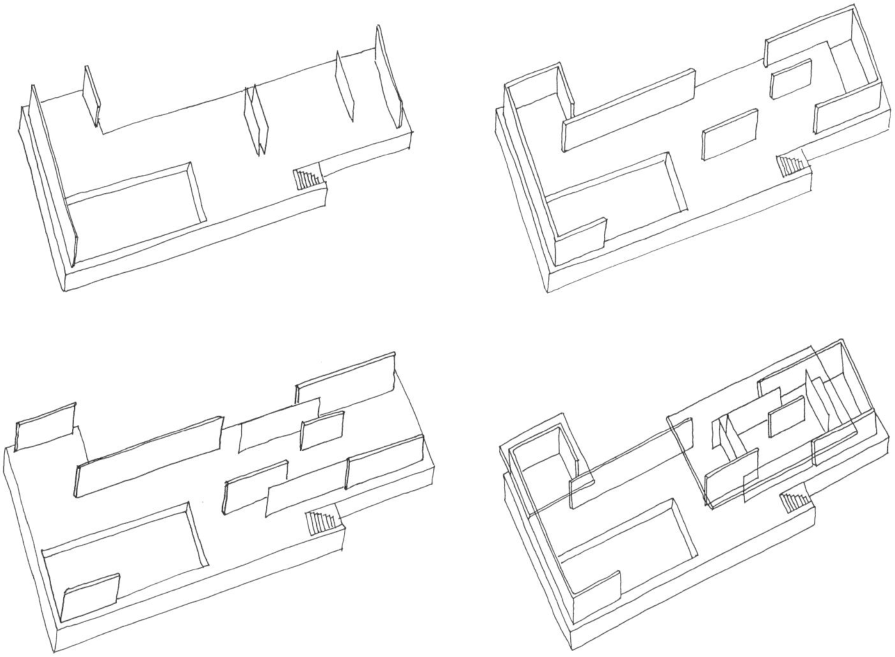

The configuration of wall planes attribute several qualities, like mystery and a sense of discovery with pauses and motion with points of interest to the entire built environmnet

Walls unifying and subdividing spaces

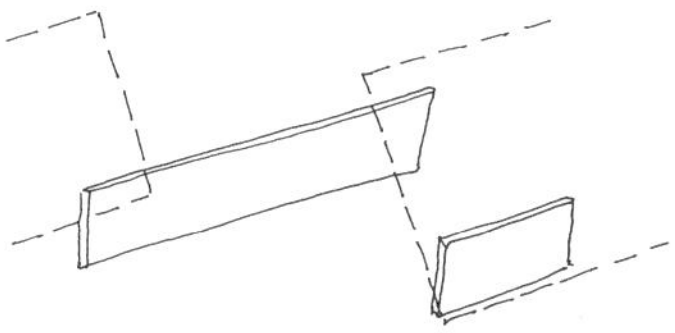

Wall also becomes an element of focus, when it is rendered with various materials and surface qualities

Wall acts as a barrier protecting the interior space from external environment

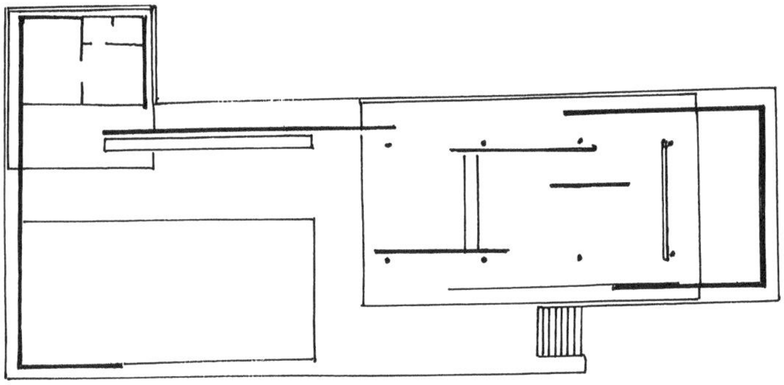

Plan-Walls creating a spatial hierarchy

Wall becomes an element communicating the overall spatial quality...

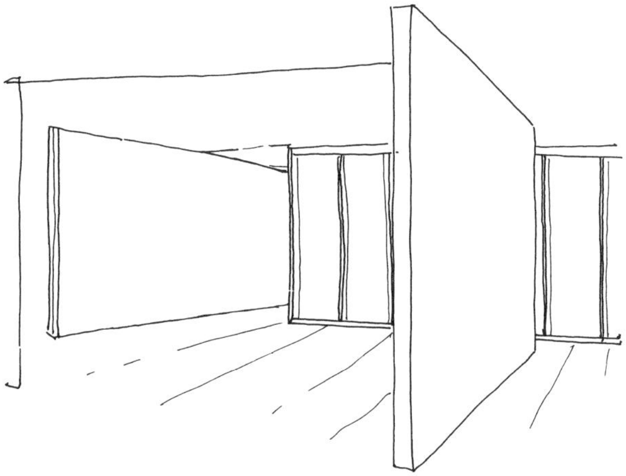

Walls forming visual frames with their interactive positions

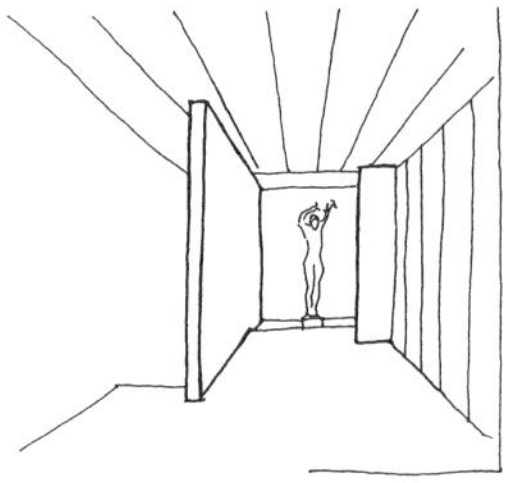

Wall becoming an element enhancing the focus towards certain corners

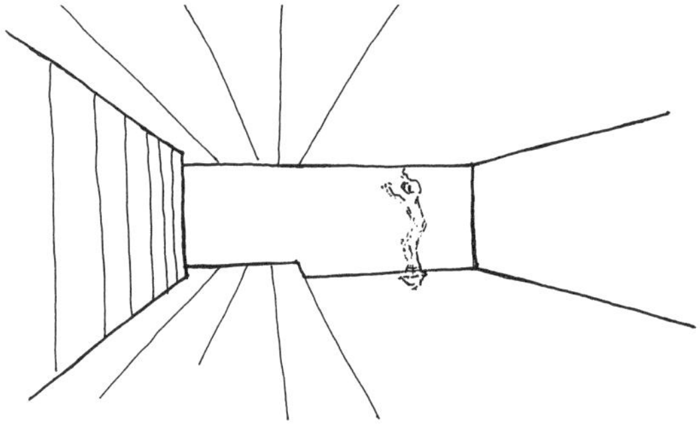

Wall guiding movement towards the pool

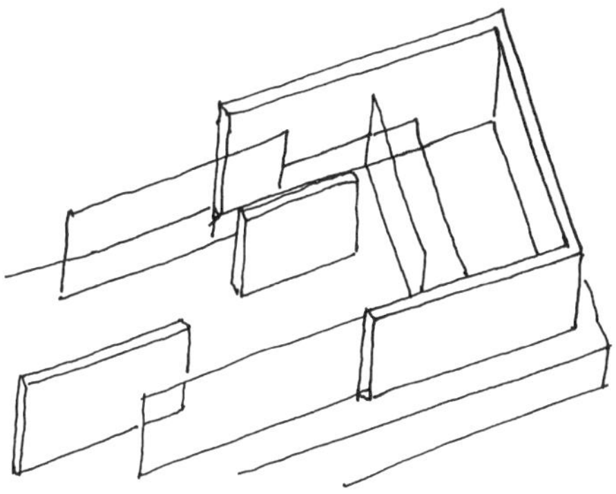

The movement pattern derived by the interactive relationships of wall planes

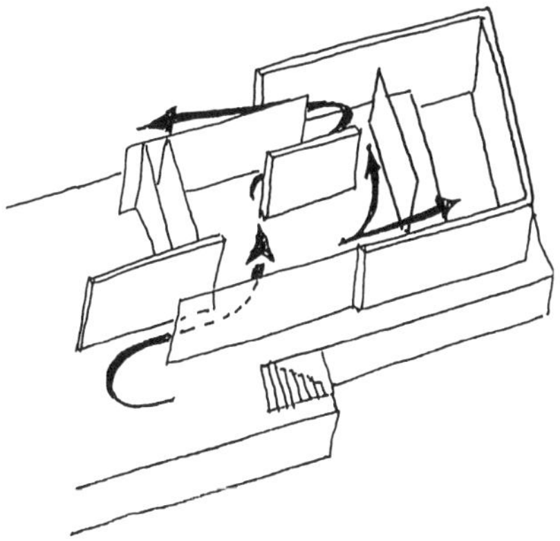

Wall as a movement guide

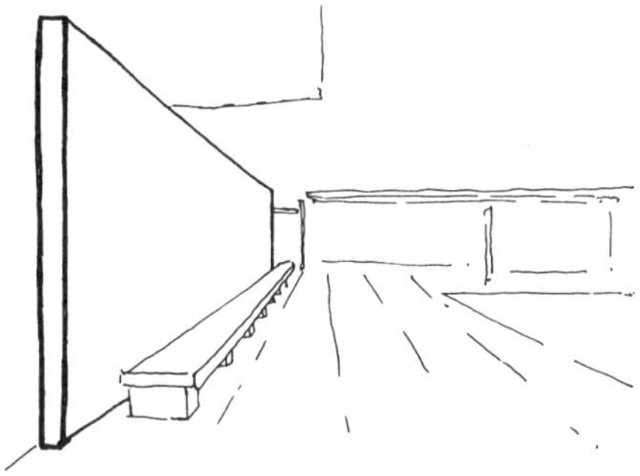

The length of walls extend the vista beyond its physical limits

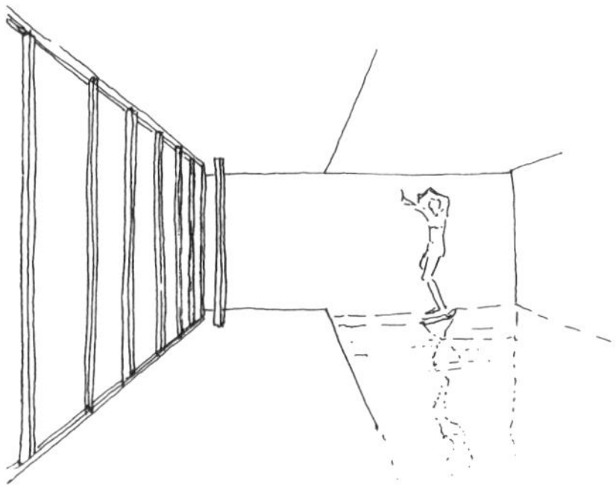

Wall performs a role of a backdrop for element of display

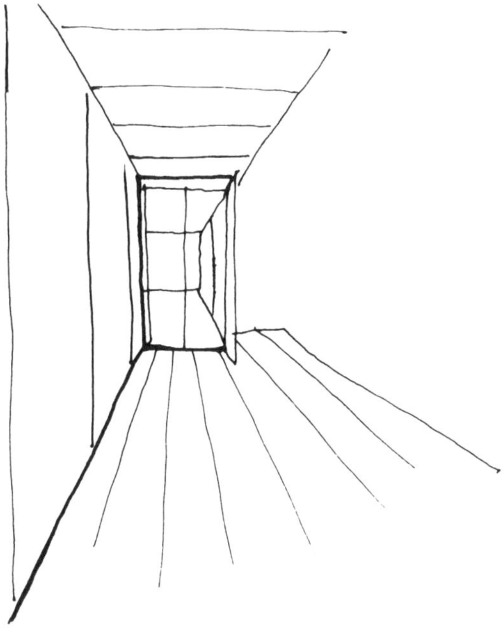

Compositions of wall planes frame the views establishing visual interaction with adjacent spaces

- Walls by virtue of being vertical planes become barriers. Their height and materials must be modulated as such, to accentuate contiguity or separation can be notional, physical or visual.

- A wall lower than knee height doubles up as seat and functions more as notional rather than physical barrier. Such walls act as space definer and threshold yet maintaining visual connection between spaces.

- A wall lower than eye level presents itself as a physical barrier but visually allows for spatial contiguity.

- A wall taller than eye level becomes a visual and physical barrier giving a true sense of enclosure.

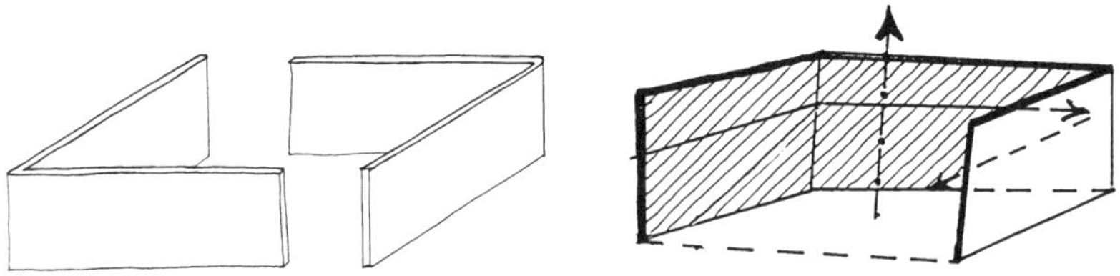

Wall as a visual and physical barrier creates a sense of enclosure yet suggests spatial extension

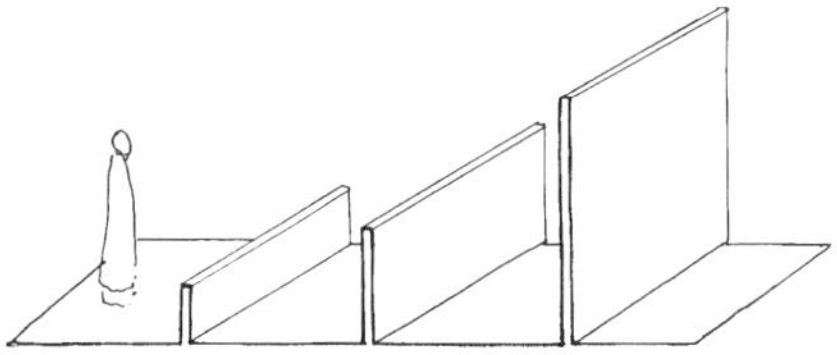

Variation in height explores the sense of physical and visual separation

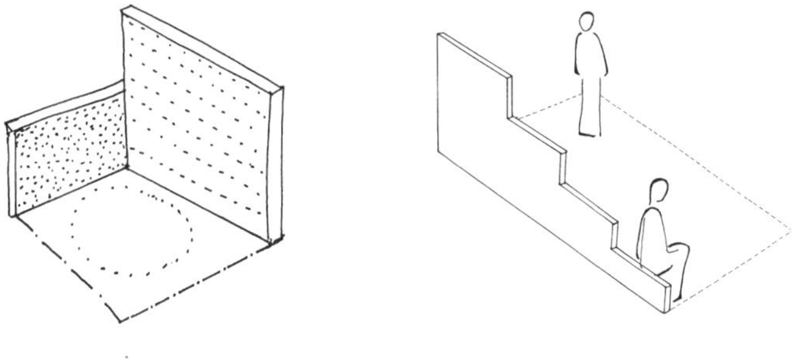

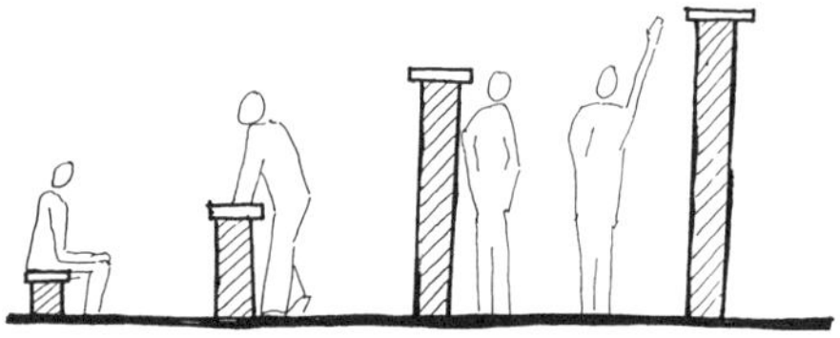

Increase in heights creates different levels of visual separation and sense of seperation as well as enclosure

- Walls in the interior spaces must have a softer and warmer overlay that invites one to touch, while the external planes of wall could recreate a hard and rough appearance to repel any encroachments or intrusions.

- Although a surface and a planar component, walls should be treated as a volume rather than as a plane. Wall offers opportunities to fold, bend and carve spaces (niches & alcoves) within. These serve not only as utilitarian devices for storage and display but also as aesthetic elements modulating visual compositions and as spatial details for sub-scaling volume. Therefore, not treating walls as simple vertical protrusions of the footprint, they should be conceived three dimensionally to produce effective subvolumes through their inclination and fold or bend in a vertical plane.

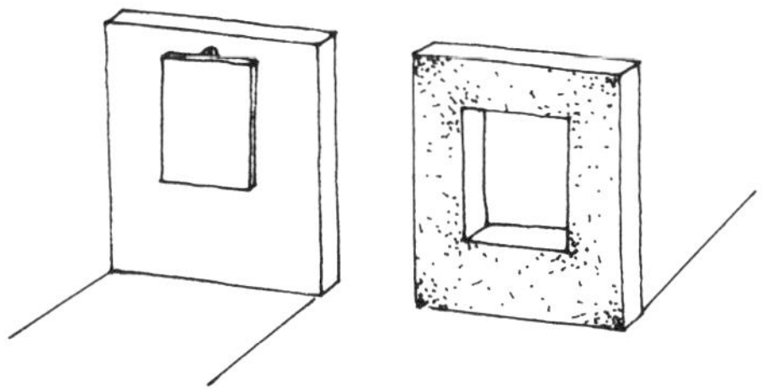

Texture defining the interior and exterior spaces

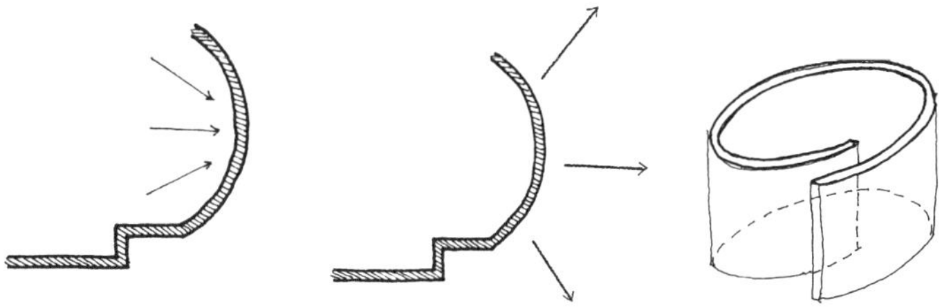

Shape and form help in generating feeling of absorption and repulsion.

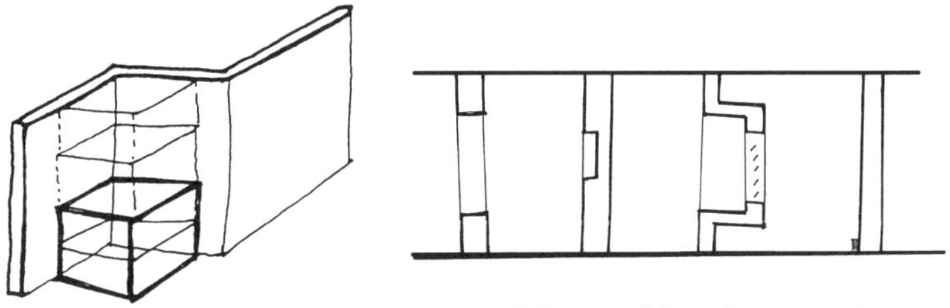

Modulating wall for utilitarian needs

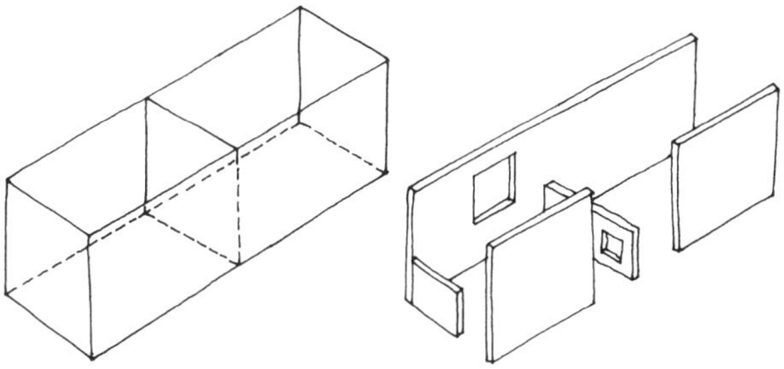

Modulating wall for subscaling the volume

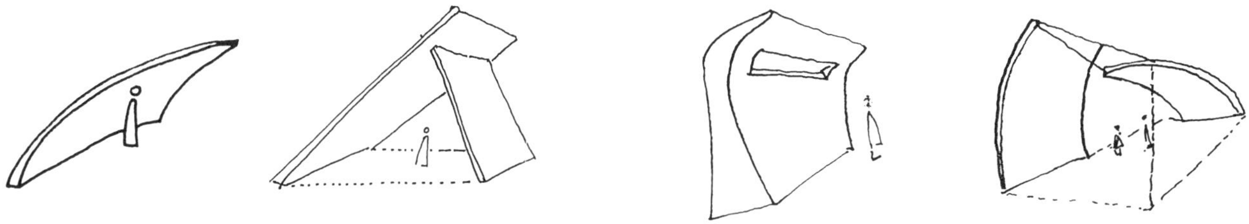

Bent walls as well as inclined/leaning or bulging walls contain volume

- Though the wall creates a sense of enclosure, it also can suggest spatial extension through the void near the base or the ceiling junctions.

- Wall surfaces up to the height of 2.1 meters are optimum for display and other forms of visual messages/clues as this falls directly in the cone of vision. This zone of wall therefore, must be used effectively for visual communication.

- Clues through relative assembly of wall planes have the most profound effect in orientation and guiding movement. This phenomenon can also be most successfully exploited through its planar as well as elevational profiles. Curving of the wall, inclination of the wall or leaning of the wall all give accent in their respective directions.

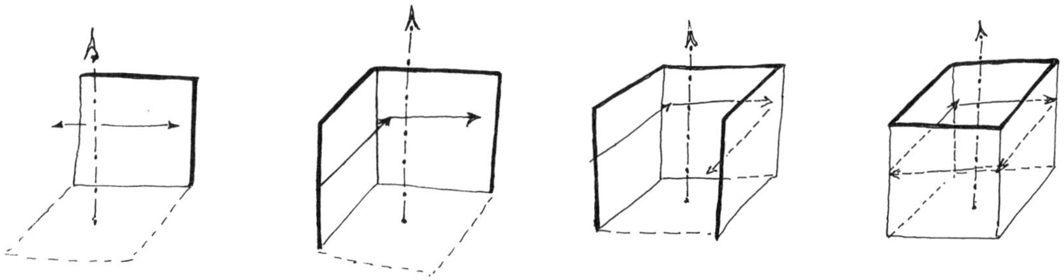

Wall for total sense of enclosure, giving sense of containment and limit

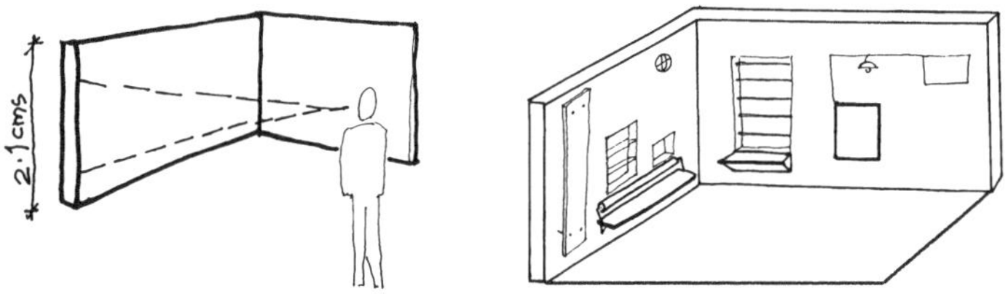

The appropriate cone of vision, where the wall surface can be effectively used for visual clues and messages

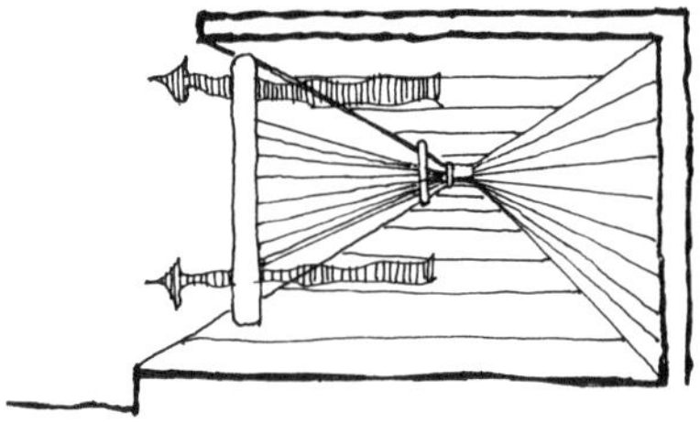

Spatial extension through modulation at the junction of the vertical plane (wall) and the horizontal planes (roof, floor)

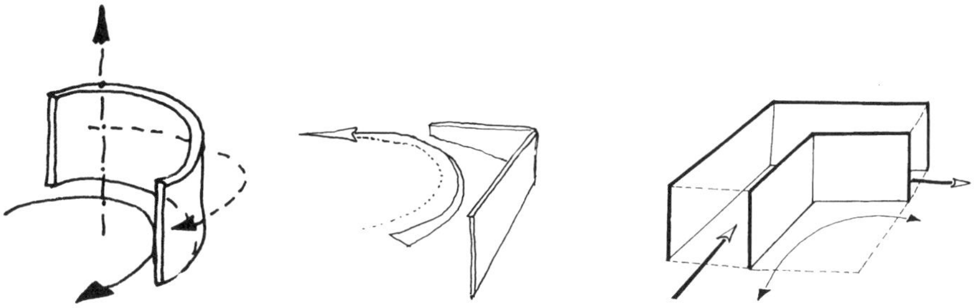

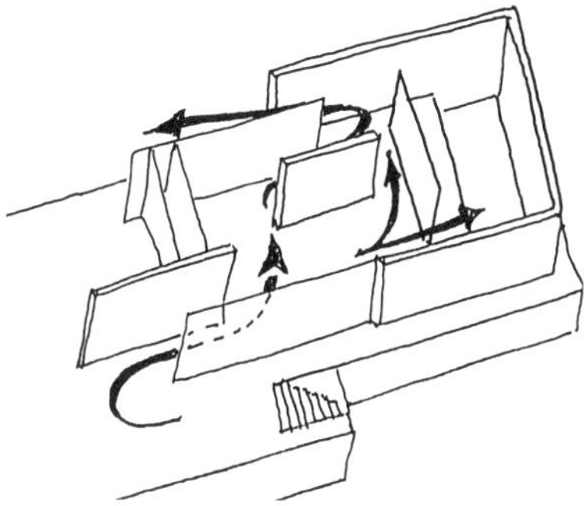

Wall defining movement zone in various instances

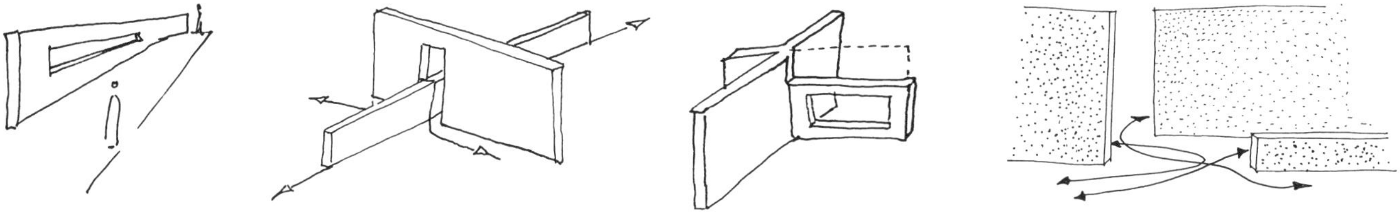

Explorations in planar and elevational dimension

DOOR

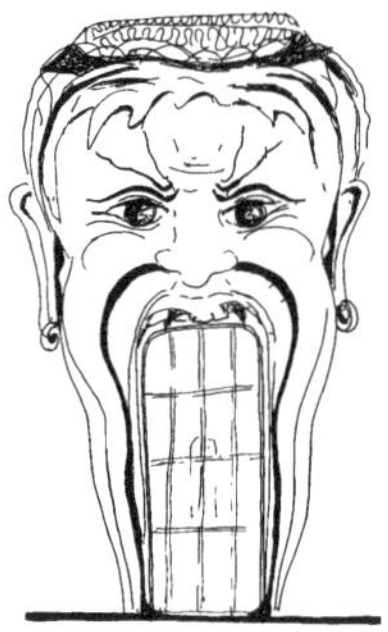

Vadnagar Toran, Gujarat

A door is essentially a puncture through a plane allowing for a passage through it. The term originates from the Japanese word *turii*, meaning gateway leading to heaven. Its Old English term is *duru* (Anglo-Saxon). The Germanic origin lies in the word *dor*. German refers to as *thor* or *thur* which means 'gate'. The Sanskrit synonym of door is *dwara*, originating from the word *dwi*—referring to "two". It pertains to the two realms; within and without, where it is often considered as an entry into darkness [inside] and the exit into light [outside]. Thus, door connotes an aspect of passage between two realms.

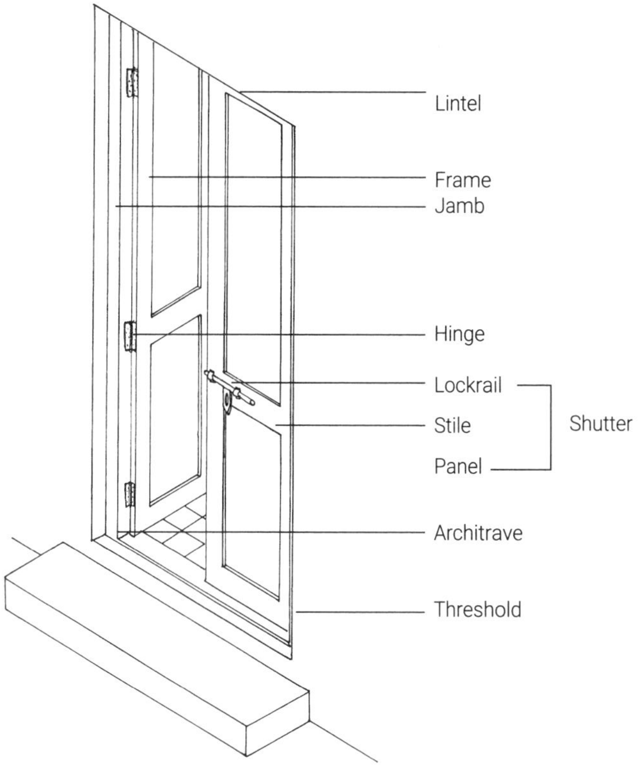

Typological Variations

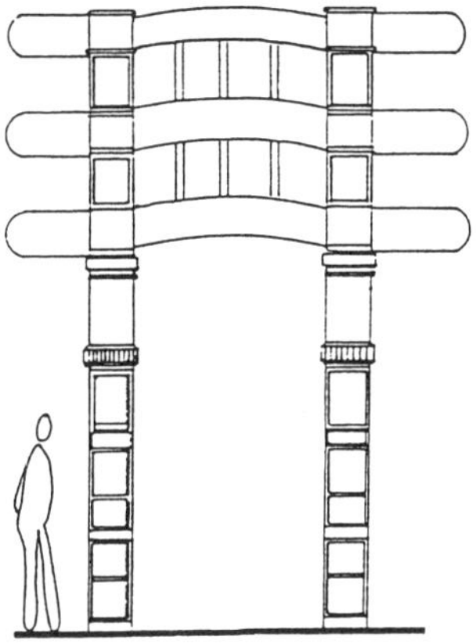

Gateway
Freestanding structure framing a notional entry passage

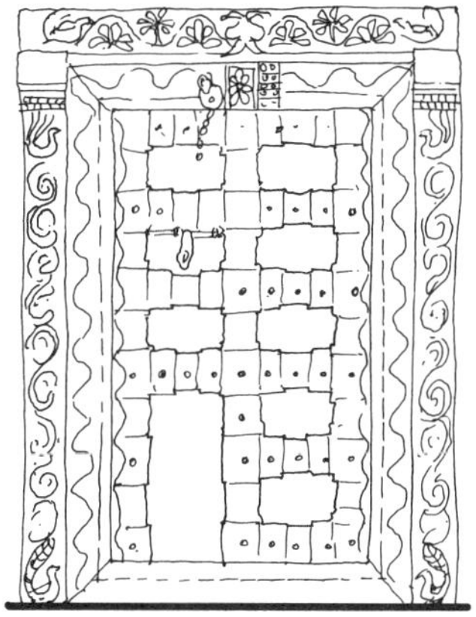

Door with shutter
Opaque shutter embedded into wall as movable plane to open or shut the passage.

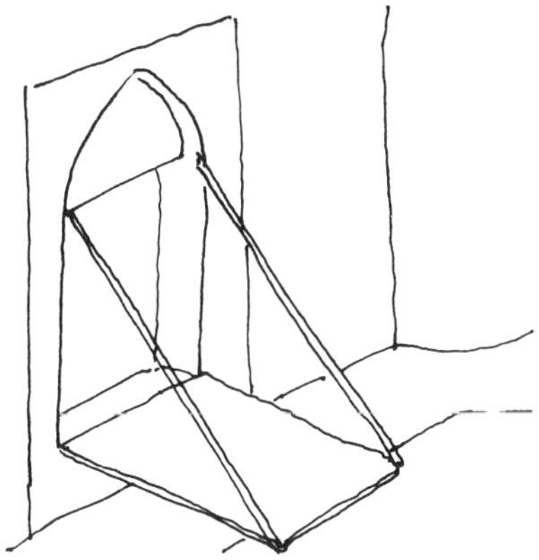

Drawbridge
An opaque vertical plane with dual functions, when lowered opens the access point by becoming a floor (bridge) to ply over.

Gateways and notional doors to mark entry for celestial elements and to demarcate influential zones

Toran of Stupa, Sanchi

Solar head and solar bird, eastern portal of temple, Baalzamin

Lion Gate, Mycenae, Greece

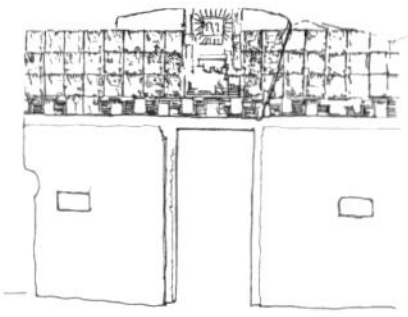

The Gateway of the Sun, Tiahuanaco, Bolivia

Egyptian temple, Egypt

Primitive man, in a hostile world with savage beasts, pugnacious tribes, and inclement weather took refuge in caves. The advantage offered by a single opening providing access into the cave reduced his vulnerability in terms of being able to block it with thorny plants and barricades. This proved to be the basis for the development of doors. The resolution of two basic requirements—the first of providing access and the second of retaining security, are the determinants of the evolution of the door. Opening sizes were controlled, allowing only singular access at a time, creating a bare minimum orifice to protect. The removable barriers evolved into the solid door shutter, tied to a frame and built into the masonry of the wall. This door opened at will and was fastened to the frame when shut. The rudimentary thongs and fasteners evolved into hinges and hardware for smooth operation. Doors acquired greater importance during the Dark and Middle Ages, essentially as a defence strategy. The drawbridge gate laid over a moat, spiked gateways aligned along meandering pathways to discourage charging elephants, and a higher placement of doors smaller than the human scale in dwellings for easy defensibility, were norms in medieval times.

Evolution of domestic doors essentially for security and defence with changing forms and functions of shutters and openings

Carved opening

Spiked branches and pile for enclosure

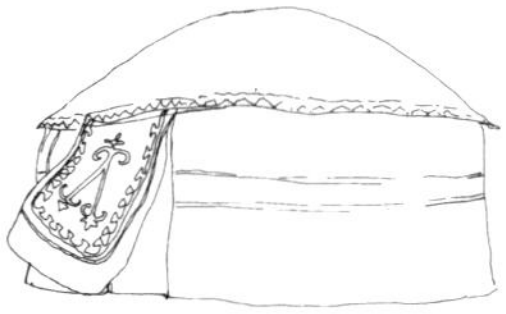

Nomad's dwelling

Portable door of log

Movable partition (Japanese house)

Gateway to a Fortress

With development of civilization, the door assumed a role of security more than that of defence. The use of the external facade of the door as an object of decoration became common. Variations in size, proportions, materials gained significance, expressing the nature of space beyond. The proportions of the door, however, have always been determined anthropometrically. The Dutch door, cut in two along the middle allowing the upper half to remain open for light and air, and the other half closed for keeping livestock out and protecting children, descends from a Flemish-Dutch type. Glazed doors first appeared in the seventeenth century as window casements extended from the floor. French doors (double-glazed) were incorporated in England and America in the seventeenth and eighteenth century. A half-door, simply supported by a two way hinge at waist height and open above neck height at the entrance of saloons/ bars etc., was popular in the nineteenth-century American West. Industrialization brought with it mechanized and automated glazed doors with notional security in the twentieth-century Automation provided standardized sections and fixed concepts taking away interdependence of scale, form and function.

Doorways elaborated to mark entry point and visual composition

BY FRAME

Keystones defining the doorway

Use of double shutter in solid bronze, Roman Era

BY FORM

Chaitya door, near Lonavala

Tiger Cave, Udayagiri

BY SHUTTER

Use of jamb doorways, St. Martin's Church, Worms, Roman Era

Decorative profile, Baroque Era

Notre Dame Cathedral, Paris, Gothic Era

Dutch door

Half door hung

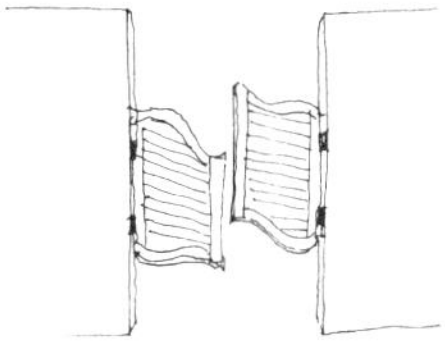

Casement door

Regency terrace-building, Hove

Glazed door

Chester Cathedral, London

Industrialization bringing glazed and automated doors

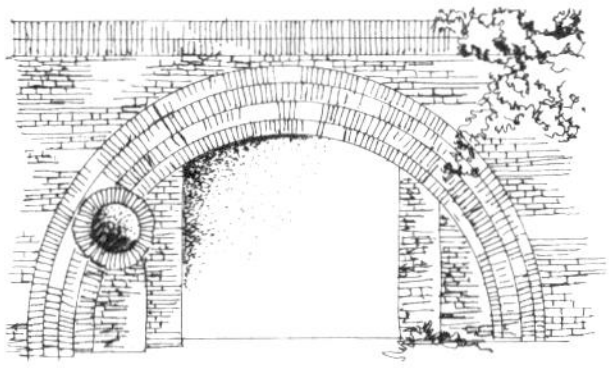

Japan Folk Arts Museum, Tokyo

Clore Gallery, London

PENETRABILITY

As a puncture in the barrier plane, the fundamental aspect of the door is to provide a passage and access through the barrier plane.

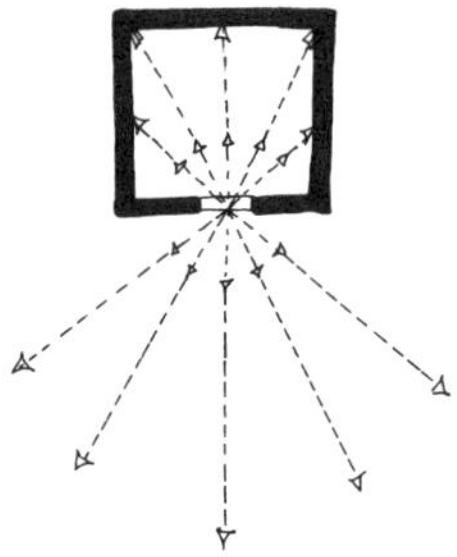

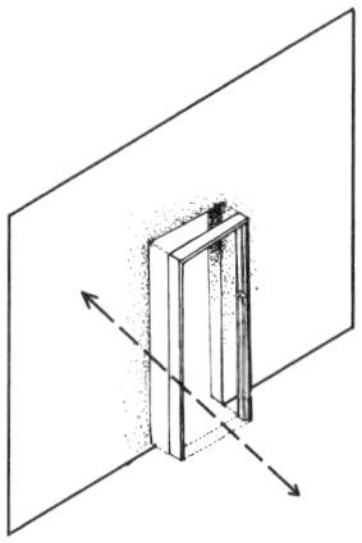

Various scales of penetrability

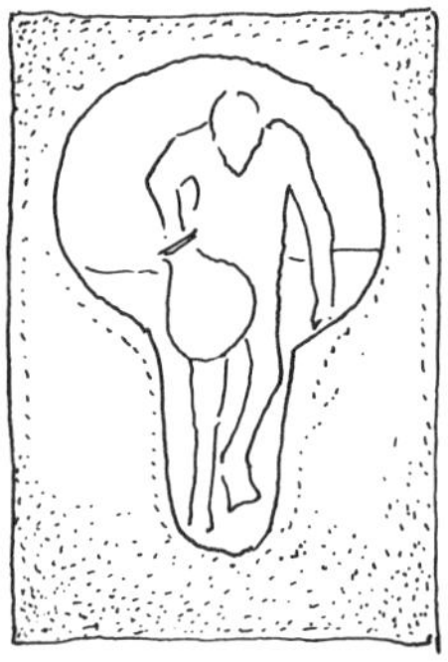

Entrance of a vernacular dwelling, Africa

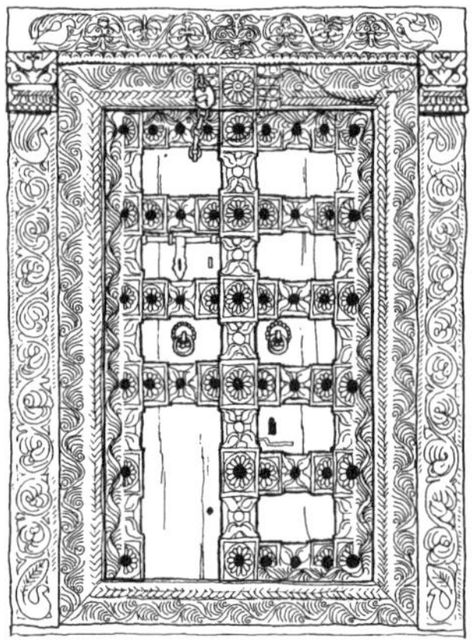

Door with a small inset opening for daily access, Northern India

Arsh house, Toda community, Nilgiri

Door as a small puncture, Middle ages

The Mission Church of San Fransisco de Assisi

Constable's Gate, Dover Castle, Kent

DIFFERENTIATION

The door refers to two realms—the indoors and the outdoors. It becomes the point where the differentiation is felt most acutely since it is the transition where one is brought into direct contact with both the realms. The differentiation between the two spaces is maintained totally by the door plane when closed and notionally when open through the threshold.

Collective scale—sacred/mundane

Toran at Sanchi Stupa, Sanchi

Mukteswar Temple, Bhubaneshwar

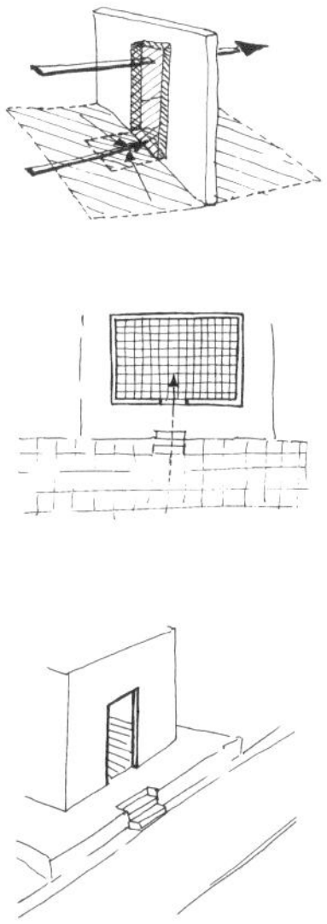

Door defining private/public territory

Door differentiates the inside from outside through its own different proportions and formal language

Opening through vestibule, Japanese house

Street view of Haveli, Rajasthan

Point of differentiation—modified as for defense and personal entry (as wicket gate)

Gateway to a *haveli*, Rajkot

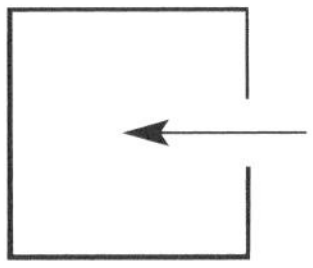

DOOR AS POINT OF ACCESS

As a definite point highlighting the penetrability within the wall, the door manifests a puncture within a plane, allowing physical permeation perpendicular to the wall plane. This act simultaneously involves the two realms. The external doors differentiate between 'out' and 'in' and internal doors, between two zones of different characteristics.It signifies arrival and entry.

Door as an access to house

Entrance of a pol dwelling unit

Gateway to cluster

Gateway to a chawl, Kolkata

Gateway to precinct

Main gate, Bikaner Fort, Bikaner

Gateway to city..

Teen Darwaza, Ahmedabad

Gateway to country..

Gateway of India, Mumbai

Gateway to an era..........................

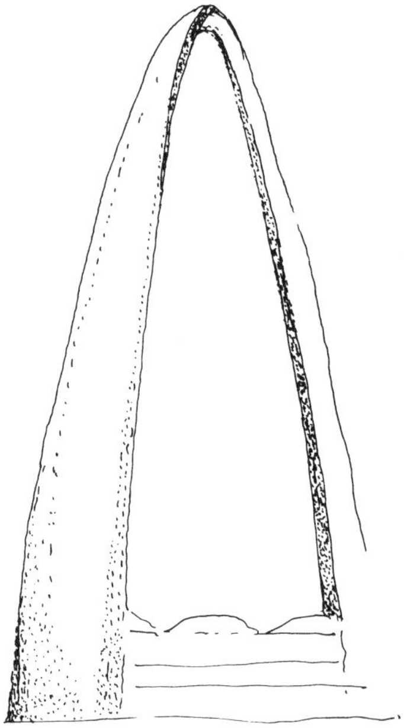

The Gateway Arch, St. Louis, Missouri

Gateway from profane to sacred

Toran, Vadnagar

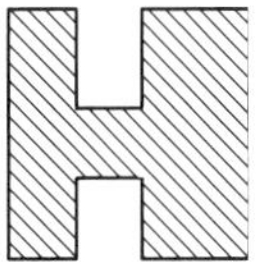

DOOR AS THRESHOLD

Being access points to one realm from the other, doors establish the sense of transition of moving from one to another realm—from public to private, in to out, sacred to profane etc. differentiated by the wall plane. But the thickness of the wall constitutes a volume, which in many cases has been elaborated into an 'in-between' subspace, allowing for a smooth transition between the two major spaces. This threshold, thus, buffers or diffuses the notions of territoriality set up by the distinct zones. It de-conditions one from the past realm and conditions one for the upcoming realm. This is accentuated with visual information, symbols and signs, thus completing the notion of transition both physically as well as notionally.

Physical transition

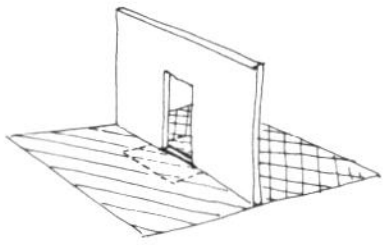

The access point creating a realm between 'in' and 'out'

Elements of doors, with variation in jamb or mass

Brixworth Church, Northamptonshire

Brihadeeswara Temple, Thanjavur

Palazzo Sciarra, Rome

Projecting/Recessed lintels or frames

Canopy

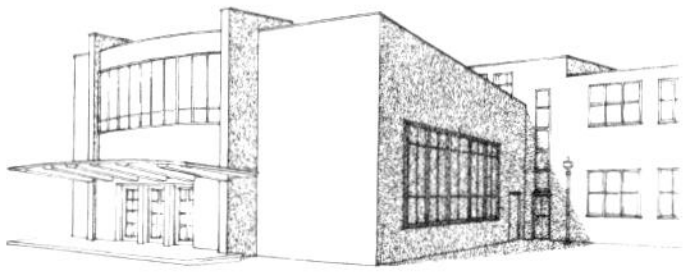

Impington Village College, Cambridgeshire

Door on an elevated plane creating threshold and plinth plane

House in Sam Desert with hierarchy of thresholds, Rajasthan

Symbolic motifs and form, at the threshold

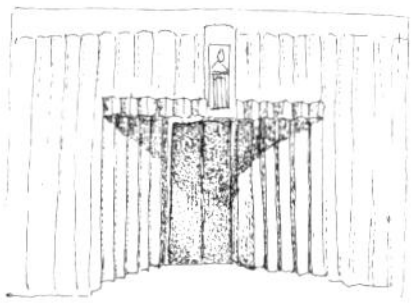

Church of St. Nicholas, Burnage

Renaissance door

Tiger Cave, Mamallapuram

Facade view of a *haveli*, Rajasthan

Guildford Cathedral, Surrey

DOOR AS GUIDE TO MOVEMENT

As the only nodes in volume allowing penetration of the wall plane in a direction perpendicular to the walls, the locations of doors in the room determines the direction and scheme of circulation within it. It offers a sense of direction and thereby articulates the interiors as subzones such as functional spaces and circulation path.

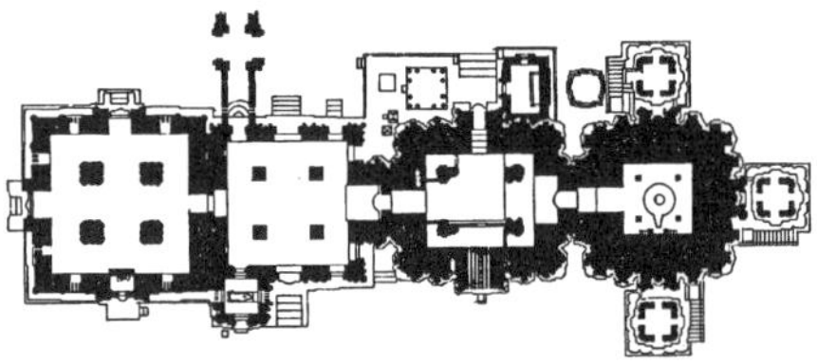

Mukteswar Temple, Bhubaneshwar

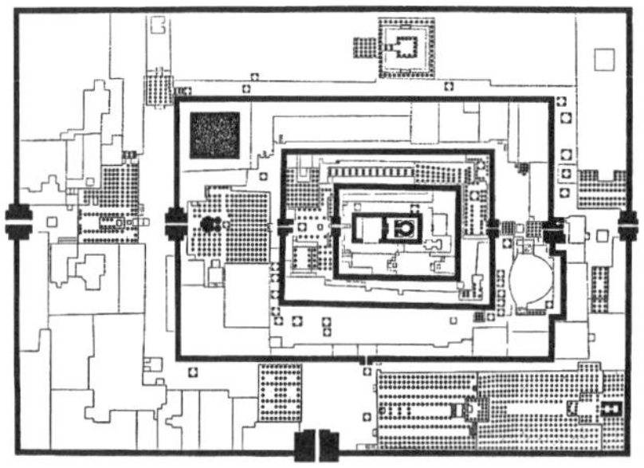

Temple of Srirangam

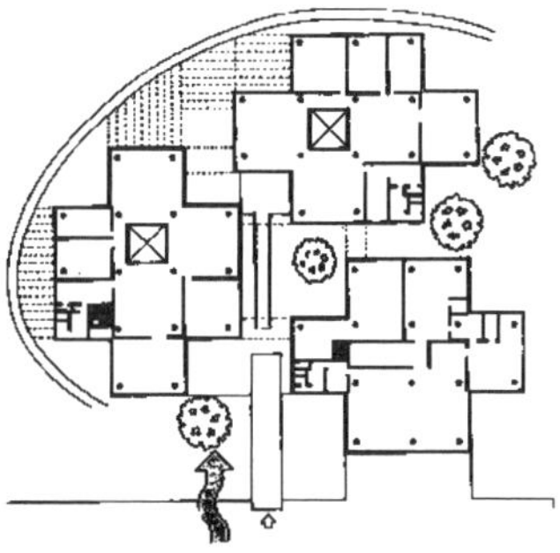

ECIL Office Complex, Hyderabad

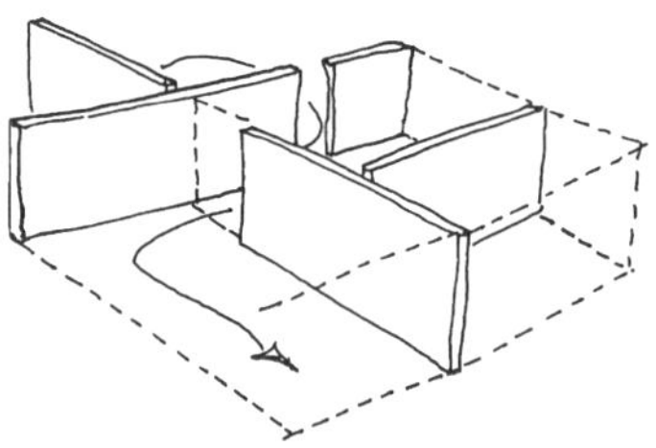

Doors as punctures in surfaces give direction for movement

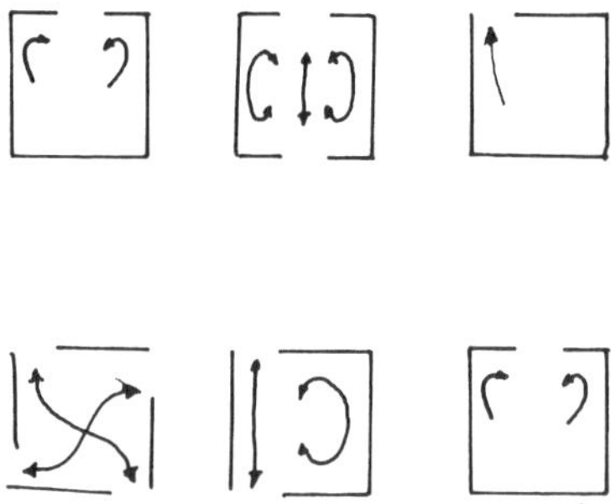

Door to subscale space...

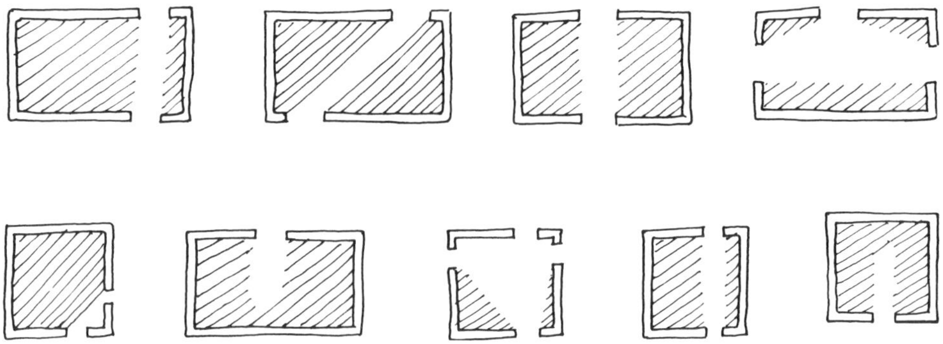

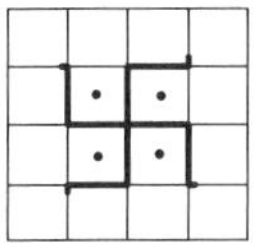

DOOR AS IMAGE-MAKER

The main door, especially, denoting the entry into a built form from the outside has, through time, been accorded the highest priority both by the vernacular and the master-builders. It manifests as the most noticeable element on the facade offering great potential in creating first impressions and conveying a projected image of the aspirations of the inhabitant. The door, therefore, often gets copiously adorned to invite, to provide identity of place and person, as well as to portray the status and wealth.

Diversity in the scales of the door reinstates the image of the building

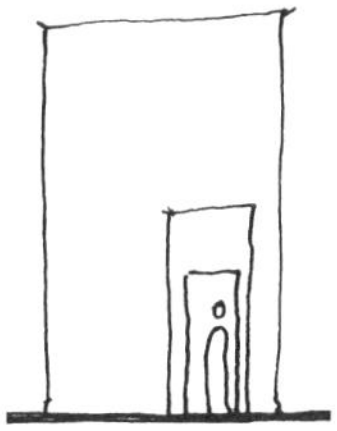

The British Library, London

Gopurams, Srirangam

Embellishments on door

Traditional motifs at the entrance

Image of the building rendered by the doors and gateways..

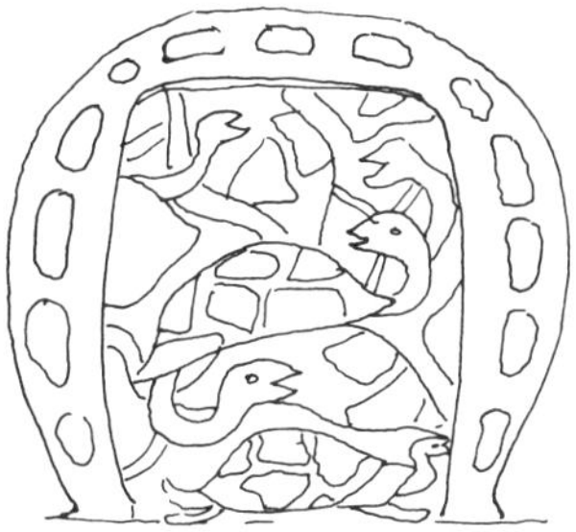

Amdavad ni Gufa, Ahmedabad

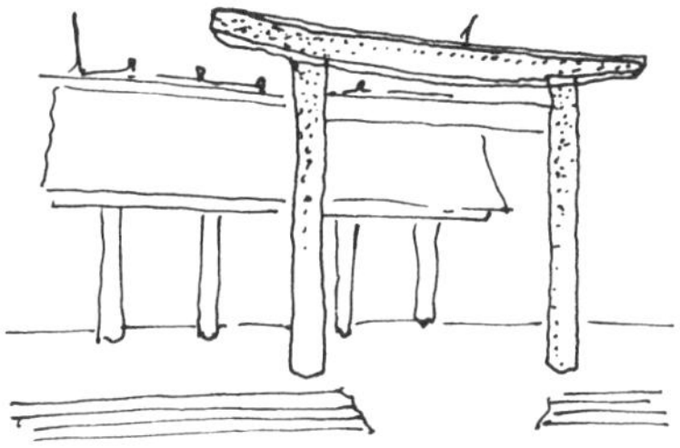

Torii, Gateway to a monastery

Gothic cathedral

City Hall, Swansea

DOOR AS MODULATOR OF FACADE

Just as any void scooped out of a solid mass automatically relates to the mass, the door too becomes an integral element of facade aesthetics. It helps to modulate form and compose facade through its vertical nature. As a mandatory point of access, often it becomes the key reference in the making of facade and composition.

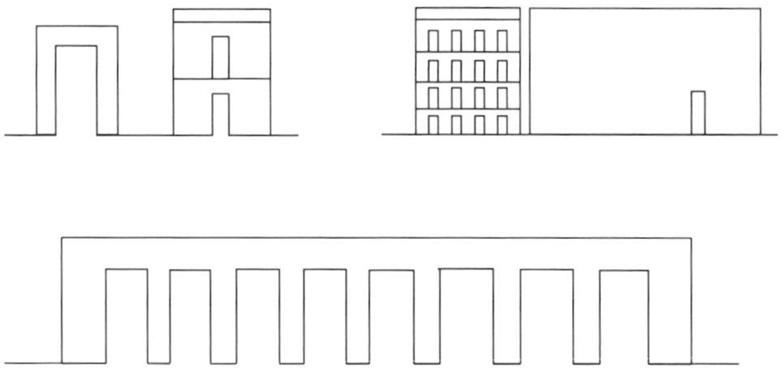

The essential point of access, the door becomes a pivotal element in the composition of the building facade

Cidade de Goa, Goa

Mahindra United World College of India, Pune

The Corn Exchange, Leeds

Tithe barn, Bradford-on-Avon, Wiltshire

Various scales of the door, attributing unique aesthetic qualities to the facade

Milan Cathedral, Milan

Facade demarcating only the door openings extensively,
Trulli (beehive dwellings), Alberobello, Italy

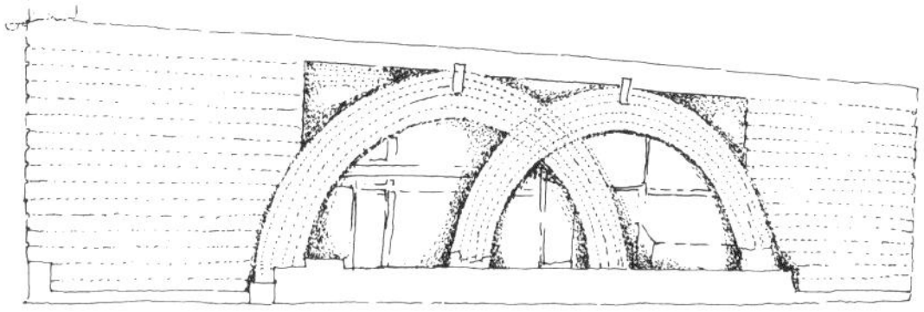

Private house, Manno

The rhythmic language created by solid and void

Buland Darwaza, Fatehpur Sikri

High Court building, Chandigarh

BULAND DARWAZA, FATEHPUR SKIRI

Fatehpur Sikri was built between 1571 and 1585 to commemorate the birth of Akbar's son and heir Jehangir. The Buland Darwaza marks the entry point of the complex. The gigantic size appropriately reciprocates to the space it engulfs within, the scale of the complex and the status of the emperor who built it. It is strongly supported by the high plinth and succeeds in creating an awe-inspiring impression. From within, the scale is reduced to the human reference and is defined by three entry nodes. The spiked gateways were used for defense purposes with details reinforcing the strength and solidity.

Door as a free standing sculpture

Door as an element differentiating two realms of inside and out

The form of the door is attributed with the magnificent scale of a gateway

Door as a point of access

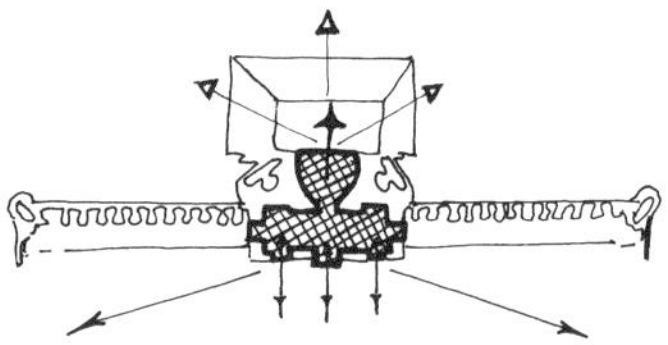

Axis of penetrability with omnidirectional accessibility

Door as threshold—a transition by depth, steps and plinth

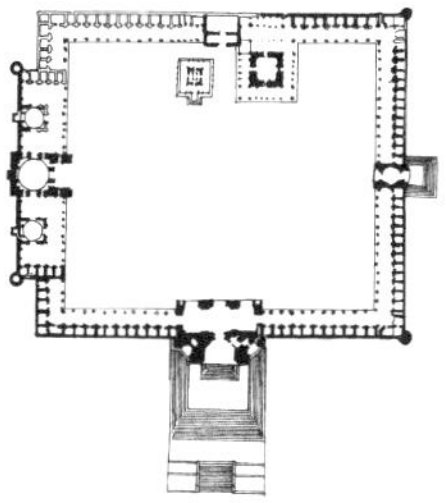

Door as an entry to capital complex

Door becoming an element of grandeur..........

Gateway with its elevated position and volumetric composition attributes an outstanding image to the entry

Door as a scaling element..............................

The elevated platform gives the majestic appeal to the form of the Darwaza

Door as movement determinant......

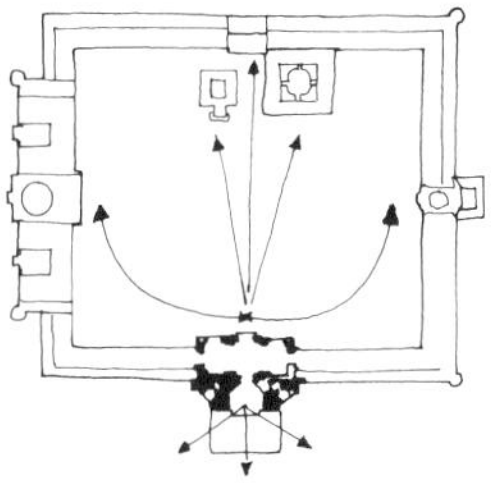

Through small puntures within the Darwaza the movement inside the complex is further oriented

Door as a facade....................................

Articulation of *chattris* and Islamic elements like arches and motifs give a distinct feacture to the darwaza

Door within the door.................................

Door as a threshold..

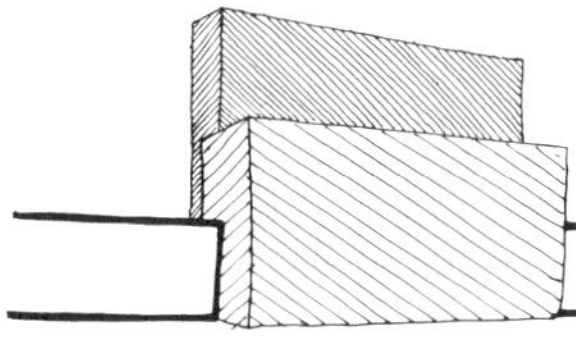

Darwaza with its gigantic structure and mass creates an overpowering sense of threshold

By breaking the solid plane and making punctures, it humanizes the entry node and becomes the point to access

The position of door generating a focus in the entire schema

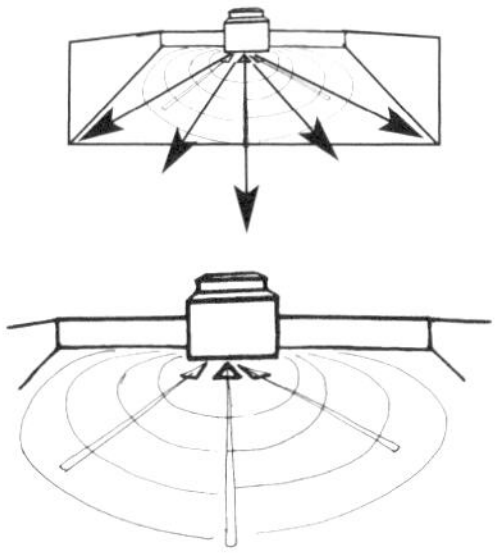

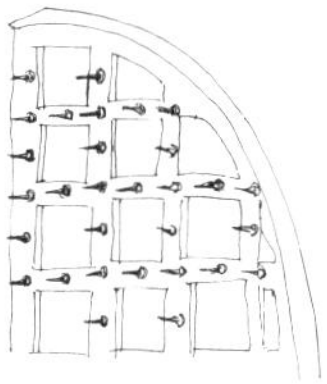

The spike door way for defense

ASSEMBLY BUILDING, CHANDIGARH

The Assembly building, built in 1956 by Le Corbusier, has a facade essentially comprising of a parasol-like shelter. The elevation of the main axis is a monumental, framed structure. The third and fourth bays open right through as a mammoth door into the bowels of the structure. The door frames within the facade plane enhance the scale of the structure along the horizontal axis, conveying the magnanimity of the institution it is a part of.

Door as an image-maker

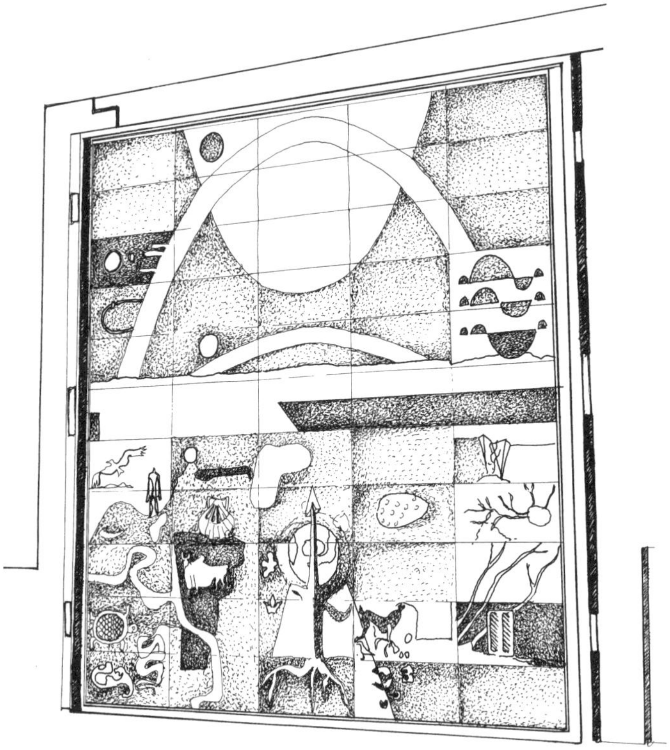

Door as point of access..

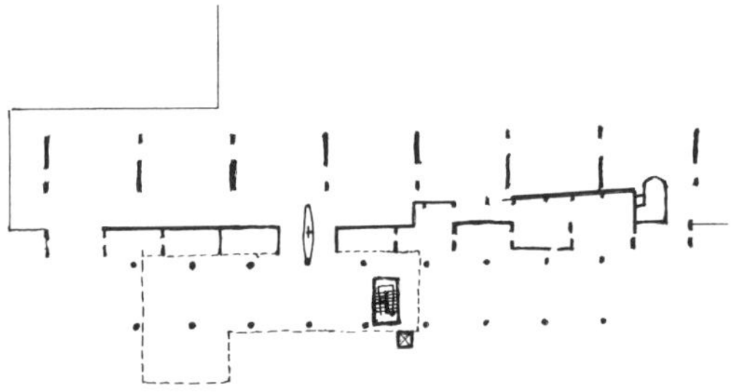

Door as one of the most conspicuous elements in the geometry of the facade determines the spatial characteristics of the overall expanse and creates a field of interest around it

Door as a modulator of facade................................

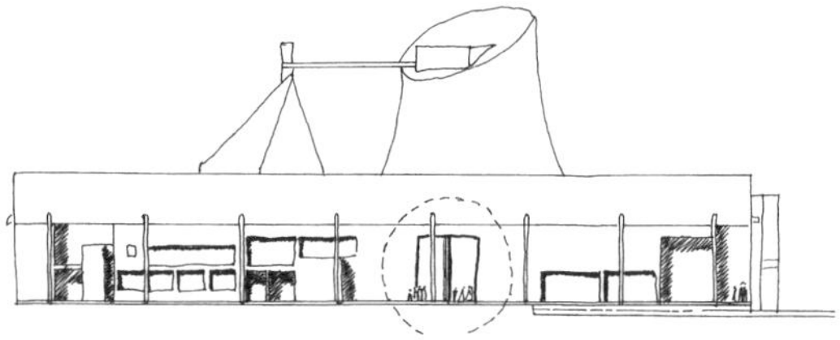

In scale and grandeur with the total mass of the structure

Door commanding the space around...

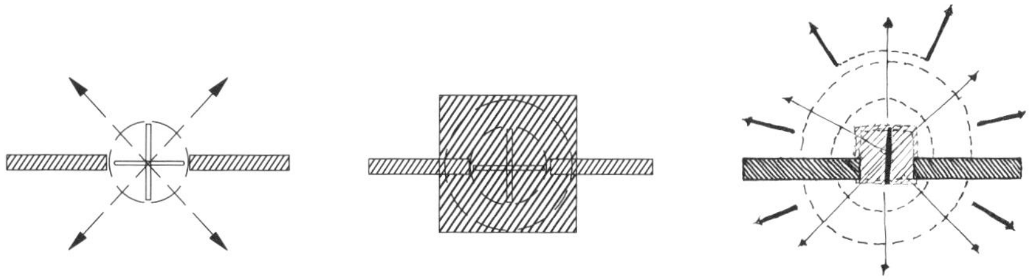

Node of differentiation—between two realms

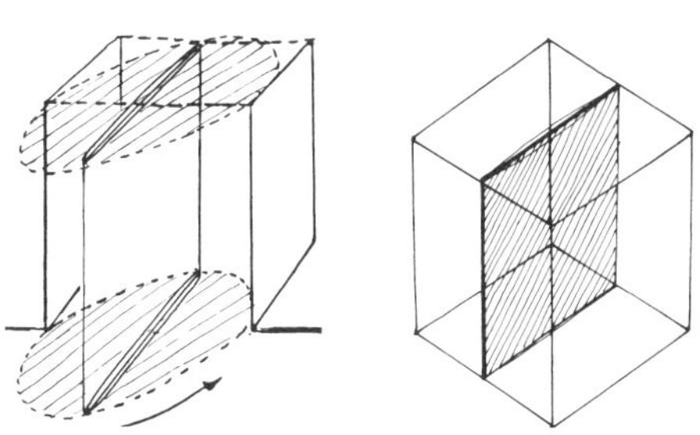

Being a pivotal door, it encompasses the volume within itself, creating a realm of its own

Door with its position creating the movement zone...

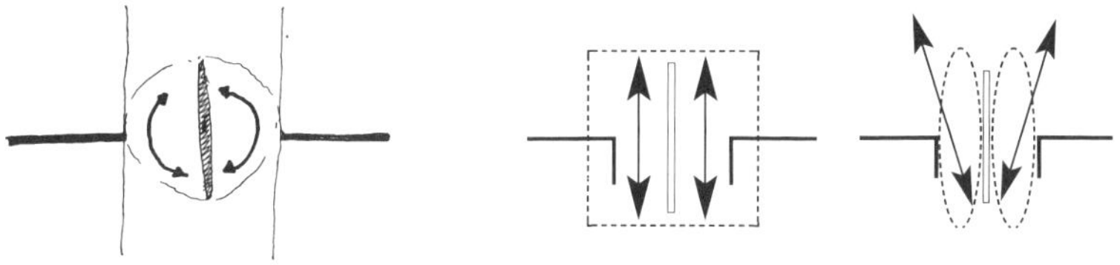

Pivoted type of doors create movement patterns encompassing the volume

Door as a penetrable plane..................................

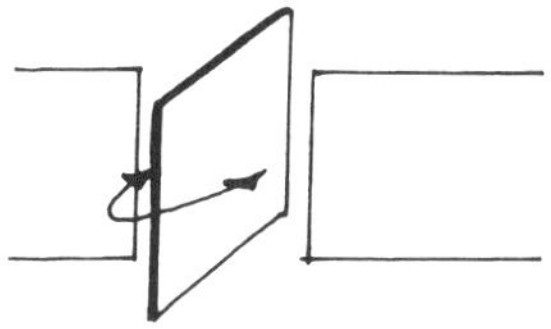

Movement between inside-out

Door depictings icons and symbols...

Icons depicting characteristics of the space and time of the built-form and the contextual scenario

Door as a threshold..

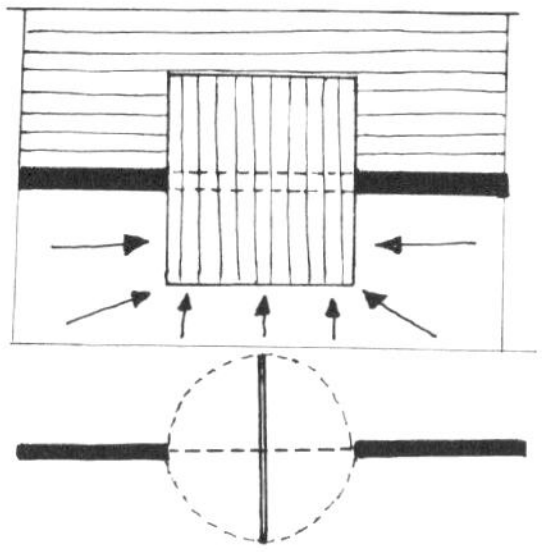

Door becomes a threshold allowing visual and physical allusion to the inner volume

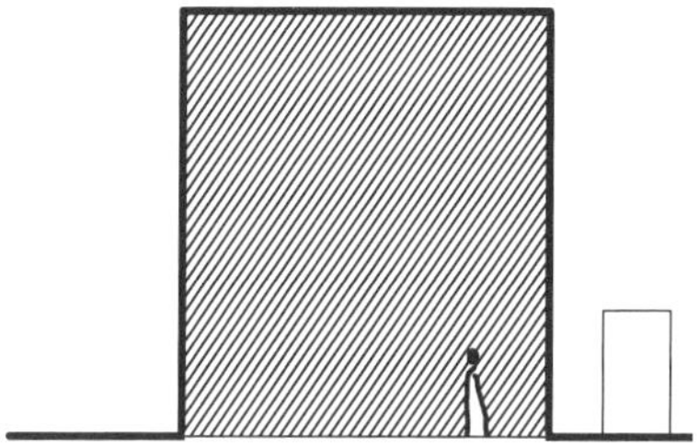

Door with its gigantic scale, creating an impactful statement of the entire built environment

GOPURAM, MADURAI

The Meenakshi-Sundereshwara temple complex at Madurai was built in the 17th century by the Chola dynasty. It has 11 *gopurams*, literally meaning the gateways, surrounding the campus along concentric entry points which lead into an inextricable labyrinth of courtyards, galleries and hypostyle halls. Embellished with numerous images of the deities they tower above the town, as if heralding the onset of the religious realm even as one enters the city.

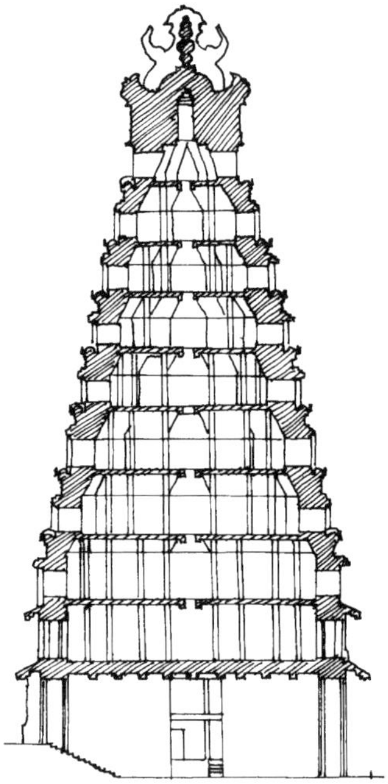

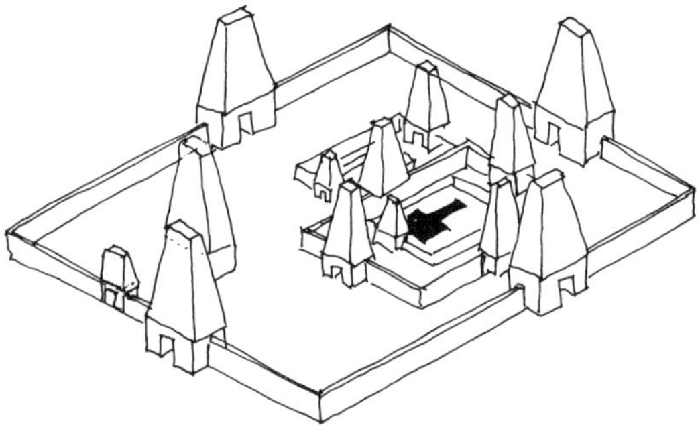

Details of *gopuram* depicting the terrifying visage of monsters, as for protecting the temple, motifs of gods and goddesses are seen as victory over evil spirits

Door as an element of differentiation

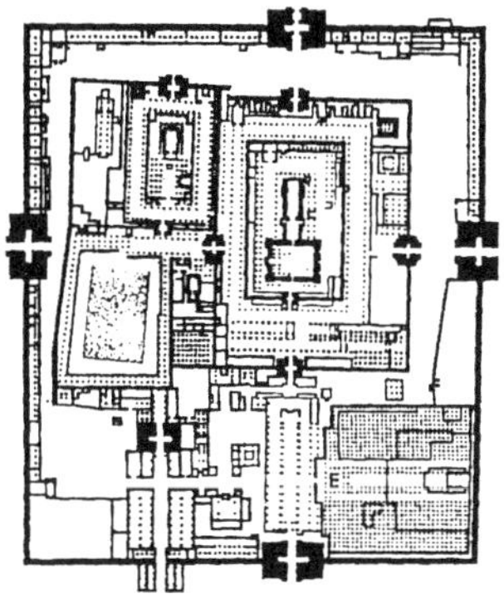

Plan of the complex

Gopurams as punctures in the barriers, distinguishing two realms, from sacred to profane

Door as point of access and movement generator

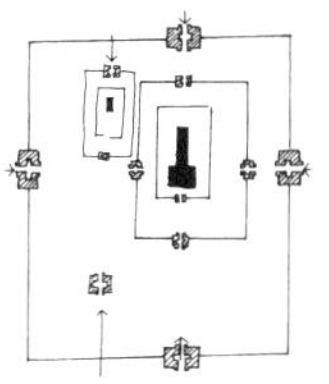

Defining point of access with its mass

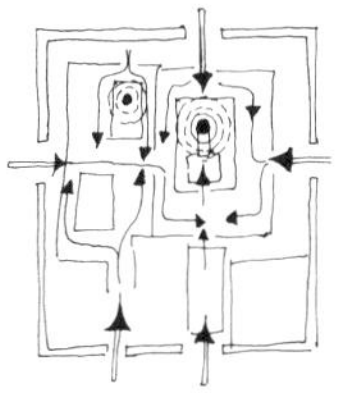

Placement determining the movement pattern

Gopuram creating sequence of thresholds

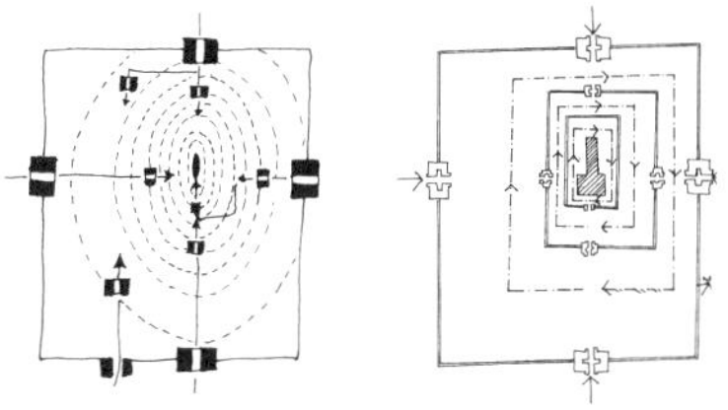

Denoting the hierarchy of thresholds within the temple complex by defining multiple intermittent zones between inner and outer worlds

Door as a modulator of overall builtspace...

Gopuram creating an image of the complex by modulating the facades with diverse scales and positions with an inherent structure of concentric realms of baffle planes

Door as a strong axis focuses the shrine—the *garbhagriha*..

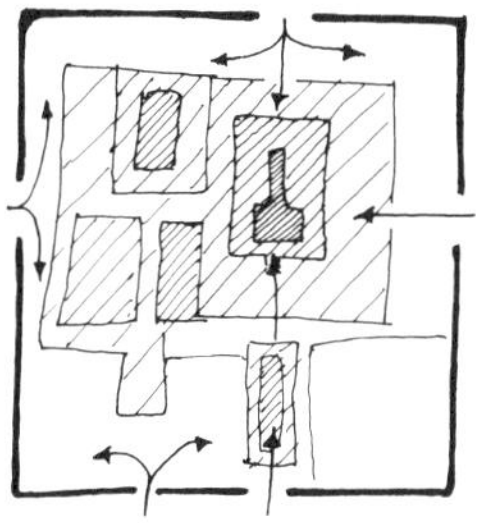

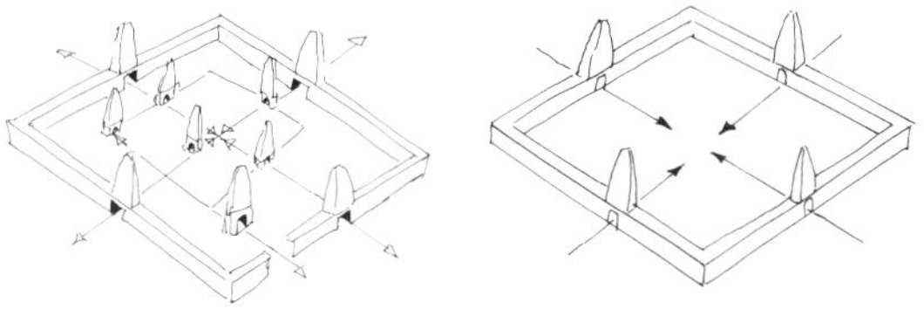

With evolving scales and mass, Gopurams become visual reference and physical link

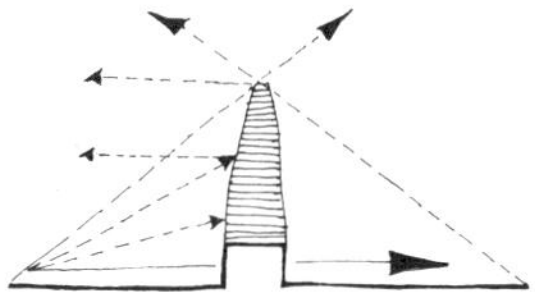

Being node of access, the doors eventually become the movement determinants

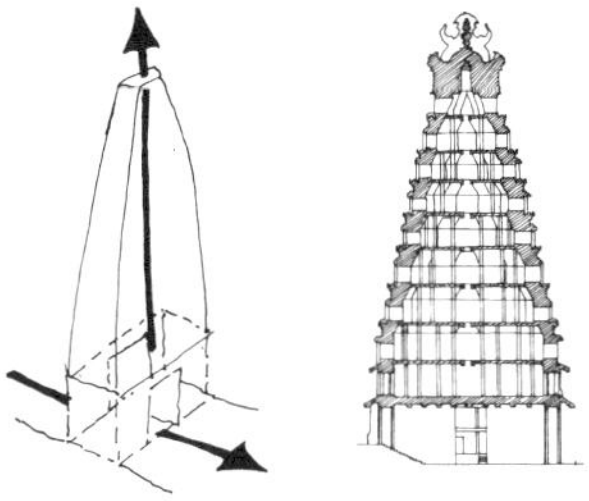

With the inbuilt mass Gopuram becomes analogous to the entire built complex

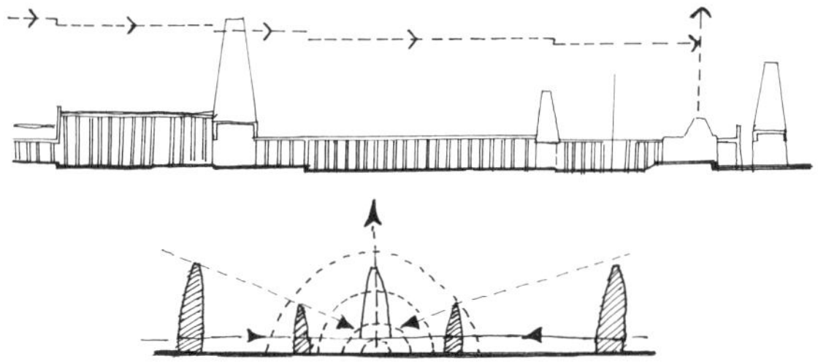

Gopuram becoming the point of entry from one realm to another, thus accentuating the transition from in to out—heaven to earth and vice-versa

HAVELI, AHMEDABAD

*Pol*s, typical residential precincts of traditional urban centres in Gujarat, are labyrinthine in nature with residences on either sides. The *pol*s confirm to long linear contiguous plots, internal courts, and wooden structure with masonry walls.

Some houses within these, belonging to the upper classes, have an elaborate scale and are referred to as haveli. Normally the clusters are formed with immediate family having dwellings clustered together around a court. The haveli being ensconced within the surrounding houses encompasses of doorways in a hierarchy, starting from the gate (*pol*) to the cluster gate (*khadki*), the house door and the internal door to subspaces.

Doors here play a vital role in defining the hierarchy of zones and often have intricately carved details to enhance the importance of the entrance.

The hierarchy of entry nodes inside the traditional dwelling

At the *pol* level

Khadki defined by gateway

Door in various scales of clusters (macro level as housing to micro level as unit level)

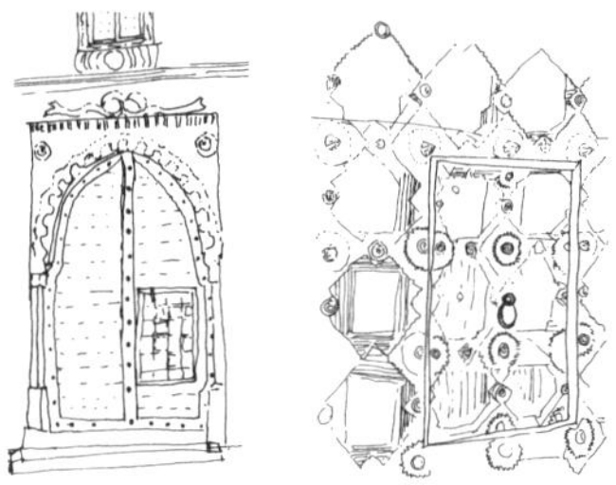

At the entrance to the housing

Entrance door to a dwelling—haveli as a wicket gate

Door as a movement guide

Plan of the *pol*

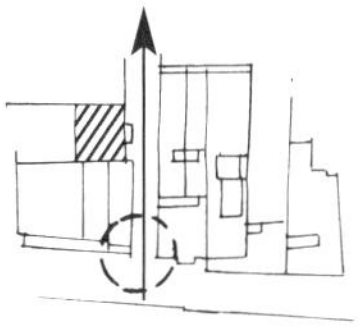

Plan of the cluster

Penetrability into private realm

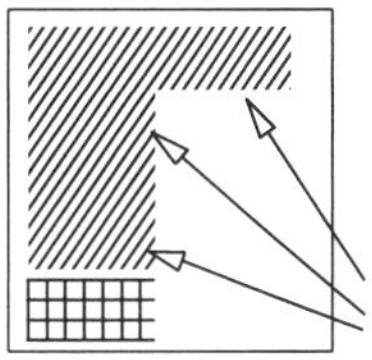

Plan of the block

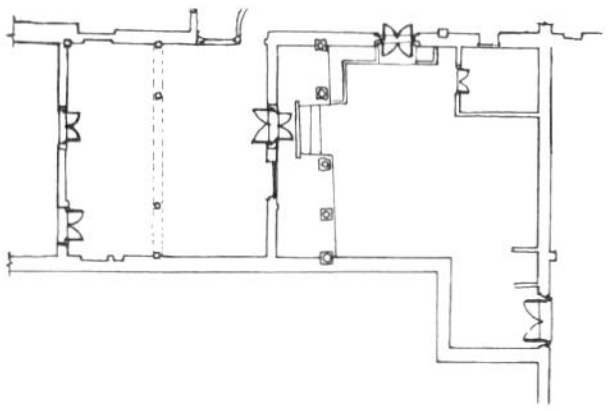

Plan of the dwelling

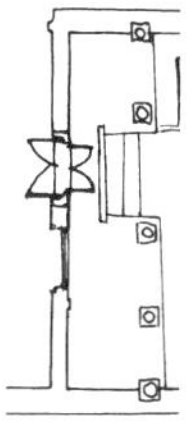

Plan of the private entrance

Defining activity zones within

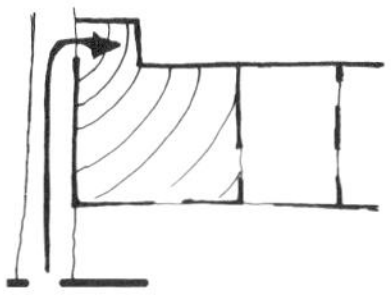

Out to in

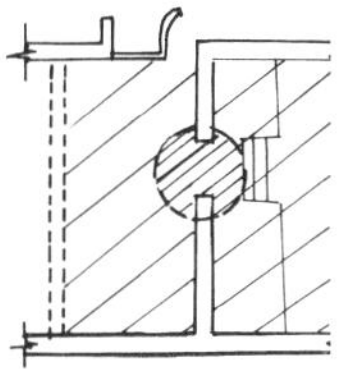

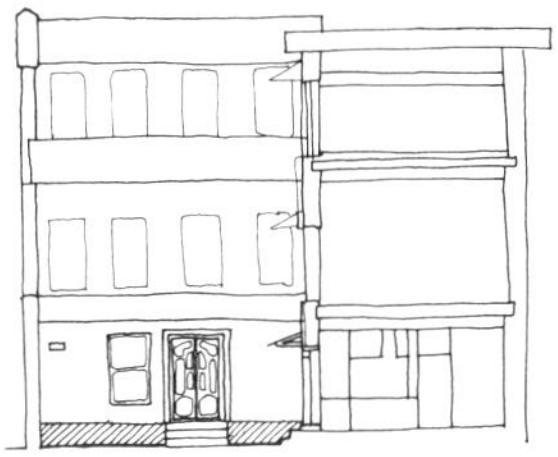

Doors opening in the open courtyard of the dwelling, connecting the built and the unbuilt nto one sequence of events

Door defining threshold

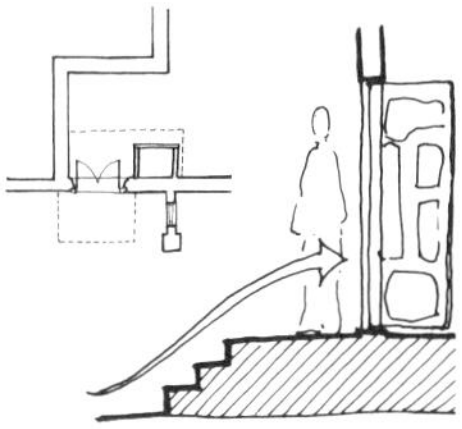

The entrance to the unit

Door becoming a threshold and a penetrable plane of the built mass attributing a sense of scale and differentiation to the entire space

Door as an element demarcating movement patterns and functional zones

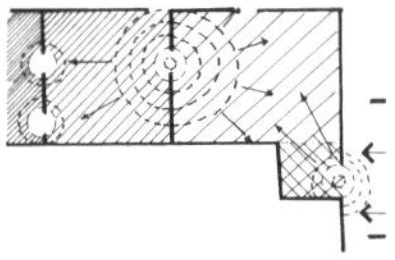

Door as a generator of pattern coherent to all spaces

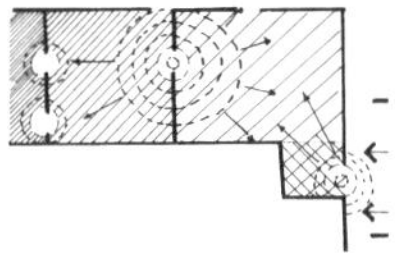

Access node defining different zones within the private dwelling

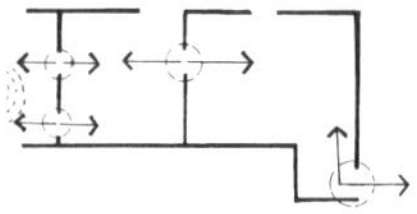

Defining axial configuration of movement

Entrance door with motifs as an image-maker

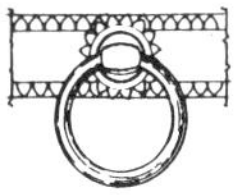

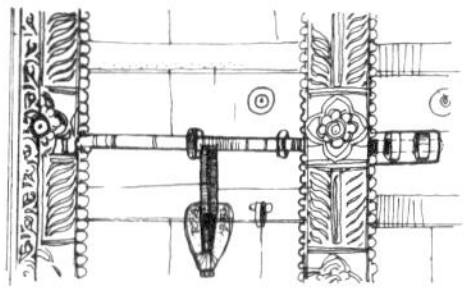

Traditional motifs and elements of door reflecting charachteristic of the culture and religion of the dweller

- The efficiency of a space, to a great extent, depends upon the position of the door. Movement patterns within the room is directly related to the location of the door, as doors become the points of access and exit.

  When a single door is placed in the middle, it divides the room into two sub-zones. In large rectangular spaces, which have a higher length to breadth ratio, locating a single door or sets of doors in the centre of the longer side helps to form proportionately scaled spaces which are contiguous in visual perception yet distinct enough to be useful for two different activities. This sort of a division classically establishes symmetry, inducing formality and grandeur.

- However, in a squarish room, two equal subzones may create not so proportionate living zones as two halves are not sizable or discernible subspaces. This reduces effectivity of space.

- The door located in a corner defines a linear circulation leaving a larger lateral portion as functional zone.

- Placing two sets of doors more or less along the same side defines a clear movement zone and leaves the most of the room undisturbed by the movement.Rather than placing door right at the corner leaving some distance in corner regions provides for storage or display zone besides the circulation.

- Doors mark the threshold for interface zones and thus, condition the mind. It is prudent to consider the door as a space of transition and treat it accordingly. Extended planes of roofs, walls or floors combined with elements like seats, thresholds, niches and steps, with the door will help to accentuate the much-needed transition.

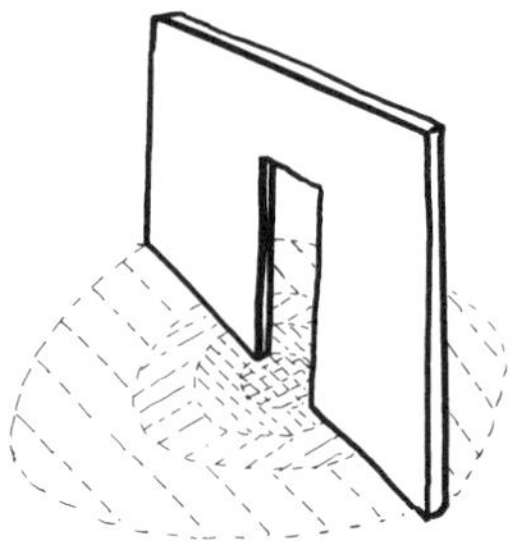

Space divided into subzones in a squarish module

Centrally located door, defining two sub zones in a rectangular module

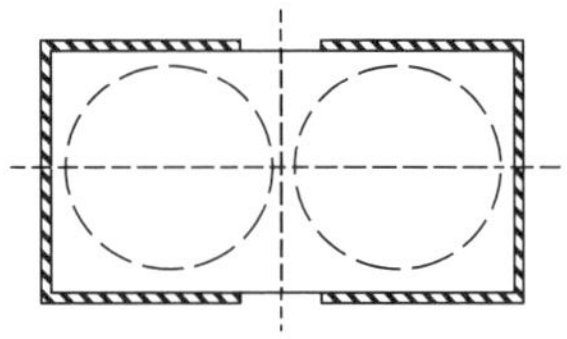

Doors in larger rooms with forming two distinct activity zones

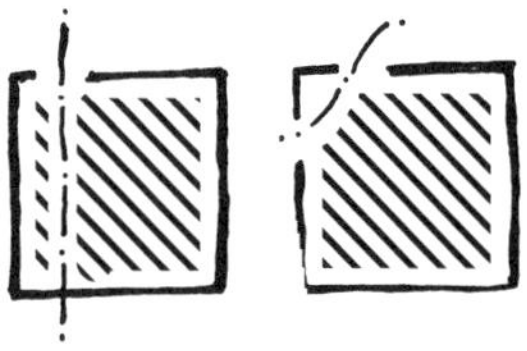

Door located in a corner, define larger zones as functional zone

Space with two sets of doors

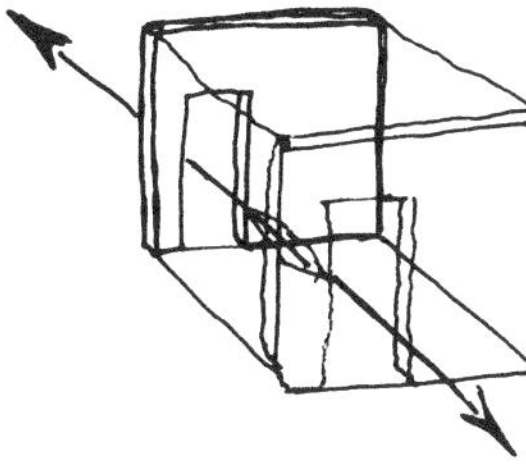

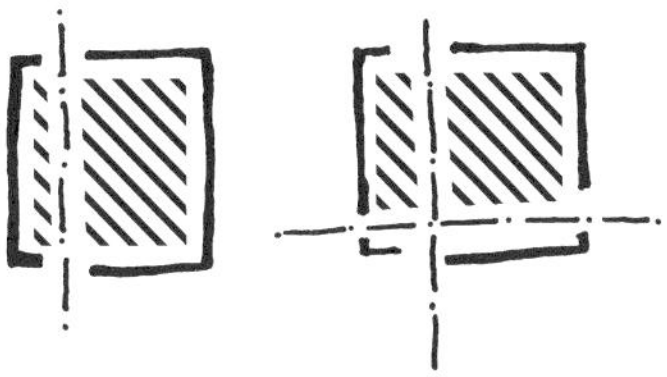

niche for storage/display

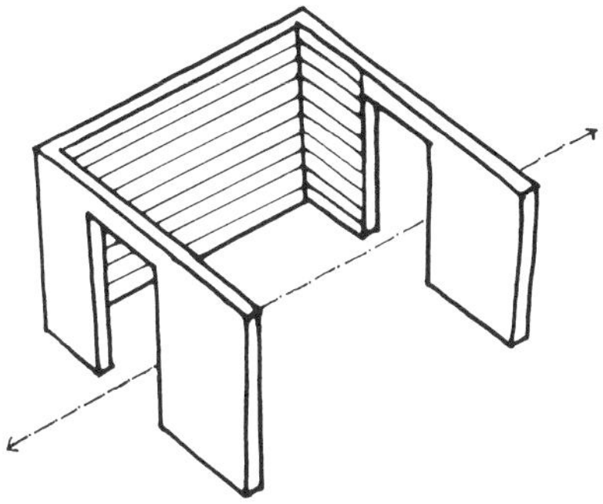

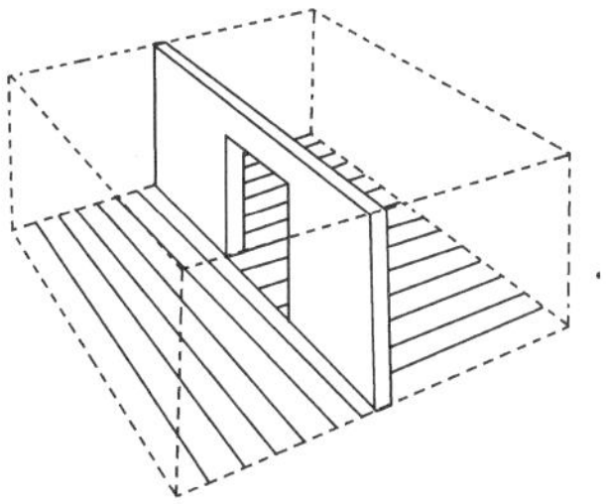

Door as an element establishing a threshold between spaces

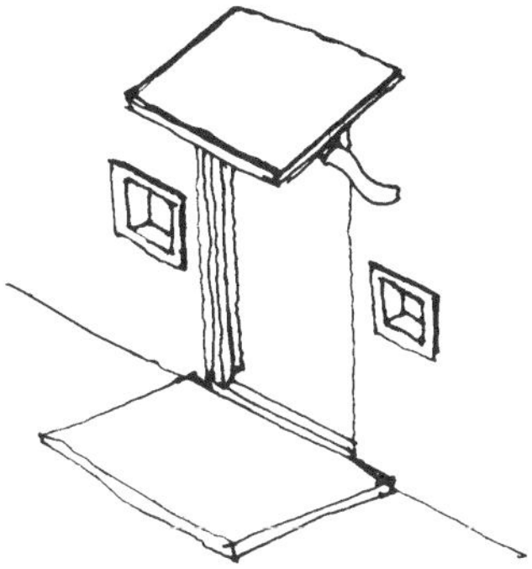

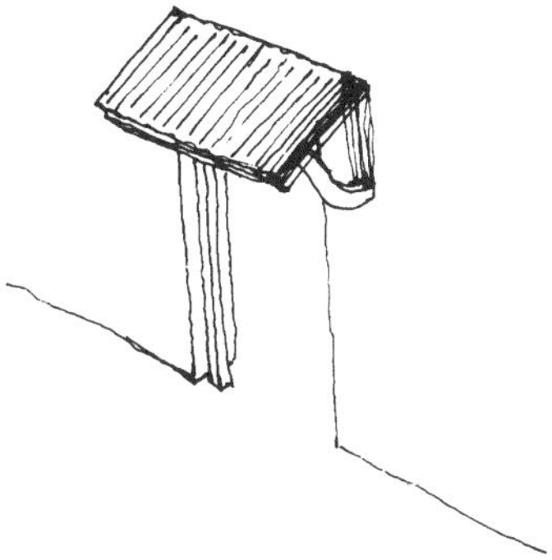

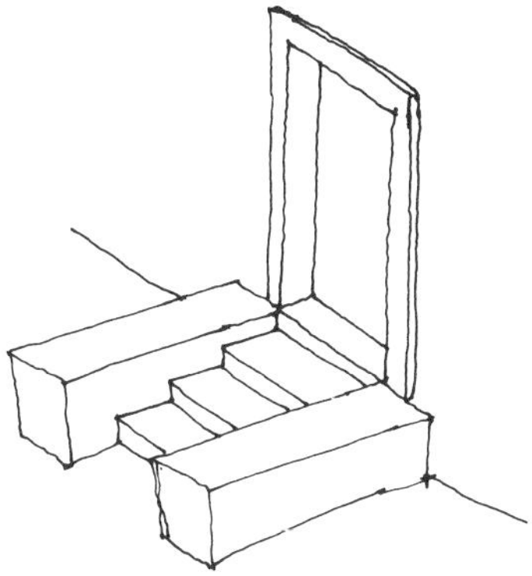

• The door is a link as well as a separator and needs to be designed for the entry as well as exit sequences appropriately. Therefore, it must not be seen as a puncture and element of interest not only from outside but should also be treated respectfully from inside. The depths created by jambs and the shutter swings along with communication potentials of shutter plane could be exploited for transition sequence while exiting.

• Doors of the same kind can be emphasized individually by way of additional openings of the sides or above, changing the scale and giving

• Very large doors can use their multiple shutter combination and composition effectively to express nature and frequency of use. For example, door within a door or wider versus narrower shutter leaf etc. Transparency or opacity of shutters also help signify door's function and space beyond.

Door as a node for entry and exit

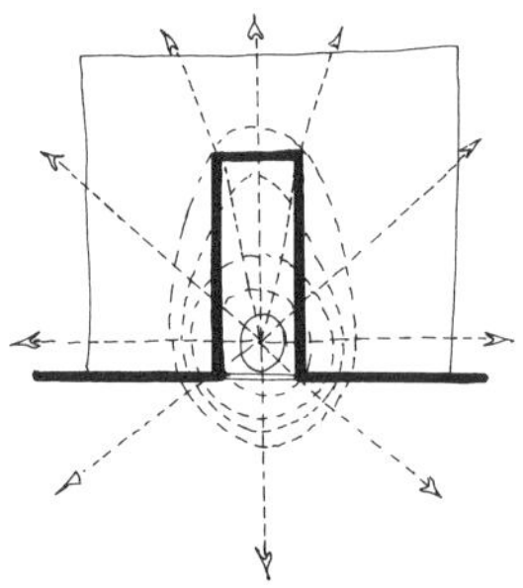

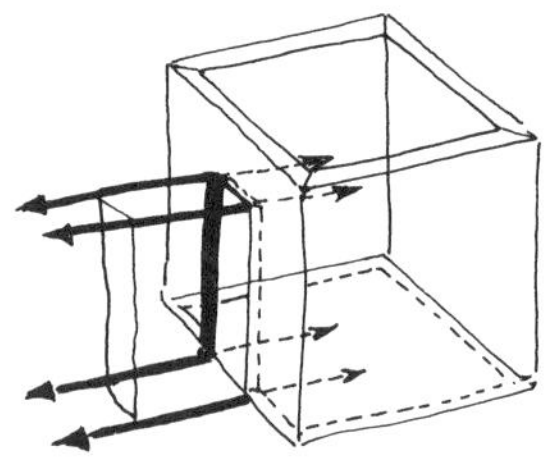

Entry node rendered by additional embellishments

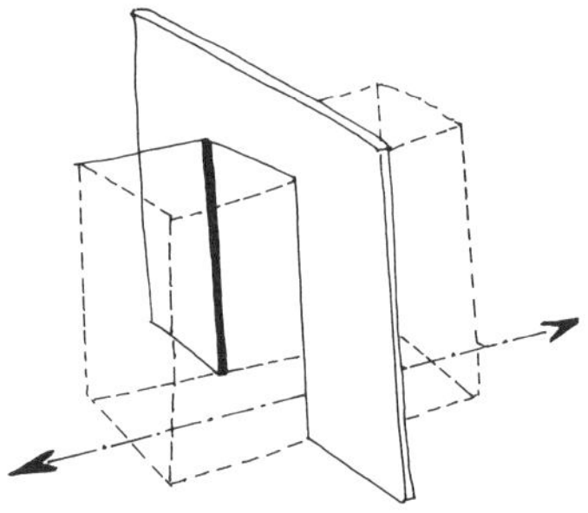

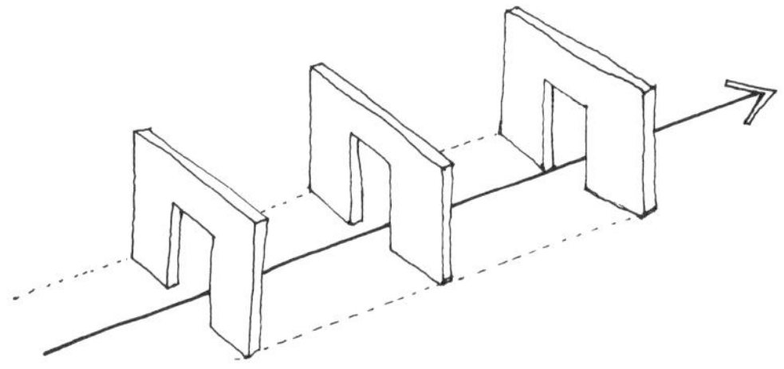

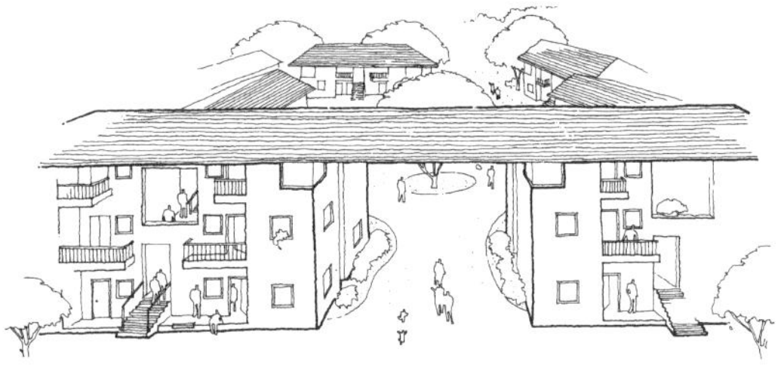

Door as a point of entry denoting a shift and transition from one realm to another

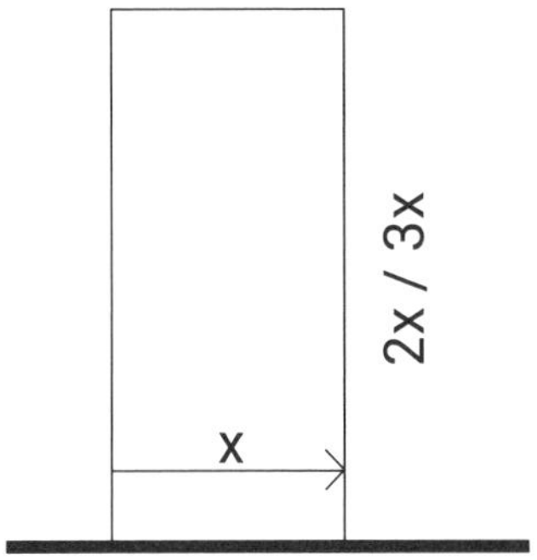

Thumb rule for proportioning of a door

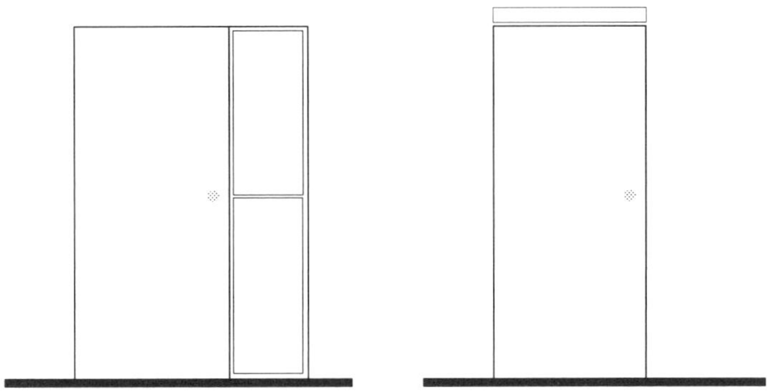

Door emphasized by additional opening and elements

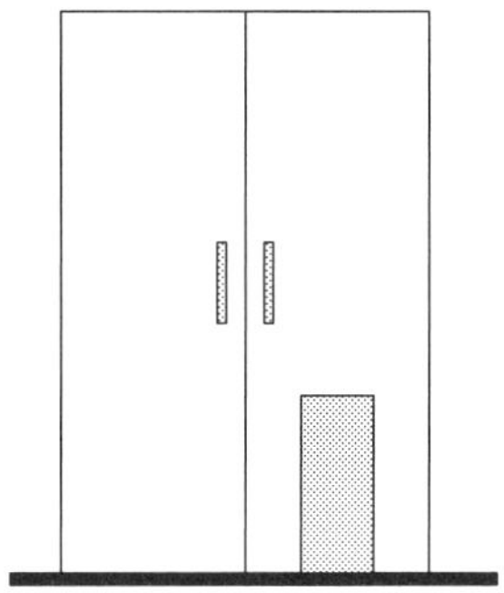

Larger door with door within a door

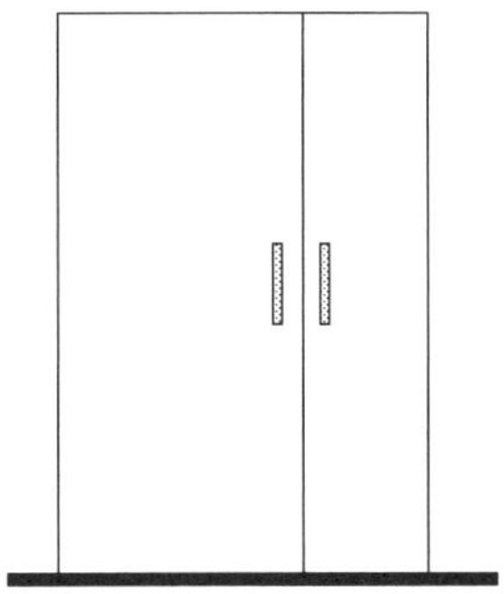

Larger door with narrow shutter leaf

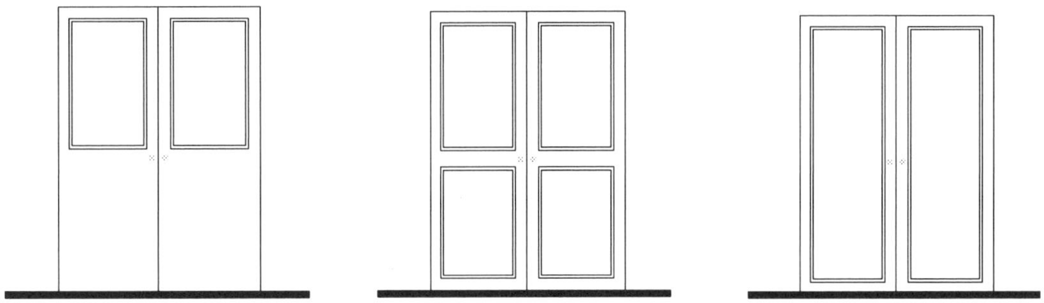

Transparency and opacity for signifying the function space beyond

WINDOW

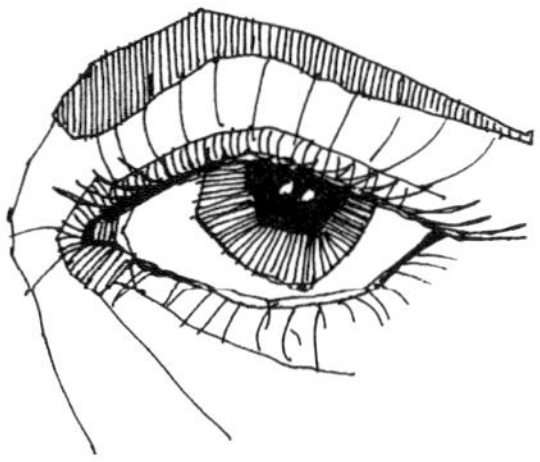

Tripartite window of a pol house, Ahmedabad

Windows, to buildings, are as eyes are to the face. They are the visual links between the inside and the outside world. While the door facilitates access into the building, windows, by controlling light and ventilation, make it habitable. The window is defined as an opening in the wall made to facilitate ventilation, light and view. The word window derives from the Old Norse word *vindauga* (*vindr+auga*=wind+eye), meaning eye for wind. The Scandinavian word was replaced and finally superseded in Old English as *eyethurl*, but the French derived *fenester* was in concurrent use as recently as beginning of the Modern Period. The Sanskrit equivalent of window is the term *vaatayana* (*vata* + *ayana*) where, *vata* means wind, *aayan* means to come. Thus, the window, even through nomenclature, suggests an apparatus to facilitate exchange between the internal and external.

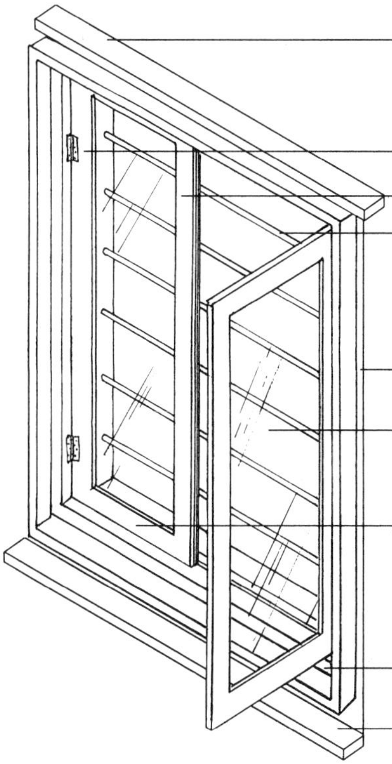

Typological Variations

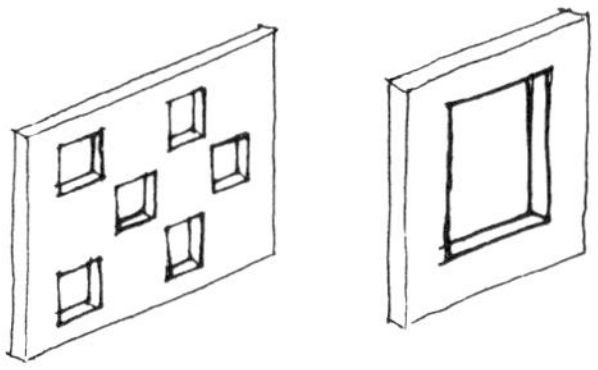

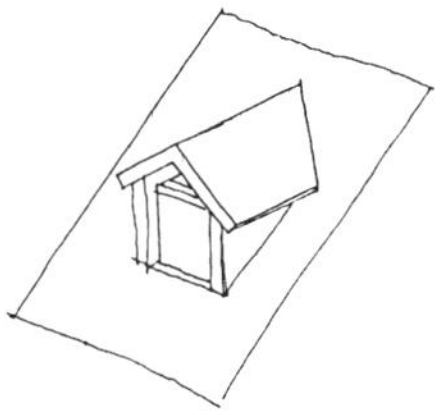

PERFORATION (*JAALI*)
In situations where privacy, harsh sunlight and ventilation are primary concerns, the window takes the form of perforated screens, or small-embedded apertures, these offer controlled visual connection and light without affecting ventilation. Also, these devices make effective use of the Venturi effect. As the air passes through the small apertures, it is cooled due to differential pressures.

CASEMENT
The most commonly found typology of window, this is the regular planar opening puncturing a flat wall to generate through connection with adjustable shutters for light, air and visual communication as per the requirements. In most of the cases, the security requirements are taken care of by grilles which form part of the ensemble.

BAY
A projected alcove in the wall, creating a subspace of its own, this window thrusts outwards, with openings on the three sides allowing for interaction with the exterior. It extends floor space into the exterior generating an intermediate space with the qualities of both the interior and the exterior while offering increased views outside.

DORMER
Essentially invented as a device to make use of the volume lost due to the pitched roof. An intersection of two prismatic solids, the vertical face has an opening which functions as a ventilator, a vertical operable opening creating a vertical aperture in the steeply pitched roof, this facilitates light and ventilation of the attic spaces.

Caves, the primitive dwelling form, had apertures carved out of living rocks to allow illumination and ventilation into the dark interiors of the caves. Windows in the form of punctures came about with masonry construction systems and can be found depicted in the early wall paintings of Egypt, Assyria and also in terra-cotta plaques of Crete.

Greek urban houses, introverted in nature, did away with the windows, and the court became a window to sky. The trabeated construction also imposed restrictions on the opening size in view of the spanning capabilities of compressive materials. The Dark Ages and Medieval period articulated the window essentially for defense as well as attack by its higher placement, smaller size, splayed jambs and positioning. The Roman invention of the arch, with different technology and increased spanning capabilities changed considerably the scale and character of window. It became a means of facade articulation and expression.

Initial window, as an aperture in the heavy and opaque wall planes

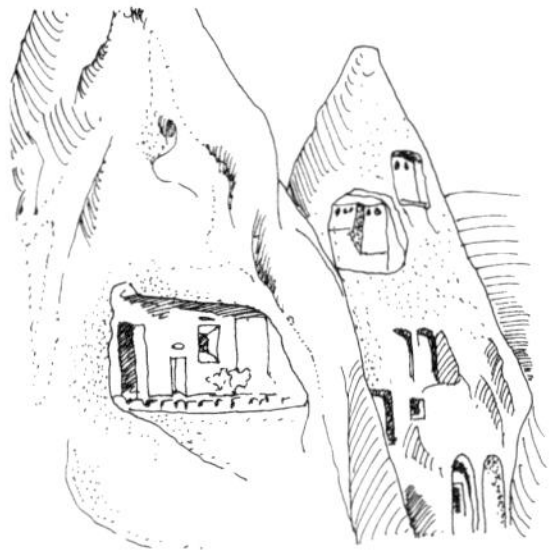

Cappadocian cave dwelling, Turkey

Urartian Relief, Kefkalesi

Courtyard working as a window to sky—a shaft for light and ventilation

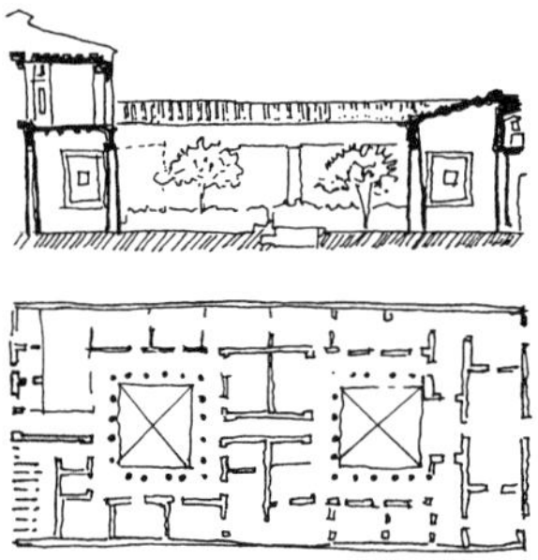

Greek houses

Imperial Abbey of St. Cyriakus, Gernrode, Germany

Narrow opening in the walls with the trabeated structural systems prevalent

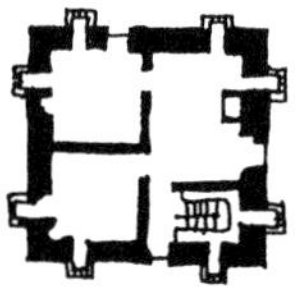

Plan

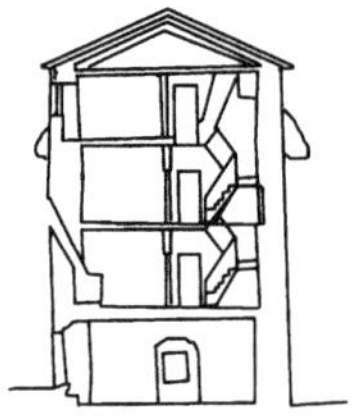

Section

Dwelling Tower, Saint-Luge-De-Tallano, Middle Ages

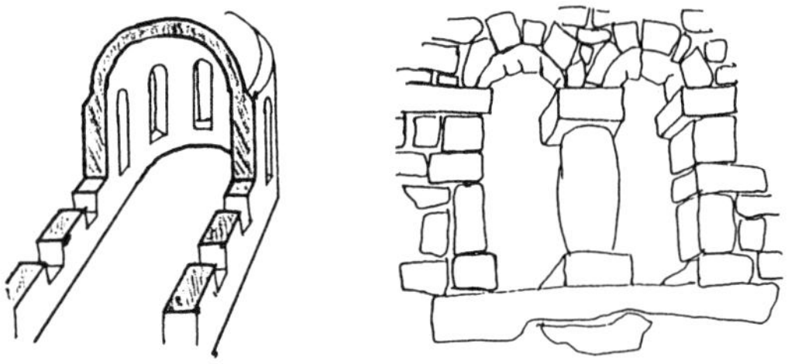

Thick structural walls having smaller puncture, Roman Era

Detail

A complete reversal of its manifestation took place during the Gothic period. The Rose window, circular in form with geometric floral patterns and stained glass, became typical of Gothic cathedrals. Such windows were pictorial. Backlit, they were often inoperable with stained glass and line composition. The introduction of stone mullions helped in making them longer. Windows, in high Renaissance period conformed to classical proportions. They were divided by a single mullion across and decorated with architraves, cornices and pediments. Ornamentation in the form of human figures and masks came to be in Baroque period. During the later Renaissance period large casement windows were introduced.

Window as an element articulating and composing the facade

Rose window

Introduction of buttresses, gave flexibility in size of the opening

Reims Cathedral with Rose window, Gothic period

Detail of Reims Cathedral

Windows identified with human figures, and decorative embellishments—Baroque window

Classical proportioned windows and decorated Renaissance windows

Detail

Palazzo Strozzi, Florence

The Royal Crescent, Bath

Second Leiter Building, Chicago

Wainwright Building, Missouri

During the early twentieth century, in the wake of modernism, with standardization and mass production, windows became austere and universal in expression. As an assemblage of pre-manufactured kit of elements. The extensive use of reinforced concrete in structure, allowed for larger opening spans. The introduction of thinner steel sections and glass in windows created large and thin planes of fenestration, almost becoming a transparent enclosure.

Skyscrapers of twentieth century relied largely on such vocabulary of the curtain wall while articulating the facade.Present day materials and technical know-how have rendered the element virtually free for endless applications and expressions. The element instead of appearing as an opening into the solid wall face now appears as a continuous skin of transparency with the supports within.

Window as a transparent wall plane and with many other visual expressions after industrialization and modernism became an exclusive element of a building

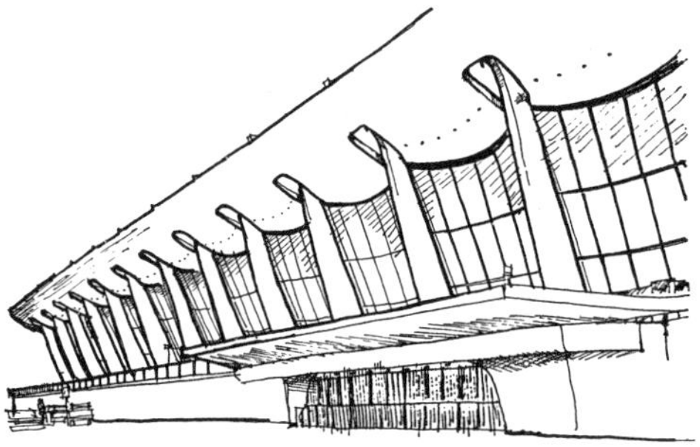

Dulles Airport, Washington D.C.

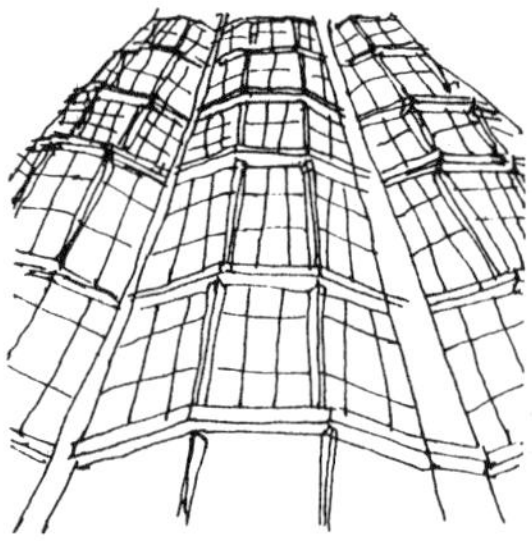

Lion Chambers, Glasgow

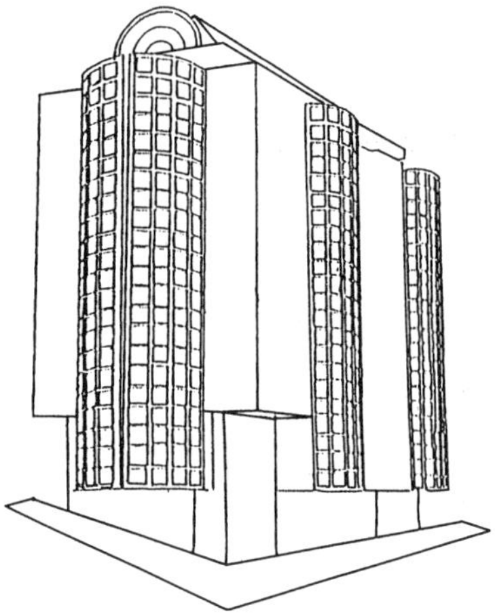

Óbuda Újlak, Budapest

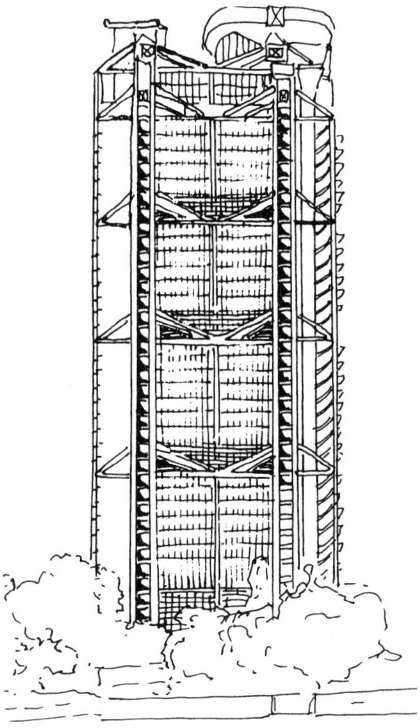

HSBC Head Office, Hong Kong

INDIAN CONTEXT

Horseshoe shaped windows known as Chaitya windows were carved out of solid mass in rock cut architecture during Buddhist phase. The arch developed during Indo-Saracenic phase, and pointed arch became conspicuous in Islamic phase. Jaali—stone lettice was also characteristic element of this phase. Multipointed Mayur arch was elaborately used in Hindu, especially Rajput, architecture. Jharokha—a projecting balcony with screened windows all around was iconic of Indian architecture both in Hindu as well as Islamic phase, as it supported notions of privacy and helped create effective microclimate. Hindu trabeated construction combined with Islamic construction.

During Colonial phase, large windows were widely seen in Indian architecture, whereas Tripartite window became a unique characteristic of vernacular architecture.

Eventually with modernism, Le Corbusier, Louis Kahn, and other modern masters brought a new meaning to window, where it became an iconic element with various languages of facade modulation.

Carved out of rock.............

Chaitya window, Pandava Caves, Nashik

Trabeated type—the sill and lintel emphasized

Mosque, Ahmedabad

Composite arch....................

Baz Bahadur Palace, Mandu

Different types of arch emphasizing the openings—Islamic Period...

Qutub Mosque, Delhi

Alai Darwaza, Delhi

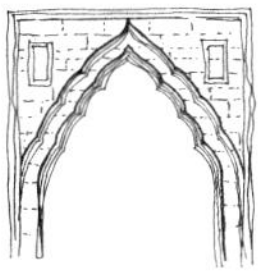

Ajmer Mosque, Ajmer

Tomb of Tughluq, Delhi

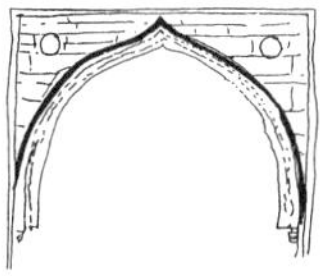

Jami Masjid, Ahmedabad

Mughul arch

Mughul arch, Shah Jehan

Typical pointed arch

Modernism bringing a new characteristics to window form.................

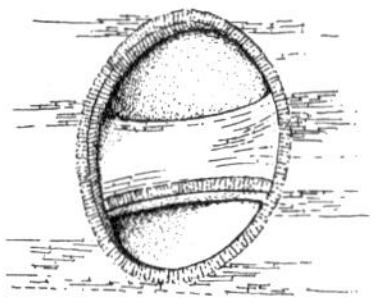

Indian Institute of Management, Ahmedabad

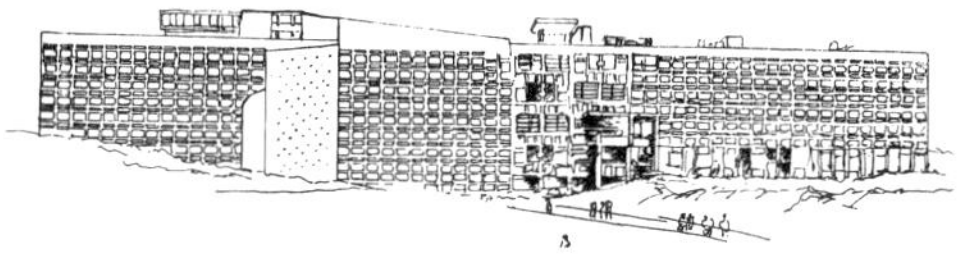

The Secretariat, Chandigarh

Vernacular windows...

Typical Mayur arch - Hindu Period

Tripartite opening pol house, Ahmedabad

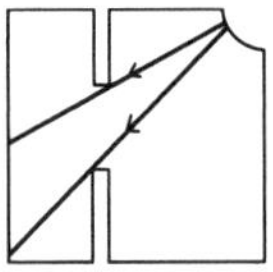

TRANSPARENCY AND POROSITY: APERTURE FOR LIGHT

Walls, essentially for defence and protection are often solid and opaque. Securing the interior against various dangers renders the space dark, claustrophobic and unfit for healthy habitation. Windows, as adjustable apertures, while confirming to the boundaries set up by the walls, illuminate the interiors with natural light from the sun, without losing out on the notion of enclosure of security. The size of the openings must be determined by considerations of security and spanning.

Window as a puncture illuminating and enlightening the space within...

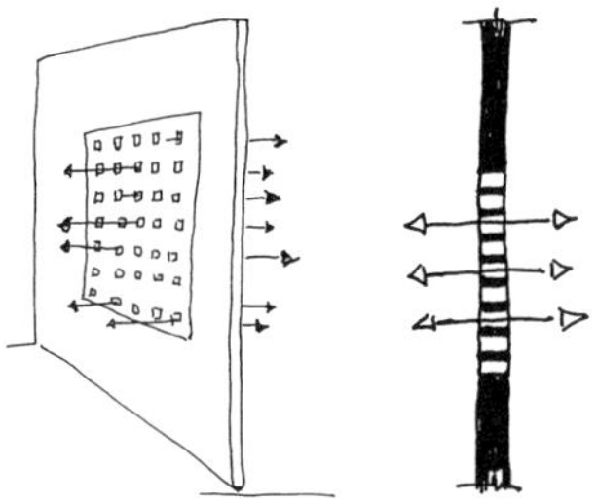

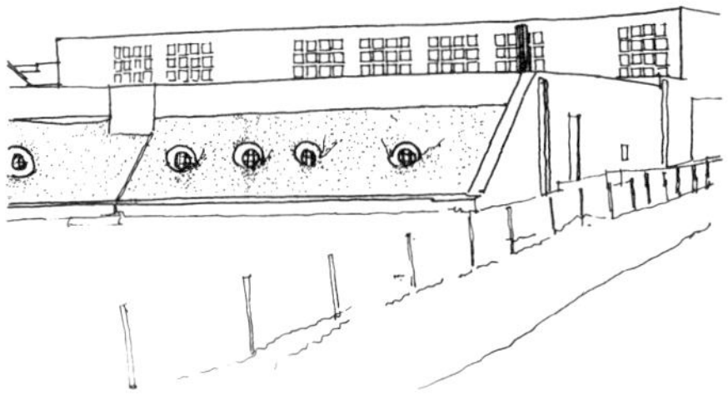

Food crafts institute, Bhopal

School of Architecture, Ahmedabad

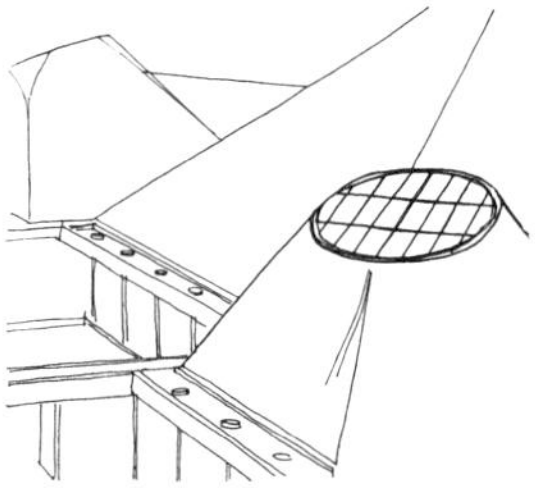

Bharat Bhavan, Bhopal

Window with its varying size and opacity dramatizing the space...

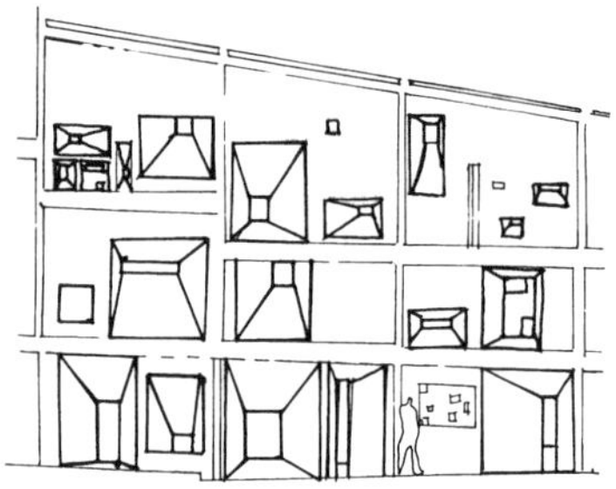

Interior of Notre Dame du Haut chapel, Ronchamp

A Bohra house, Siddhpur

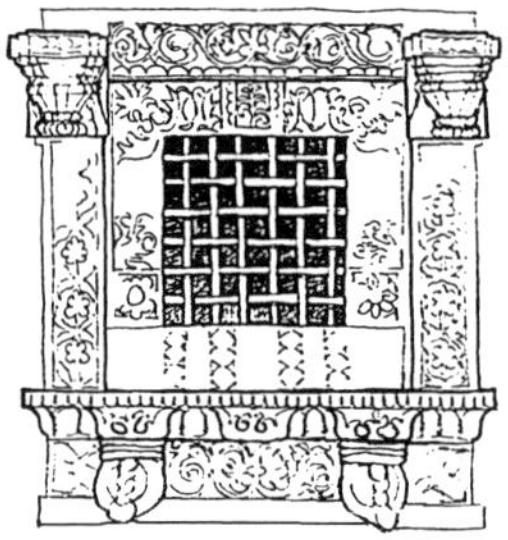

Opening with interwoven metal rods forming defensive *jali*

Pierced stone window with icons of swastika and lotuses

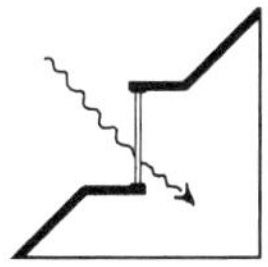

PASSAGE FOR AIR

Apart from providing light, the openings in the wall also allow the diffusion for fresh air into the room. The ionised, draft of air not only replenishes the stale air with fresh, but also evaporates humidity lowering the temperature and thus increasing the comfort levels indoors. Pragmatic attempts aided the design of windows in their location so as to facilitate cross ventilation where the natural breeze is captured to maximise circulation. In warm, humid conditions, movement along with shade form the primary determinants of habitability of buildings. In hot dry conditions, windows are modulated to wind escape on the leeward side and as small apertures on the windward side to let in the air, cooling it, and exhausting it from above, channelling prevalent winds into the interiors. Location of windows according to the principles of aerodynamics and with knowledge of the wind directions determines the wind flow in a room.

The positions of window in the space, determine and govern the air movement creating a peculiar environmental conditions in the space.

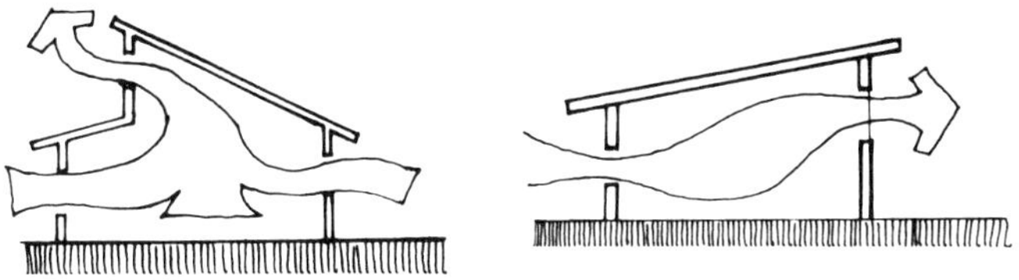

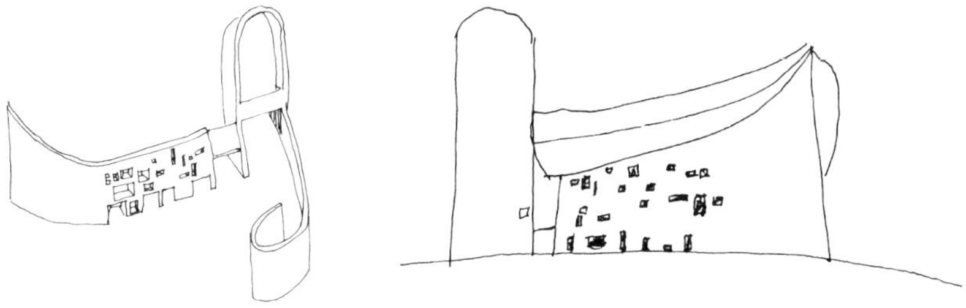

Interior of Notre Dame du Haut chapel, Ronchamp

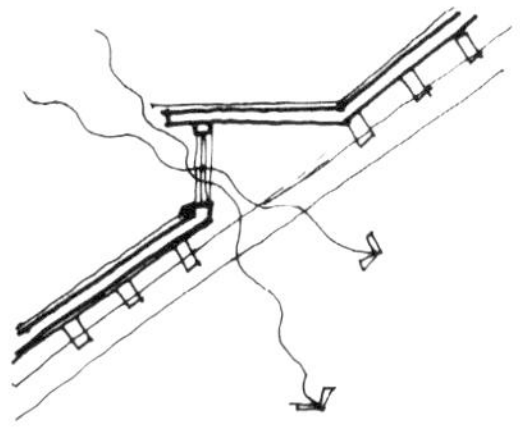

Dormer window- at typical example for passage of light and air

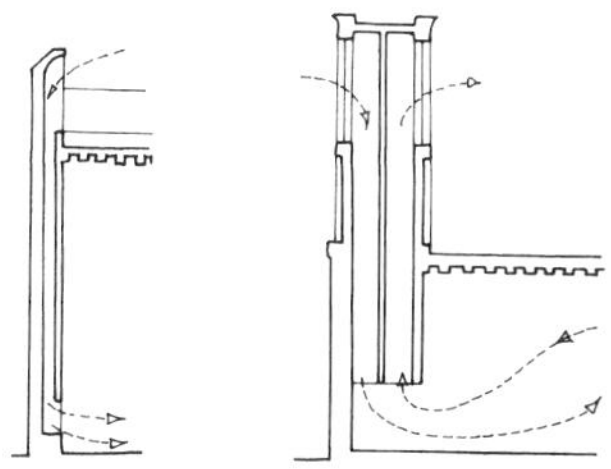

Alternative 1 Alternative 2

Wind Scoop

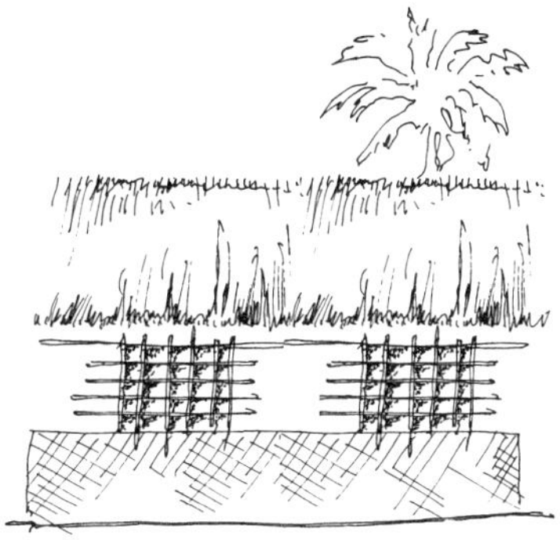

Punctures for air, Vernacular House, Kerala

WINDOW AS COMMUNICATION LINK

Windows, as openings in the wall, owing to their transparency, form the visual interface with the exteriors communicating with the outdoors. Depending on the nature of use of the spaces that they separate, windows could govern either one-way or two way communications. Where the privacy of the interiors is maintained while allowing view outwards. *Jali*s or perforated screens were used to achieve the one way communication most effectively. The aspect of increased communication and interface with exterior conditions has given existence to bay windows and window *Jharokhas*, which project from the wall to give a bulge from the wall into the exterior.

Apart from the typology of window, the location and scale of window influence the type and intensity of visual communication and link to the natural elements and outdoors.

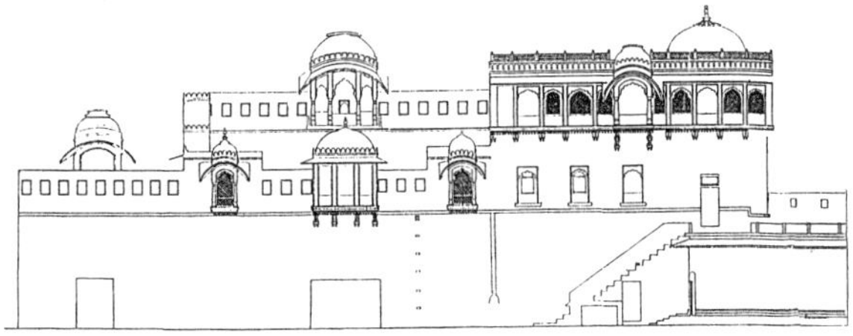

Street profile with *jharokhas*, Jaisalmer

Villa Savoye, Poissy, France

The propensity of the window to enhance or constrict the visual links between inside and out
In to out

in to out

Outside to inside interaction

Jali—one way communication

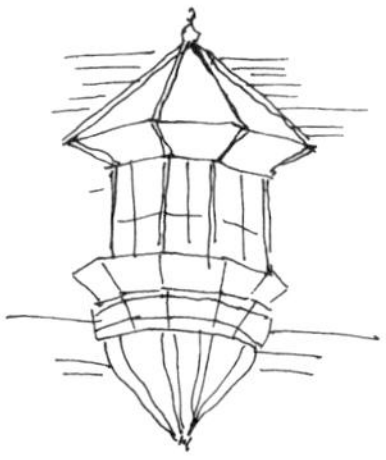

Padmanabhapuram Palace, Thiruvananthapuram

Chhatri window, Jodhpur

Street view,Rajasthan

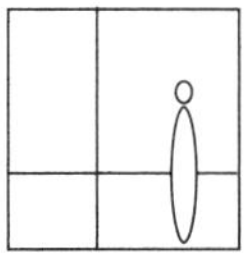

WINDOW AS SCALING ELEMENT

As a puncture in the contiguous surface, windows become visual reference. Contrasted against the texture of the wall surface, the voids they represent, their modulation as tall or wide, their spacing and implied rhythm, their stretch and alignment in vertical or horizontal direction, all contribute towards scaling the built-mass. They break the surface continuity and sub-scale the mass. The visual orders of the external skin is often derived more through windows and in some of the cases the window therefore is designed according to the scale of the facade so as to compose it more than the internal requirement. Once the void is generated, it can be internally modulated through other devices.

Residential street, Cairo

Window reflects the scale of the space within to the outside making the two realms homogenous

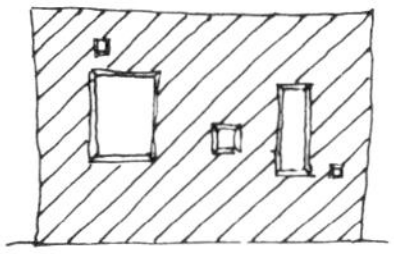

Window behaves as a device scaling the space inside the built form

Indian Institute of Management, Ahmedabad

Shibam, Yemen

Window becoming an element sub scaling the space outside..

King's Cross Station, London

Coleshill House, Berkshire

Facade of Bohra House, Siddhpur

Entrance porch of Bramshill House, Hampshire

WINDOW AS FACADE MODULATOR

From the exterior, the primary elements constituting a buildings facade are the roof and the wall. Windows, as elements, which adorn the wall, play a significant role in its modulation. Depending on the size, form, number, placement and articulation, windows alter the perception of a building, bringing in aspects of lightness, rhythm and sculptural quality. These also may clue us about the nature of functions, spaces and environments within. Even in the roof as seen in the European towns, the windows, as dormers in the steep roofs, have played a major role in accentuating the roof-scape.

With the porosity created by the articulation of opening the building acquires lightness and transparency

The Secretariat, Chandigarh

With the formal language and the rhythm followed by the window the built space gains significance

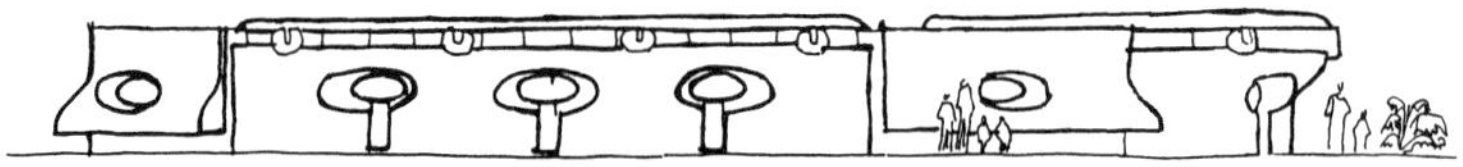

Sanskrit school, Auroville

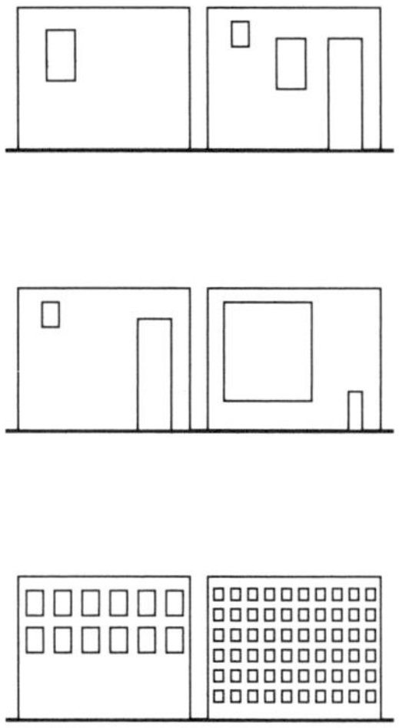

With unique characterization, window creates a built space having sculptural quality..

Hawa Mahal, Jaipur

Casa mila, Barcelona

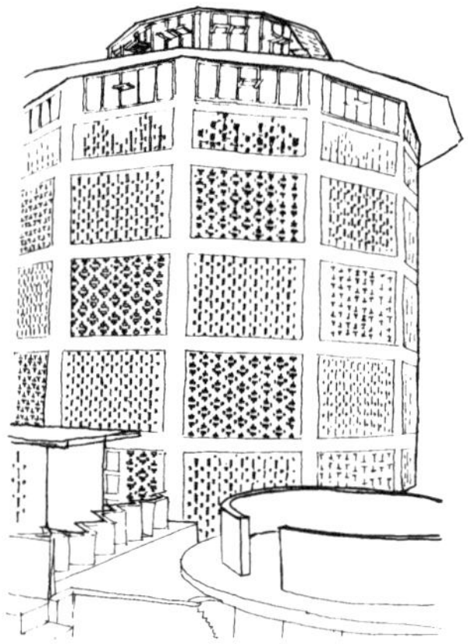

Centre for Development Studies, Thiruvananthapuram

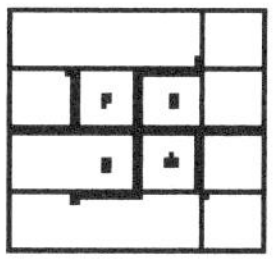

WINDOW AS IMAGE MAKER

As an external element and nearly mandatory for every building, the window often becomes a key element in the visual imagery of any building.

Windows frame views and also gets framed within the facade surface. Often buildings get recognized and identified through the image portrayed by these characteristic windows.

The image is not only conveyed through their visual characteristics but also by their proportions implied through numbers and translucency of the windows. These indicate the notions of security, privacy and introversion - extroversion.

Cathedral of Our Lady, Reims

Sidi Saiyyed ni Jali, Ahmedabad

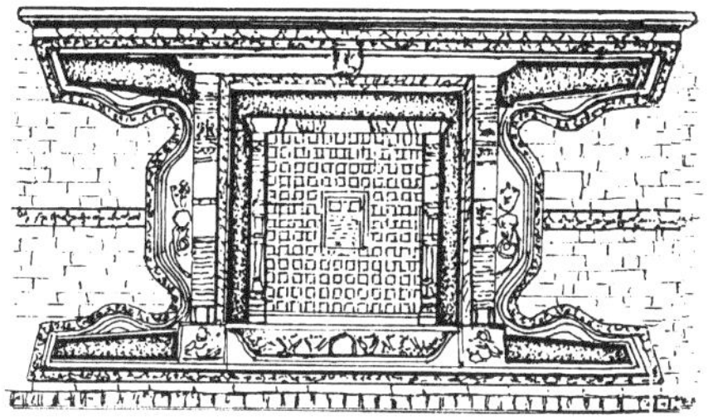

Newar window, Nepal

Form and characteristics of the openings assist in establishing building's identity and projecting unique symbolic quality

Residential alley, Cairo

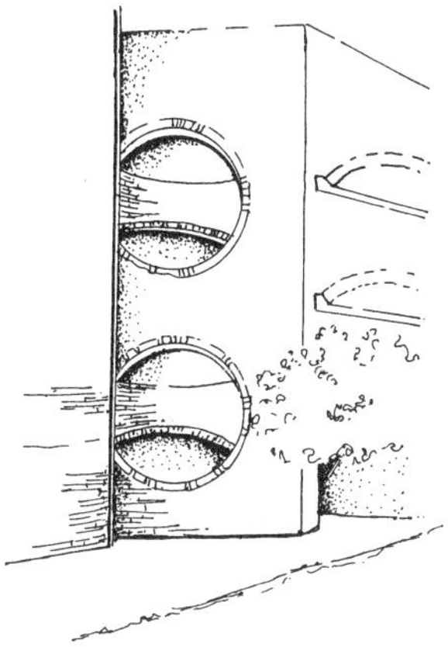

Indian Institute of Management, Ahmedabad

Chaitya window, Ajanta Caves

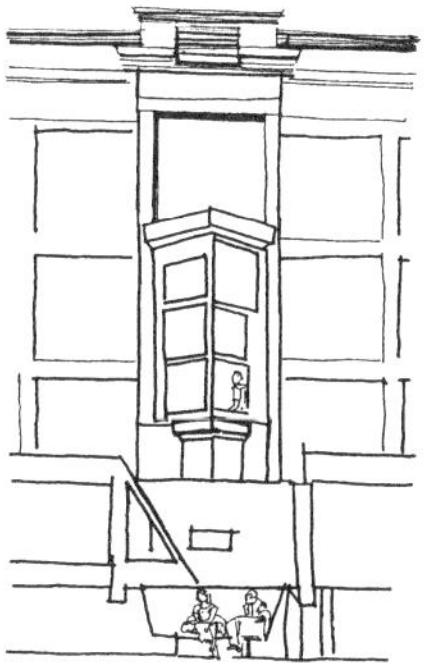

Clore Gallery, London

BOHRA HOUSE, SIDDHPUR

Dawoodi Bohras of Mustalian division of Islamic sect came into existence in around 1047 A.D. Their houses are grouped together so as to form their own domain, with gates at entrances. In Bohra dwellings, the sense of privacy is extremely high and, therefore, windows as connectors to the exterior are more sensitively modulated. Scale and arrangements were laid very much with the human concern of shapes and proportions. The openings were grafted on the Gothic style, an image of the lands visited by these traders. Shapes of openings vary from floor to floor, changing from square-headed at lower levels, to segmental, semi-circular and pointed at upper floors. This probably was the result of engineering skill establishing harmony between load and support since safety of an arch increases the closer its thrust approaches the vertical and decreases conversely. In addition pointed arch enables enhancement of the desired verticality more than the semi-circular ones.

Within the voids, openings were often further divided into tripartite shutters. The lower one from floor to parapet level often as louvered shutters, offer visual communication while in a seated posture from the floor and allowing for breeze at floor level.

It also maintains privacy by keeping the communication one way. The middle ones are in opaque surfaces which are opened and closed as per the climate and user's choice of communication with outdoors. The top one is a stained glass ventilator allowing for light and air even if rest of the window is shut for privacy reasons. They also prove to be an aesthetic component modulating facade as well as offering imageability and identity of its owners. The permutation and combination of these give users tremendous control to mitigate diverse conditions of climate and privacy.

Window as an image-maker

Window giving the facade an exquisite individual quality communicating the cultural influences on the community

Window as an aperture for light and air

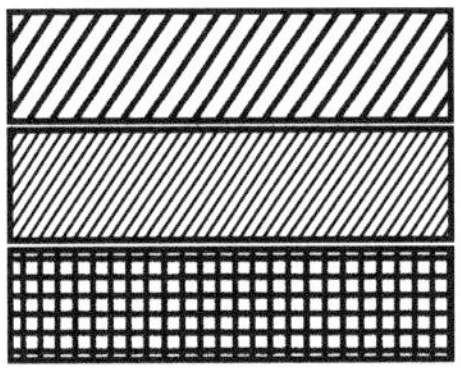

Allowing light and air, and functioning as an aesthetic element

Allowing for visual communication

Allowing air at floor level and keeping one way communication

Window creating different levels of interaction on various floors

With varied porosity and transparency establishing hierarchy in privacy levels

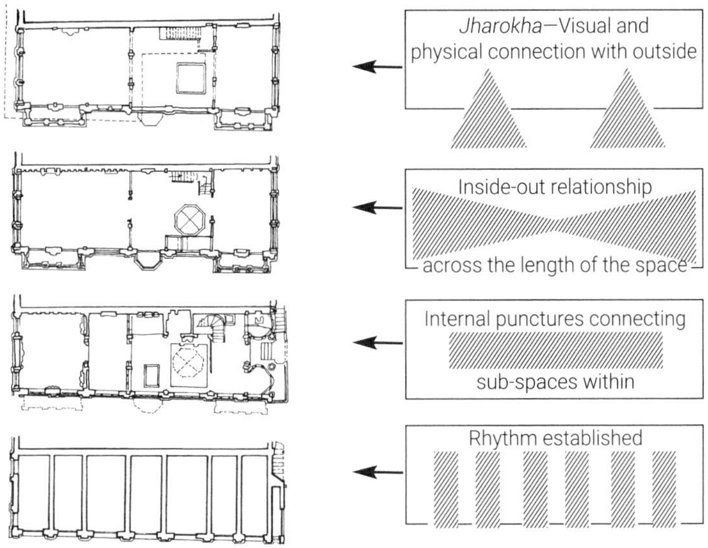

Window as a communication link

Jharokhas with ornate parapets as subspaces projecting out of the otherwise protected facade

Colourful decorations and stained glasswork as aesthetic expressions

The pragmatic divisions articulated to govern visual and physical interaction with the outer environment
Windows as facade modulators

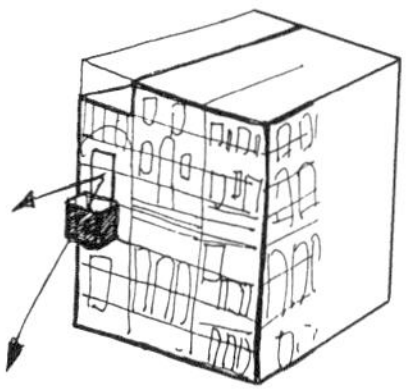

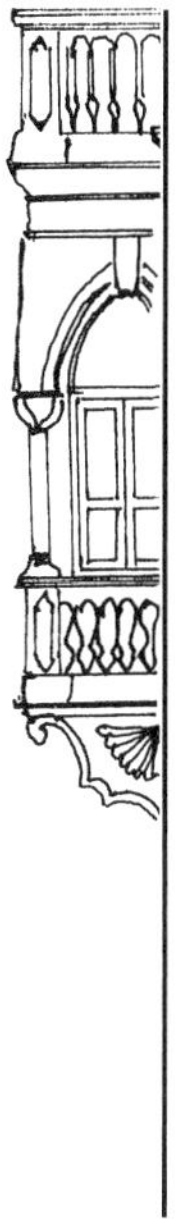

Window as a scaling element

Window as facade modulators

SHODHAN HOUSE, AHMEDABAD

Architect Le Corbusier in 1951 designed the Shodhan House. The building is conceived as a box with a parasol defining the roof and the internal massing forming voids below it. On the south-western facade there are the sun-breakers which open up the facade where required and on the north-eastern facade, there are small punctures which have colored glass and the jambs splay out internally to form a graphic composition. With the concrete mass, the openings form a relief. Transparency and porosity are highlighted while modulating the facade.

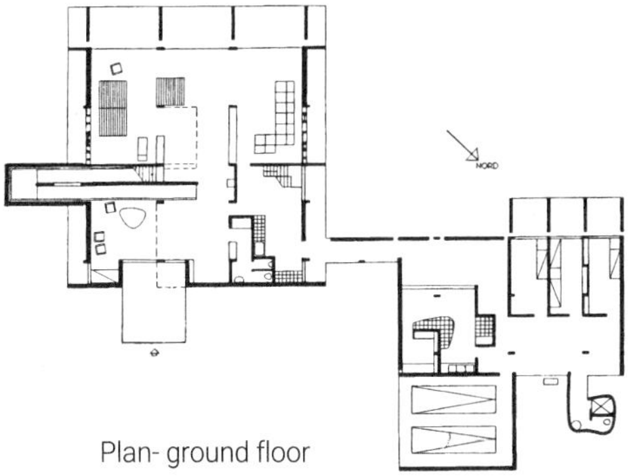

Plan- ground floor

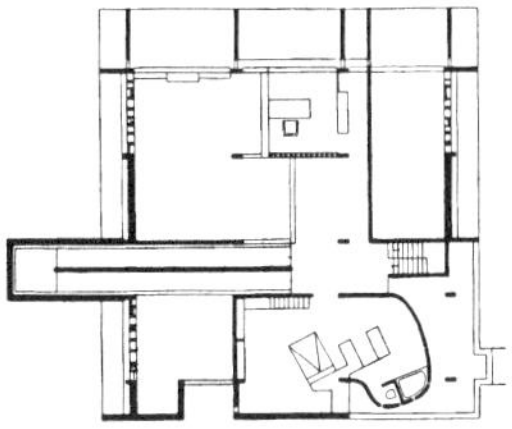

Plan- first floor

The modular

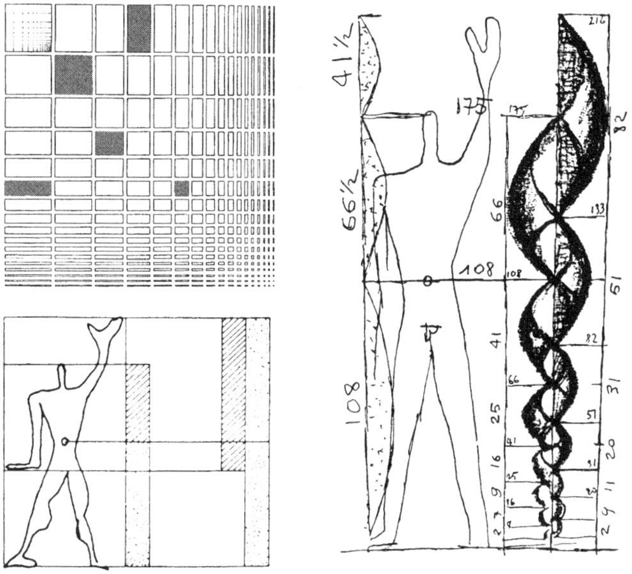

The openings following the modular system
determining the scale and proportion of void / mass

Window as a link between inside–out

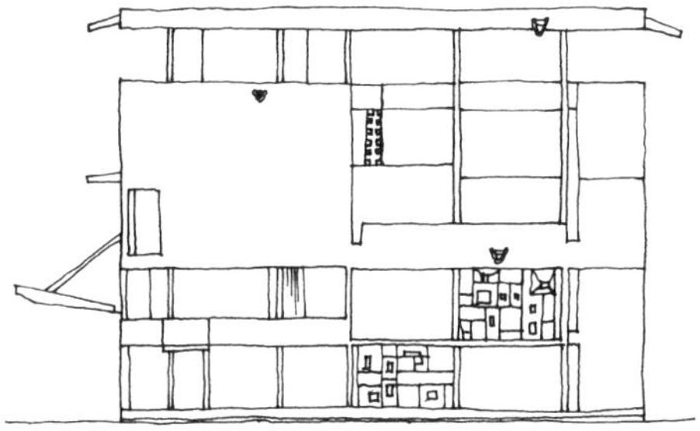

Elevation

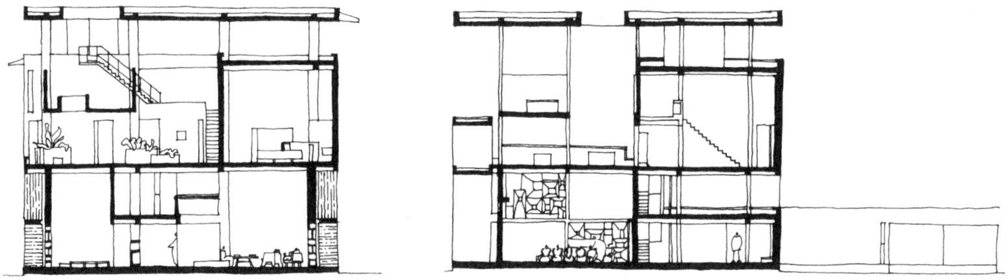

Sections

Window as an aperture for light and air..

Window, in itself being a sculptured element, forms different levels of luminosity within

Window as an image-maker...

Concrete facade punctured with openings bringing forth a sense of strong interaction between the inside and the outside

Window modulating the facade

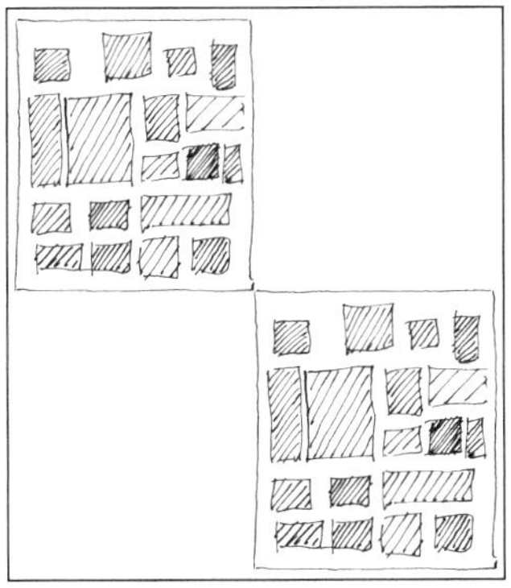

Windows with various composition of porosity and transparency

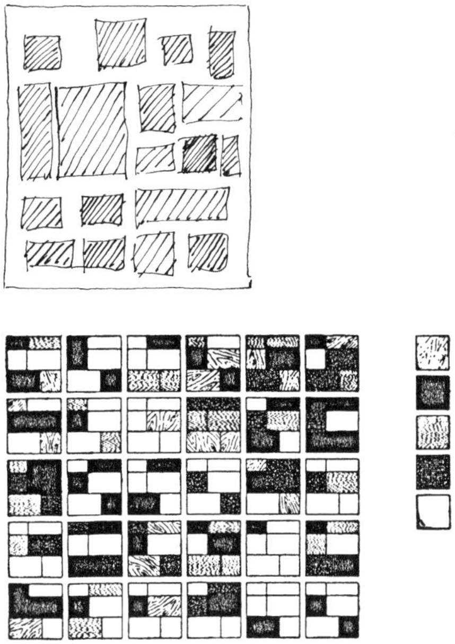

The compositions of the punctures establishing a language of scales, derived from Golden Section

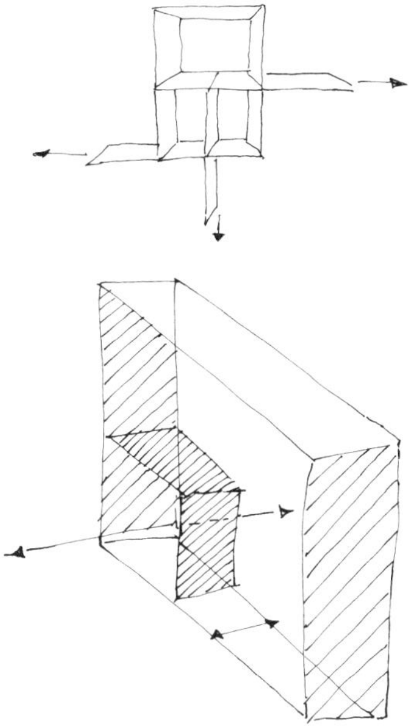

Window attributing transparency and porosity to the wall surfaces

INDIAN INSTITUTE OF MANAGEMENT, AHMEDABAD

Architect Louis I. Khan designed the Indian Institute of Management in 1962-67. The academic complex follows strong geometry and is surrounded on two sides by the student hostel and faculty housing, resulting in a variety of courts and squares. The complex is a textbook on the variety of arches and makes use of these, in the most poetic and appropriate manner, to generate voids for windows and other apertures for a variety of uses. The deep recesses and openings are varied devices to control the natural light, permit ventilation and modulation of the built mass. Ordinary construction materials such as brick and concrete, in this built space, have a very special meaning in the form of three-dimensional flying arches and buttresses. Solid insulating planes of exposed brick, shaded corridors as internal streets and austere plazas give the institutional campus its dignity and monumentality.

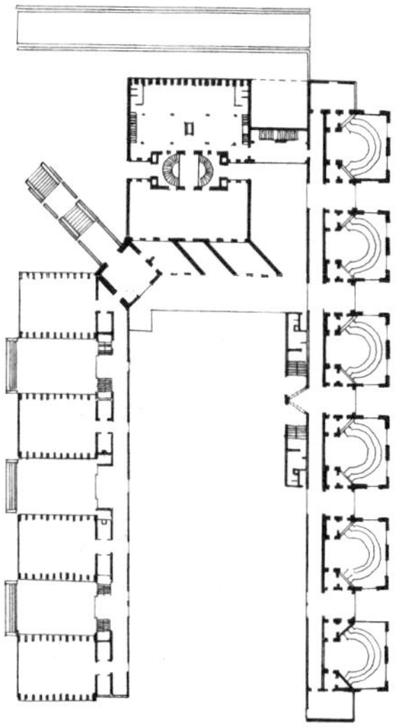

Plan

Window as an eye to the world..

Composition of openings rendering individuality to the entire complex

Openings frame the view towards the courtyard window for view

Window as an aperture for light, air and view

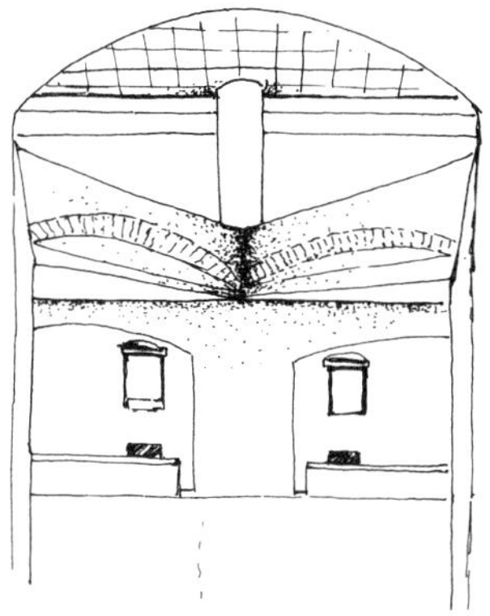

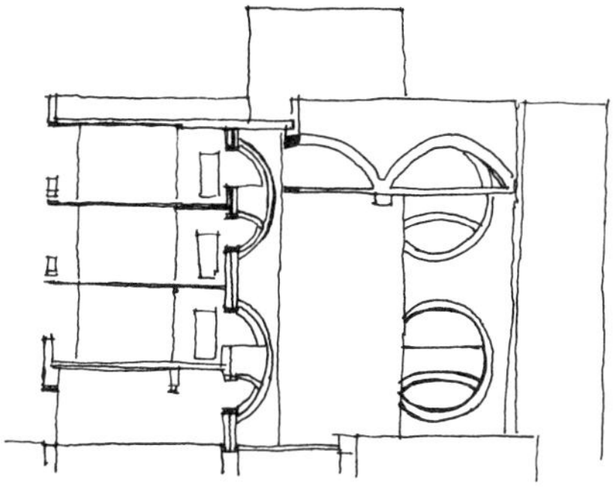

Window marking the visual references

Sectional elevation of the opening

Window as a modulator of facade

The circular window behaves as an image maker for the entire complex

Window as visual link with the outside

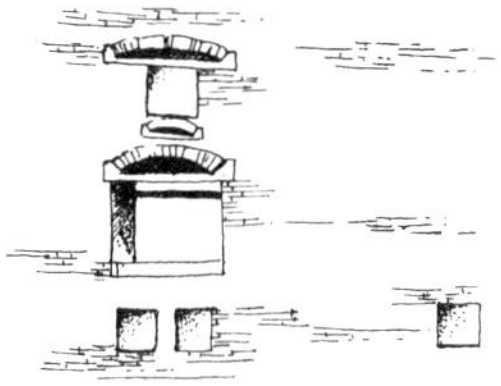

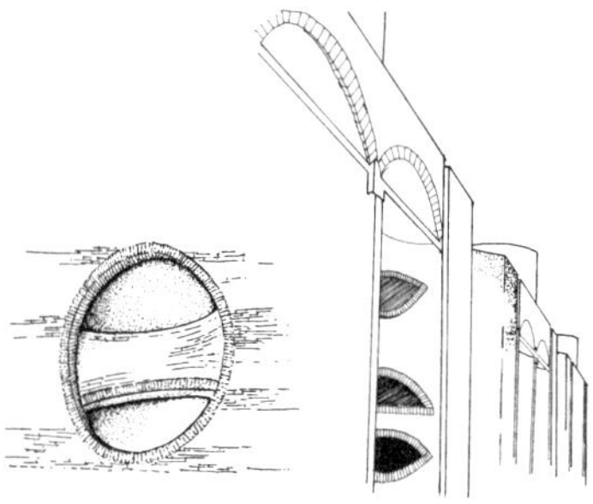

Window as an enhanced device conjuring varied sequence of visual communication

Window as a scaling element

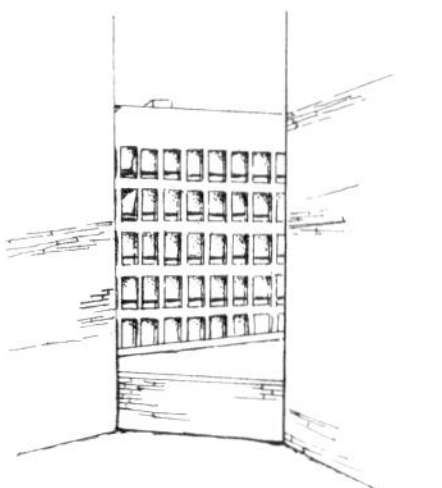

Facade with its rectangular module

Facade with its arch module at the lintel

NEWAR WINDOW, NEPAL

Newar architecture was founded by an ethnic group of Tibeto-Burmese in the valley of Kathmandu during the mid-18th century. In such built forms, the higher standards of craftsmanship and decoration are more apparent than the exuberance of form and detail. Openings, as windows, form an axial arrangement on the facade with modular design patterns and define the verticality or horizontality of the facade.

The ground floor windows are small openings of hardly any functional use other than to complete the facade and attribute an aesthetic element to it. The first floor windows internally have a higher sill; mainly functioning to permit light as the floor is used for storage of grains. The second-floor windows are operable and reach out as extensions leaning out. This is defined as projecting balconies.

The window frames itself, as a picture frame, upon the facade with intricate carving.

The structural technique used here comprises two frames, the primary frame-sill, lintel and jamb and the secondary frame-*toranas* (a decorative structure). A band of moulding communicates the character of the window with motifs as snakes, dragons etc., which are referred to as the guards of the entry node. It also defines an edge between the inner space and outer world.

Window as an image-maker

Street elevation resulting from the configuration of windows with formal language unique to Newar windows

Windows as a modulator of the facade

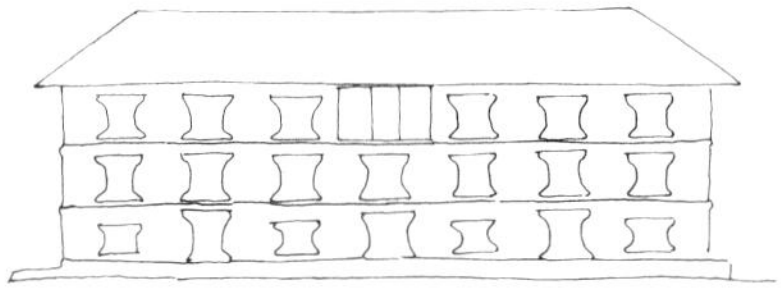

Windows as a scaling element

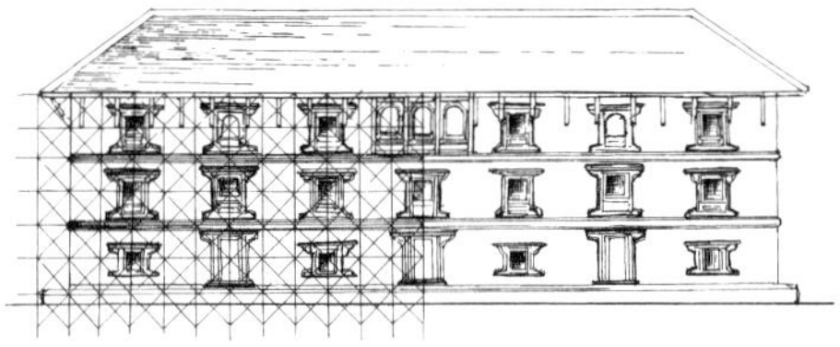

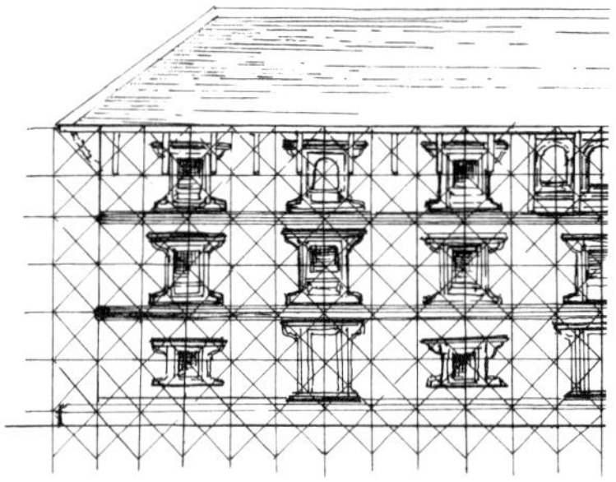

Proportions of the facade - Division into 24 vertical and 6 horizontal sections based on a module of 1.42 meter. Cornices at ceiling level as well as mouldings in the middle of the three storeys stress the horizontal arrangement.

Motifs in the window reveal the world into three realms, as the essence of life, the cycle of life and rebirth. Sill with demons signifying the underworld, the opening signifying the middle world, and the lintel signifying the upper world.

Window as a visual link

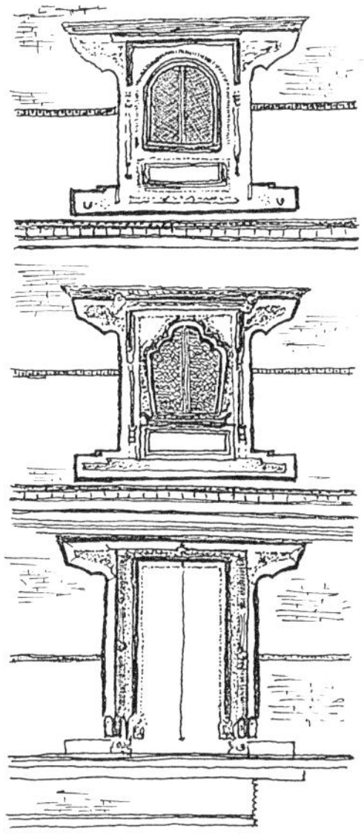

Intricate carvings with different frames dominating the facade

Module of a window

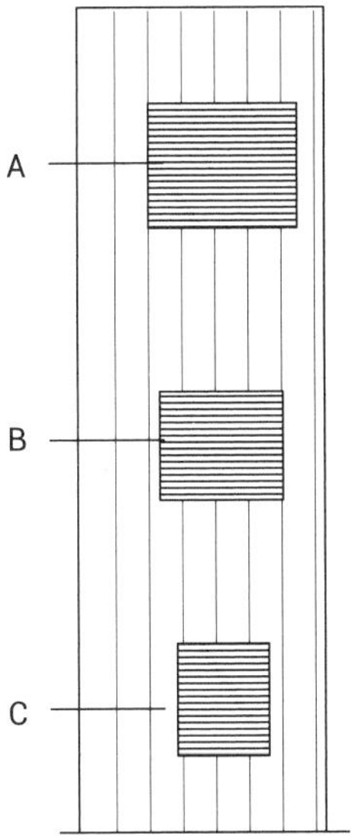

A Visual interaction
B Light and ventilation, also used for storage purpose
C Facade modulation

The structure

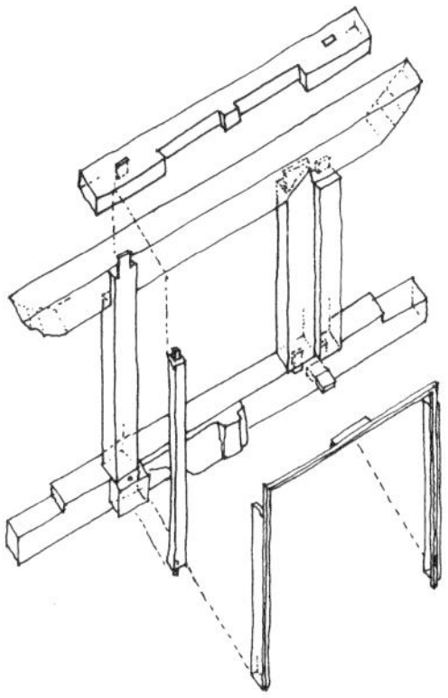

Window having squarish proportion, with more width than height

Structural form

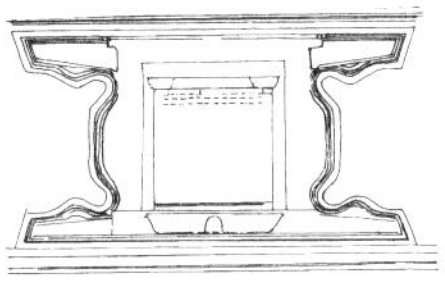

The opening of the window with its grillwork has its own frame with sill and lintel

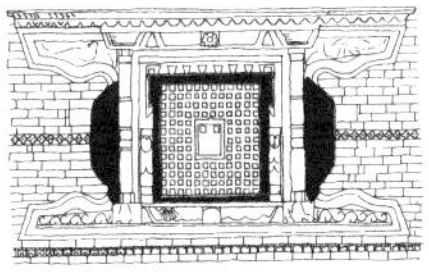

Two frames mediate between different structural parts

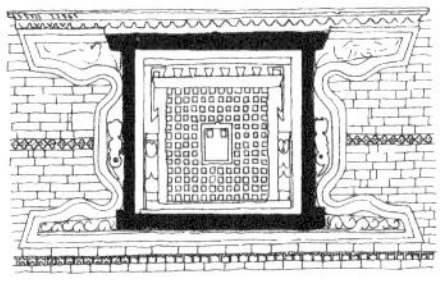

The bearing frame of lintel and jambs

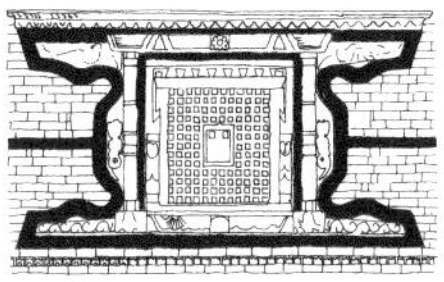

The secondary window frame with its sill and lintel

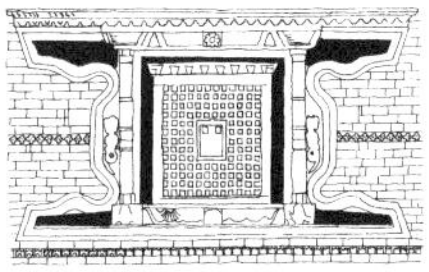

Interpretation of the window as heaven, the middle world and the underworld

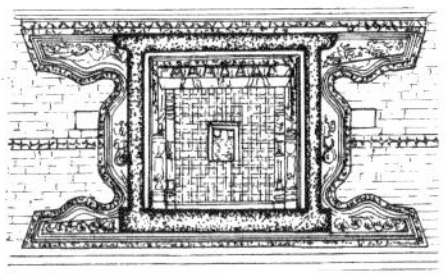

- As the window is a connection between the internal and the external realms, there needs to be a proper understanding of the requirement from inside to the situation outside. Thus, if 'view' is a criterion then the window needs to be placed and proportioned in such a position affording maximum exposure of the external spaces to the inside. If visual communication is a criterion then, it can be achieved by placing the window along the movement route or overlooking an active zone. If privacy is an added consideration to this then screen walls can be adopted to provide one way communication to the spaces within. Easy view and communication, necessitates a low sill especially since in some cultures most of the seating is on the floor. Low sill also expands the cone of vision to include more of out door areas in visual frame. Windows at upper floors of the habitable space can also afford to maximize views by lowering the sill, without affecting the privacy within.

- Windows generate 'place' by forming an alcove or a bay-projection with a seat. Often at ground level, if view is required in a busy street, privacy within the space is at risk. This conflict can be resolved by raising plinth and getting the sill above the eye level outside while retaining the windowsill level within.

- The window inlets for cool breeze should be placed lower, while the outlet (exhaust) windows must be placed higher, as hot air being lighter rises up. For further penetration of the natural light within the interior spaces and to diffuse the glare of harsh light, it is effective to introduce horizontal ledges or louvers in upper part of the windows, which provide maximum penetrability through internal reflection. For the effective flow of air it is preferred that windows are positioned in opposite planes.

- Windows having all three functions as of light, view and ventilation simultaneously, can be treated as a tripartite element.

- The requirement of conditional usage divides the fenestration into separate operable shutters for appropriate reasons respectively.

- Here the uppermost part, placed above the eye level as opaque louvers, is for passage of low intensity light and change of air. The middle part is largely for the view and breeze. Essentially, an operable shutter, it should have controls to open and close.

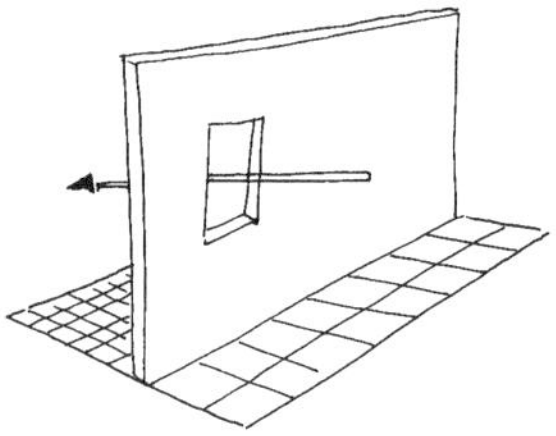

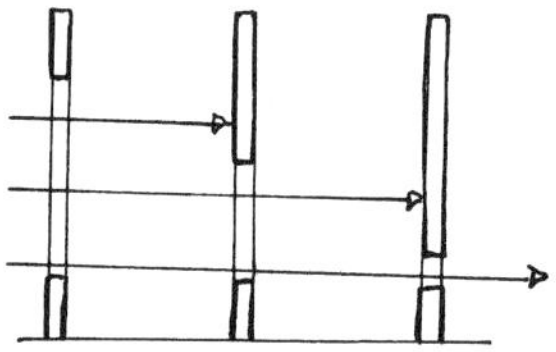

Window as a scaling element

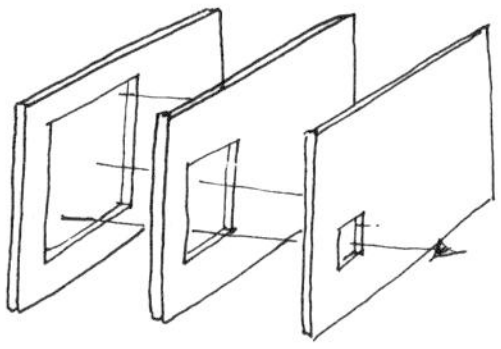

Window as a screen wall for one way communication

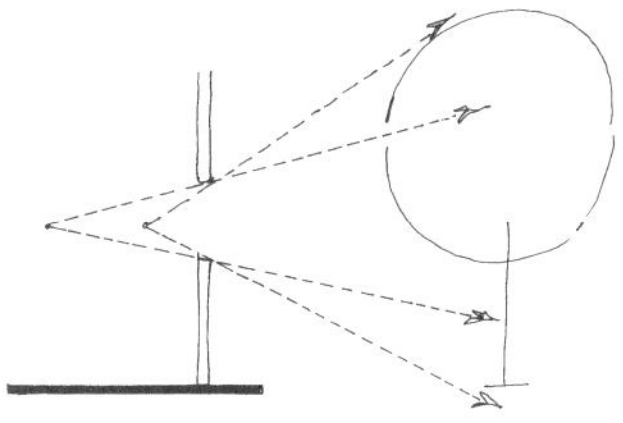

Window frames the view from inside

The low sill enhancing communication with the outside

Increase of the total plinth of the building

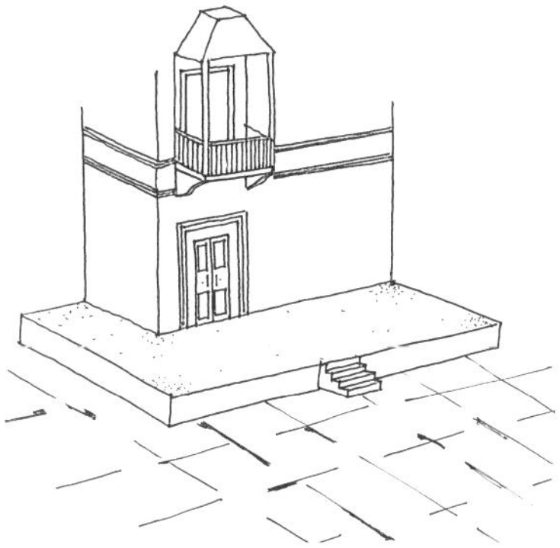

Jharokhas projecting as spaces from the facade enhance visual and physical link with the outside

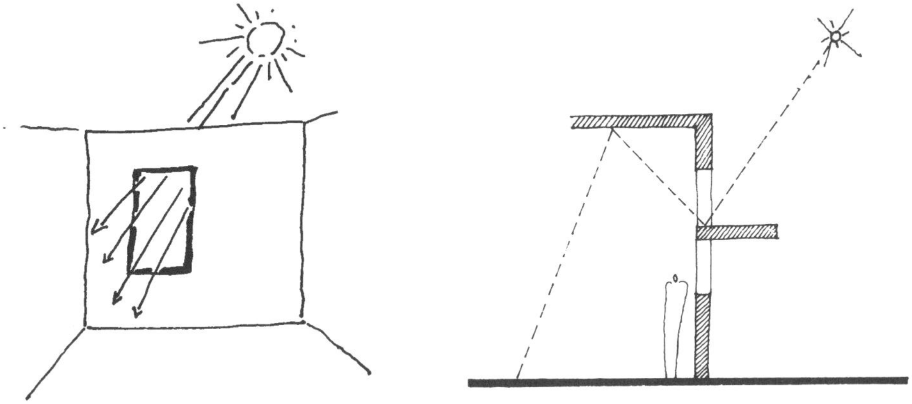

Light is diffused by decreasing the ceiling height or by introducing system of horizontal ledges/louvers in the upper portion of the structure

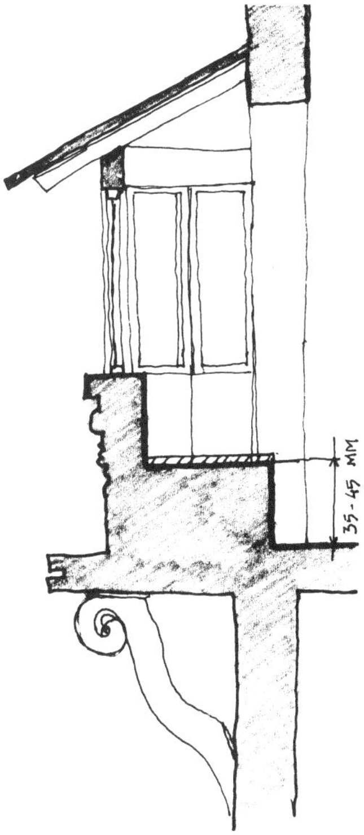

Alternative placement of window for easy flow of air

- The lowermost part is primarily assigned for breeze and extension of the internal space outwards, but it also helps visual proportioning of mass from outside and modulates facade. It also provides view and ventilation while in sitting/squatting/sleeping postures on the floor. Such a tripartite arrangement through varied permutation and combination helps mitigate the outdoors in different seasons and for different activities effectively.

- To prevent the glare around the opening, or conversely to enhance spread of light within, the splaying of jambs could be done at 50 to 60 degrees, and upto the depth of 30 cms.

- Spatially, it is advisable to have the amount of openings in a room such that they resolve the subtle conflict created by the opening as exposure (punctures) versus the sense of enclousre offered by the built mass.

- Being a link to external environment and the internal enclosure, windows form an integral part of the facade and can be used effectively to compose, scale and modulate the facade.The placement of windows near floor versus ceiling, can respectively lower or raise volume through implicity increased intensity of light in lower and upper zones accordingly. Similarly, their form can proportionate the building more horizontal or vertical. For example, ribbon like bands make facade read horizontal while vertical slits make it appear taller.

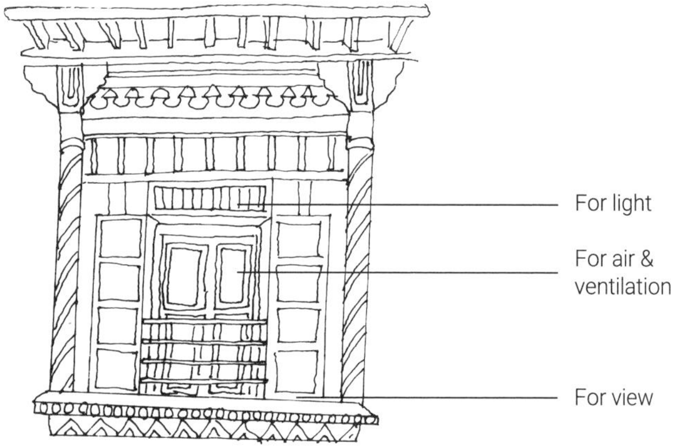

Window in three parts for light, air and view

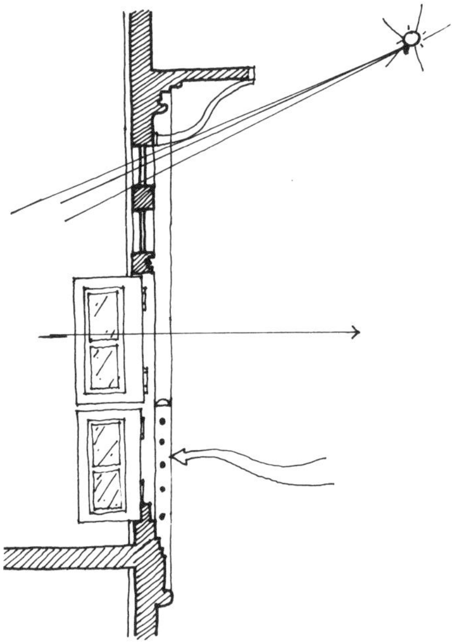

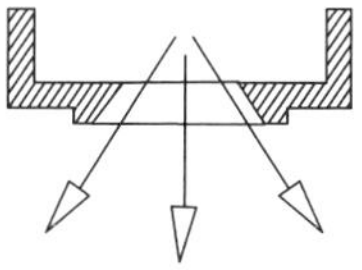

Plan

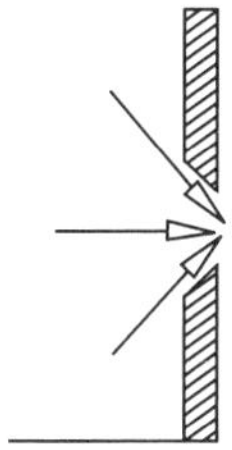

Section

Preventing glare within the internal space by splaying the jamb - splaying could be designed on all sides of the opening to bring still more light and prevent the harshness of glare

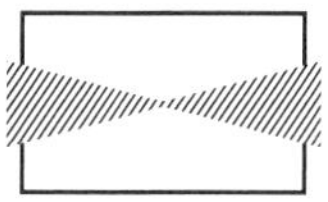

Opposite directions

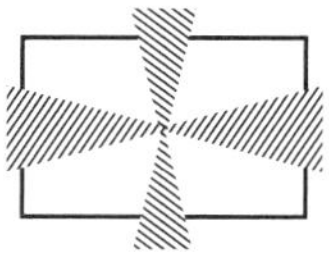

All four directions

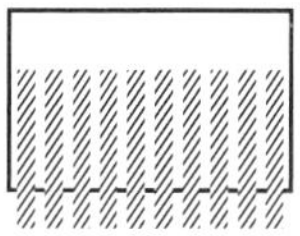

Multiple openings in one direction

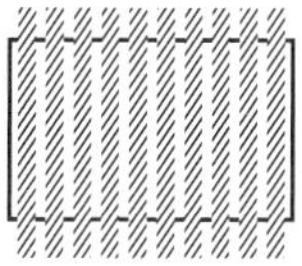

Multiple openings in opposite directions

Window positions changing in different instances creating varied transparancy inside the space

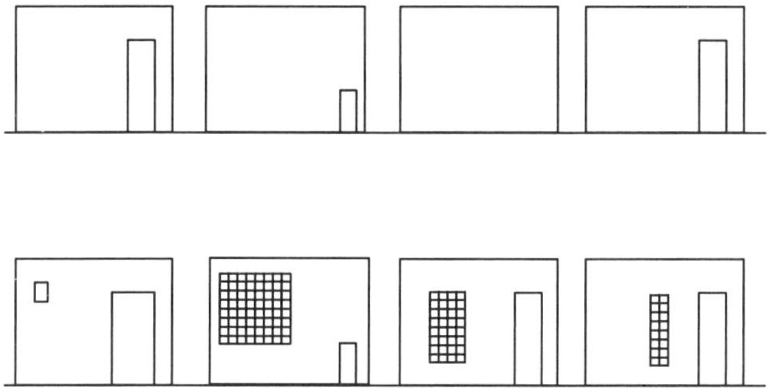

Different modulations of openings contribute to the visual appearance and disciplined relationship of the building facade

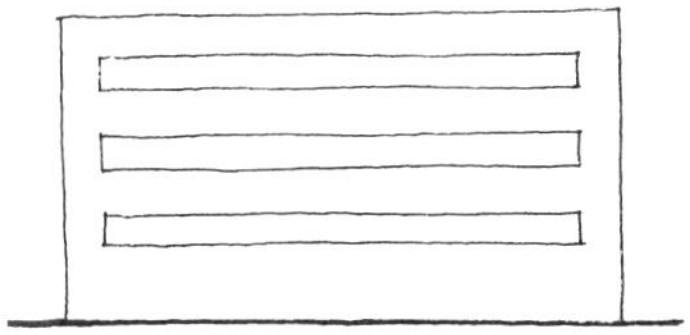

Ribbon windows modulating the facade profile horizontally

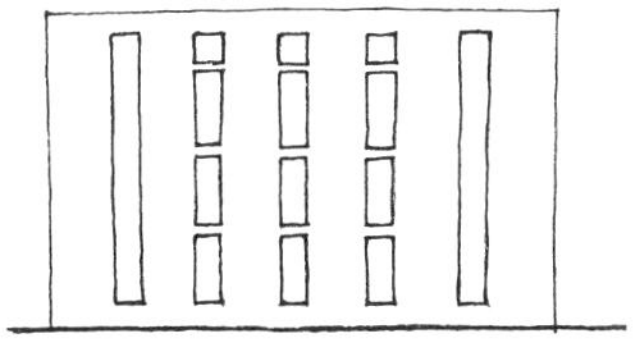

Stilts modulating the facade profile vertically

STAIR

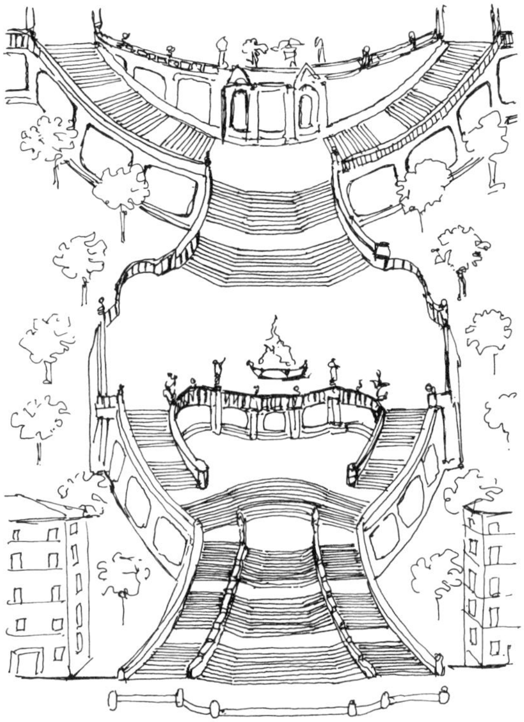

Piazza di Spagna, Rome

Stairs are vertical circulation elements, used to effect movement between two horizontal planes at different levels. Stairs make easy the transition of large vertical distances by breaking it up into a series of smaller vertical pieces of humanly negotiable size over a specific horizontal spread. This ties up the dimensions of the parts of the stair to standardized anthropocentric considerations. The origin of the term lies in Old English and Old Higher German word '*stigan*' meaning 'to rise'. It is akin to the Greek term '*steichein*' implying 'to walk'. The primitive form of the stair is the ladder. The term has reference to Old English '*winion*' meaning '*to lean*'. It is also defined as '*streger*'. Its Germanic origin is as 'stiz' meaning 'to climb'. In Low German it is defined as '*steiger*', '*steger masc*' meaning 'scaffolding', 'landing-stage'. The Sanskrit counter part of step is '*Padasath*', while that for the stair is 'Sopana Pad'. 'Pad' means foot/step and '*sap*' means to rest/support. Thus, the step refers to an element upon which the foot can rest and take support.

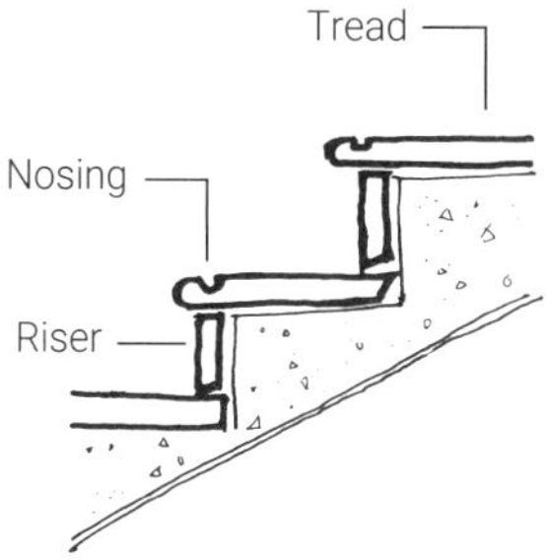

Detail

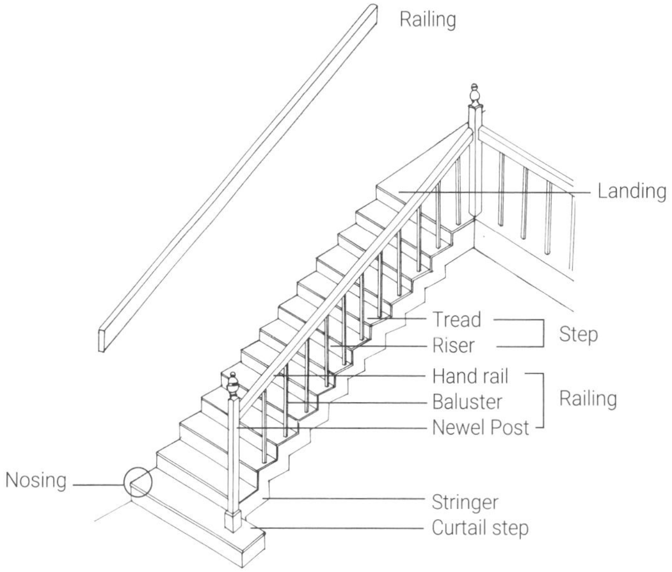

Typological Variations

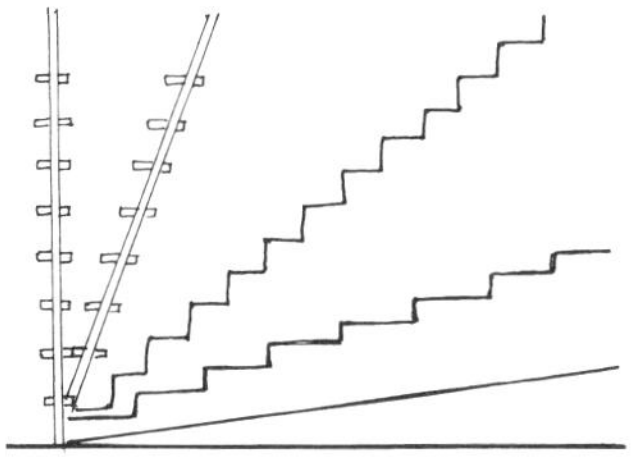

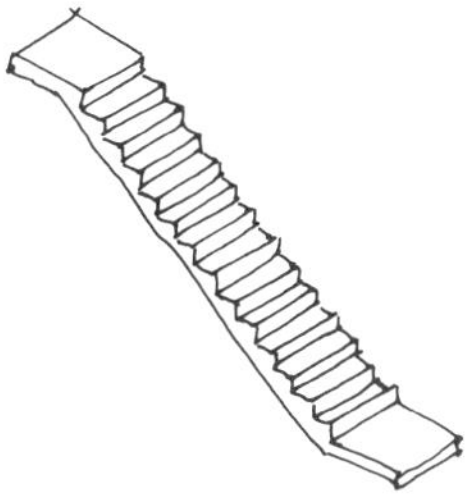
STRIAGHT FLIGHT

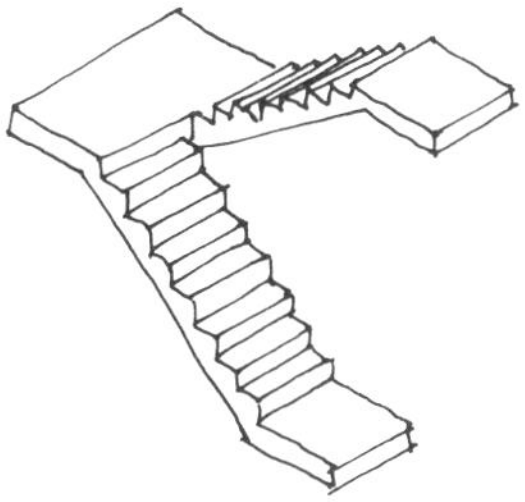
DOG LEG STAIR

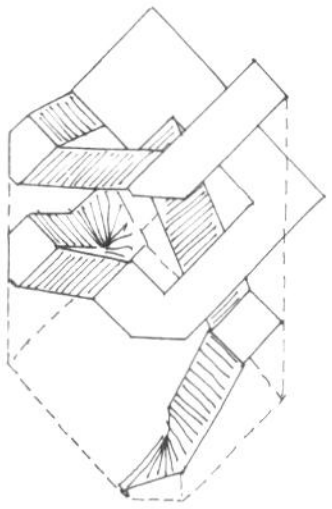
STAIRWELL

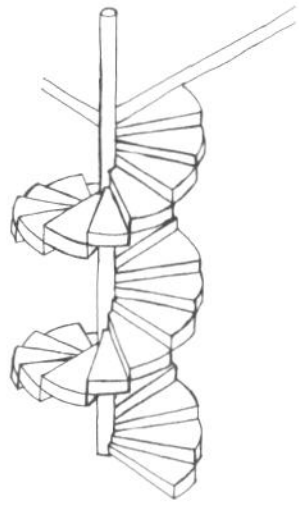
SPIRAL

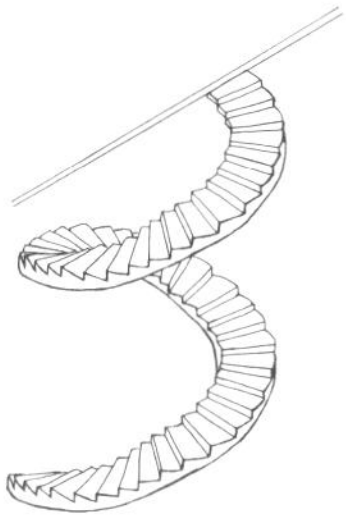
HELICAL

LADDER

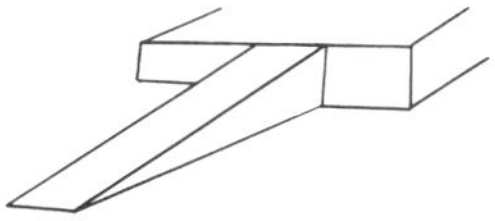
RAMP

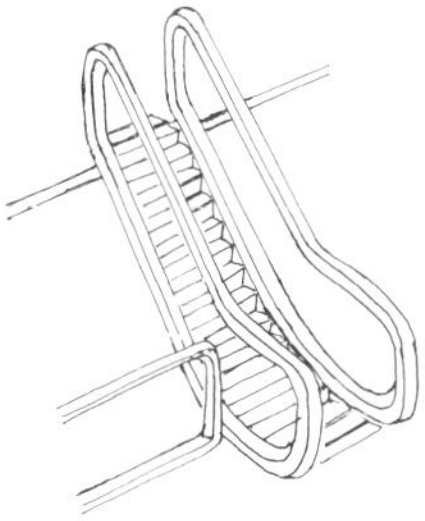
ESCALATOR

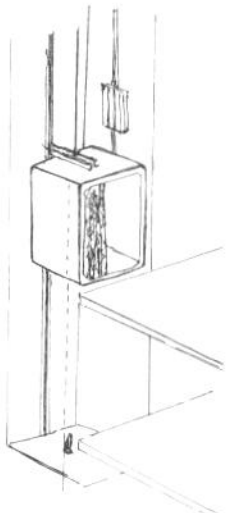
ELEVATOR

Primitive man elevated his dwellings for protection from the wild animals. He created houses upon the branches of the trees. In order to make his ascent and descent he used the vines for leverage. Over time, braided ropes were made with knots to serve as footholds. Sometimes notches were cut into the bark of the tree and these were then used for leg grips, and the rope, for hoisting with the hand.

The wooden ladder was devised with stout twigs tied together. Functional needs accomplished, the search began for the ease of operation. The same principle was used in the larger edifices, which had by then gained currency, as attractive massing of small levels, which one could walk up. Rudimentary building technology in the early days required the steps of the stairs to be supported from the ground as a built-up mass, making the stairs seem like the floor modulating vertically. Stairs also define semi-built spaces in amphitheatres and stadia, wherein alterations in the vertical modules of risers adapt themselves for seating.The Greeks and Romans have extensively used this aspect of stairs in their monumental and public architecture, where external stairs and the plinth embellish the lower part of the facade just as the entablature decorates the upper.

Stairs built between parallel walls liberated the steps from apparent dependence upon the floor. The stairs were confined to the walls, which not only supported the steps but also demarcated a room dedicated to the act of going up or down within the building envelope. The genesis of this stairwell saw its usage in other ways such as a light well and ventilation shaft and as atriums. With densification and urbanization, buildings of more than one storey became common and hence, staircases became an integral part of the schema. Internal staircases gained importance for protection from the weather. Initially, internal staircases were considered only as service elements. Enclosed in masonry with poor light quality, these staircases broke the 'roofline' in towers often to gain access to the terrace. With changes in building technology during the Gothic period, staircases became lighter and better lit. They also began to assume an identity of their own, though still integrated within the wall. They were treated with embellishment and began to compete for attention, though more as a structural resolution than due to element of space organization.

Stairs as built-up mass, with religious associations of journey towards the heavens

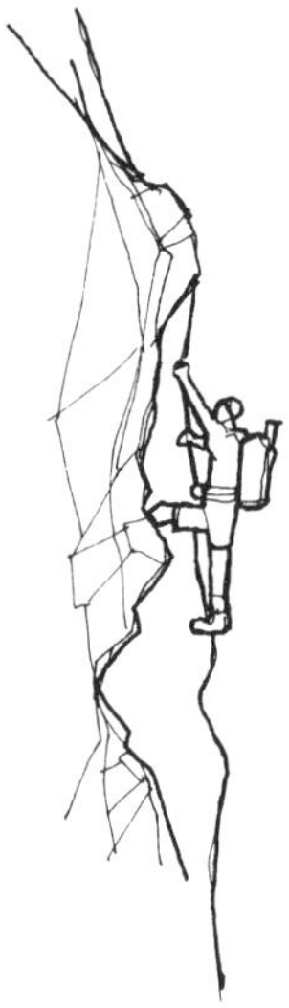

The Great Mosque, Iraq

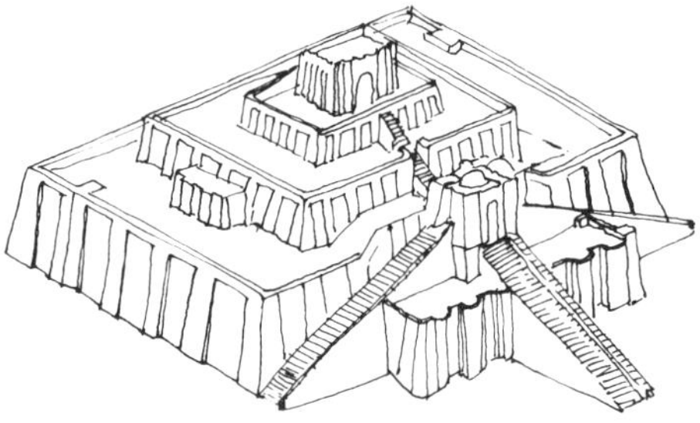

Ziggurat of Ur, Iraq

Temple of Tlahuizcalpantecuhtli, Peru

Semi-built spaces as amphitheatres

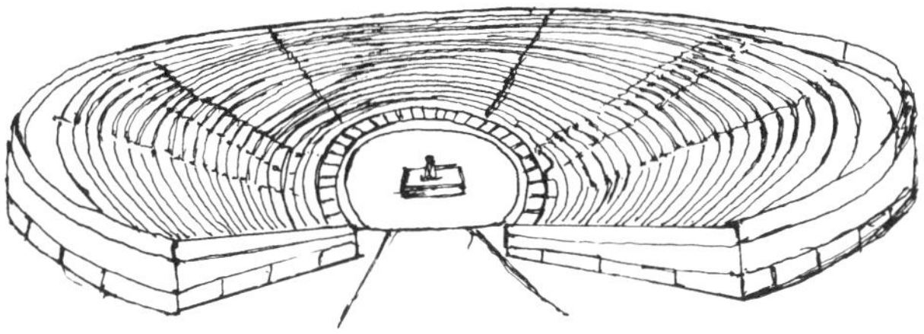

Roman Theatre, Segesta

Staircase with restricted light and enclosed in masonry

Early Medieval and Romanesque period Tower of London, London

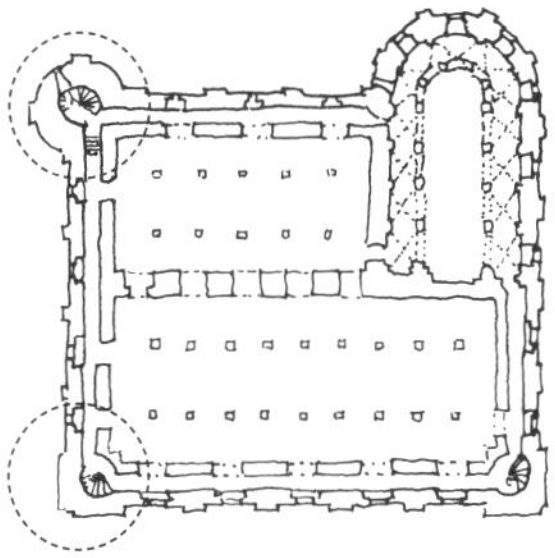

Plan

Steps liberating as staircase and functioning as a service element connecting different floor levels

Greek Temple, Palace of Persepolis

Taos Pueblo, New Mexico

Stairs as an architectural expression, in form of a raised platform

Temple of Hera, Paestum, Italy, Greek Temple

St. George's Hall, Liverpool, Roman Era

The Renaissance period saw the glorification of the stair. The internal stair, exquisitely embellished, became the primary feature of the layout, often dominating the double height arrival halls.

Stairs then began being resolved as a sculptural element, its degree of embellishment denoting the social status of the owners.

The balustrade being more perceptible upon the stair became the most decorated element, and thus manifested a multitude of treatments. Different materials were used for their construction, from seasoned timber to fine marble, and techniques specific to them were refined and exacted. With the Industrial Revolution, iron and steel were identified as new and promising materials. Wrought and cast iron were used in decorative and intricate ways, continuing and developing the treatment of the Baroque and Rococo periods during the Arts and Crafts as well as Art Nouveau Movements.

The Modern Movement with its rejection of applied decoration, ornamentation and glorification of materials and technology, emphasized sleekness of appearance and lightness in construction. Steel construction, structurally and visually lighter, could be assembled with bolts freeing the structural obligations of position and support system. This helped giving flexibility with respect to internal location.

With the introduction of reinforced concrete and the framed structure, the staircase integrated structurally with the frame. Their inherent structural advantages saw a burgeoning of these kinds of stairwells. Speed and comfort of vertical movement resulted in the development of elevators and escalators, basically as functional substitutes to stairs. The staircase form was mechanized whereby the horizontal plane itself traversed the vertical interstice. They often found places in atria and external facades as elements of attraction. Elevators with their continuous vertical shaft influence space planning, creating circulation cores. With travelators, as surfaces capable of moving in all the dimensions, mechanized movement is possible both in vertical as well as horizontal axis without having to transit from one to the other.

Staircase getting identified with formal expressions and decorations..............................

Internal view, Louis XII, Royal Chateau de Blois

Notre Dame, Paris, Gothic Period

Louis XII, Royal Chateau de Blois, Gothic Period

Stairs getting sculptural quality with ornamentation and embellishments of various components

Newel Post, Ornamented Stairs

Pulpit in a Cathedral, Renaissance Period

Queen's House, Greenwich

Hotel Tassel, Brussels

Use of wrought Iron, Post Renaissance, Art Nouveau

Industrialization brought flexibility in form and use of stairs

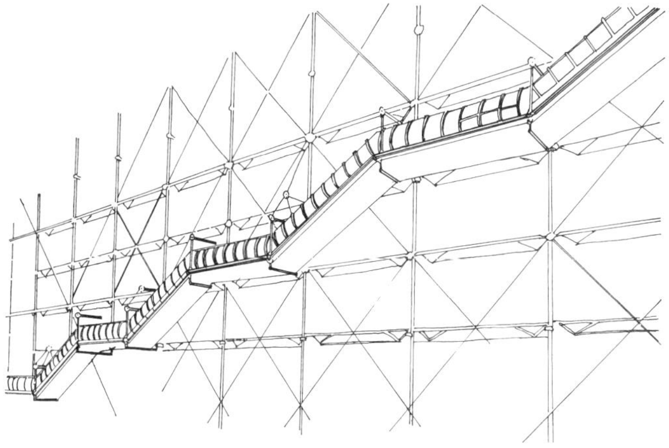

Centre Pompidou, Paris

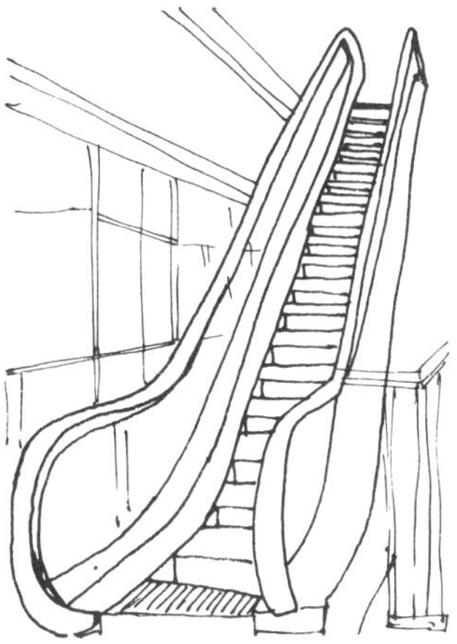

An Escalator

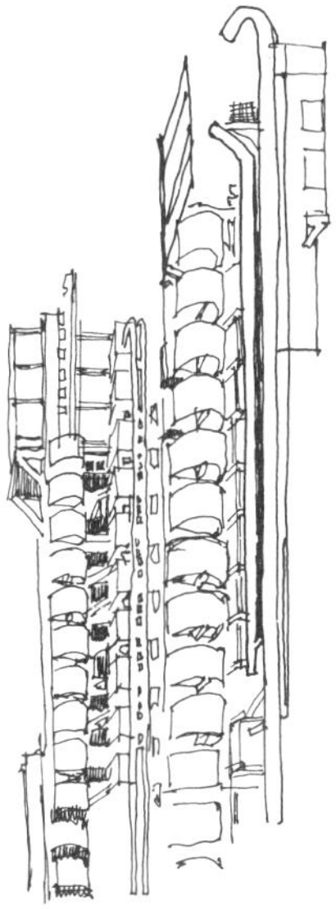

Lloyds Bank, London

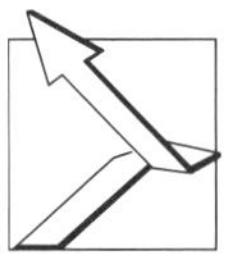

MOVEMENT IN VOLUME

Movement in the horizontal plane requires the least physiological effort as opposed to movement in the vertical plane, which requires the maximum effort. But vertical displacement is mandatory in certain natural conditions like changes in terrain or man-made situations of different floor levels in the built environment. The stair becomes a negotiation of the vertical displacement as its oblique component ensures the break up of the height over a particular horizontal distance. It is thus manageable in smaller units dictated by the standardized human anthropometric studies, specifically the size of the foot, comfortable angle of inclination, size of a step etc. This makes horizontal movement a part of the ascent. There are two major components in the stair, the tread (horizontal) and the riser (vertical).

Displacement in volume: Simultaeous movement in X and Y axis

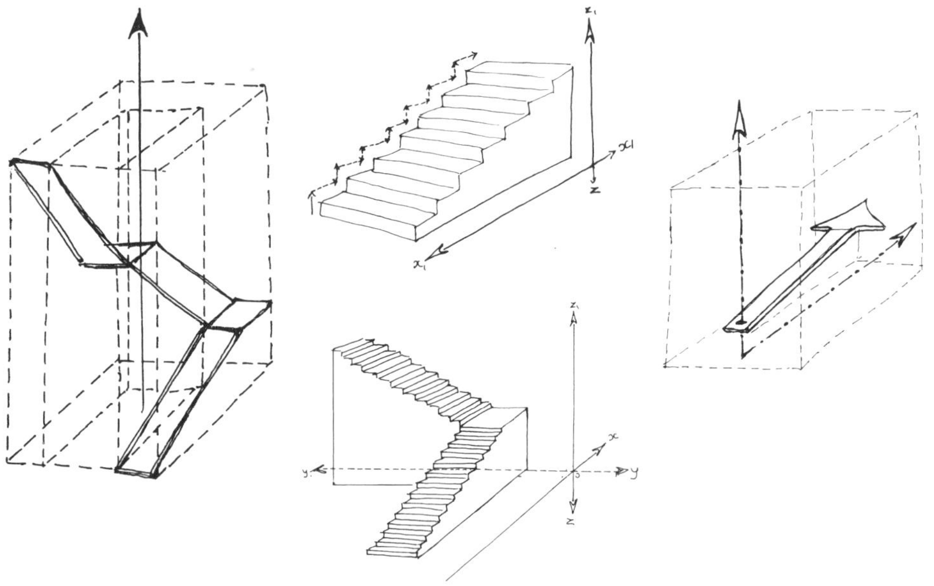

The ideal proportion between the two is 2R+G=60 cm (R=rise & G=going). Thus, the stair attempts to camouflage the vertical movement through horizontal displacement, integrating the climb into the traverse, thereby allowing for movement in both Z and the X or Y dimensions.

The simultaneous displacement in horizontal as well as vertical axis is a typical characteristic of a stair. The implied significance of this attribute is the changing points of view and references to orientation.

Movement in three-dimensions and enclosing the volume below...

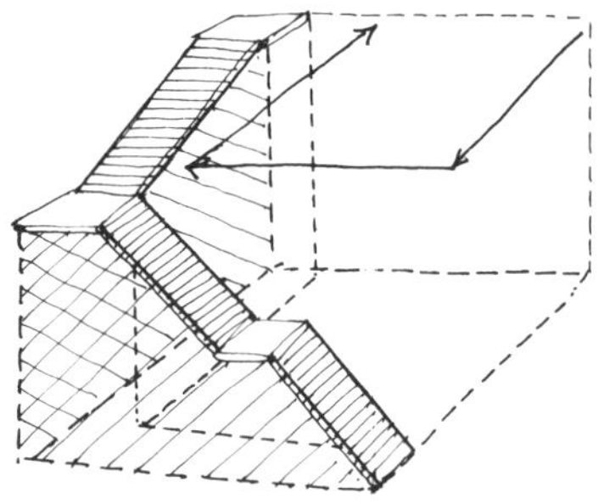

Various pause points in the ascent of the staircase

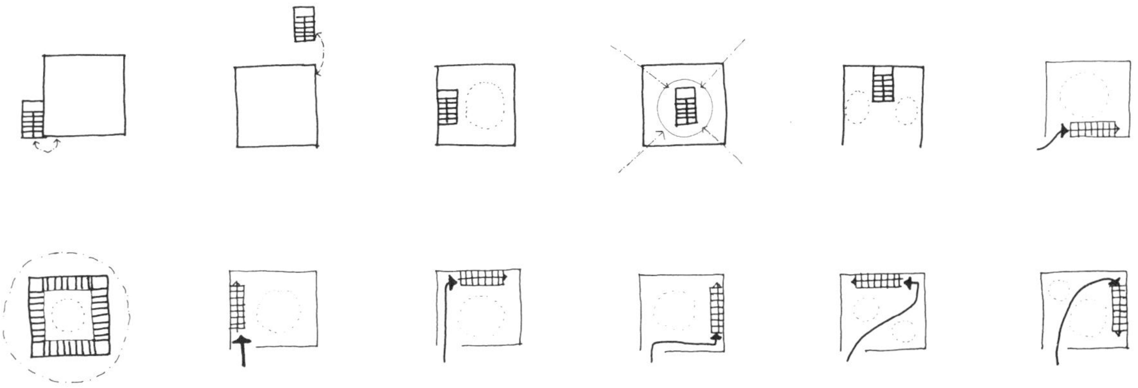

Movement in space and orientation

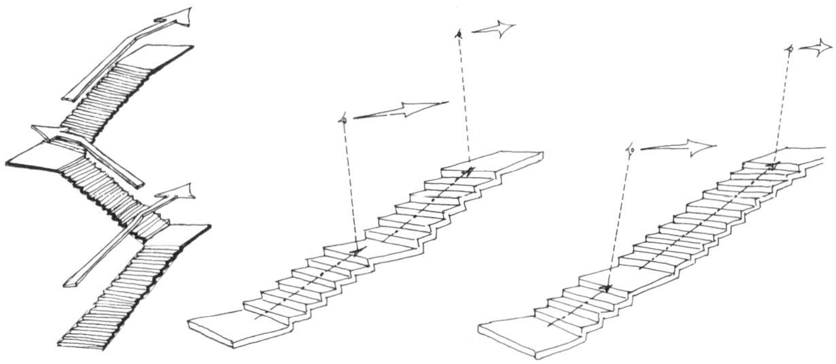

Stairs as a physical and visual connetor

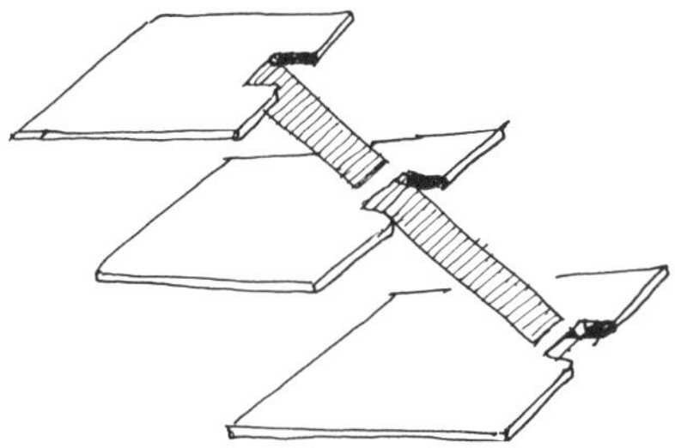

Disciplined flexibility

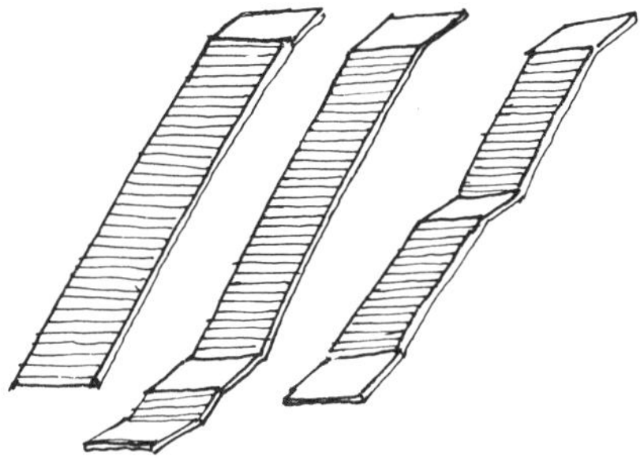

STEP AS PEDESTAL

Step as an element to negotiate the plinth becomes the most obvious feature of the building. This is often pronounced in the facade as an invitation to access the buildings. A series of steps negotiates the plinth, a pedestal upon which the building rests, to reach up to the building from the base.

Steps in front or around the building elevates the sense of entry with the formal and monumental language

Spanish Steps, Rome

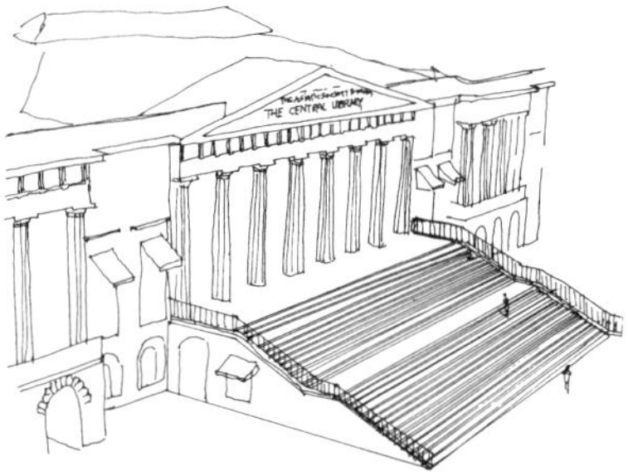

Asiatic Library, Mumbai

Jami Masjid, Delhi

Steps as an element negotiating plinth translates a casual entry into a ceremonial event

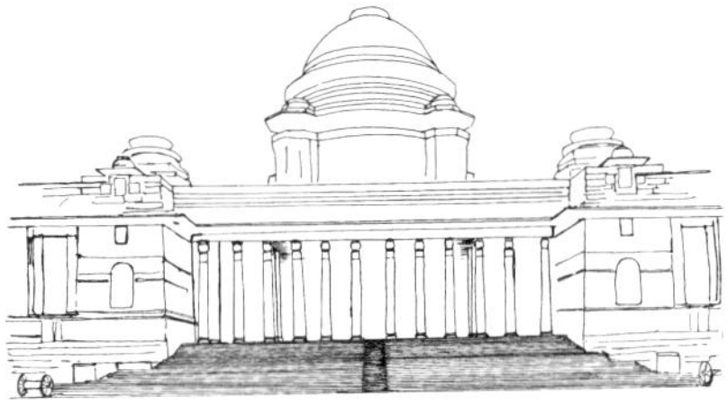

Rashtrapati Bhavan, New Delhi

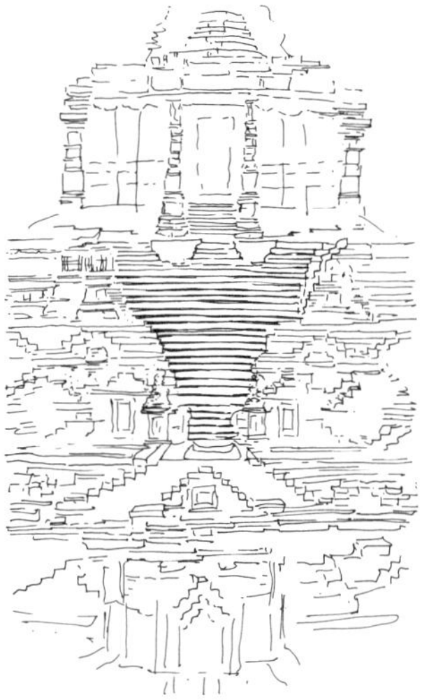

Rudabai stepwell, Adalaj

Kandariya Mahadev temple, Khajuraho

STEP AS SEAT

Stairs consist of comfortable negotiable small platforms for ascent. These platforms if modulated accordingly also can double up as seating since they recreate the ambience of a theatre at a smaller scale. Depending on the arrangement of the stair, groups or individuals can sit, together or in isolation, facing each other or towards a focus. This in-built flexibility combined with the nodal position of stairs for the movement make the stair multipurpose and invariably used for seating apart from just movement. Wider stairs allow both of these functions simultaneously. Clean, hard paved surfaces of treads provide impromptu seating space.

Steps with their multidimensionality act more like an element catering to varied functions

Steps as seat

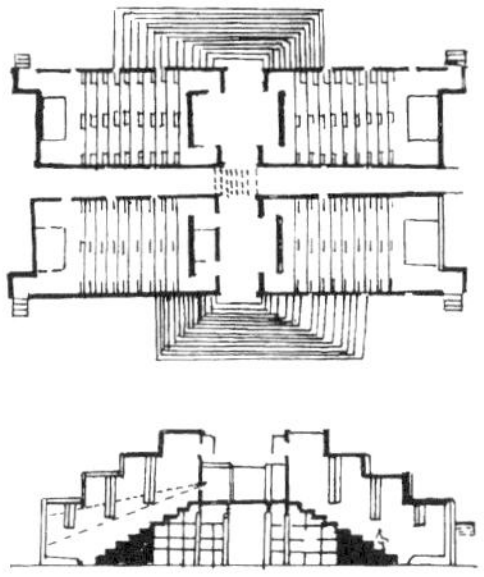

Plan

Section

University of Jodhpur, Rajasthan

Nehru Memorial Pavilion, New Delhi

NIFT, New Delhi

Steps acquire a module conjuring the possibility of a convinient seating...

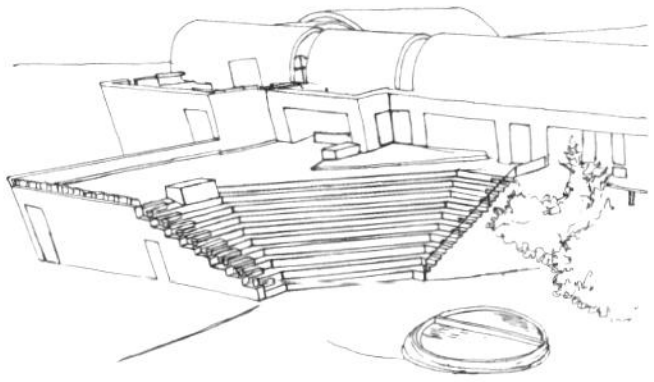

Mahatma Gandhi Labour Institute, Ahmedabad

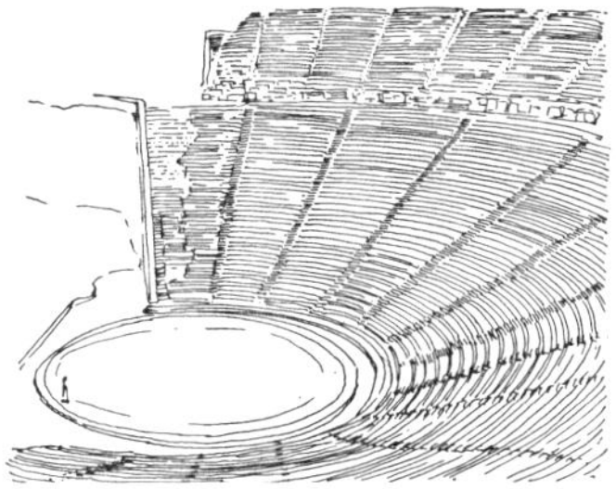

Theatre Aspendos, Turkey

Section of an opera theatre

Steps at the ghats, Banaras

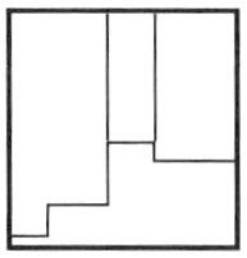

STEP AS THRESHOLD

As buildings are raised on the plinth, steps form the natural link to negotiate these level differences. This provides the first most important transition from outdoors to within, from unbuilt to built, from horizontal to vertical. Thus, steps become a threshold for both linking as well as dissociating two realms.

Flight of steps with its formal and notional articulations create a link and simultaneously a distinction, which could be defined as built and the unbuilt

Street- Pol house, Ahmedabad

Steps and Plinth, Jaisalmer

Steps creating subtle boundry between two realms of inside-out

Transition-from profane to sacred

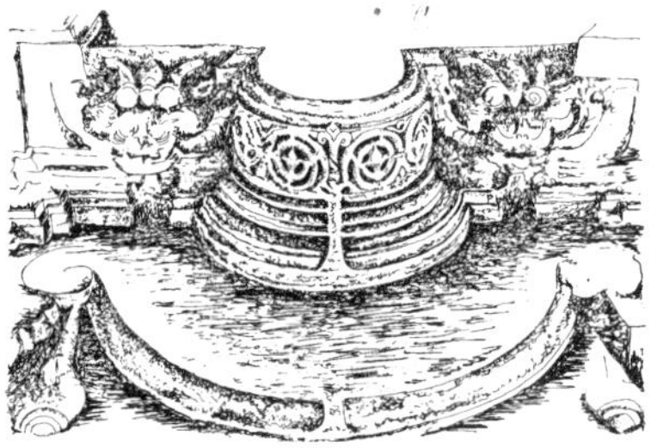

Threshold within the temple

Stairs with the physical variations create a symbolic and literal definition

Indian Institute of Management, Ahmedabad

Laurentian Library, Florence

The Erechtheion, Athens

Sun Temple, Konark

STAIRS AS MOVEMENT GUIDE

Stairs is a physical link between two levels. As a result it assumes nodality as the confluence of horizontal and vertical movements. Its placement is always determined with respect to the movement path. This junctional position upon the movement path gives a special reference value to the stair. The location of the stair by itself becomes visual as well as physical pause point to attract movement towards it and the space within which it is located. The stair form and profile can further attract movement over it towards next destination or also adjacent to it by becoming a backdrop.

Stairs becoming the node for horizontal and vertical movement

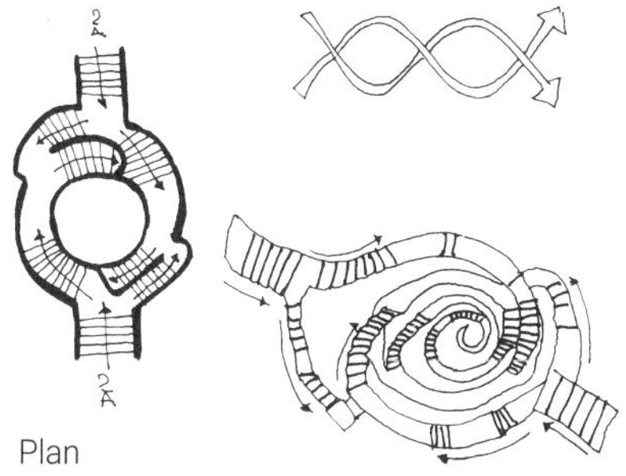

Plan

Halisa Kuva, Halisa, Gandhinagar

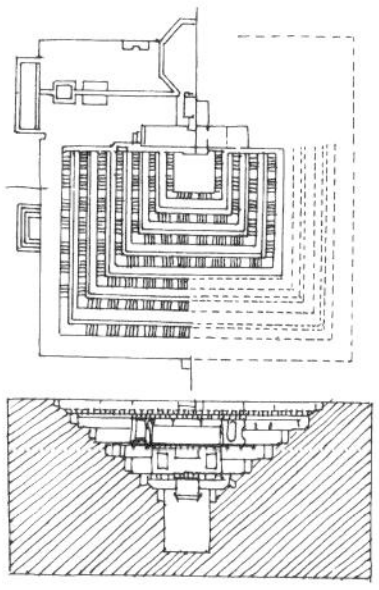

Amber stepwell

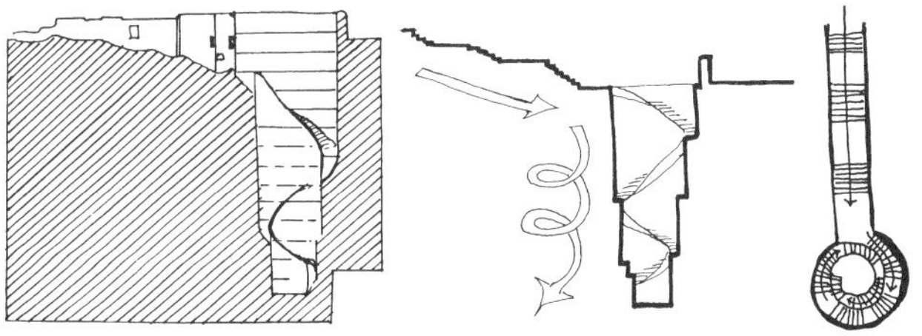

Bhamariyo Kuvo, Bhatpur, Rajkot

Plan

Baoli (Stepwell), Madhya Pradesh

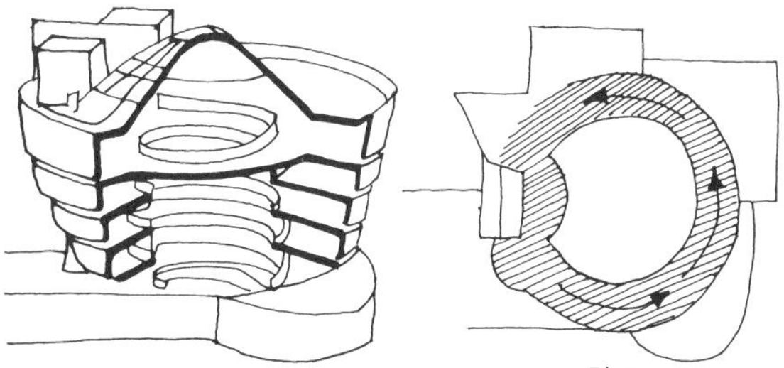

Plan

Guggenheim Museum, New York

Indian Institute of Management, Ahmedabad

STAIRS AS PHYSICAL LINK

Stairs has evolved, but essentially still retains its primitive function of translocation from one horizontal plane to another at a different level. It physically connects two different planes and serves as the means to link the, otherwise disparate, levels either within the same building or between two building blocks. In this process of connecting, the location and arrangement of the stair also disciplines and directs movement. In multi-storeyed buildings, the stair acts as the primary circulation link between the various floors. Stairs designed with certain features like a stairwell, for instance, exploits the potentials of this connectivity in terms of visual communication between floors, ventilation, light percolation etc., becoming an atrium unifying the floors, which would otherwise be dissociated from each other. In modern buildings, stairwells double up as a service shaft reaching all floors or an elevator duct too, being able to optimize and centralize resources.

Stairs is 'the' element connecting two levels and establishing visual communication respectively

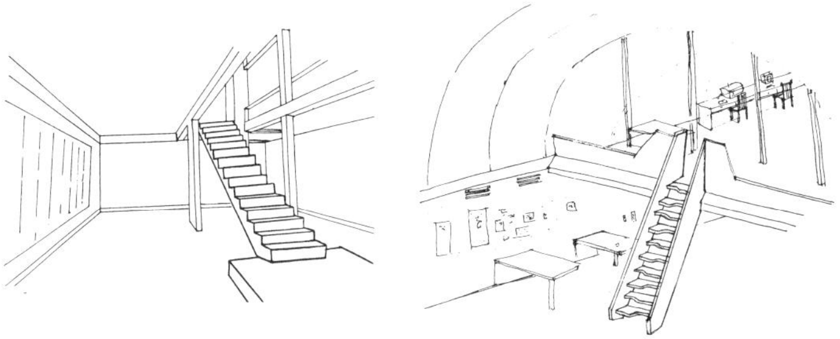

Sangath, Ahmedabad

House in Jaisalmer, Rajasthan

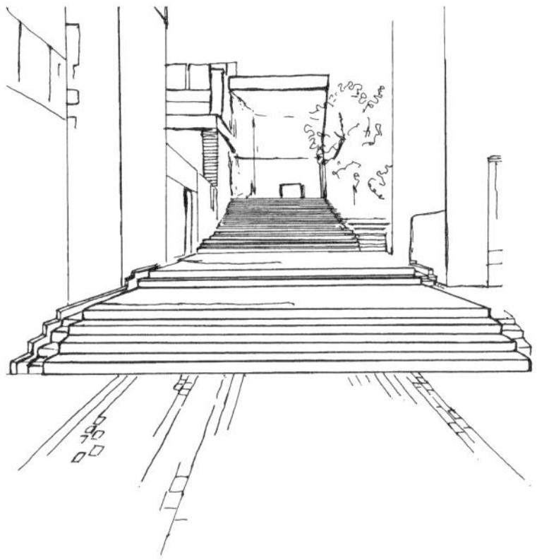

School of Architecture, CEPT University, Ahmedabad

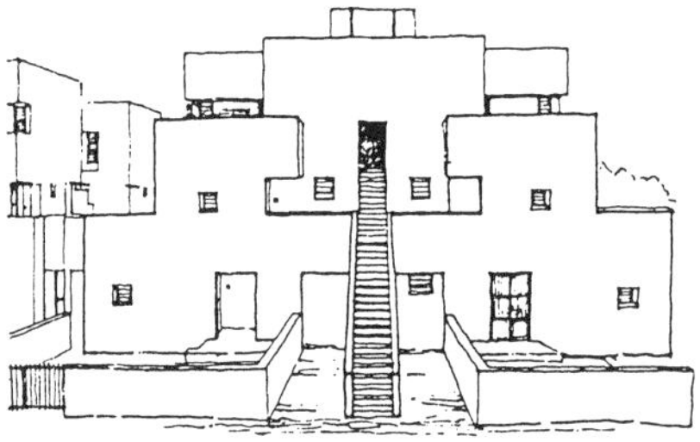

LIC housing, Ahmedabad

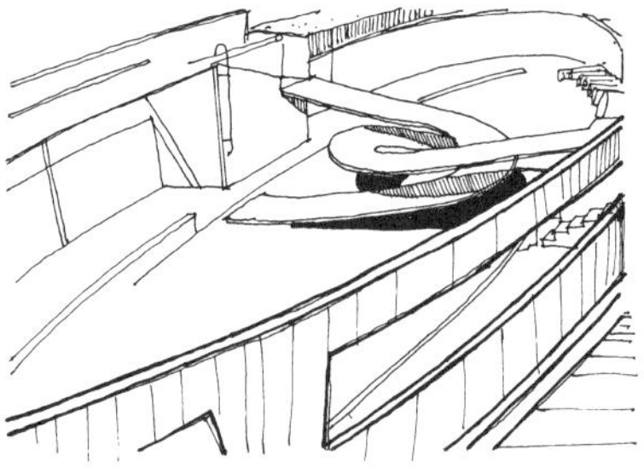

London zoo, London

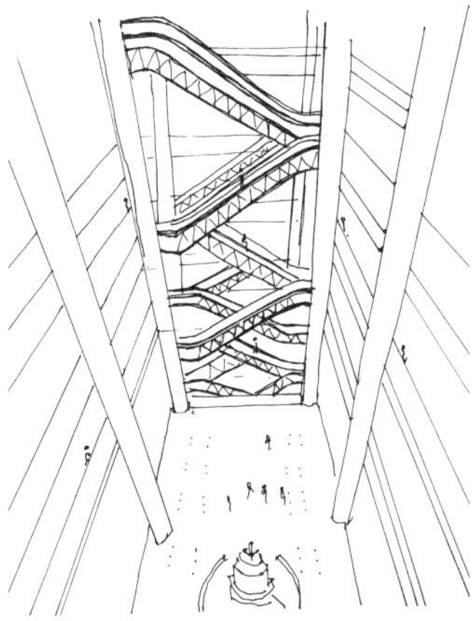

Lloyds Bank, London

STAIRS AS AESTHETIC ELEMENT

Steps, stairs as well as elevators due to their basic obligation of connecting various levels, remain essential ingredients of space at each level as they are the only elements which connect the otherwise autonomous floors with no connection whatsoever. Due to this advantage of being visually and physically evident and realising the inevitability of its presence, this element has often been aesthetically integrated into the building through the continuity of stylisations and entablature. The sculptural form due to its volumetric connection becomes an additional aspect to treat it as a visual and aesthetic element in composing space from within or externally as a facade element. In the course of negotiating the heig ht the stair may wind upon itself to conserve other usable floor space. This dimension causes changes in rhythm through landings and assembly of number of sub-elements like steps, railings, balustrade etc, creating dynamic architectural spaces.

Stairs defining the massing and form of the building

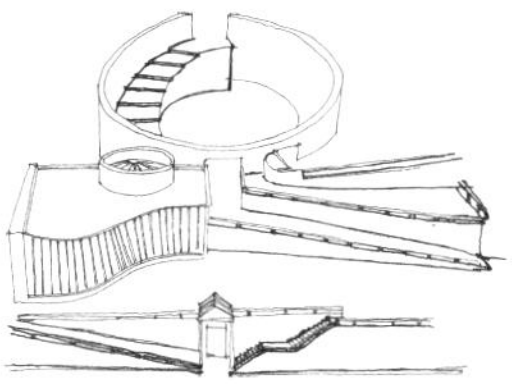

Staatsgallery, Stuttgart

Guggenheim Museum, New York

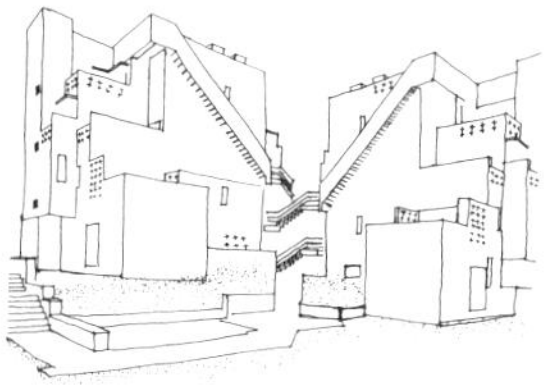

Housing of National Institute of Immunology, New Delhi

Bom Jesus do Monte, Braga, Portugal

Stairs being an integral part of the facade

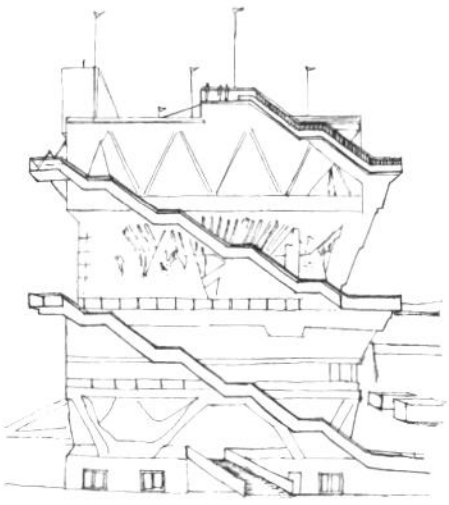

Expo Building, Japan

Chiswick House, London

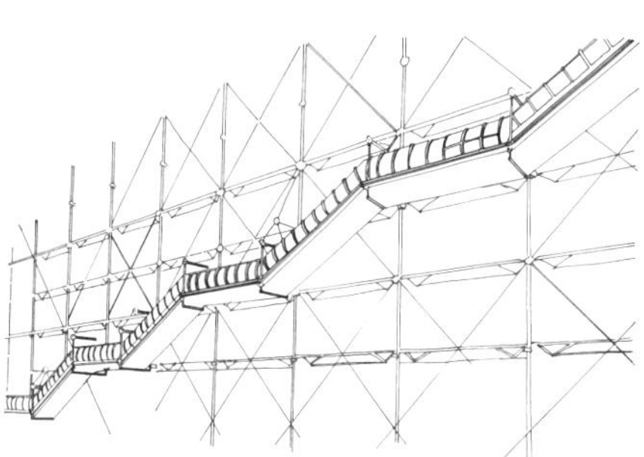

Pompidou Centre, Paris

Stairs marking the node in interior

Interior of a residence

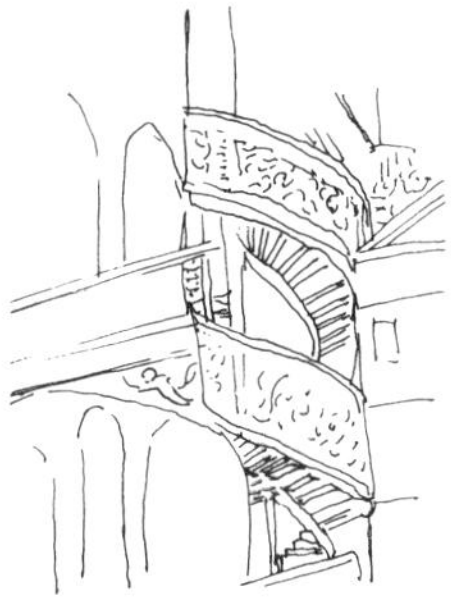

A Church Pulpit

STAIRS AS SPACE MODULATOR

Essentially being the link between two levels, a stair becomes an unavoidable component with reference to volume. The diagonal stretch across the volume and its influence upon the horizontal as well as vertical perspectives can be exploited for enhancing or delineating subspaces. For example, the stair can contain volume within itself between the inner edges of stair flights—within the stairwell. A compact stair designed as a shaft can command surrounding space radially. A vertically linear flight as a barrier can divide the space into two. A stair with floating treads allows visual continuity but cuts off physically axial movement whereas a stair as a mass only seen from front gives itself to the undulations of the floor plane and becomes an extension of it. As an entry to the upper floors, the stair automatically determines the emphasis and suggests the hierarchy of spaces in an otherwise democratic spatial organisation.

Stairs dividing the space

School of Architecture, Ahmedabad

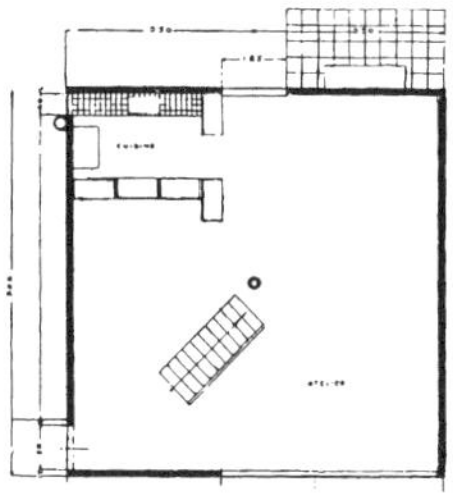

Ground floor plan

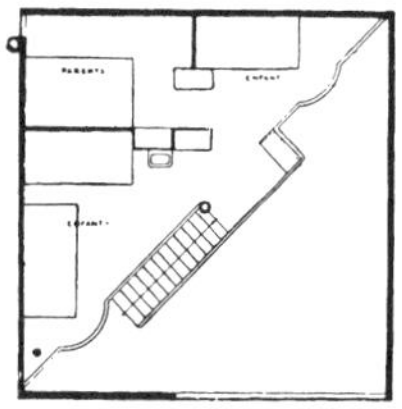

First floor plan

Stairs containg / defining the space

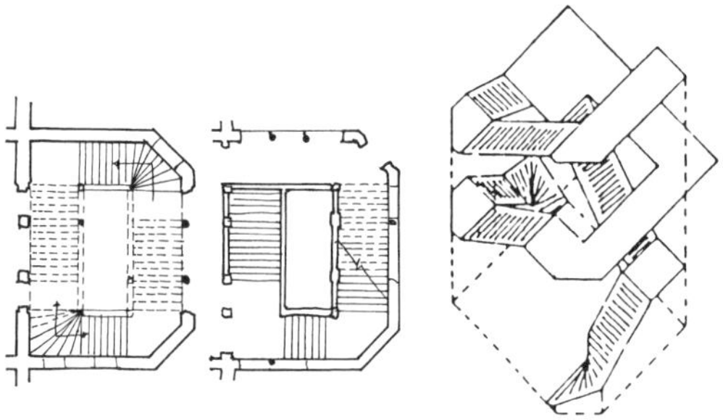

Ranjit Vilas Palace, Wankaner

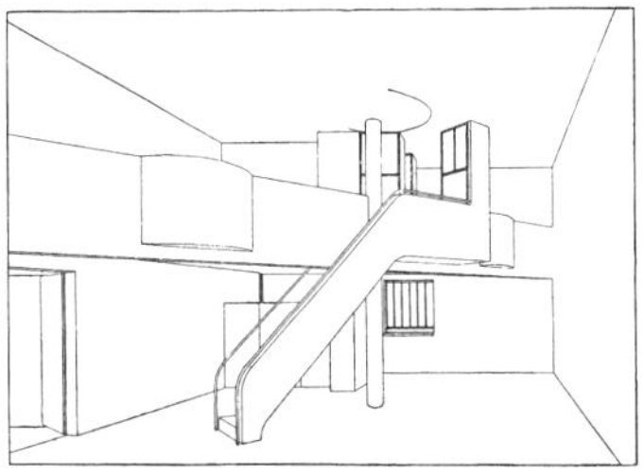

Residence by Le Corbusier, Paris

Stairs commanding the space

Mahabat Maqbara, Junagadh

STAIRS AS DISPLAY AND STORAGE

Vertical surfaces adjacent to the floors are generally useful for storage. Inadvertently the stair also stretches from the floor to the ceiling of any respective floor, giving a vertical surface in the, otherwise unusable, volume below the treads, which can be exploited as display or storage depending upon its position in the overall configuration of space below it. In case the space does not have any other obligations it can be cordoned off and used as a storage space below. The mass generated below the stairs can have small niches, which can be used to displace elements inside. Similarly, the steps as elevated platforms are also successful display systems due to their consecutively raised levels and corresponding sight lines.

Vertical volume space treated as for display or storage...

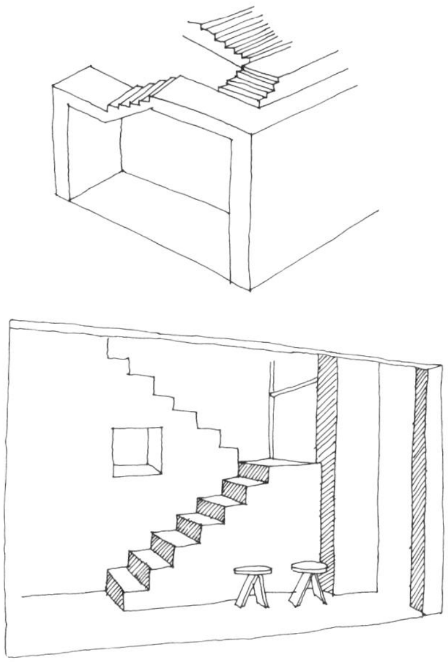

House of B.V. Doshi, Ahmedabad

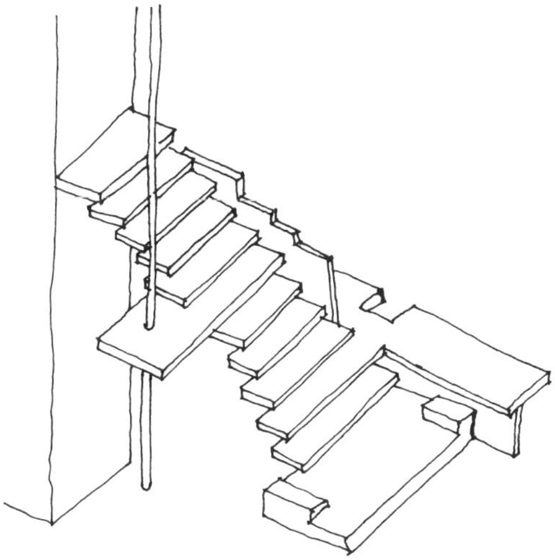

Stairs at Olivetti Showroom, Venice

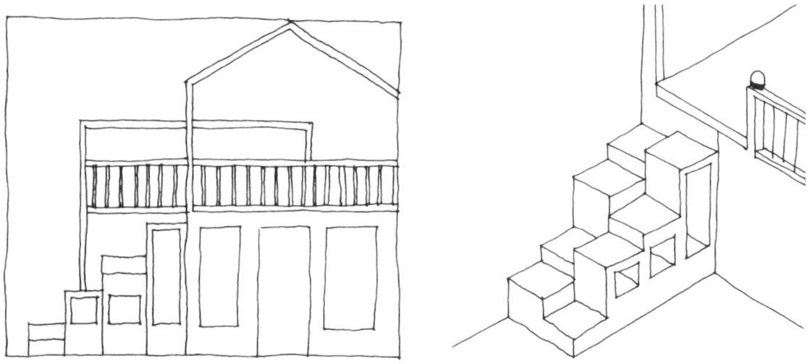

Vertical volume of stair being reflected

Stair mass expressed externally and through section like atrium shaft

STAIRS AS VENTILATION SHAFT

The stair cuts across the multiple levels of the volume. As a result it becomes a link volumetrically connecting the spaces. This aspect inherent to any stair combined with its resolution as stacked core creates a vertical shaft penetrating the entire vertical dimension within the volume all the way from ground floor to roof. This provides for an excellent opportunity to take in or exhaust light and ventilation through this aperture and relieving the individual floors of their static nature.

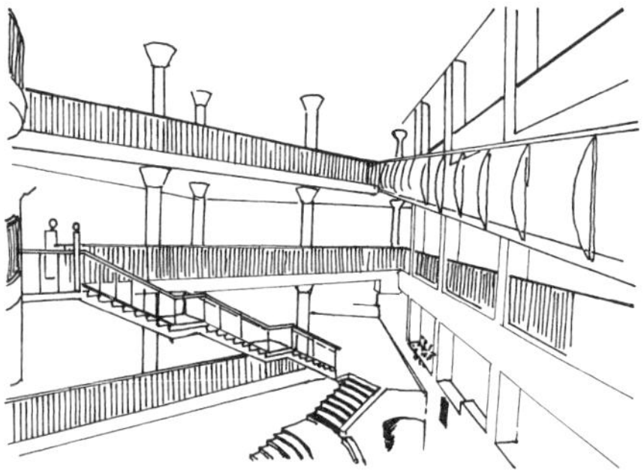

IIS Infosystems, Noida

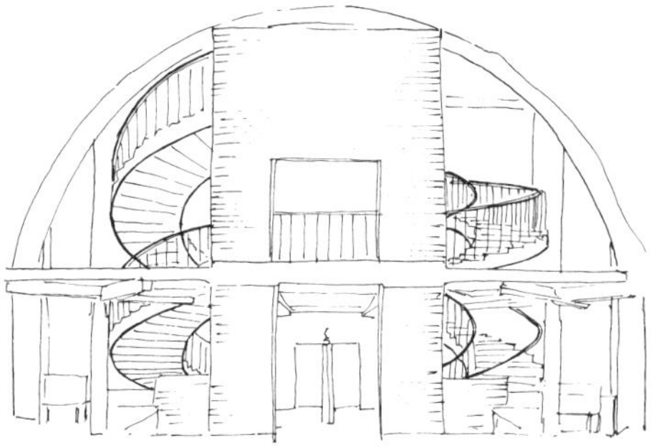

Indian Institute of Management, Ahmedabad

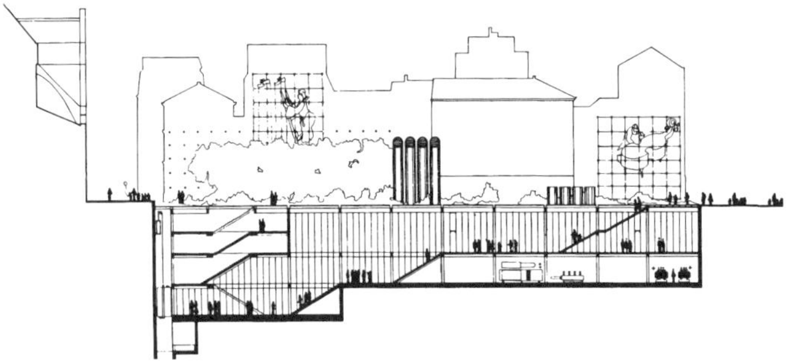

Section, Institute for Research and Coordination in Acoustic and Music, France

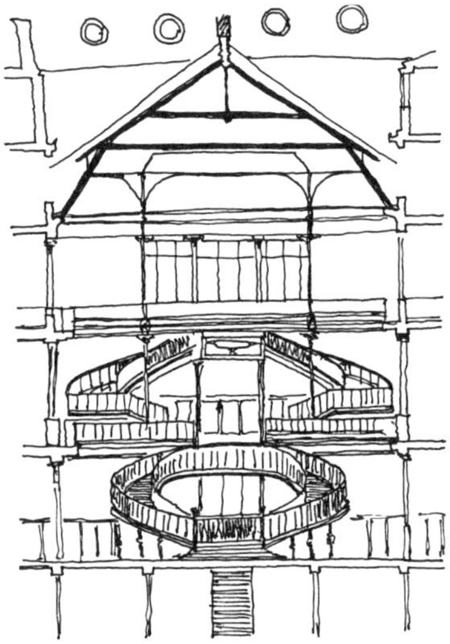

Bon Marche Department Store, France

STAIRS AS DEVICES/ INSTRUMENTS

Instruments developed to study astronomy mostly make use of the Sun and its positions with respect to the earth. The forms developed for such studies defy all principles of space planning, as the intent is different. However they must be at every point accessible. The aspects of verticality, simultaneous displacement in vertical as well as horizontal axis and the stair being composed of modular components (steps) has made the stair as an indispensable element to take readings and to service all the parts of such scientific instruments and devices.

One of the first attempts in this regard was to create a gadget to reach the sky—the heavens—at the tower of Babel. King Jaisingh created number of scientific installations in Delhi, Jaipur, Benaras, Ujjain and Mathura to calculate time, measure the position of Sun as well as other planetary constellations and heavenly bodies.

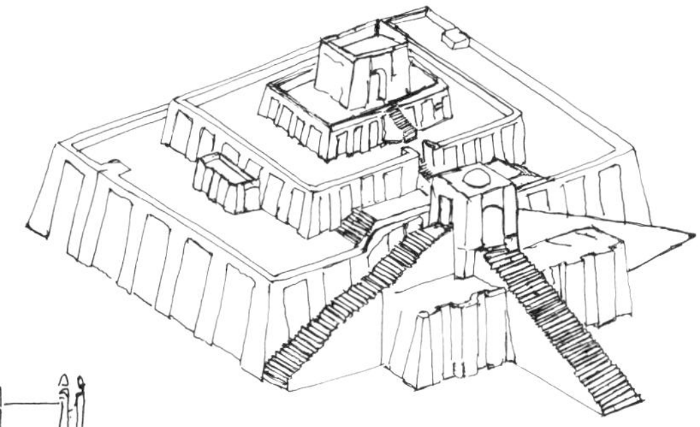

Ziggurat of Ur, Iraq

Rama Yantra, Jantar Mantar, Jaipur

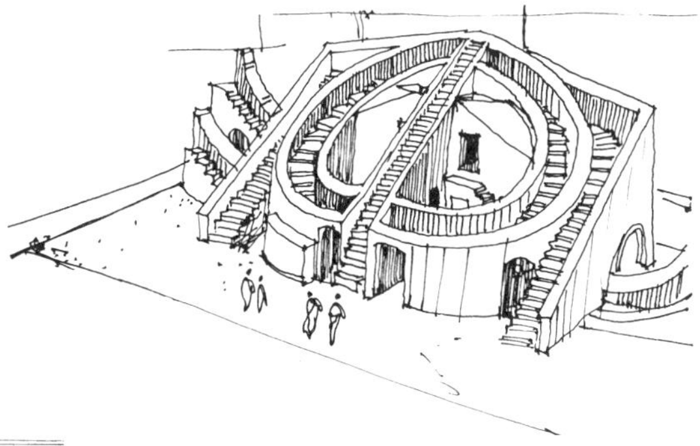

The Mishre Yantra, Jantar Mantar, Jaipur

Samrat Yantra, Jantar Mantar, Jaipur

SUN TEMPLE, MODHERA

The sun temple at Modhera in Gujarat, built by Bhima I, of Solanki dynasty in the 11th century, is a classic example of a typical architectural composition being transformed by the element of steps, stairs and staircases, adding another dimension to the ensemble. Otherwise a typical typology of the North Indian temple form, this Sun Temple is made unique due to the presence of the stepped *kund* or ablution tank, the first of the tripartite organization of the overall scheme. Essentially, it is a large tank with a steep pitch, determined by the angle of reflection of the *shikhara* in the water. The *kund* is the best example of subterranean architecture of steps with linear and cross-linked platforms, levels and shrines that continuously weaves the movement through the volume within. Physical, graphic and spatial roles getting overlaid with spiritual and metaphorical allusions, the *kund* exemplifies the potential of stairs as an altar to the divine.

Steps modulating the overall spatial configuration with their geometry and position

Plan

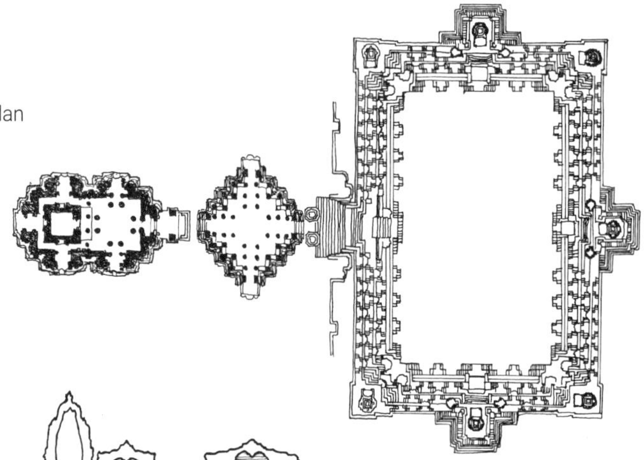

Section

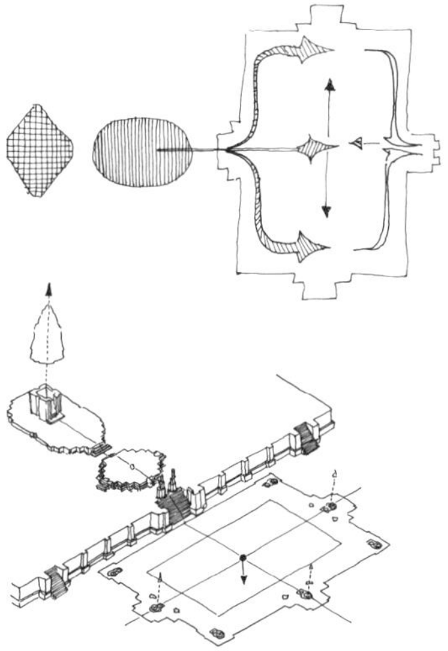

An axial stairway from the *kund* to the temple connects the two different planes serving as a linking element to the otherwise disparate levels.

Stairs connecting two realms physically and notionally as up–down, sacred–profane, inside-outside

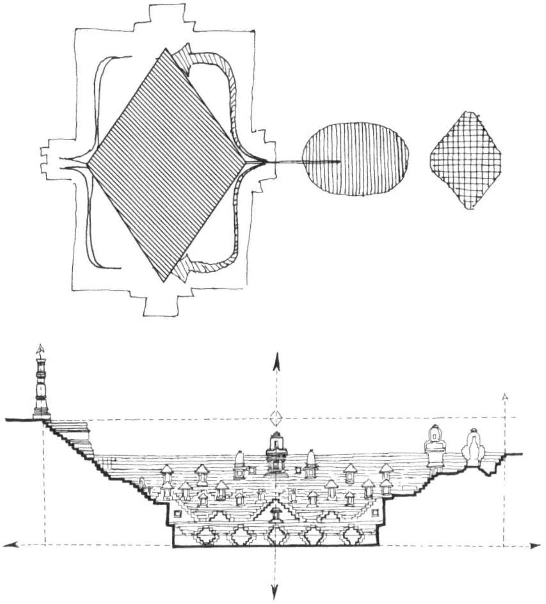

Stairs with the vertical movement in the volume, integrating the climb with overall schema of the complex

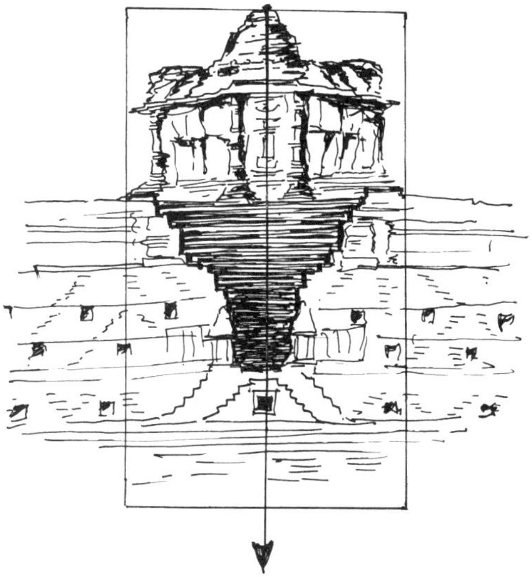

The vertical axis formed between *kund* and temple.

Steps as physical link

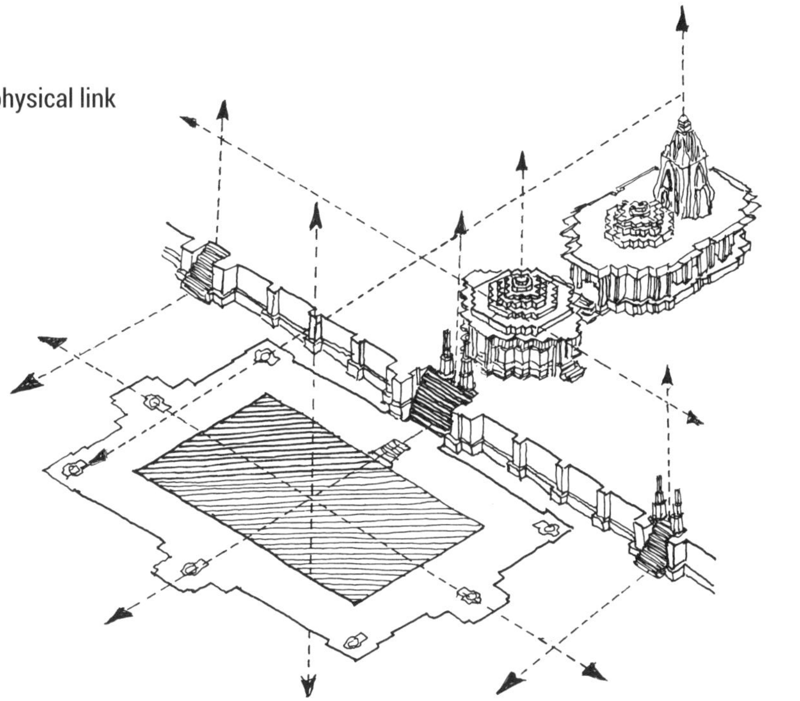

Steep angle of steps descending to the water and the ascending steps to the temple connects the two realms

Scaling of the step in a module

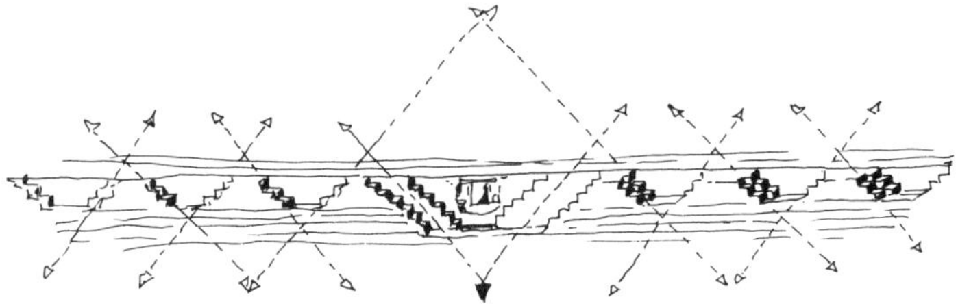

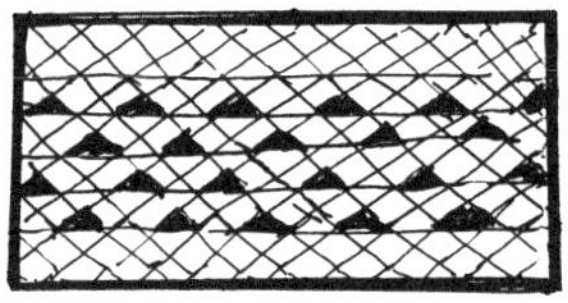

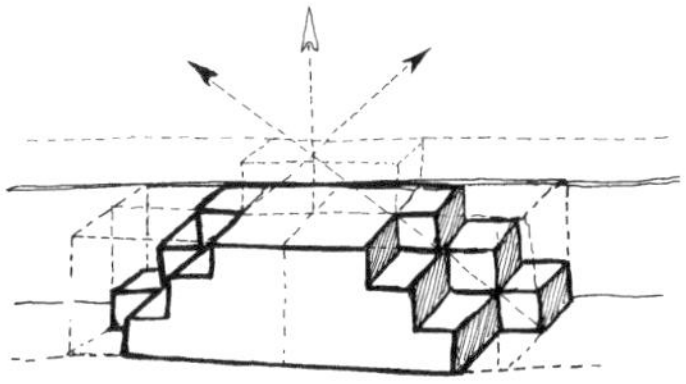

The composition of steps creates a unique movement pattern

Steps as pedestal

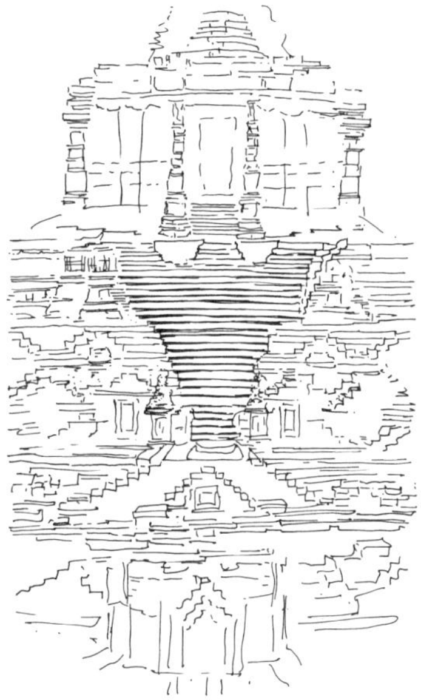

Steps as aesthetic elements

Steps containing the volume with a defined movement within...

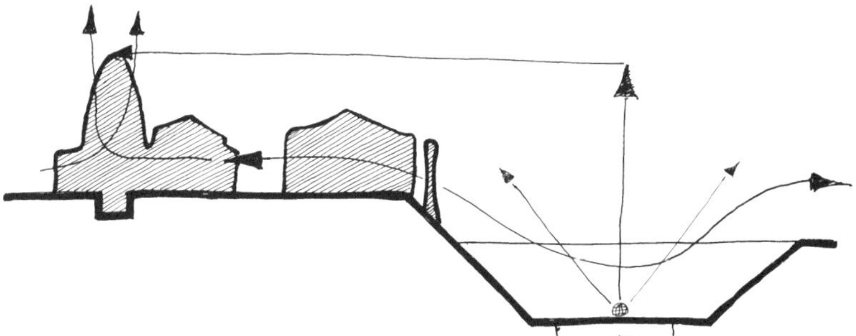

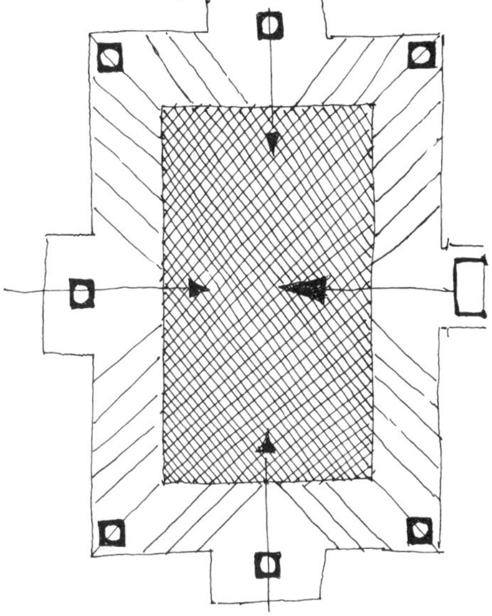

Steps as a physical link...

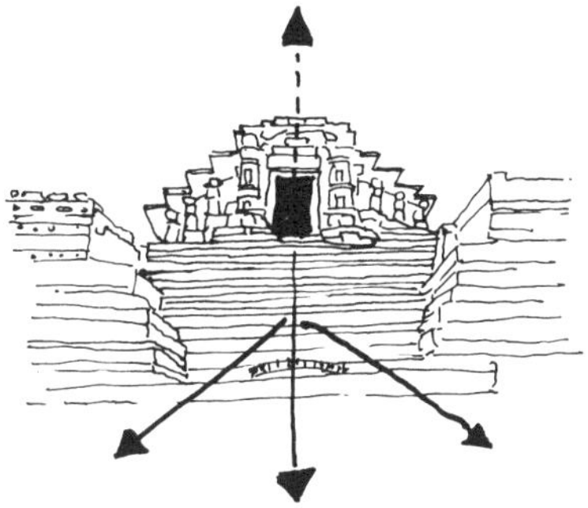

Kund—transition from profane to sacred

Section—connection established between the horizontal distance and the vertical movement

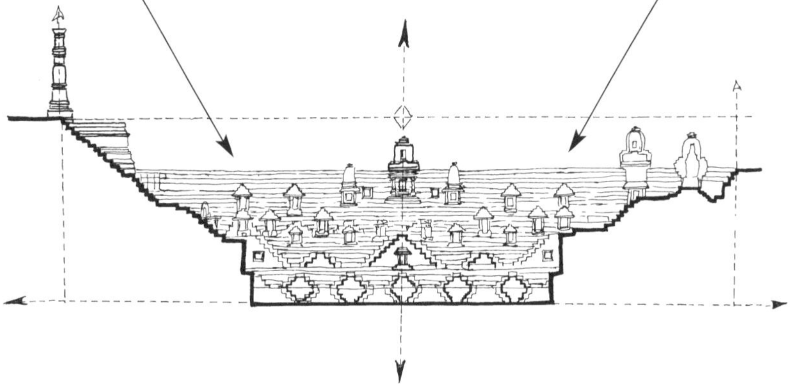

RUDABAI STEPWELL, ADALAJ

Rudabai, wife of the Hindu Rajput king Vikramsinh Vaghela, built the stepwell at Adalaj in AD 1499. The five-storeyed structure is braced with crossbeams all along its length to retain earth. The only visible clue above the ground is the pair of large outcrops flanking a small flight of steps up a plinth. Steps descending to a square platform provide pause in-between involving a shift in the visual axis. A linear, symmetrical organization of elements along the horizontal axis at each of the intermediate levels due to the stone crossbeams, the visual references continuously and radically change due to inclined downward movement at every step.

Each step reveals only the next while the subsequent flights of steps and water are concealed from the cone of vision by platforms.

Plan

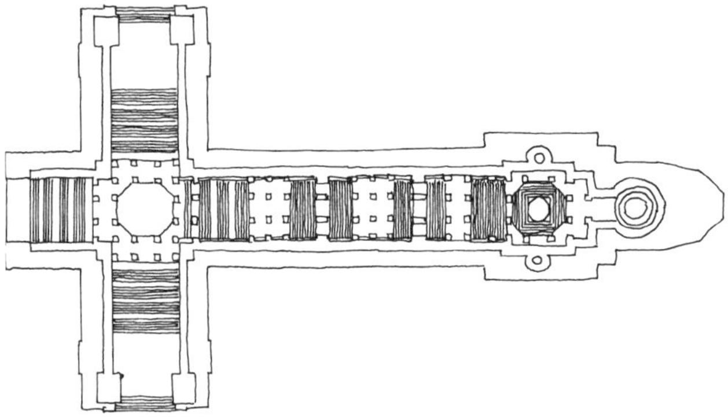

Section

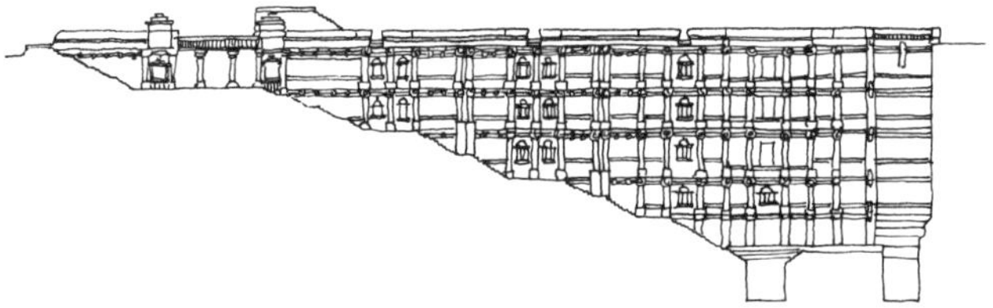

Stairs enclosing volume underneath

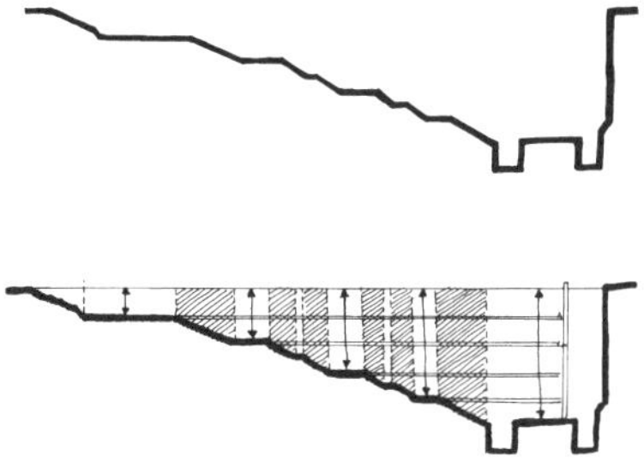

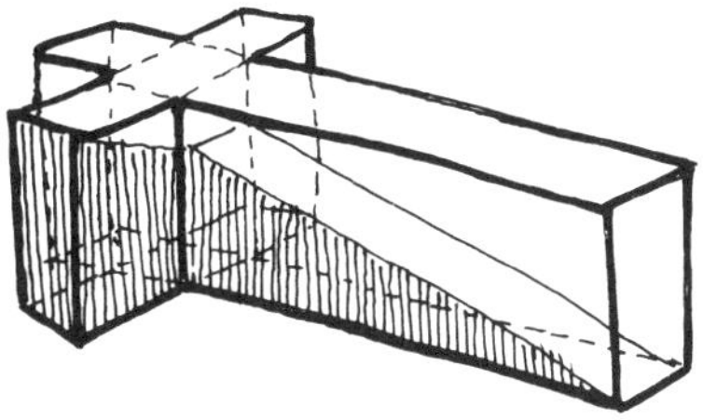

Stairs as a threshold creating platforms

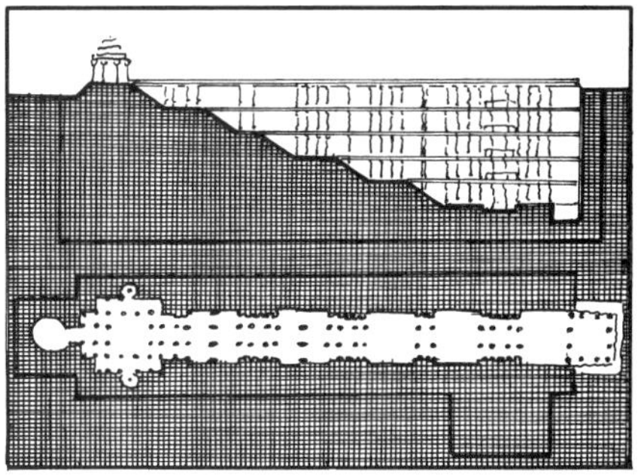

Stairs as seat and pedestal

The entrance view

Stairs as a space modulator

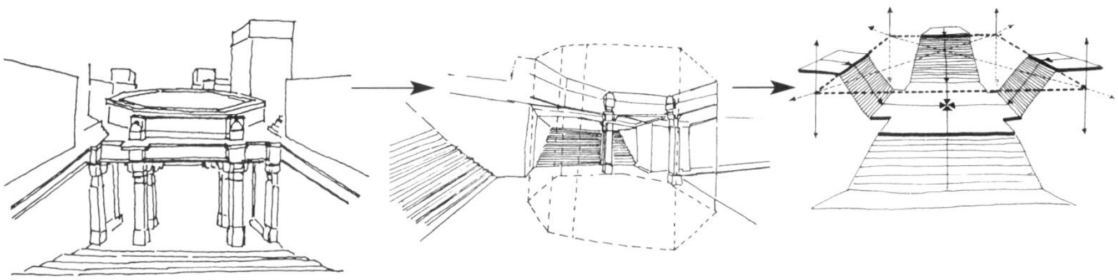

Stairs orienting towards the centrally located shaf

Stairs as a linear axis

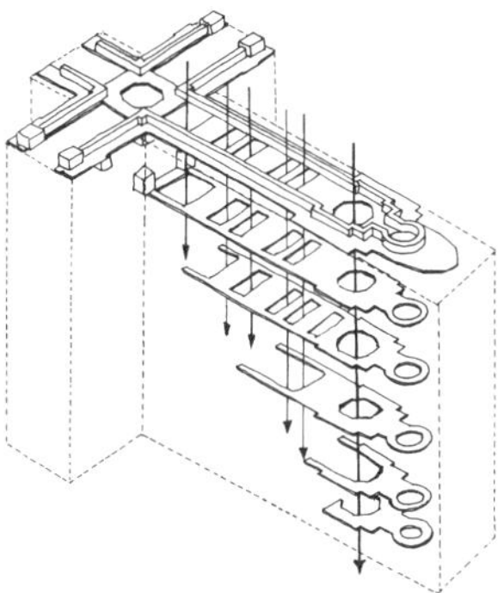

A linear axis from temple to the *kund*

Stairs as a movement in volume

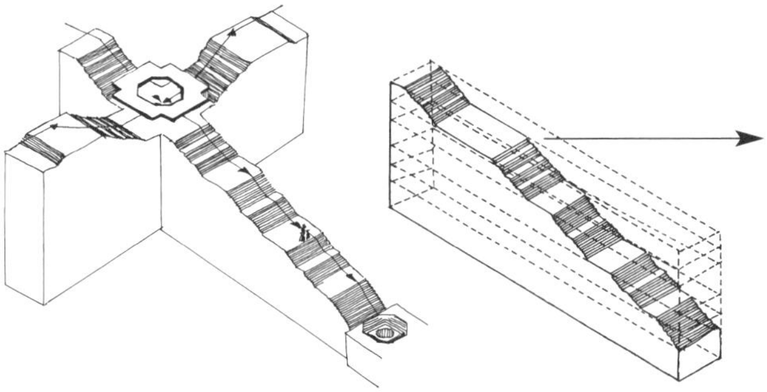

Movement guided by steps, their structure and formation

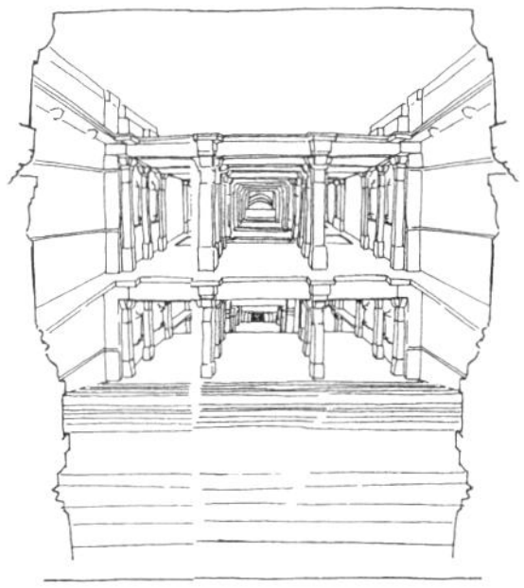

Enclosed volume into a number of subspaces sets a successive visual frame, connected by stairs as a vertical element

AHMEDABAD TEXTILE MILL OWNERS' ASSOCIATION HOUSE, AHMEDABAD

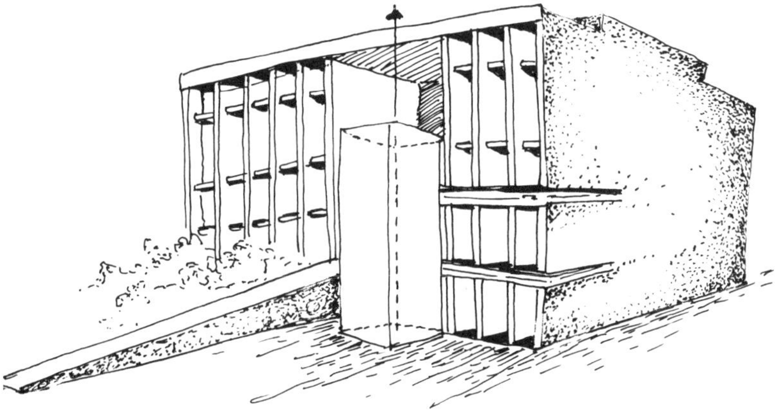

Designed by Le Corbusier in India in 1954, the Ahmedabad Textile Mill Owners' Association (ATMA) House is a perfect manifestation of the architect's idea on Promenade Architecturale. Emphasising perception while in movement, its organisation depends heavily on the vertical movement elements to serve as anchors of the overall composition. The primary components framed in the facade are the stair mass and the long ramp, both formal, which project from the built-mass. The ramp takes over the movement due to the proximity and subtly leads one up to the first floor overruling the role of the ground floor in the building. The stair mass then becomes the ever present connector to the other floors where the height of the solid railing restricts external vision and guides release only within the building and beyond towards the river. This height of the railing is also a resultant of the compositional massing required by the facade. Another smaller stair on the upper floor is totally free flowing and informal as required by the amorphous space below and above.

The five modes of transition

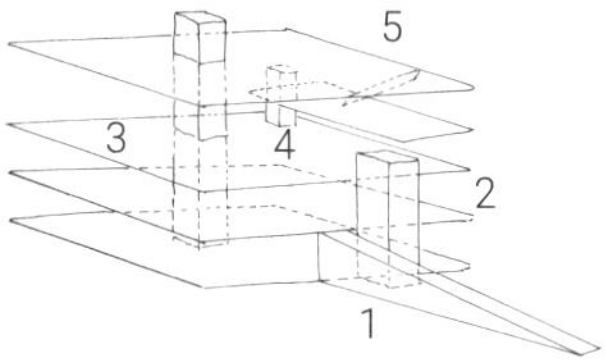

1 The ramp

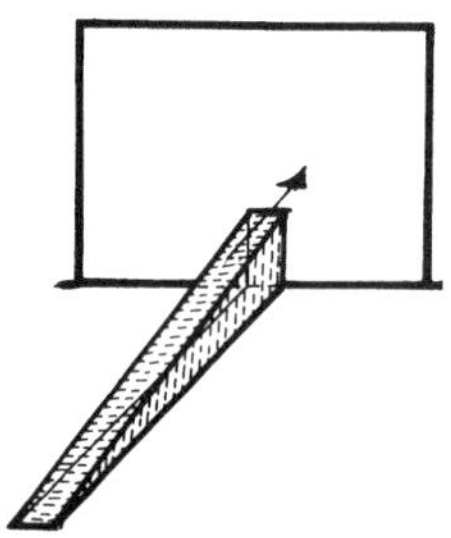

2 The dogleg stair

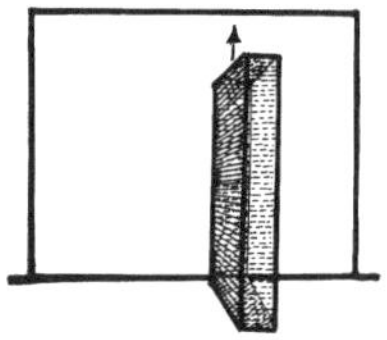

3 Lift shaft

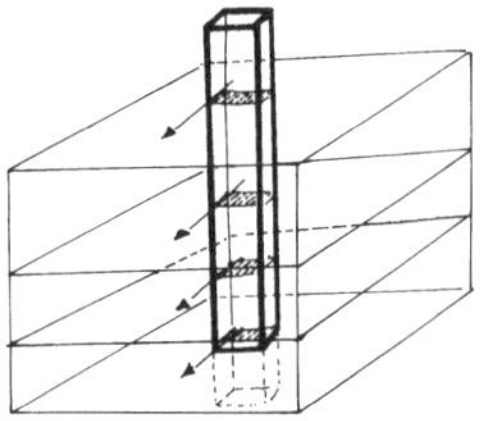

4 Staircase linking second floor to mezzanine

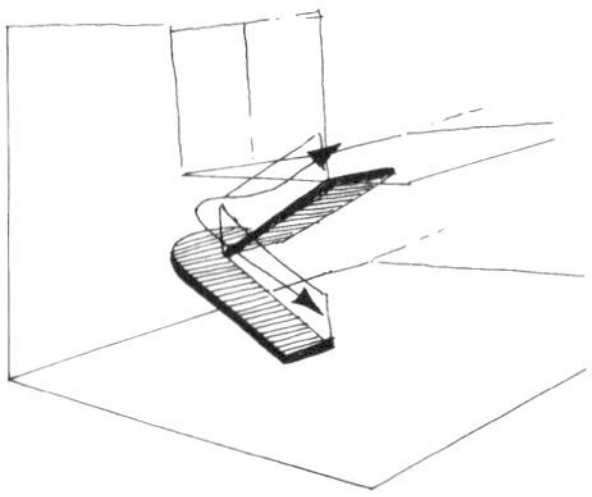

5 Staircase linking the mezzanine level to the terrace

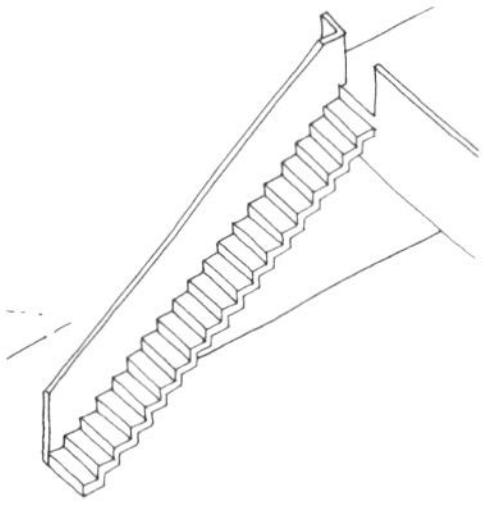

1 The ramp

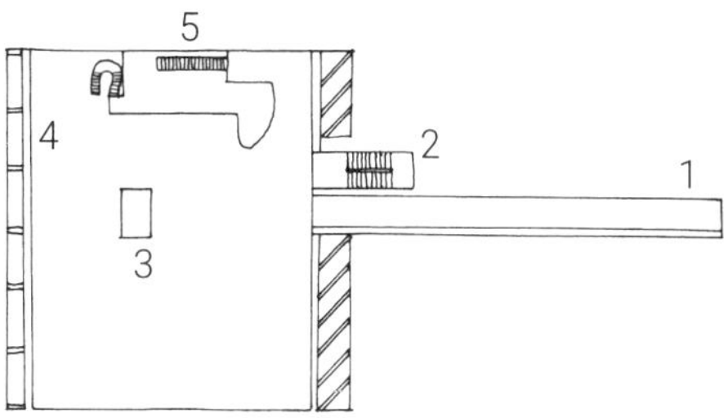

Plan

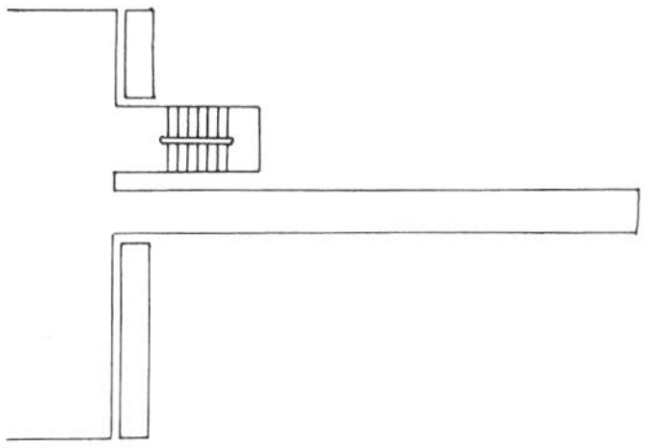

Part plan ramp and dogleg stair

Staircase manipulated as ramp to integrate with the form and enhances the form in itself

2 The dogleg stair

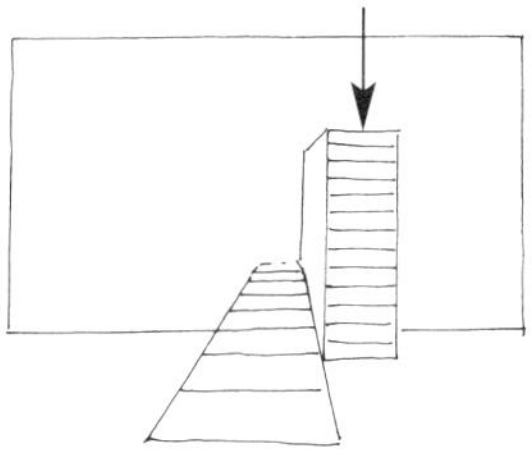

Stairs as aesthetic element

Ramp and dogleg stair forming the compositional element of the facade

Stairs defining the vista

Metal railing along the ramp

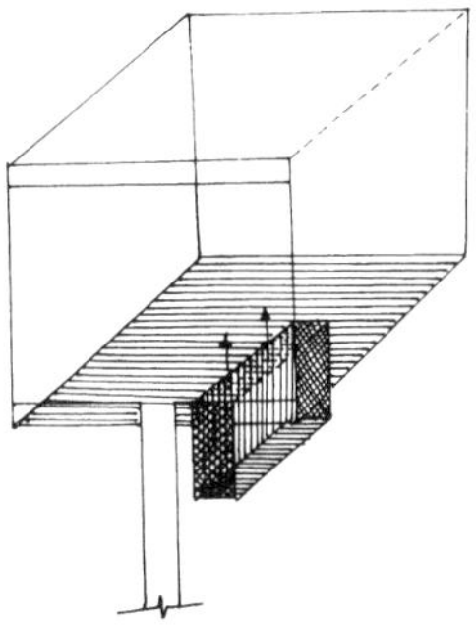

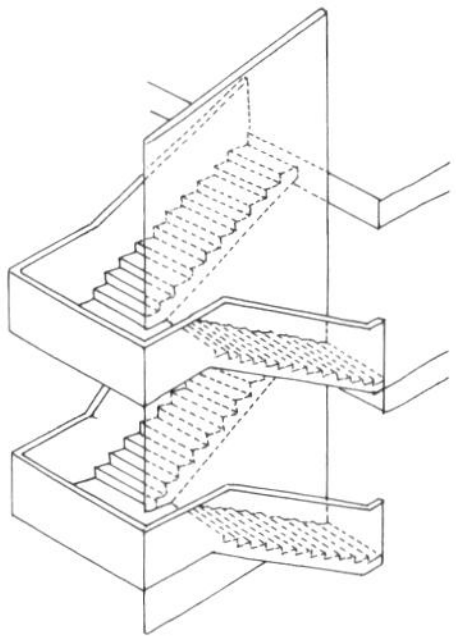

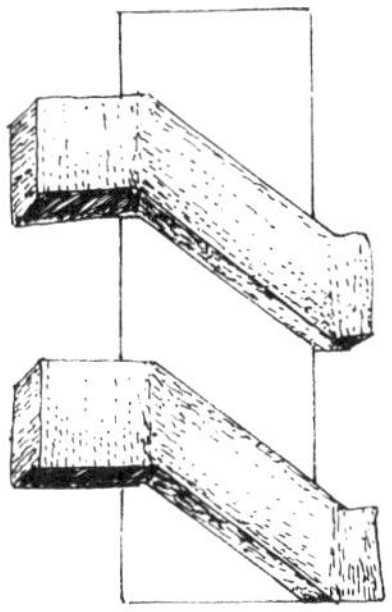

Dogleg stair perceived as a vertical mass in double height at the entrance enhances the free standing vertical mass of the staircase

Stair in its vertical mode

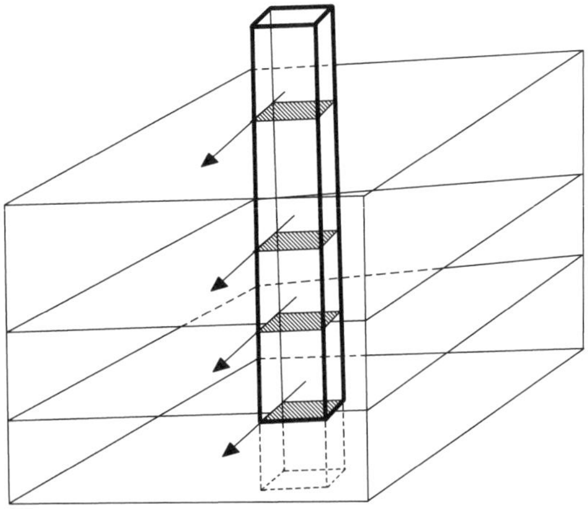

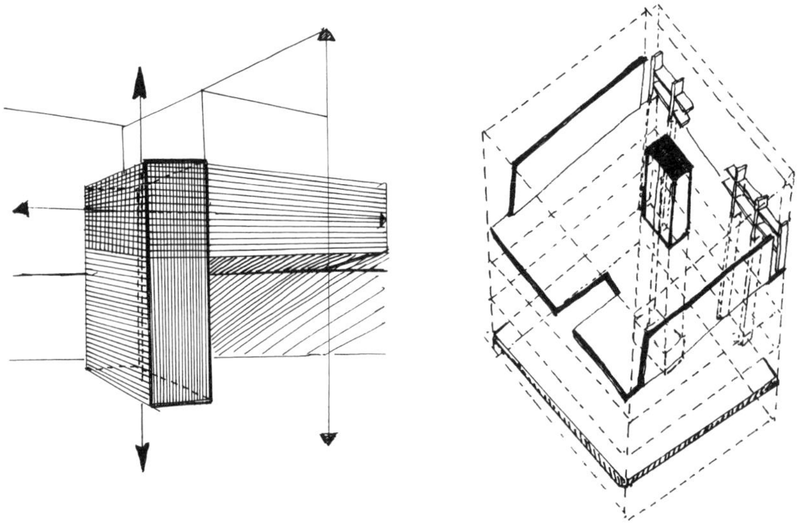

The elevator creates a strong link between all the floors, forming a vertical mass in the space in the entire volume. It forms a reference node for the surrounding space and activities

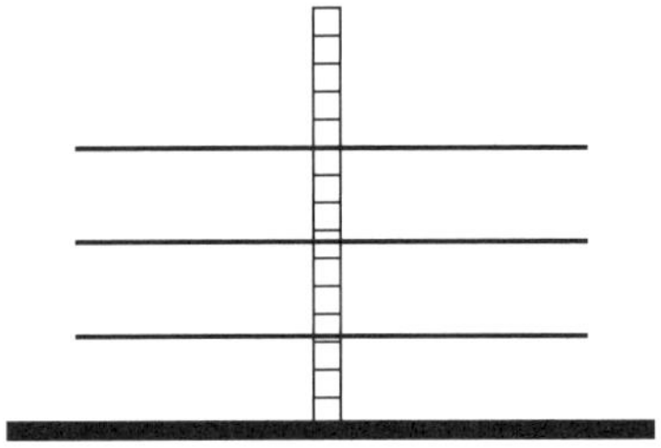

Main vertical axis of the built form located centrally

4 | Staircase linking second floor to mezzanine

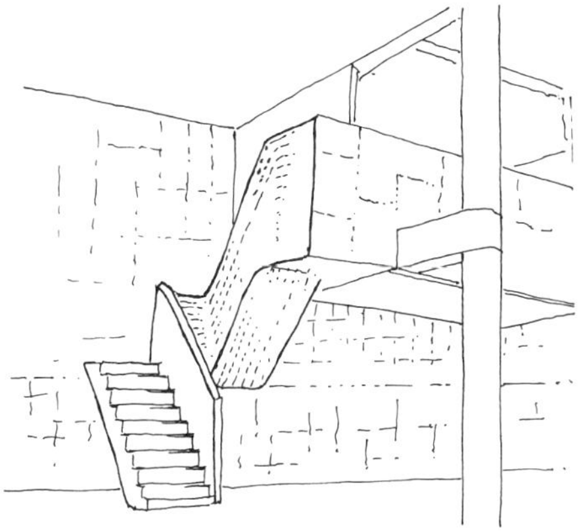

Stairs as the focus of the space....................

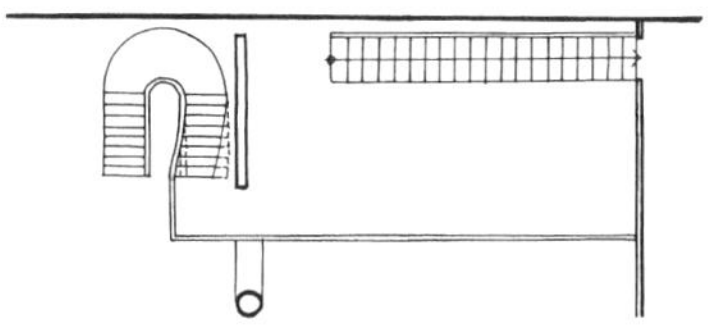

Plan

Stairs as movement guide...

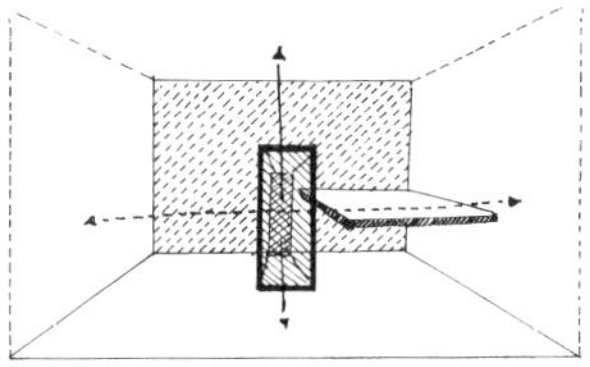

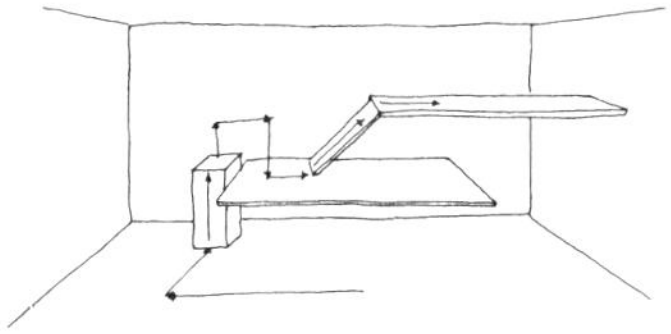

Movement is guided in a manner that unfolds a series of sequential spatial experiences

Stairs as physical link...

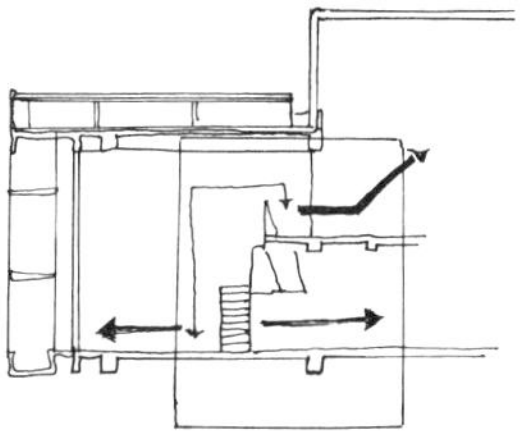

Part elevation

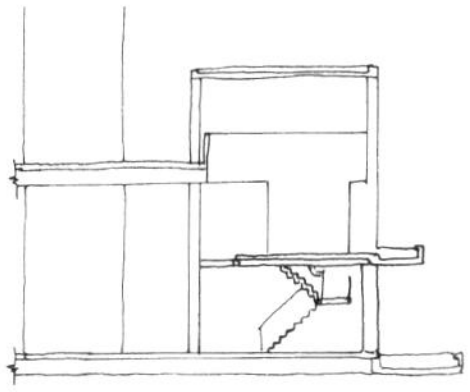

Part elevation—stairs as free standing element

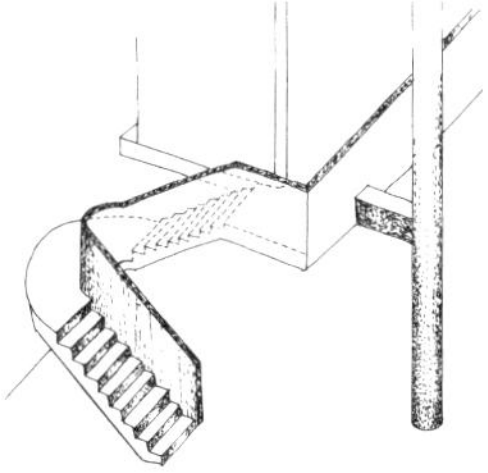

Dogleg form squeezed, emphasizing its independent quality with wall as the reference

5 | Staircase linking second floor to mezzanine

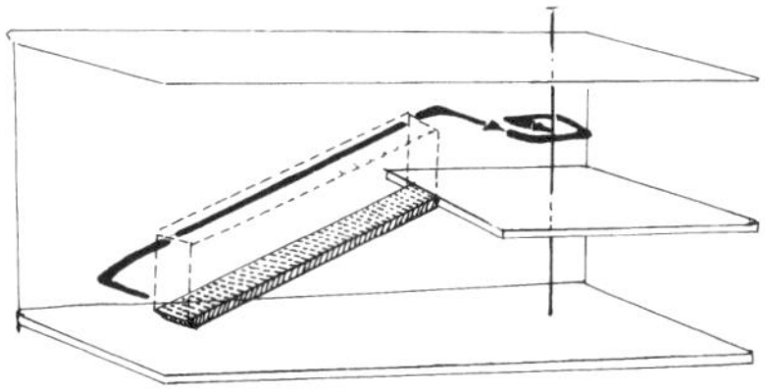

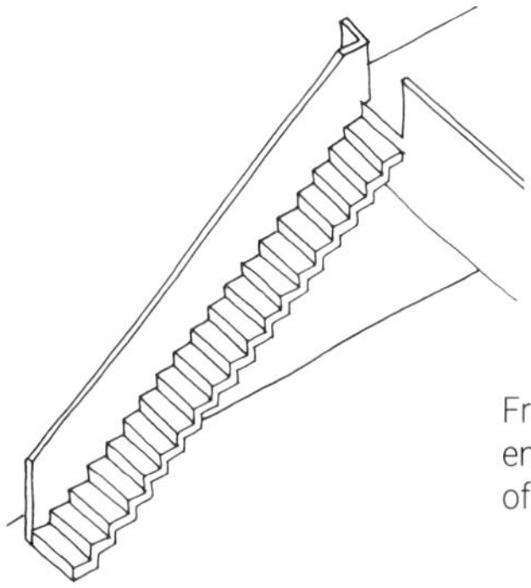

Freestanding structure enhancing the spatial experience of travelling up

SANTOS HOUSE, PENNSYLVANIA

Architect Adele Santos designed this residence for herself at Pennsylvania. The entire living space on the upper floor revolves around a central staircase element, which becomes main spatial element of the house due to the variety of functions attributed to it. The stepped platform is created in such a way that the south light filtering from above is reflected through the entire building. The stair-mass screens the private spaces behind providing storage within. The accompaniment of wider level aided in the display of artifacts while the stair itself doubled as an amphitheatre for screening shows. Thus, the stairs here not only becomes a circulatory element linking both the floors, but also performs several functions, becoming an active participant within the house.

Stairs creating a theatre within

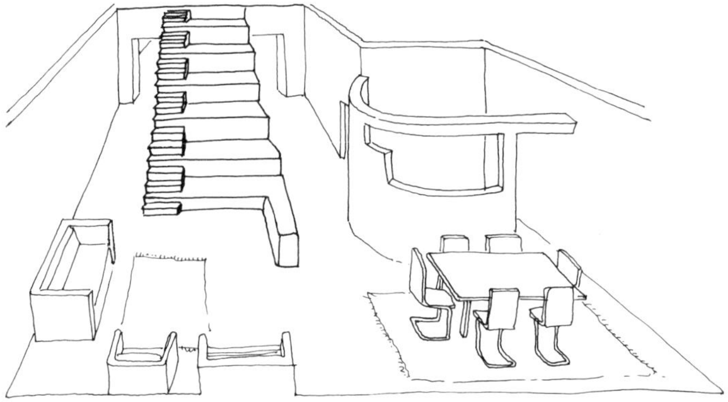

The view of the house with stairs becoming a crucial element of space making

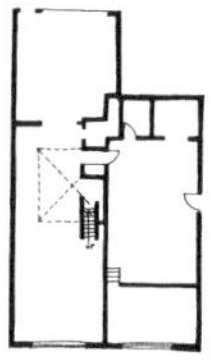

Ground floor plan

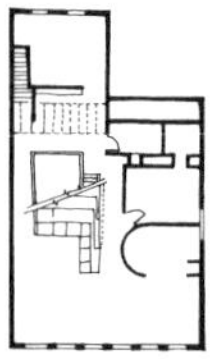

First floor plan

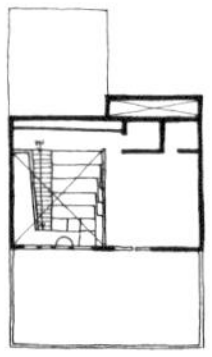

Second floor plan

Stairs with varied spatial roles

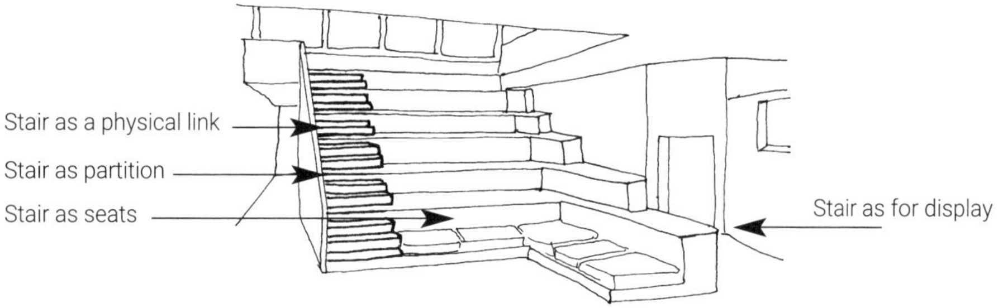

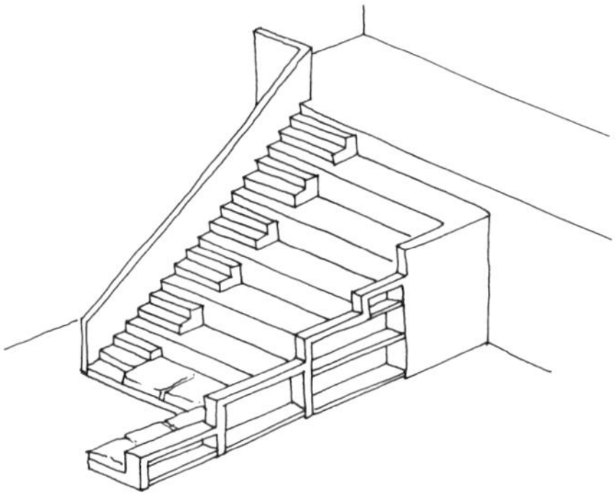

The stairs becomes an element having potential of catering to multiple spatial and functional requirements

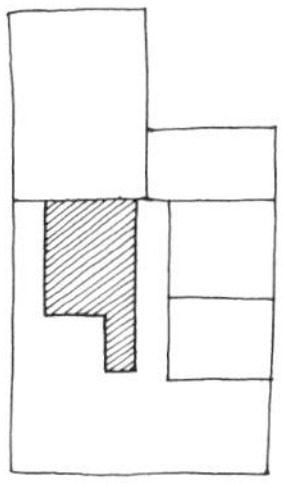

Locational plan

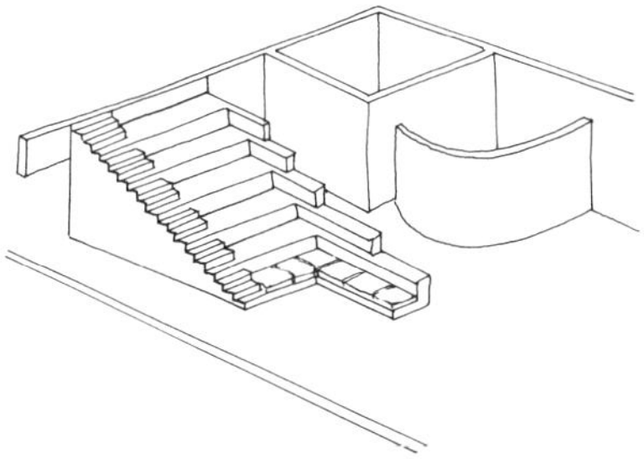

Stairs manipulates the space around it by its mass and position

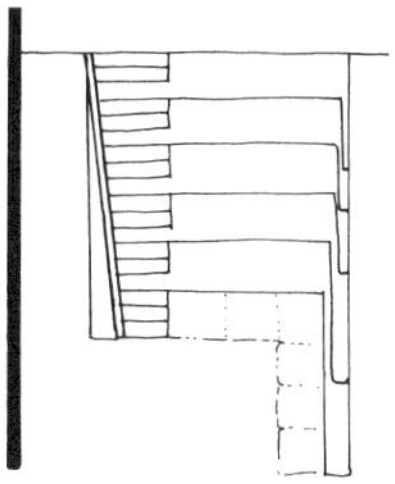

Detail plan of stairs

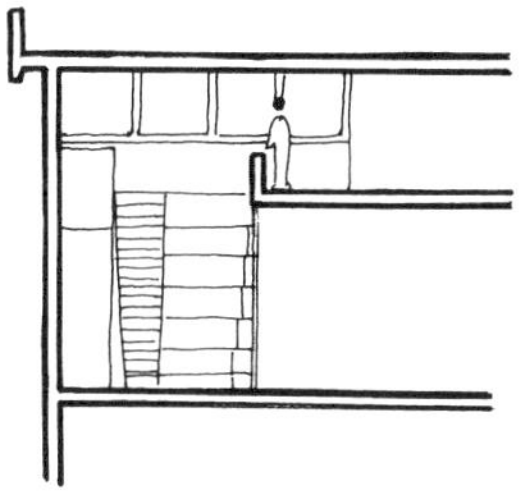

Sectional detail

Visual interaction created between two levels, by linking the physical planes

Stairs as an element defining sub-space

The stair amongst all its surrounding specifically functional zones creates a concentrated functional area

Stairs creating a theatre within

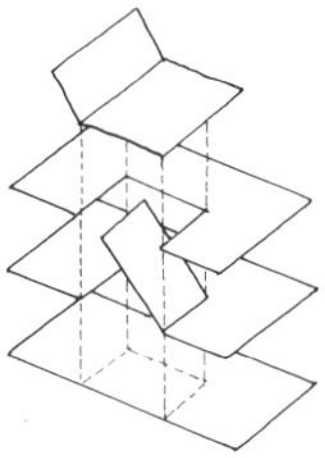

Stairs becomes a physical link between the three-level volume unifying the sub-volumes

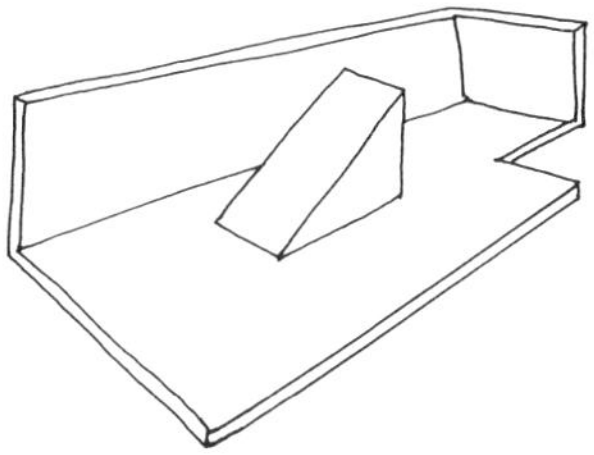

Stairs with its solidity in the volume asserts an overwhelming presence in the space

Stairs as ventilating shaft

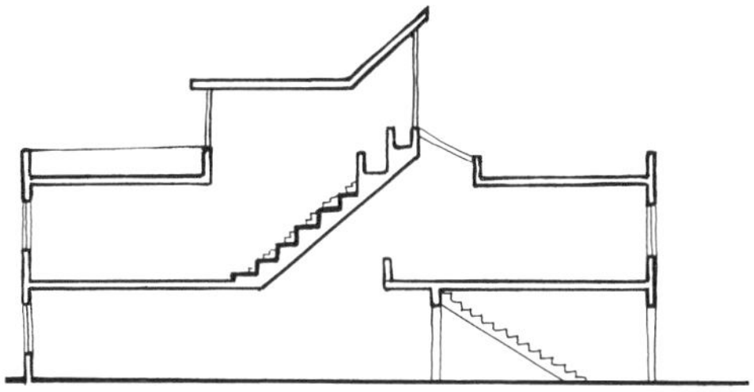

Section—a shaft drawing natural light to all floors

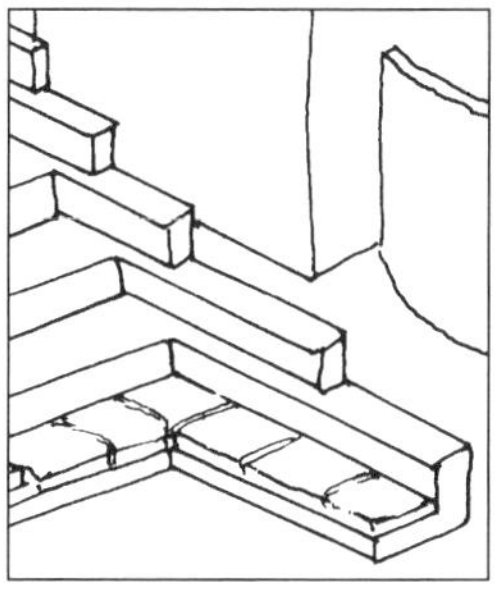

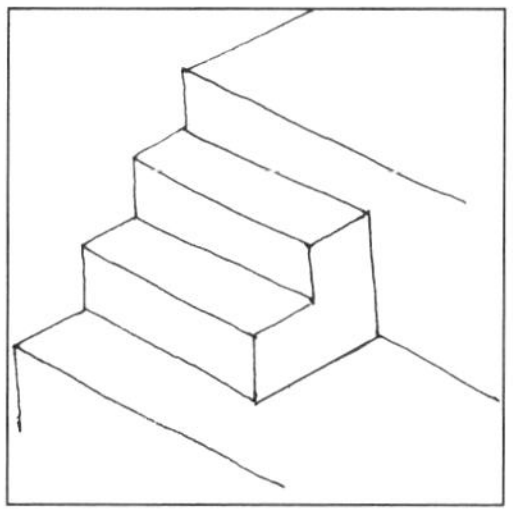

Geometry of the stairs create a language throughout the vertical axis

- Basic criteria for designing the stairs within a space are:
  - Placement within space.
  - Spatial definition of spaces flanking springing point and end point.
  - Directionality defined through rotational movement.
  - Width of the flight based upon user density.
  - Numbers, size and shape of steps according to anthropometrics
  - Aspect ratio of tread and risers.
  - The support and degree of enclosure.
  - Location, form and size of landing for the physiological comfort.

The thumb rule for the steps in stairs is, twice the Riser plus Going (tread clearance) should be equal to 60 cms. (2R+ G= 60 cms)

- Every stair governs a flow of movement. A natural flow torque is established by the successive turns of the stair. Its direction (clockwise, anticlockwise or linear) should be established in a manner that, spaces at each end get definition through such rotational flow or spin off.

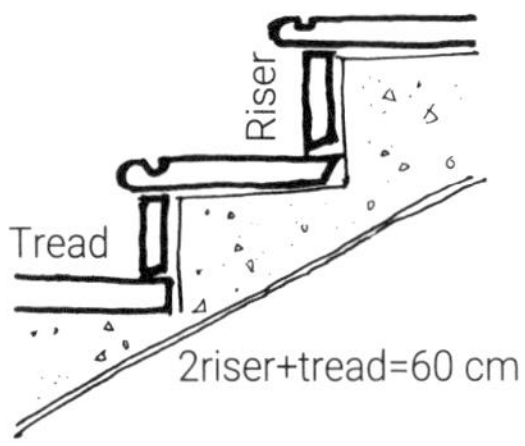

Proportion of tread and riser

Width varying according to the use

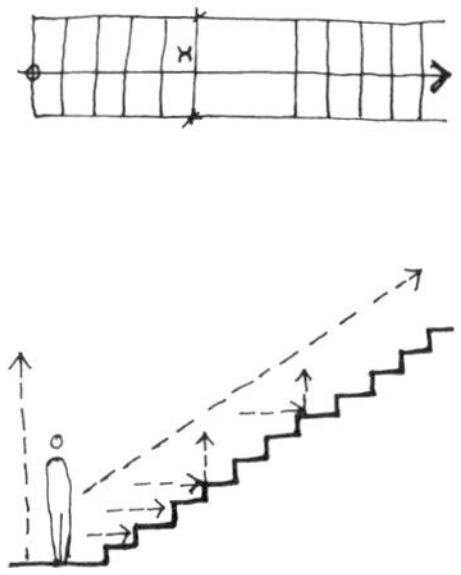

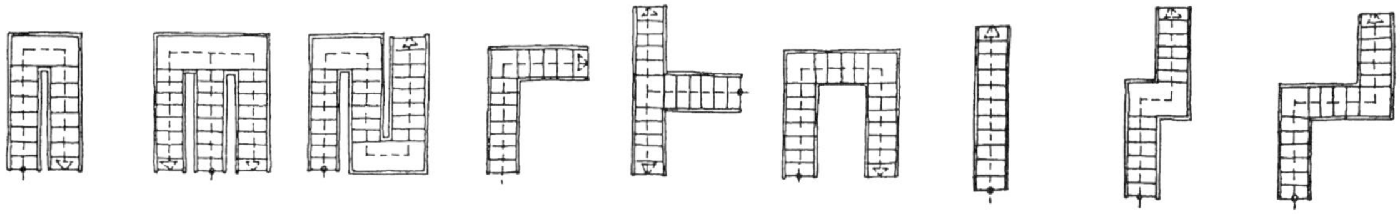

Stairs guiding the flow or movement. Placement stairs become axes of reference

• Some manipulations of steps by way of flaring the few bottom steps with open window or light railing and wide treads help people coming down the stair becoming part of the action in the space also changing the direction of flow and accessibility.

• Stairs can effectively duplicate as seats. At least the lower steps could be designed, if supported by the space below, to multiply as step, seats or display platforms.

• External open stairs act as extensions of the public realm from the street end and transition space from the private realm, and therefore could be designed as so with open edges and natural transition to both (inside & outside)

Elaborating the stairs at the base

Detailing the components of the element

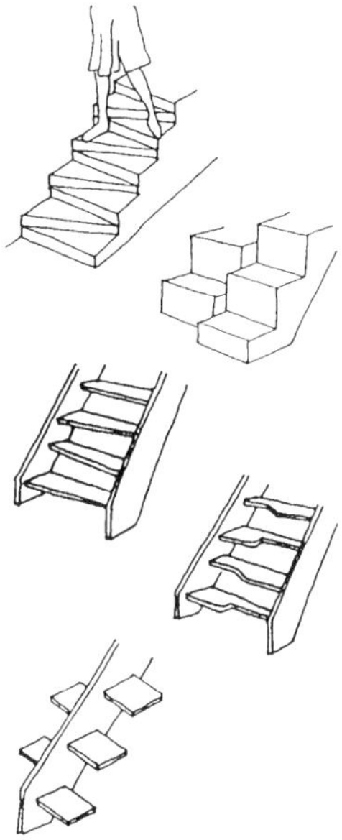

External stairs as an extension of public realm

External stairs as an extension

Stairs as storage

- Landings are spatial as well as visual pause points. Such pause platforms should therefore occur in a way that effectively exploit orientation. The placement of landing in terms of its levels as well as direction could exploit visual cone- sightline consciously such that the visual frame becomes special reward of the design through the visual frame (vignettes created at such point). A landing is mandatory approximately at once every 2 meters of climb to prevent excessive fatigue. Landing platforms can also become effective, usable and multipurpose spaces if deepened (widened) beyond circulation obligation.

- Every stair occupies a volume that is more than one storey atleast. The volume pierces through different levels and thereby becomes a unifying space. The vertical shaft of space can effectively double up as a shaft for natural light and ventilation as well as volume of visual and physical communication.

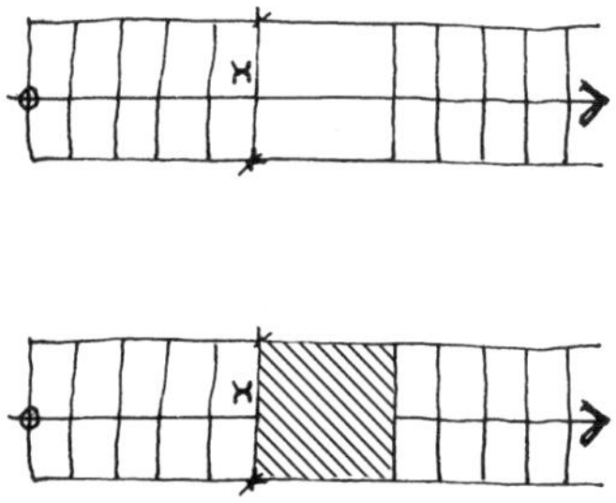

Landing providing changing points of view (sightline) and reference to orientation

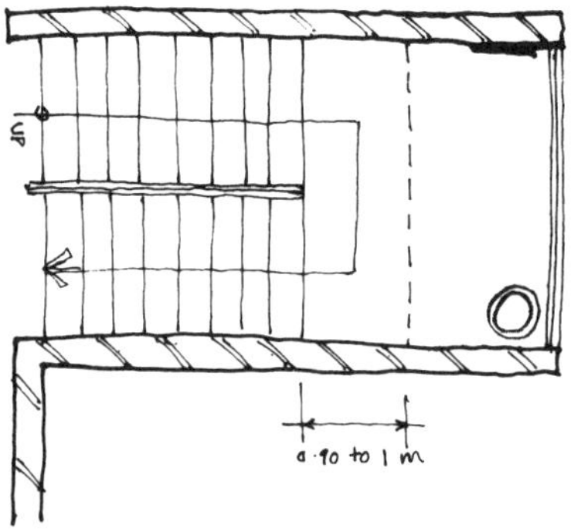

Stairs as seats and landing platform extended for multipurpose use

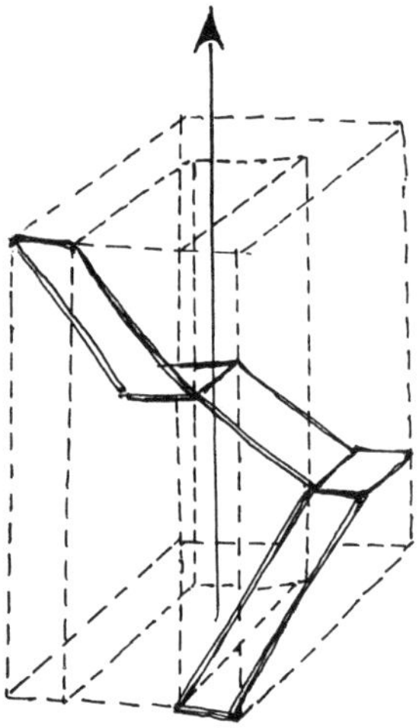

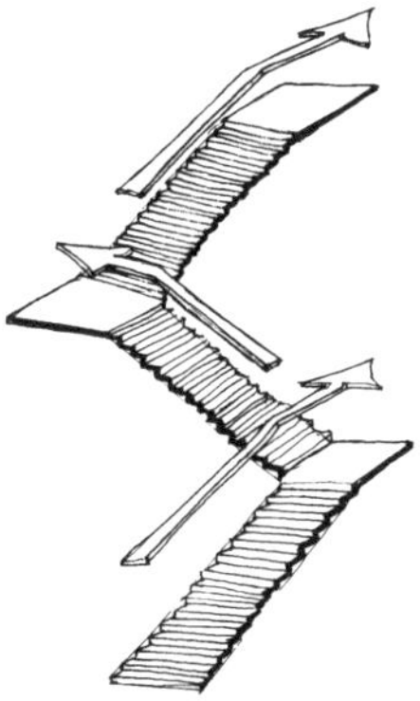

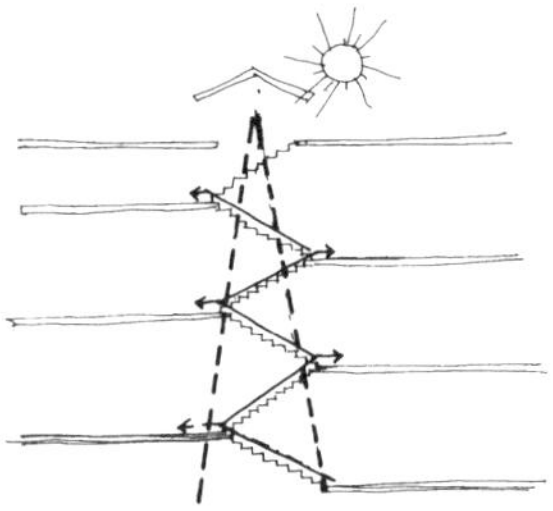

Staircase functioning as a shaft for ventilation

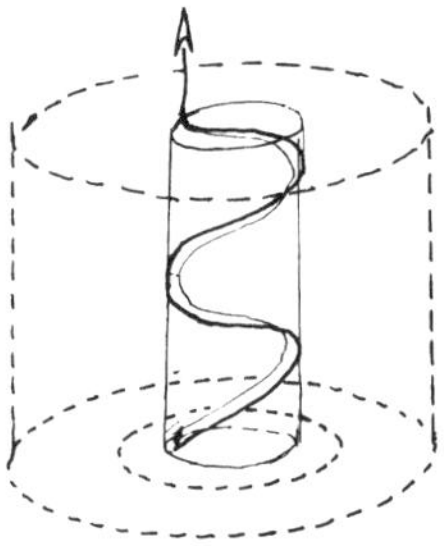

Staircase as a vertical shaft

- Being the key to movement, a stair should be in visual rapport from entrance. In a building, with different rooms upstairs it must be placed in a portion such that it forms a kind of axis that people can clearly and logically comprehend. Sucessive placement of stairs also define circulation within the floor space.

- Stair is perhaps the only node of a building, where a transition between levels occur naturally. Hence, the placement of the stair should be such that the stair is either made open to the room below it, or as embracing the room near the perimeter forming, a visually contiguous and socially connected space.

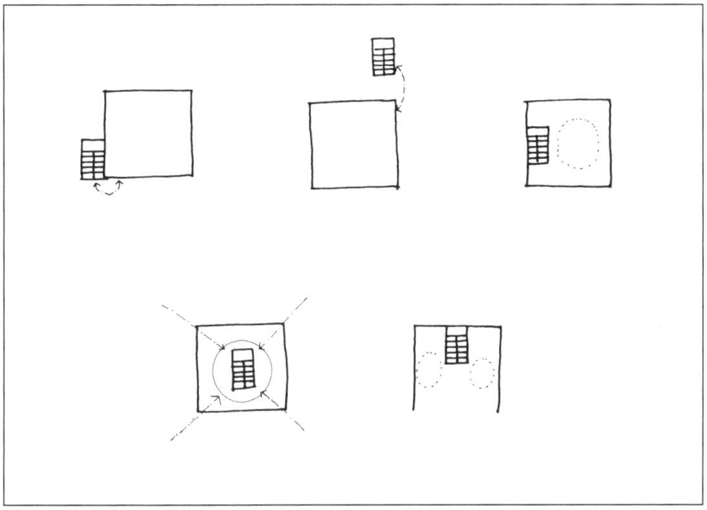

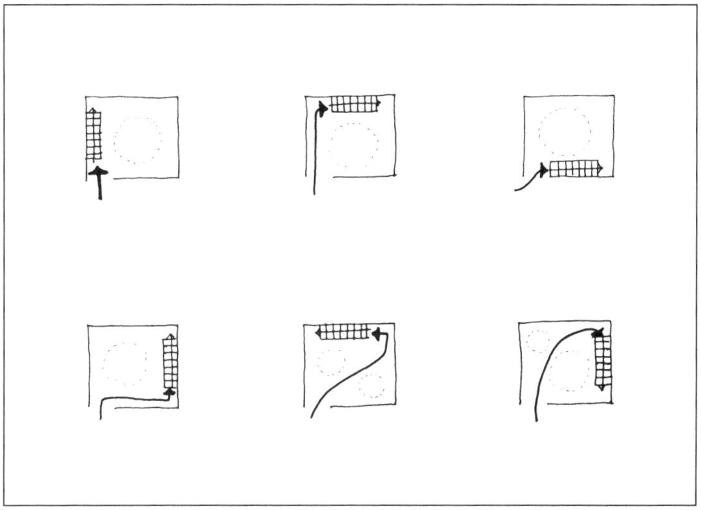

Stair being the node in a building

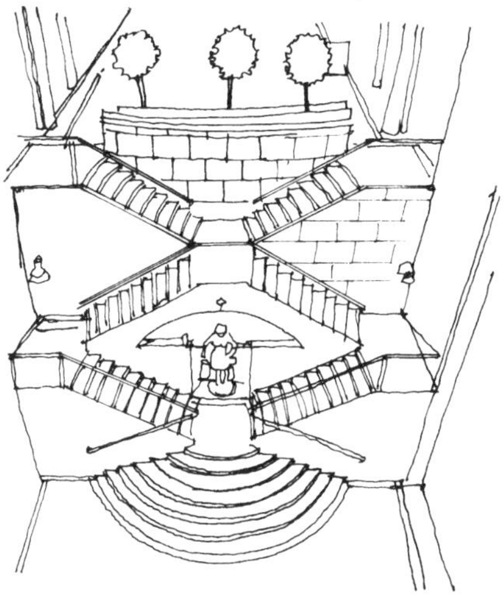

ROOF

Basically, the term roof signifies a shelter, denoting space and implying volume. The roof has been referred to as ceiling in Middle English terms such as *celynge/siling*, perhaps ultimately deriving its root from the Latin *caelum* as heaven or *celare* as hide. The term *hrof*, in old English or the Dutch *roef* mean cabin, coffin-lid or boat shed. The position of this element is such that it manifests as the first efforts to form a finite datum as enclosure, the first efforts to create a sky of one's own. Thus, the term has definite references to the sky or the envelope

Koothambalam (Theatre Hall) at Vadakkumnath Temple, Thrissur

Typological Variations

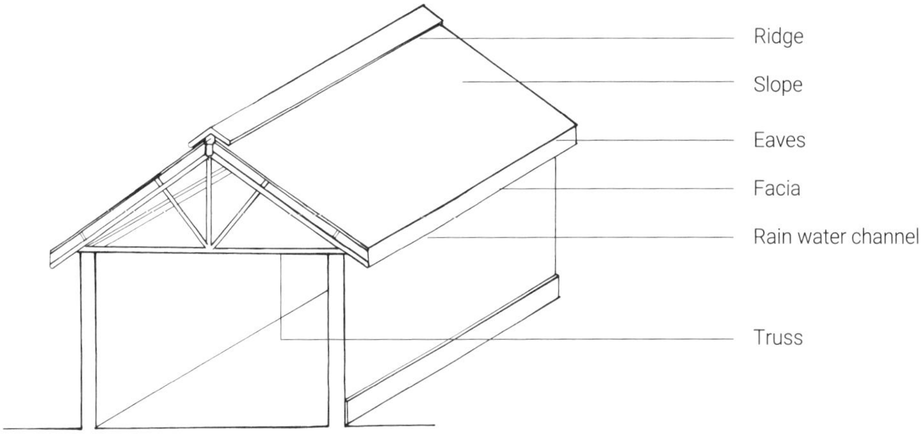

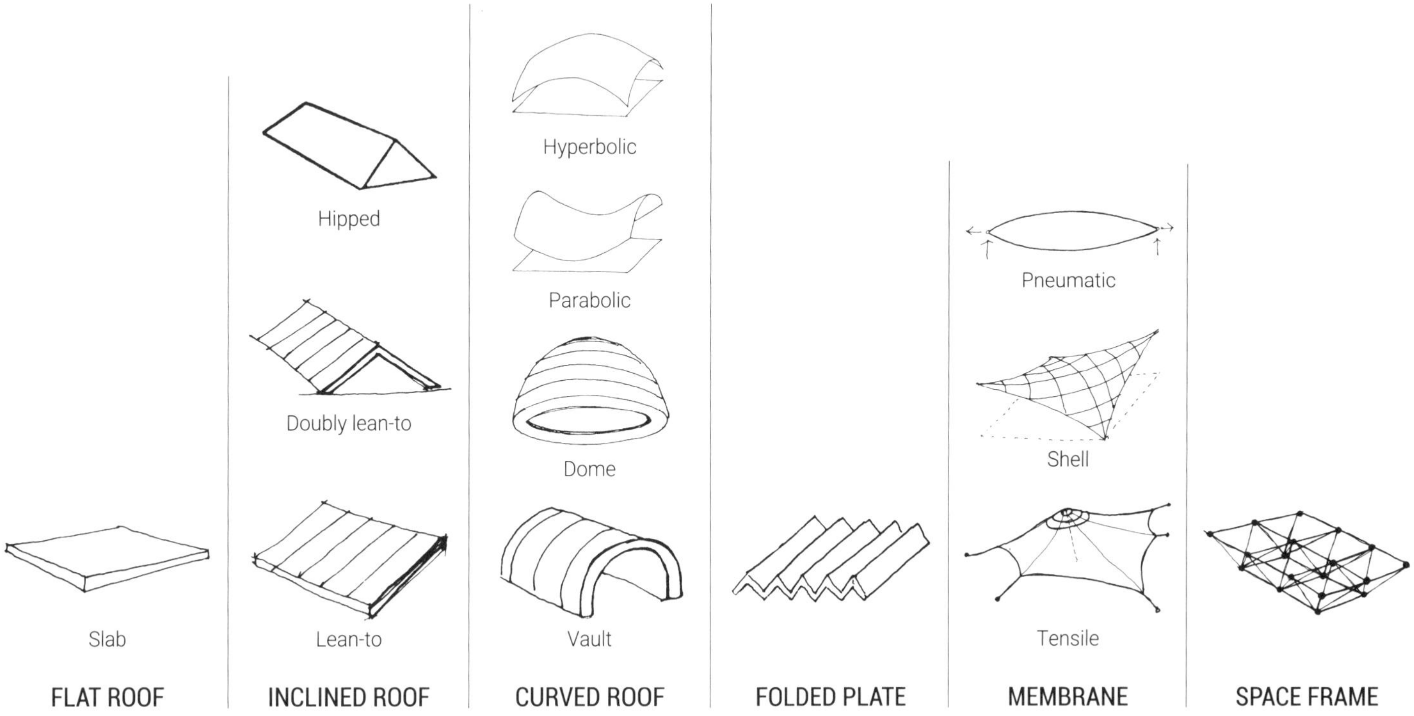

Since a time when the surface of the earth was thought to be a flat slab, resting on the back of giant tortoise and floating in a sea of water, the sky was looked upon as a finite solid canopy. Stars were fixed, and the sun and moon traversed across it. This unattainable celestial cloak started finding physical manifestation, as if in continuum, as the uppermost layer of structures built by and conceivable to man, as an intermediate plane between earth and sky. The human instinct to generate a simulacrum of the environment, rendered the soffit of the roof, with plastic treatment, inlaid with applied decoration or mosaic. Attributes given to the ceiling were not only directly representative of the heavenly but also wove in the legendary, mystic and symbolic.

Constructive attempts started primarily with the concern of protecting and preserving oneself from wild beasts, savages and the unknown wilderness as well as sheltering from the adverse conditions of climate and surrounding environment. Protection from attack and beasts manifested primarily as physical vertical barriers, while shelter from the elements of nature secured with the help of the overhead plane, the roof.

Depiction of sky as ceiling

Mausoleum of Galla Placidia, Italy

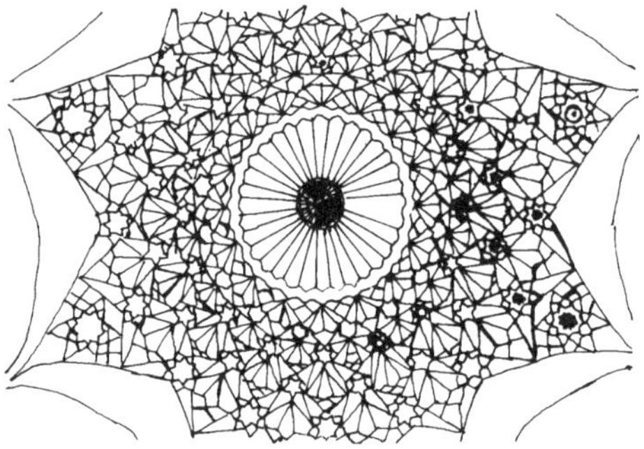

Tomb of Sultan Nithar Begum, Interior Dome Allahabad

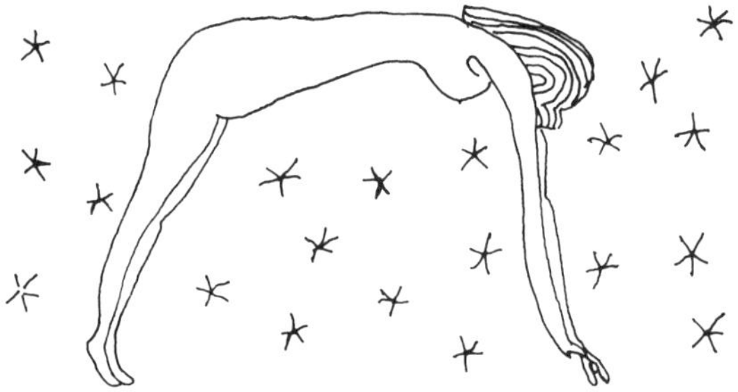

Goddess of sky depicted as enveloping the sky

Evolution of roof primarily concerned for protection against climate and surrounding evironment

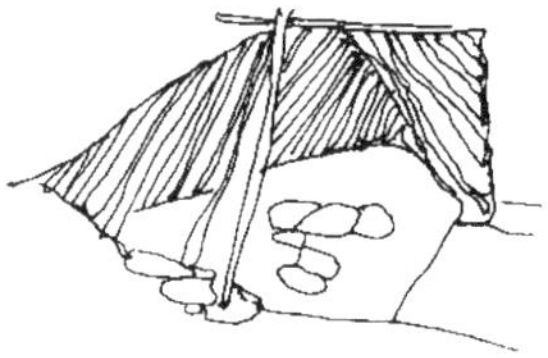

Lepenski Vir house, Serbia

Communal dwelling of Makiritare people, Venezuela

Kyrgyz Yurt

A lavvu (traditional tent) of the Sami people

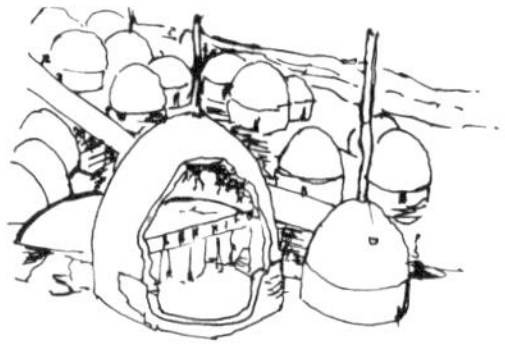

Khirokitia, Cyprus

Barabaig Gheid, Tanzania

Evolution of roof in terms of spanning capabilities and embellishments

The Nave, Southwell Minster

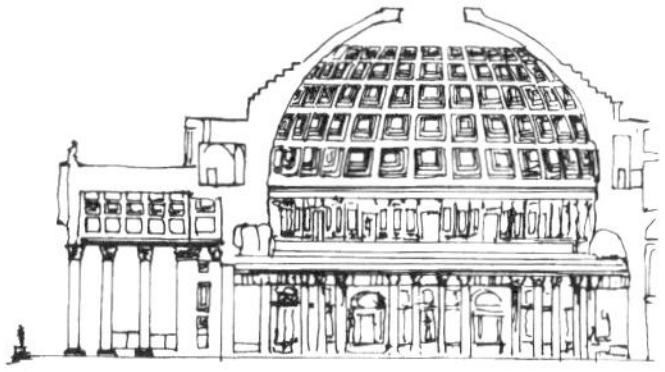

The Pantheon, Rome

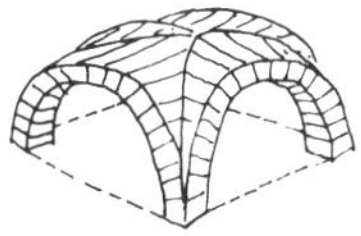

Crossed or Groin Vault

Hagia Sophia Museum, Istanbul

King's College, Cambridge

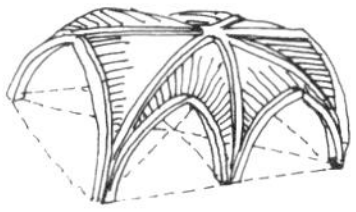

Ribbed Vault

Evolution of roof with change in material and technology

Chapel of Notre Dame du Haut, Ronchamp

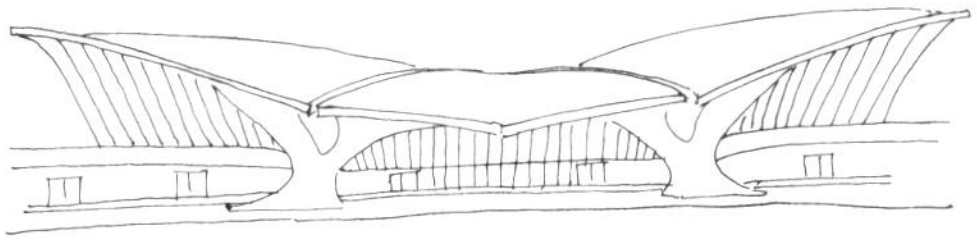

Kennedy Airport, New York

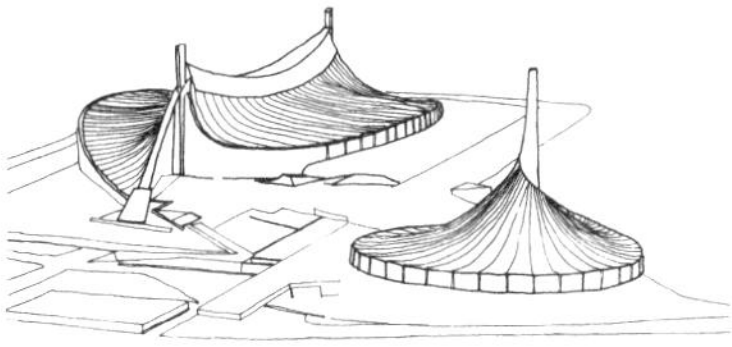

Sports Complex, Tokyo

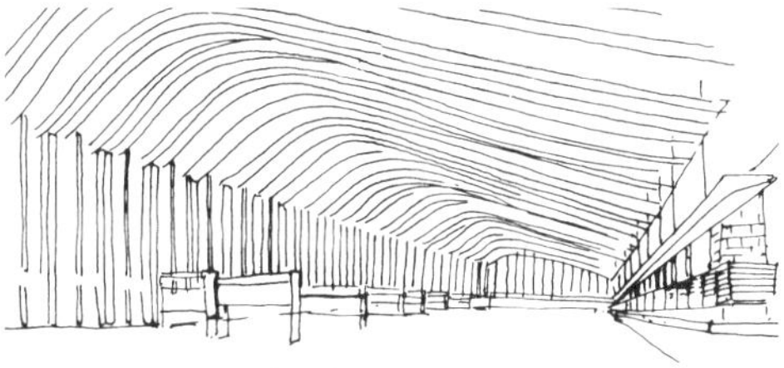

Central Railway Station, Rome

Material properties and climate conditions have determined to an extent the roof form itself. Spanning techniques, through developments overcoming the restraints, have determined, primarily, the evolution of the roof form. Early examples show the roof conceived as a solid mass, necessarily held up by a supporting system, exerting dead weight vertically downwards. Spanning capability through corbels and lintels, where gravity and material property were main considerations, was focussed upon. Later, the same material was used, but more efficiently, in arches, vaults and domes. This change in technique is also seen in the translation of large wooden beams to trusses consisting of wooden elements of smaller sections but capable of spanning greater distances. The roof thus transformed from a weighted overhead mass to a thinner plane. The form of the roof, hence, emerged as a representation of the method of its construction. With a change in material, technology guided the expression of the roof—from steel truss to shell, space frame, geodesic dome, tensile and structures pneumetic with no intermedia to support required even for the covering of stadium.

CHURCHES AND MOSQUES

Development of the roof—especially seen in the sacred and public buildings, started primarily as a pragmatic approach of negotiating material, span and to facilitate the collective nature of space.

These roof forms, with an overlay of meanings and notions, transcended from being mere physical forms to becoming icons in themselves, identifying the typology of the building by their appearance.

The evolution of church form shows an attempt at lightening the support members, bringing in natural light and increasing the open spans in space. The evolution of domes in mosques is also a gradual transition from the corbelled structure in compression to omnifarious surface structures in tension.

Churches

Onion Roof, Resurrection Church, Kostroma, Russia

Bascilica of San Michele, Maggiore, Pavia

Milan Cathedral, Milan

The Cathedral of Toledo, Spain

Cathedral of St. Maria del Fiore, Florence

Mosques

Taj Mahal, Agra

Selim Pye Mosque Selimiye, Edirne, Turkey

Gol Gumbaj, Bijapur

Mihrimah Mosque, Istanbul

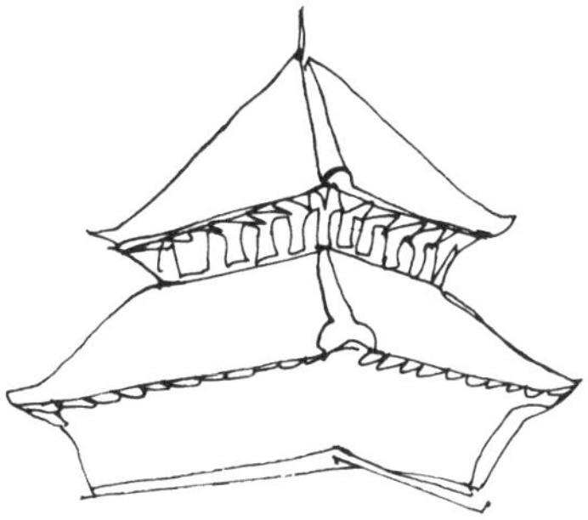

Malabar, Northern Kerala

Pattadakal, Karnataka

Bhuvaneshwar, Orissa

Jain Temple, Deogarh, Uttar Pradesh

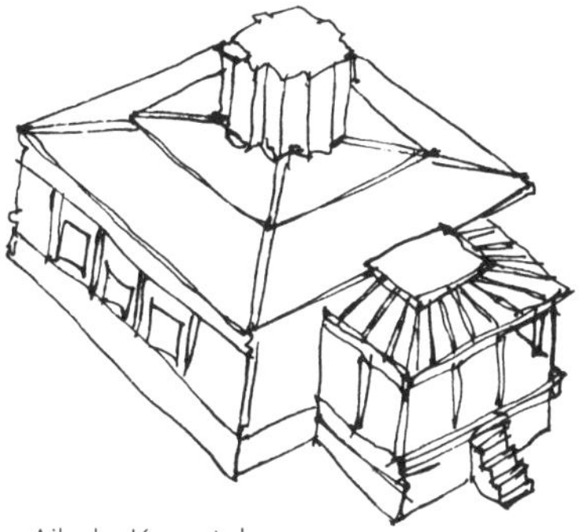

Lad Khan, Aihole, Karnataka

TEMPLES

In the subcontinent also, just as in classical Europe, the association of the roof to the sky was evident. Not only did the external envelope of the roof allude to the sky with allegories, inscriptions and embellishments but so did the ceilings, animating and annotating the experience through allusions and celestial/mythological anecdotes. The mode of communication embodied the paradoxical unity, mutual cross-references and inherent dualities of Indian philosophy.

Variation of roof form in Indian temples

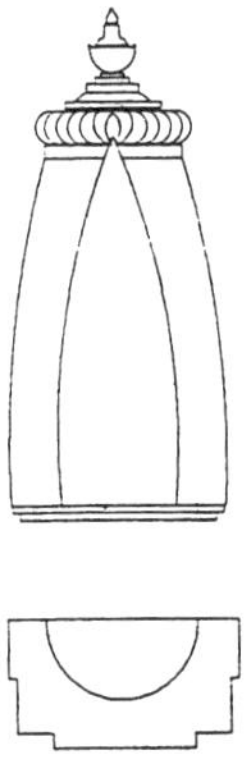

Shrivatsa

Shringa

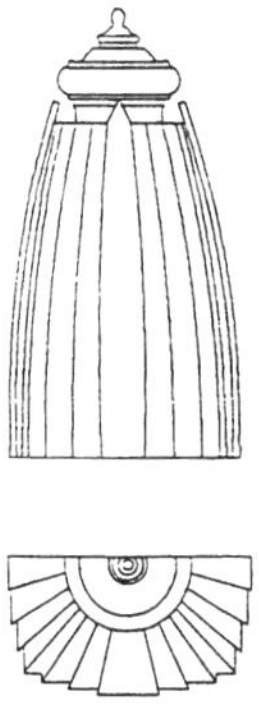

Mahabalipuram

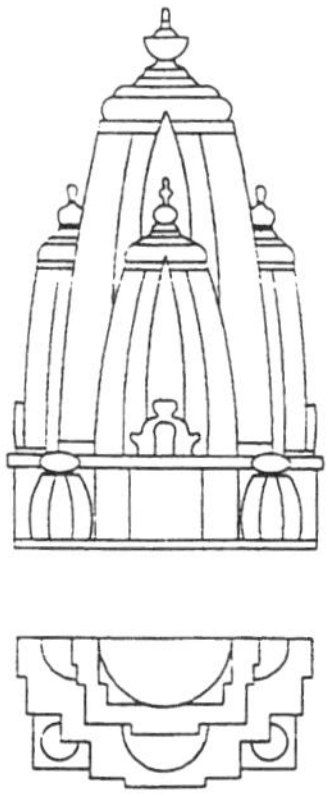

Sarvatobhadra

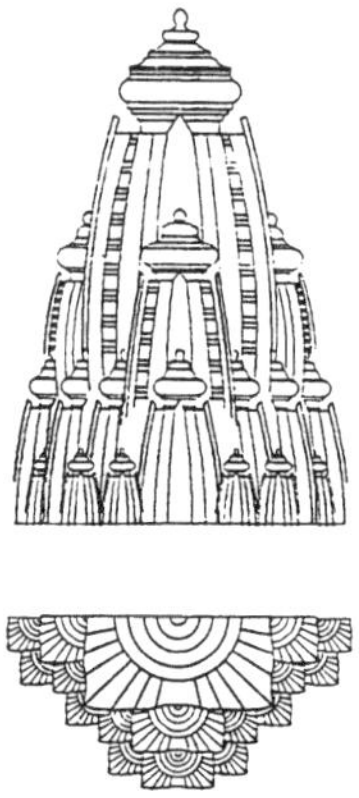

Parshwanatha

Kandariya Mahadev

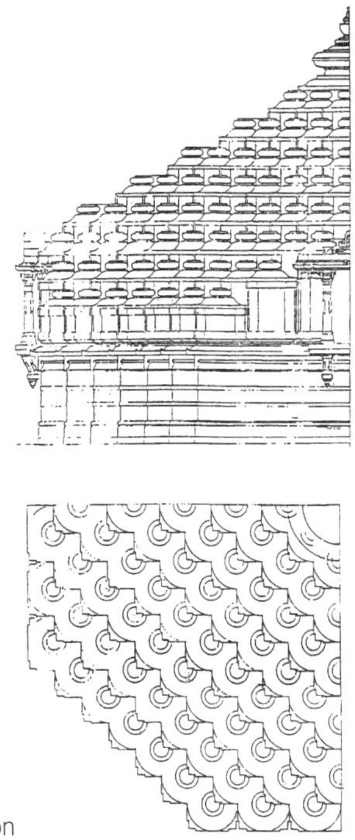

Elevation

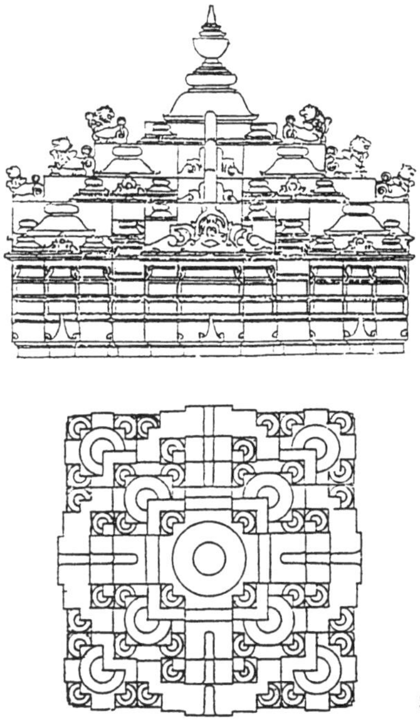

Samvarana Mandapa

OVERHEAD PLANE

The most fundamental notion associated to an overhead plane is as a shelter, denoted as roof. The aspects of planarity hovering, sheltering and enclosing are built into it. An umbrella or the *shamiyana* are, thus, the most basic manifestations that signify shelter and space.

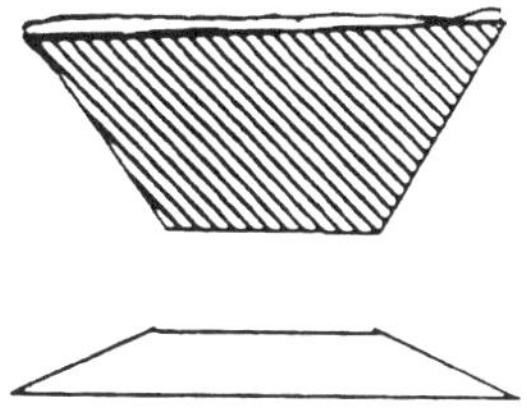

Overhead Plan

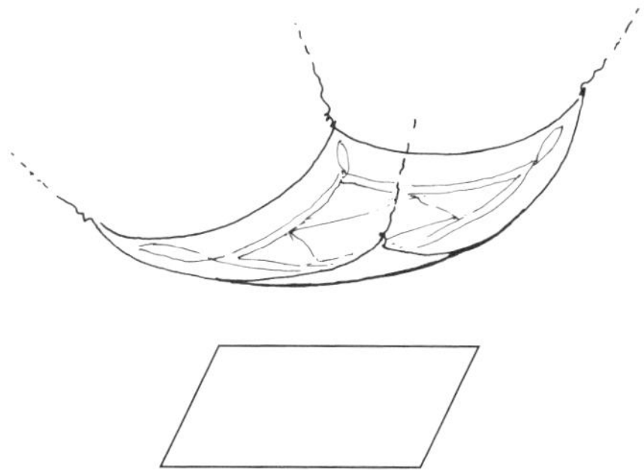

Shamiyana

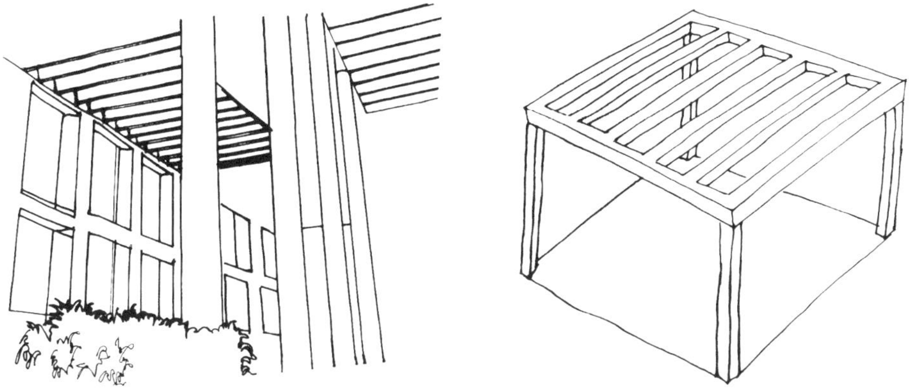

Pargola Roof, Indian Institute of Management, Bangalore

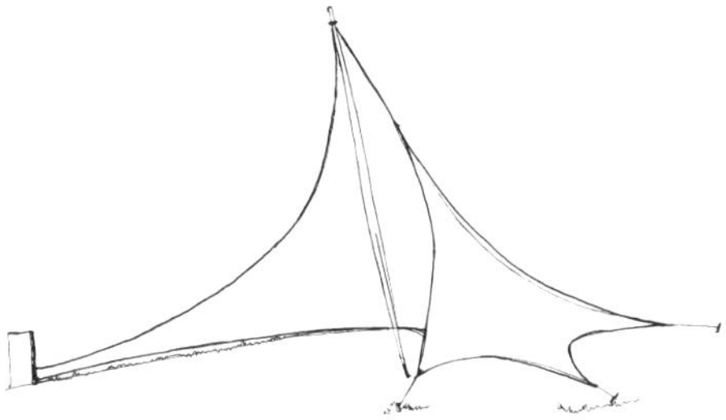

Shelter Pavilion, Cologne

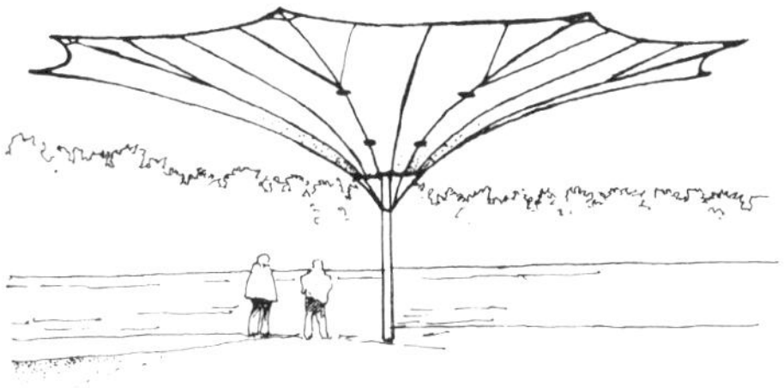

Umbrella Roof, Cologne

Retractable roof,
Open Air Theater Roof, Bad Hersfeld

SHELTER

The primary necessity of the enclosure has been to provide shelter and safety to man. This takes on defensive and protective connotations—defence against attack from beasts and rivals, shelter against the elements of nature. The early caves provided both. But with built architecture, the role as the defending agent against attacks was transferred to the walls (the vertical planes), while the roof (the horizontal overhead plane) took on the responsibility of providing shelter from sun, rain, snow etc. The necessity of shelter being both physical and psychological, the roof demarcates between the outdoors and the sheltered space by physically intervening, and also provides the reassurance of having a cover overhead for protection, giving rise to the perception of private, protected spaces as opposed to public open spaces.

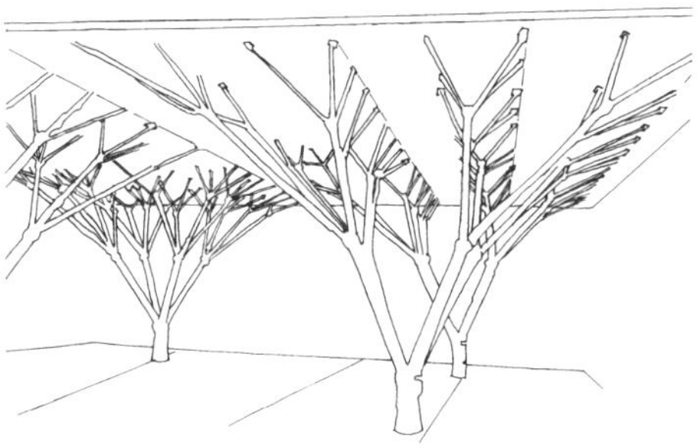

Tree canopy as shelter

Canopy

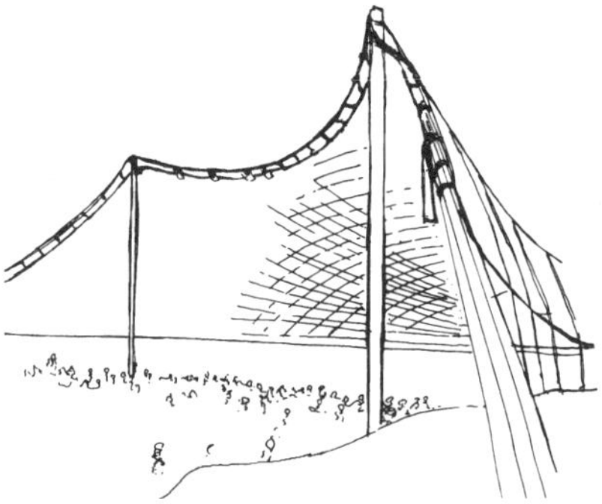

Sidney Meyer Music Bowl, Melbourne

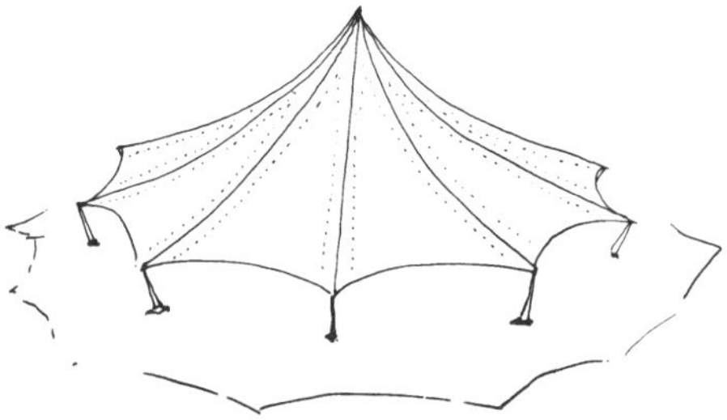

Circus Tent

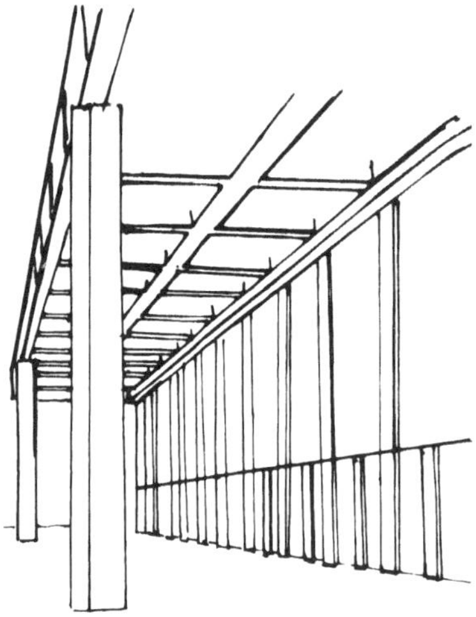

IIM, Bangalore

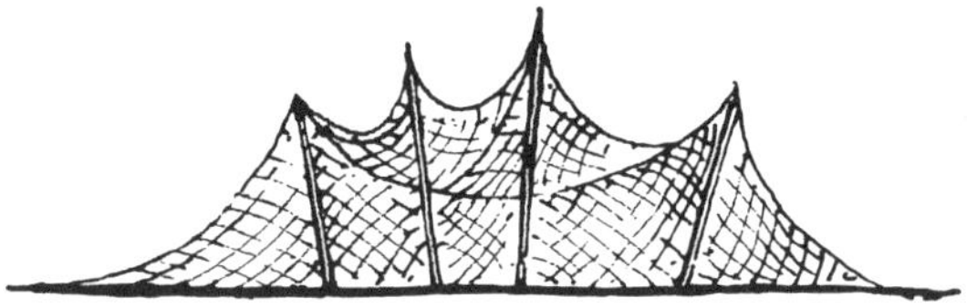

German Pavilion, Montreal

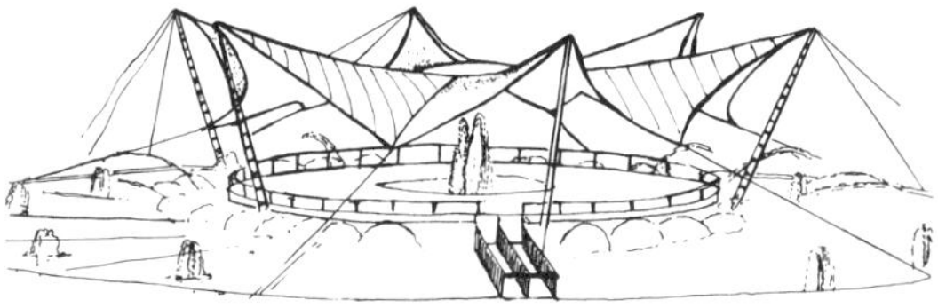

Dance Pavilion, Cologne

ROOF AS SPATIAL ENCLOSURE

The roof, canopy ceiling provides an enclosing surface, which defines and limits interior space especially and demarcates between the notions of 'in' and 'out'. The planar co-ordinates indicate the expanse and stretch of the enclosure while its relative position in space, especially its height, indicates volume. The sense of containment is often complete with just a roof device overhead.

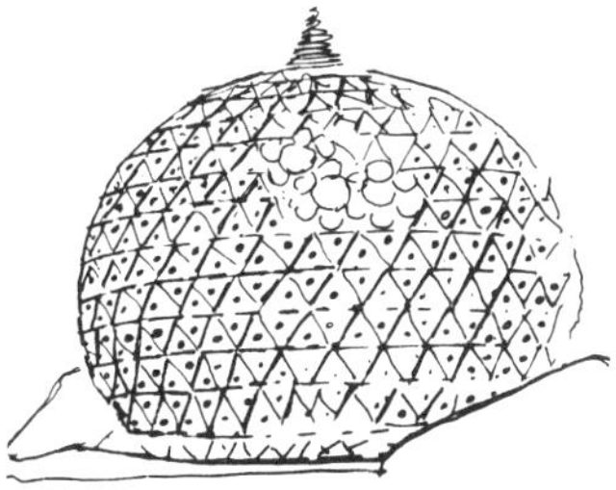
Matri Mandir, Auroville

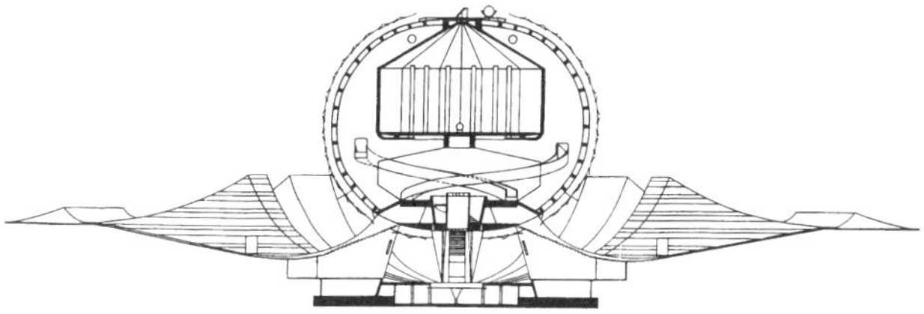
Section, Matri Mandir, Auroville

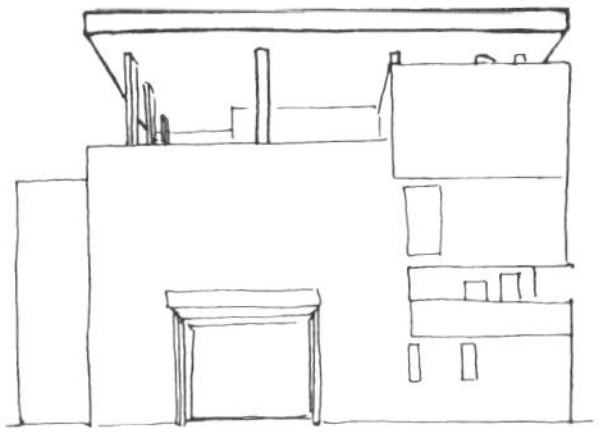
Shodhan House, Ahmedabad

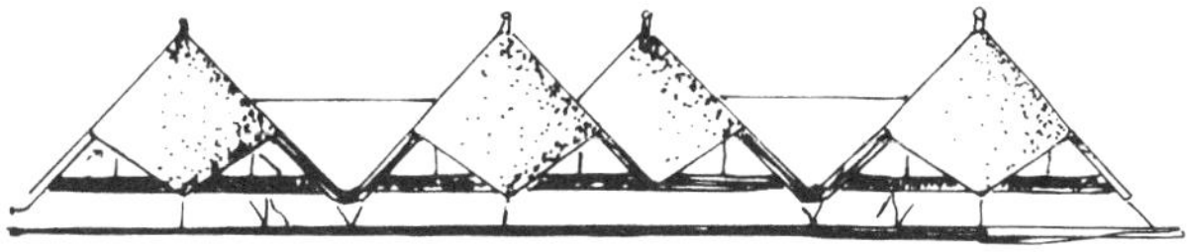
Aspiration huts, Auroville

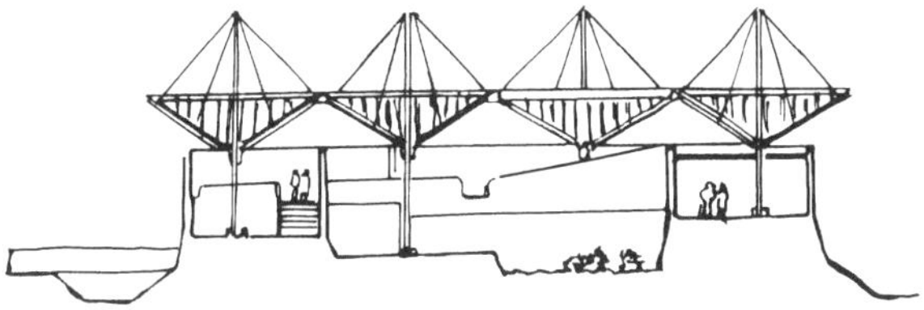
Handloom Pavilion, New Delhi

Sri Venkateshwara University Auditorium, Tirupati

Amdavad ni Gufa, Ahmedabad

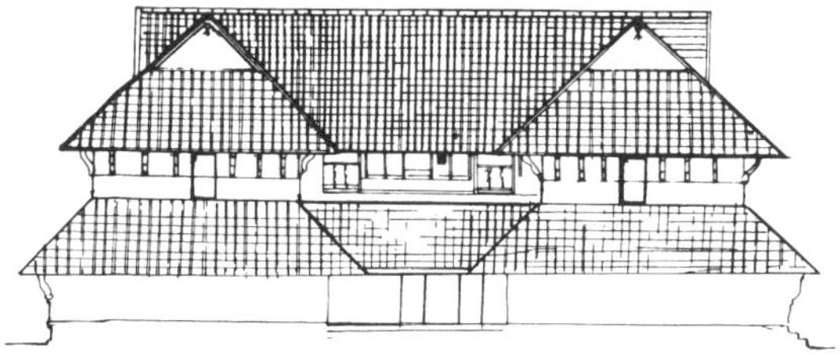
Padmanabhapuram Palace, Thiruvananthapuram

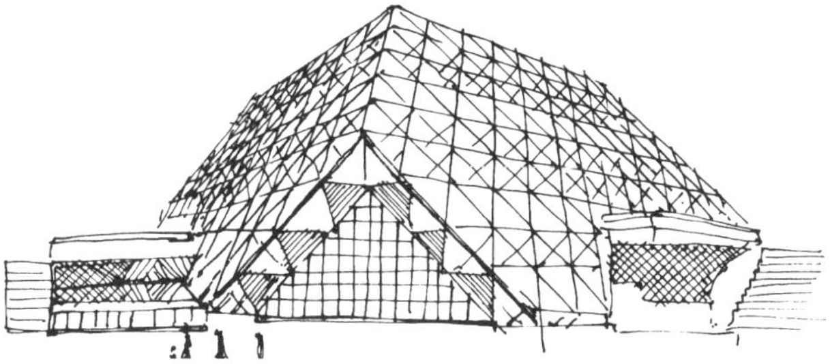
Exhibition Pavilion, New Delhi

ROOF AS MODULATOR OF VOLUME

The plastic qualities of the roof form determines the three-dimensional habitable volume contained below. Modulation of this roof profile and height affords possibility of getting a diversity of such trapped volumes both in size and shapes, which induce scale and character to the space. Modulations in the ceiling volume also help generate subspaces within a larger contiguous space.

Roof trapping the habitable volume within........

Beehive, Northern Syria

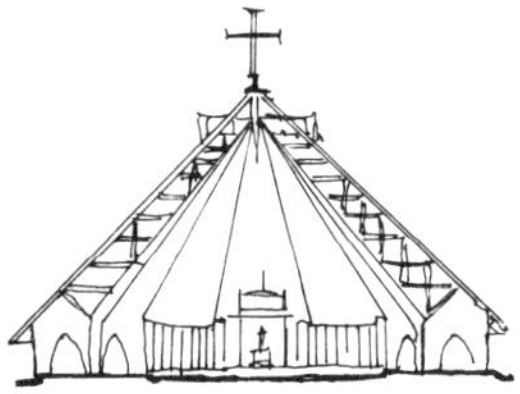

St. John's Cathedral, Thiruvalla

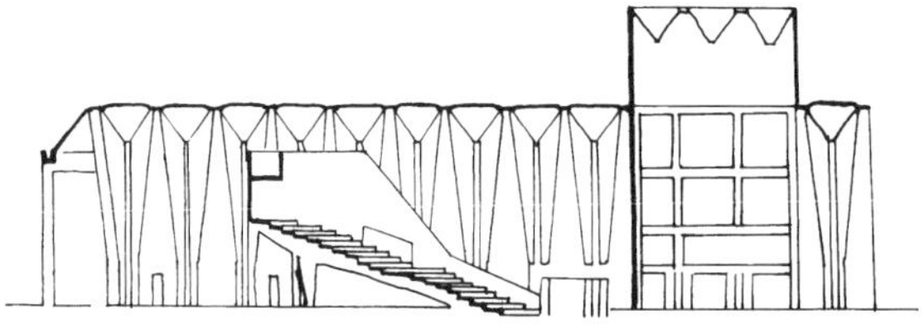

Tagore Hall, Ahmedabad

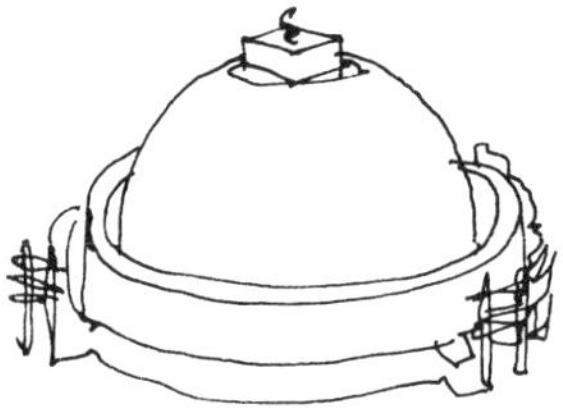

Stupa, Sanchi

Kandariya Mahadev temple, Khajuraho

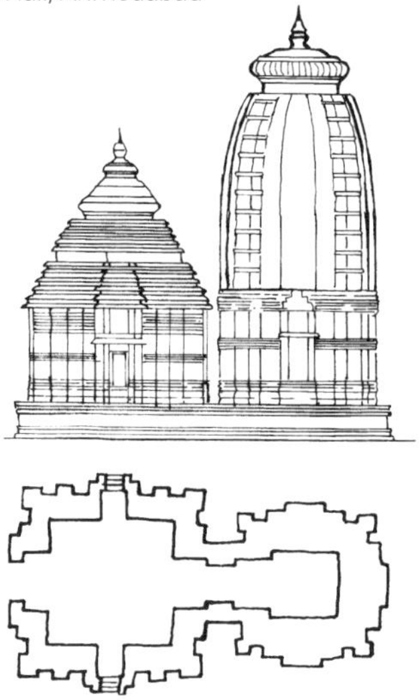

Lingraj Temple, Nagara style of architecture

Ibrahim Rauza, Bijapur

Roof-ceiling volume creating subspaces within........

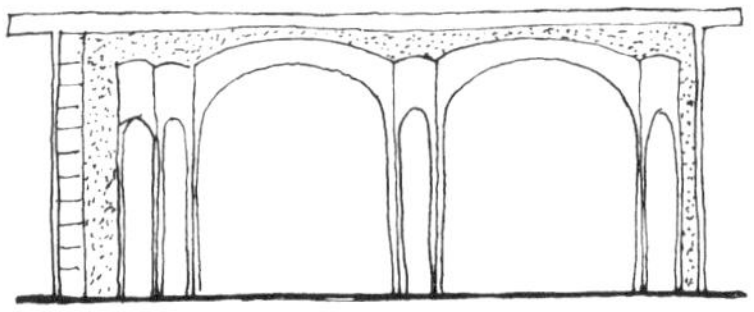

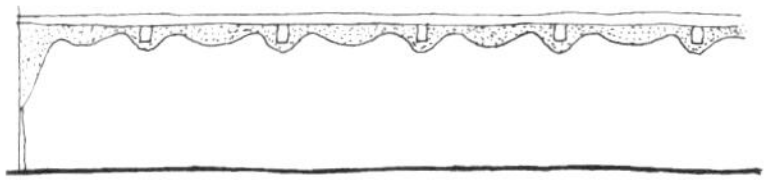

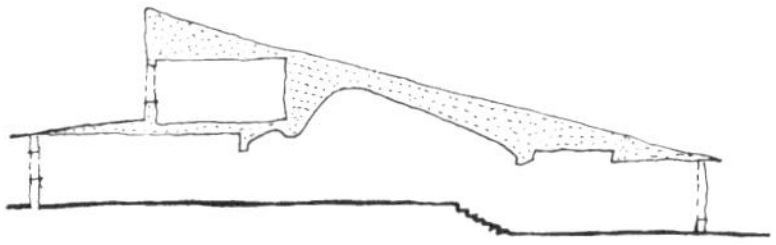

ROOF AS ENCODER OF SYMBOLS

Being detached from the ground (living zone) and notionally unreachable, inaccessible and nearer to the sky, the roof from within and without takes on connotations and treatments as befitting a celestial and fantastic realm, of an intangible metaphysical nature. It encodes myths, legends and mystique. It becomes a receptacle for symbolisation and plastic decorations representing divine activity and metaphorical expression. In addition to the outer form, the relief, stucco, frescoes, mosaics and other decorations as well as artistic statements find place on the roof as well as ceiling. This elevates the perception of the roof from the physical to another dimension of semiotics.

Roof (External form)

Sydney Opera House, Sydney symbolising sails

Bahai Temple, Delhi
symbolising lotus flower

Shikhara, Angkorvat manifests as faces

Pilgrimage Chapel, Ronchamp
symbolising a bird in flight

Kandariya Mahadev temple, Khajuraho,
symbolising mountain

Ceiling (Internal form)

Tejpal Temple, Mt. Abu. The celestial world

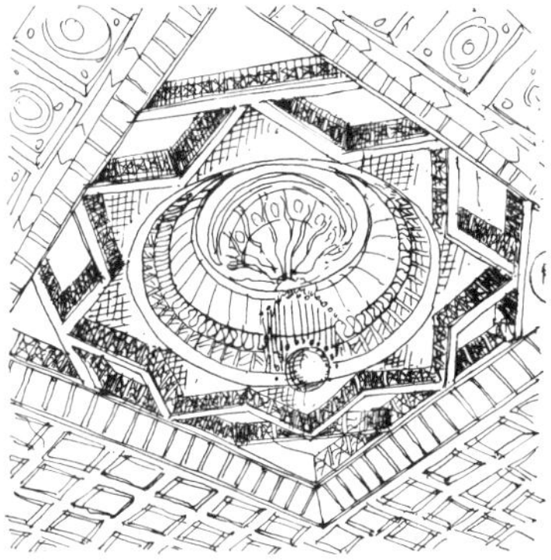

Hall of the Tai Heidan, Beijing.
The elements of sky

ROOF AS IMAGE MAKER

The roof being the topmost part of the edifice, forms the crown, the most conspicuous elements in the skyline of a city and easily recognisable from a far. The outer form of the roof therefore begins to lend the structure its identity, creating a distinct image. The outer form as well as its height and proportions therefore become critical and if pronounced, make its registration apt and from far distances.

Image of building type...

Anant Vasudev Temple, Bansberia

Keshta Raya Temple, Bishnupur

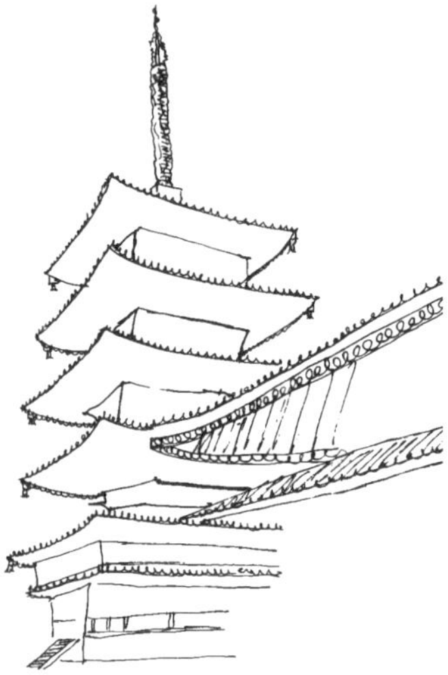

Pagoda, China

Mahabodhi Temple, Bodh Gaya

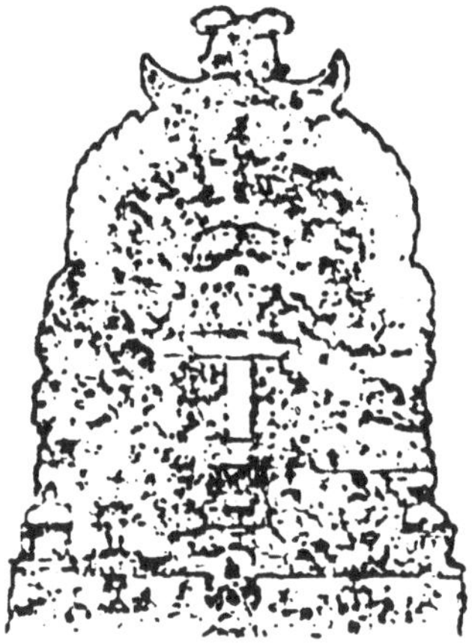

Gopuram, Madurai

Image of climatic condition

Pitched roof, warm humid climate

Mansard roof, cool temperate climate

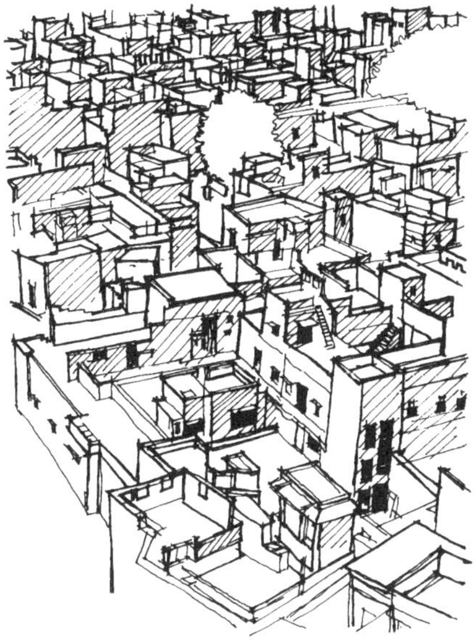

Terraces, hot dry climate

Inuit igloo, Russian tundra extrem cold climate

Image of place

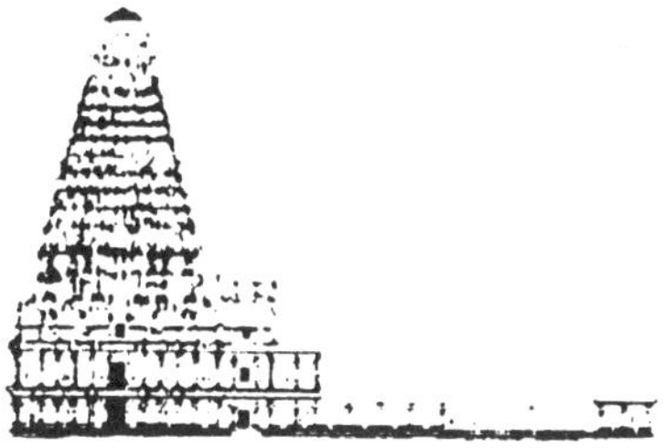

Brihadeeswara Temple, Thanjavur

Taj Mahal, Agra

St. Andrew's Church, Chennai

Amdavad ni Gufa, Ahmedabad

BAHAI TEMPLE, NEW DELHI

The Bahai House of Worship was built in 1980-86, by architect Fariburg Sahba in New Delhi .

The building complex comprises a ground structure, as a large covered hall for assembly, in the form of a lotus. Seen from outside, the lotus flower is made up of three orders of petals. The form of lotus flower is conceived and interpreted, using definite geometric solids, such as cylinders, spheres, toruses or cones. The two orders of petals called the 'entrance leaves' and 'outer leaves', the inside and outside, generate lines of thin walled elements. The lotus flower petals are finished in white to create a dazzling outline.

Roof as an imagemaker..

The aerial view

Lotus flower—the basic conception for the structure

Roof as an imagemaker...

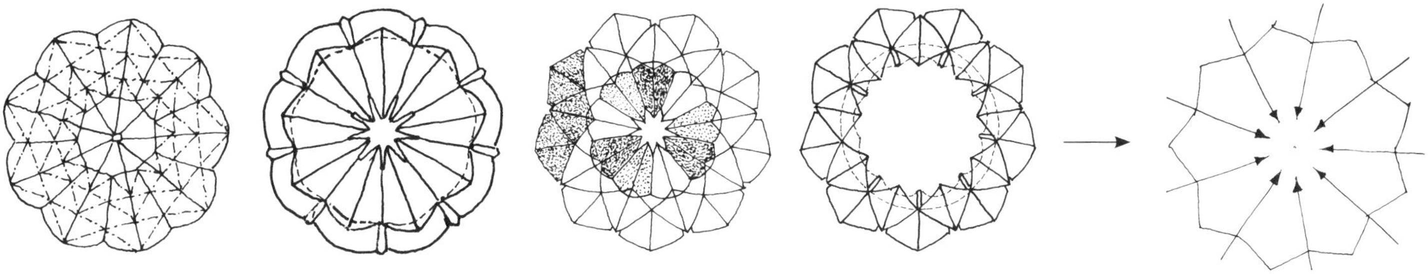

The structural system representing the structure of a lotus

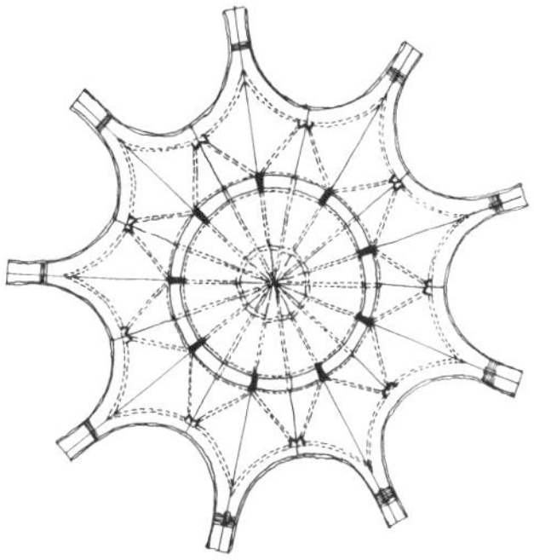

Ground plan inspired from the metaphors of petals

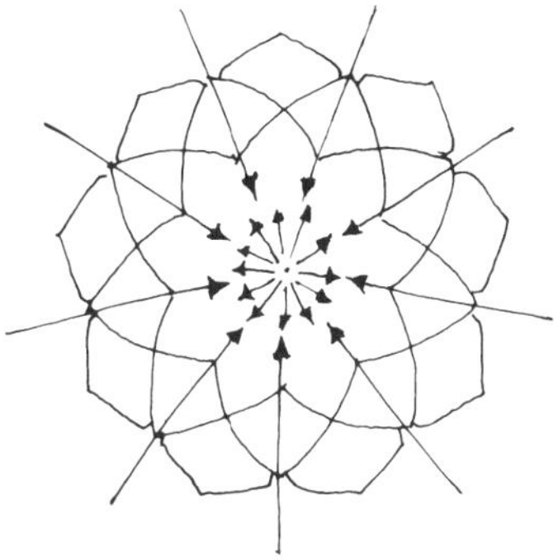

Organizer of space by the virtue of centrality and omnidirectionality

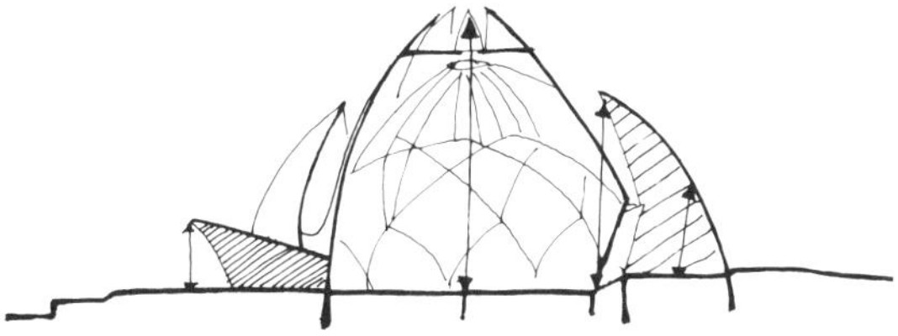

The form, with its apex, defines and elucidates the verticality, symbolizing the movement towards the heavenly form the mundane

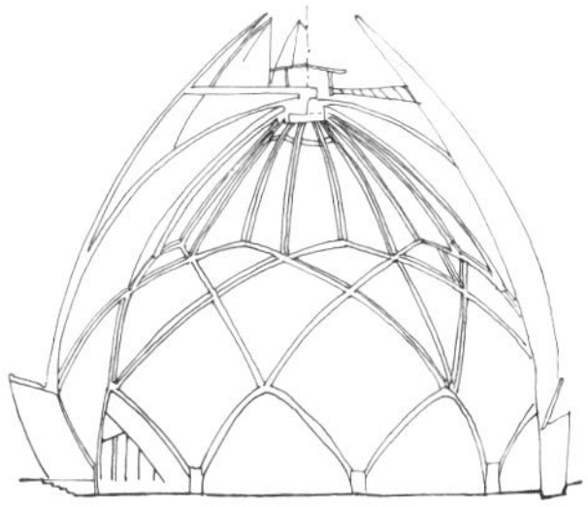

The modulations creates diversity of scales, enhancing the human existence in the infinite

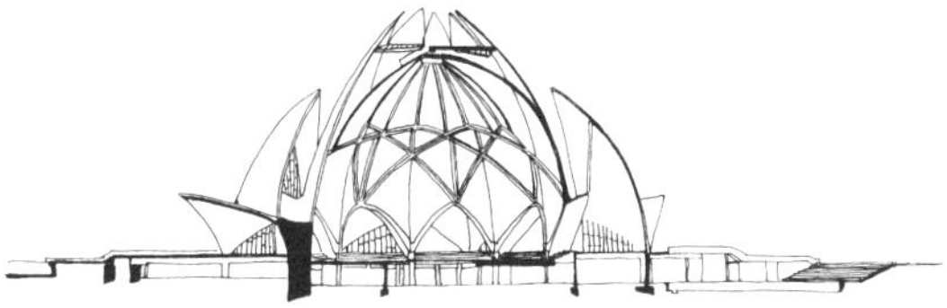

The structural propensity of the built-form creates a transcendental experience inside the space

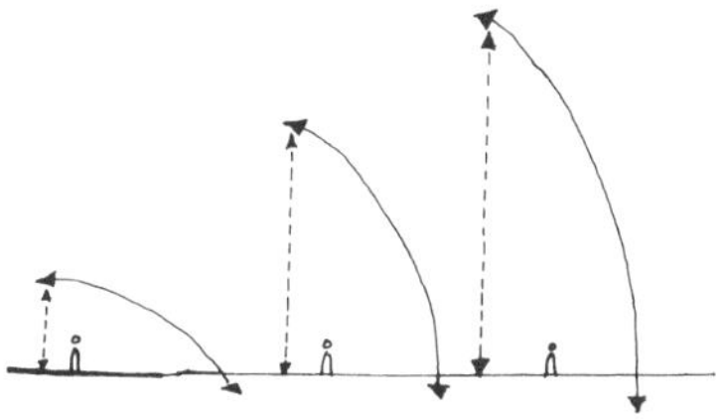

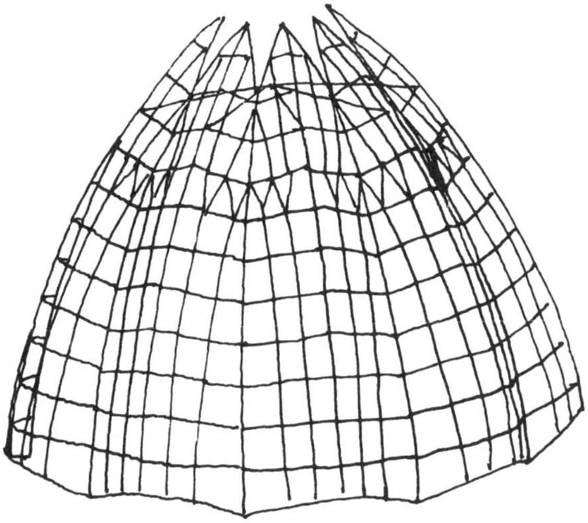

Roof behaves as an element enclosing
as well as enhancing the volume within

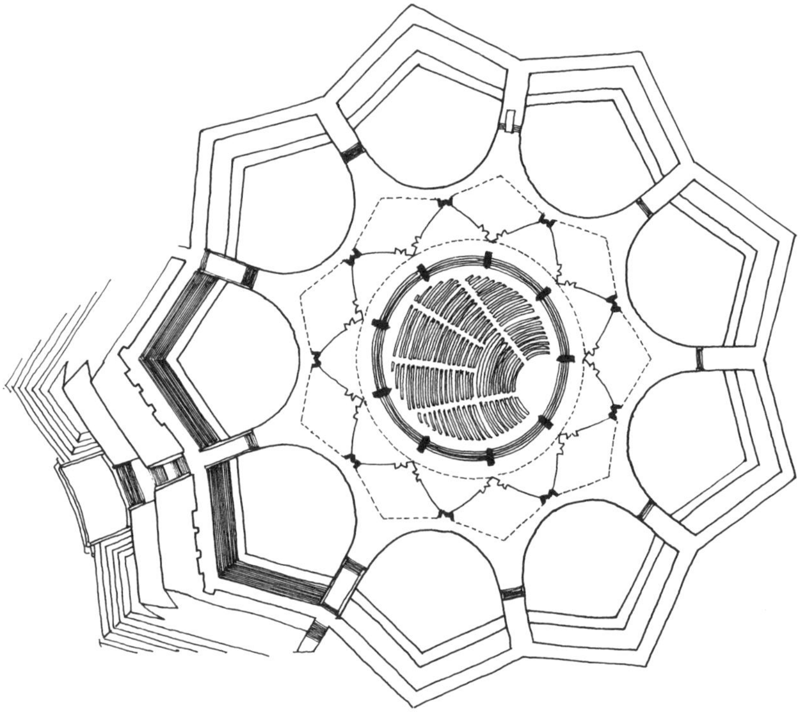

Roof as an element sheltering multiple activities inside its expanse and volume

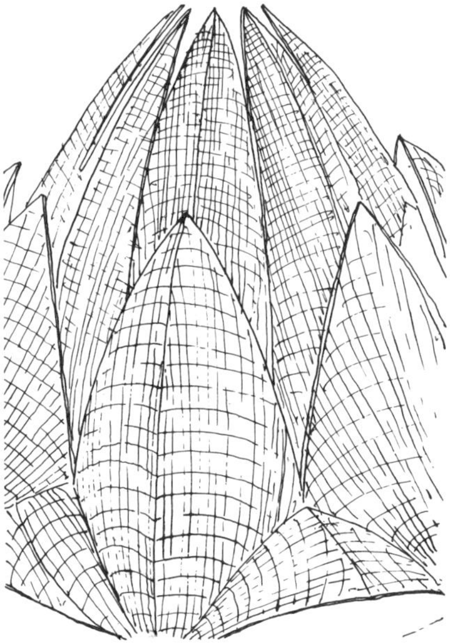

The formal languge becomes a juxtaposition
of metaphors and spaces

Roof as a device attributing light and ventilation to the enclosed space

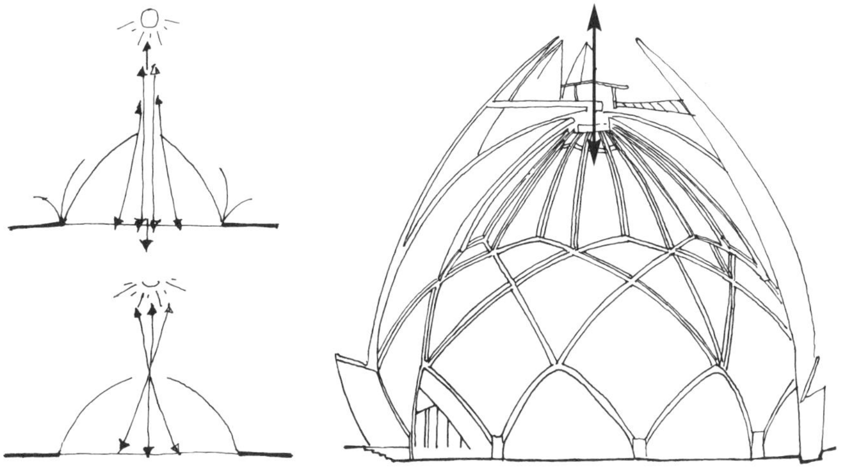

Section-apeture for light and ventilation

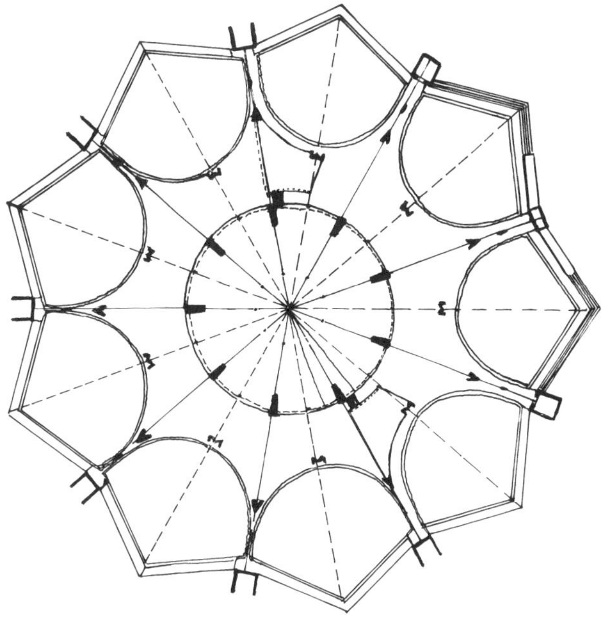

Reflected celling plan

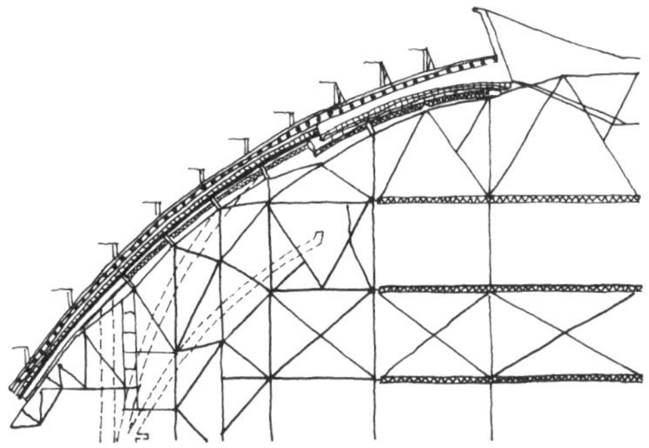

Structural modification for penetration for light and ventilation

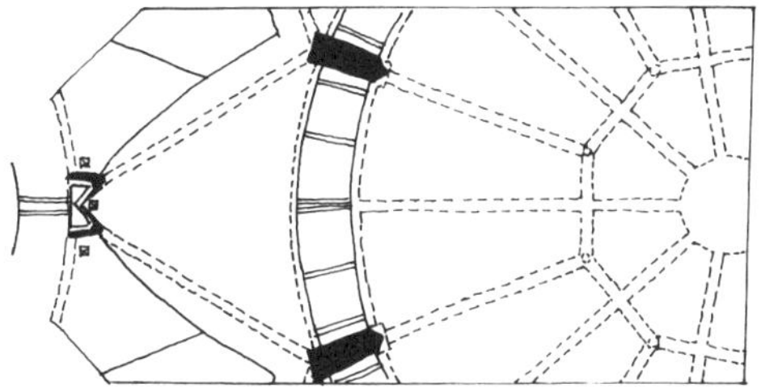

Plan detail of the roof structure

ASSEMBLY BUILDING, CHANDIGARH

The Assembly Building was built in 1953-54 by architect Le Corbusier in Chandigarh.

The main assembly hall within this building is enclosed within a hyperbolic shell, inspired from the form of industrial cooling towers. The top of this shell is terminated in an oblique section, which receives a metallic framework. This works in multiplicity for the interplay of natural light, artificial light, ventilation and acoustics. Other sculptural embellishments on the roof manifest various impressions of the architect to created interesting silhouettes.

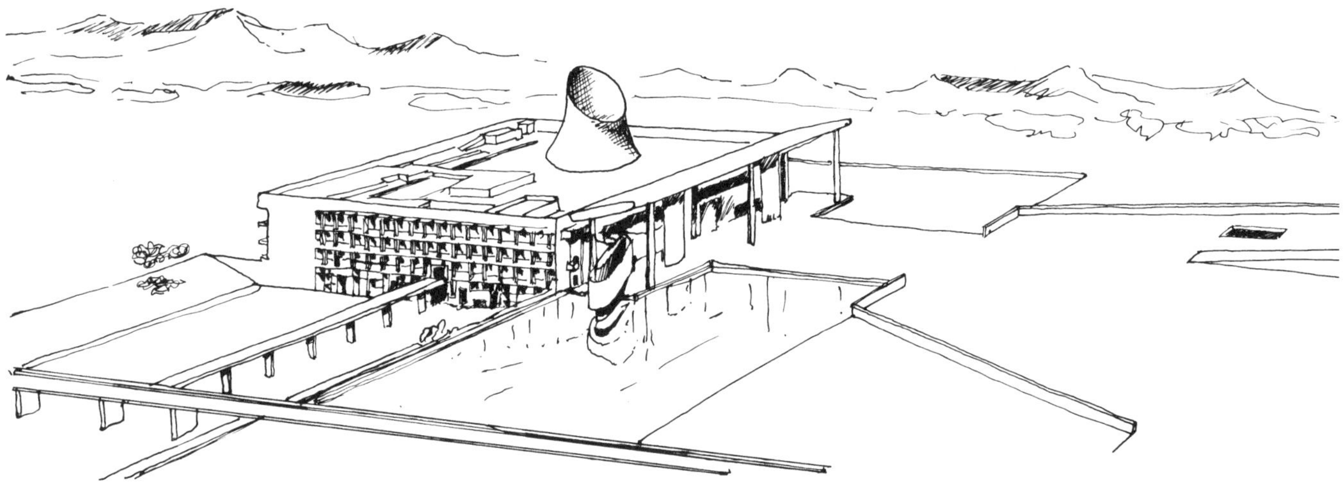

Roof as spatial enclosure

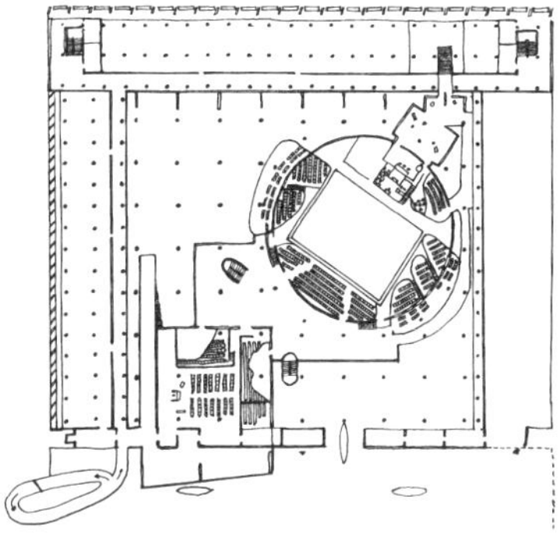

Plan

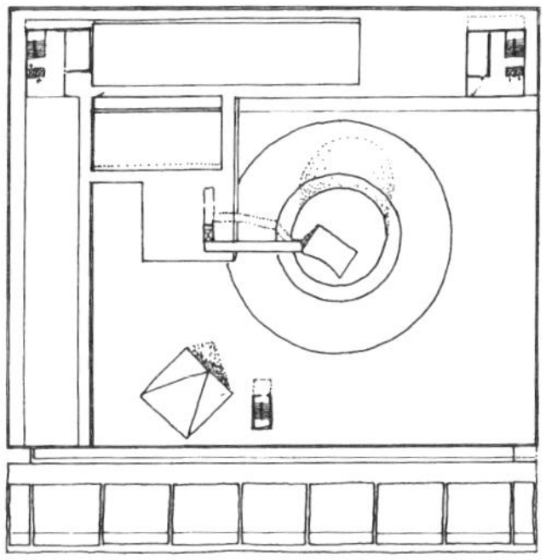

Trapping the volume inside

Roof as an imagemaker

Image of the roof inspired from the structure of the cooling towers of the power-houses

Image of cooling towers by the architect Le-Corbusier

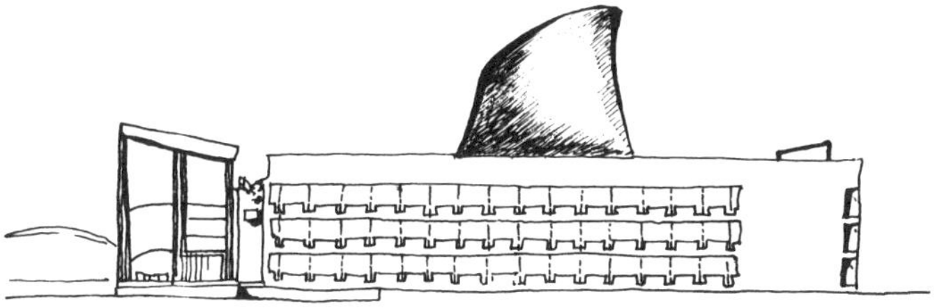

Roof as a modulator of volume

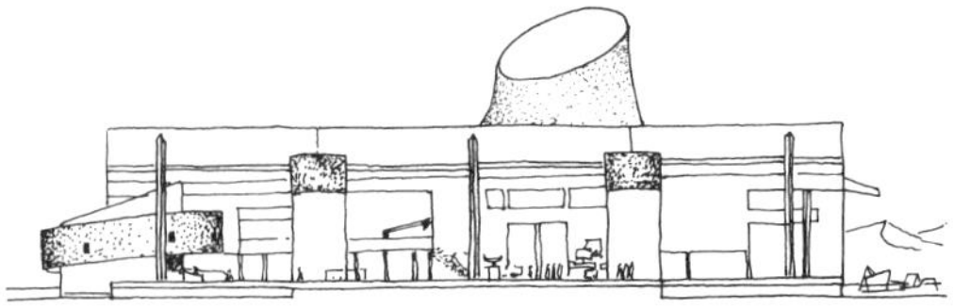

The mass of the roof attributes a strong sense of individuality to the overall scheme of the built-form

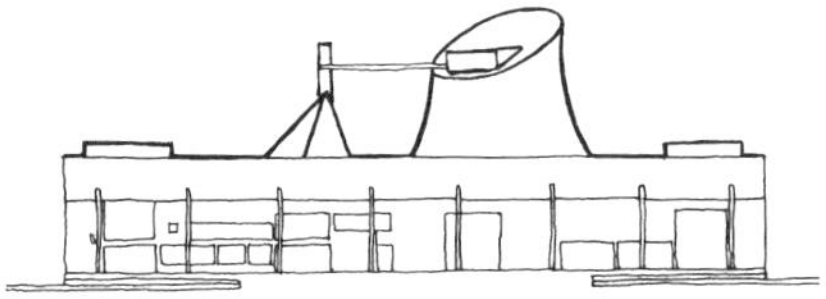

Façade with the roofline giving identity of the structure

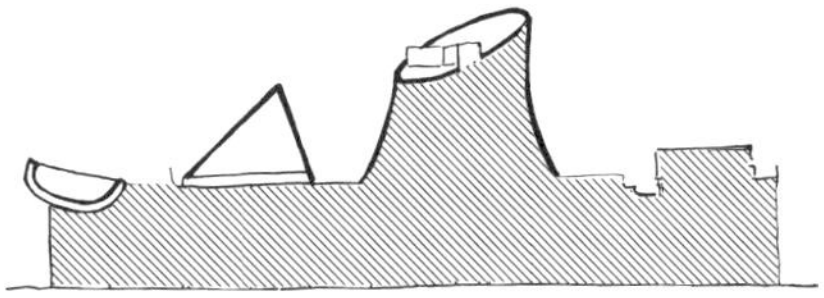

Roof with its plastic form manipulating the space within

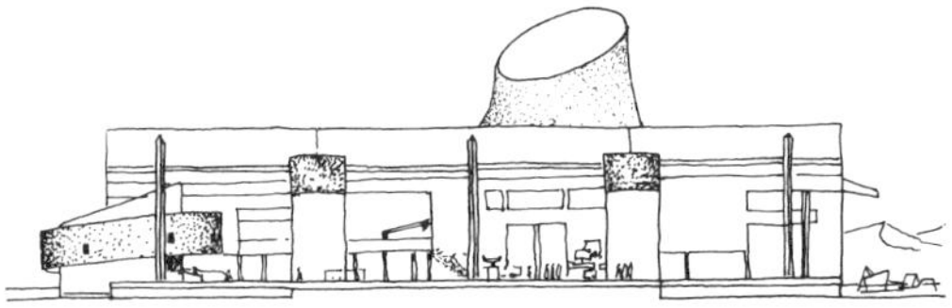

The external facade and the extended roofline shelters various scale of activities

With diverse modulations of volume, building retains its formal language

Roof scaling the defined space

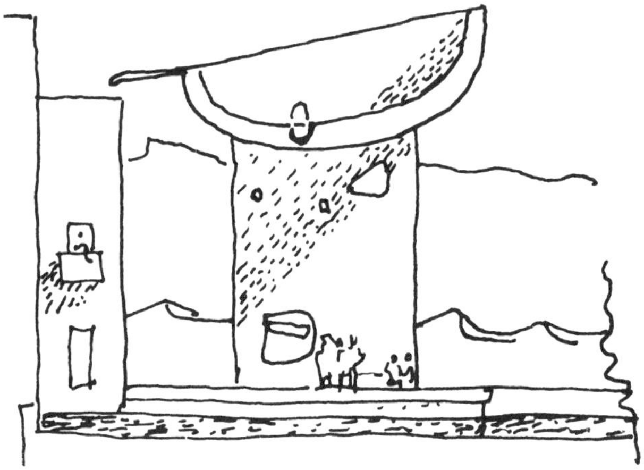

Roof as an element giving shelter and protection as a canopy overhead

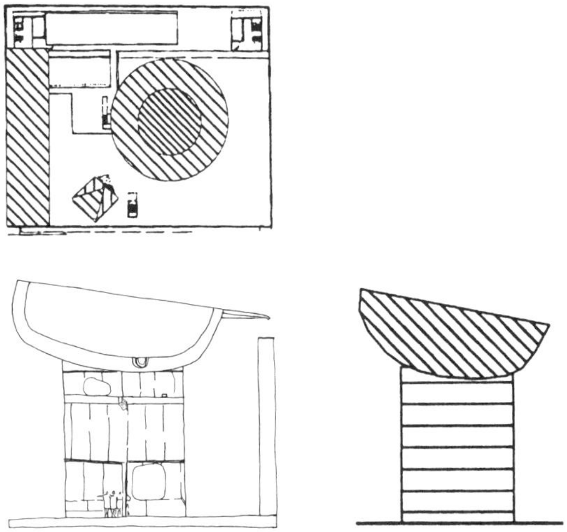

Roof enhancing the volumetric expression of the overall builtform

Roof as a symbol itself

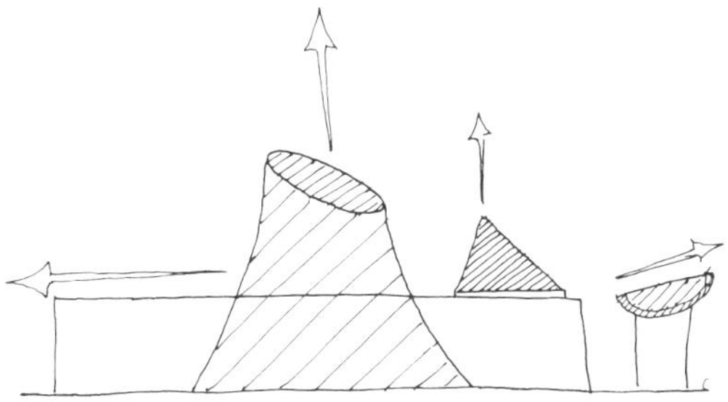

Roof as a composition of various forms in a unified whole

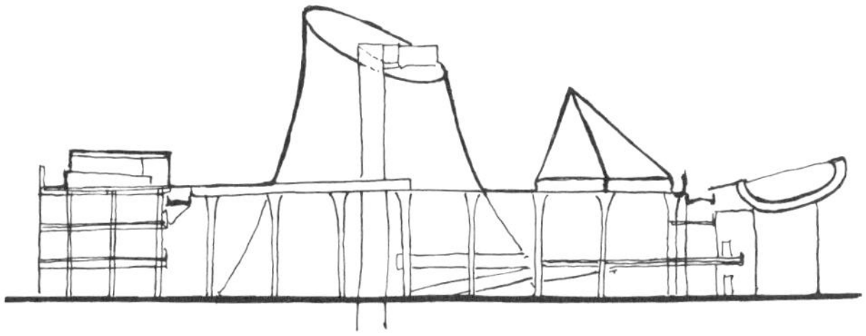

The overall schema of roof being a uniqe juxtaposition of forms, imageries, symbols and volume modulations

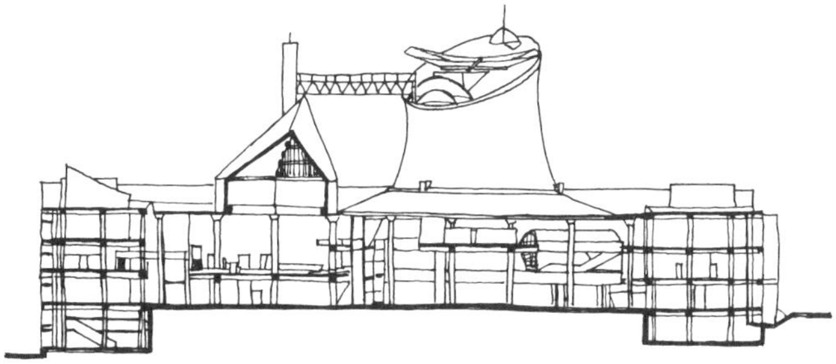

Roof as an element for light and ventilation

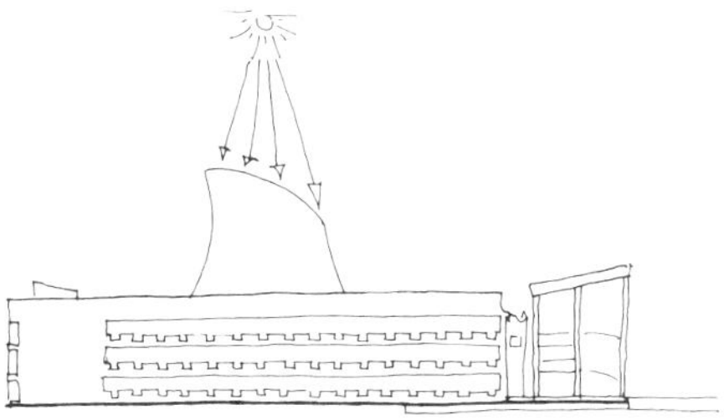

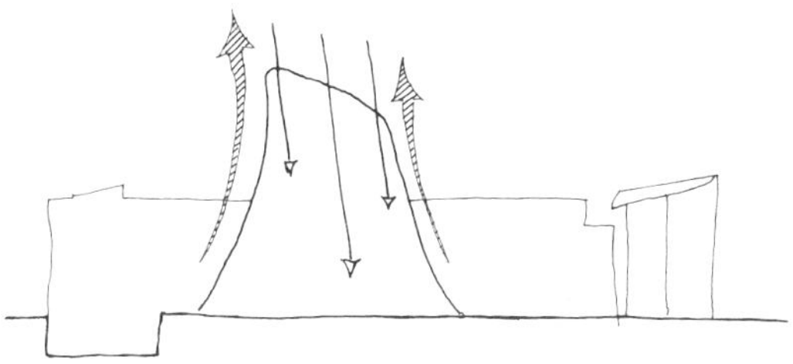

Roof as encoder of symbols

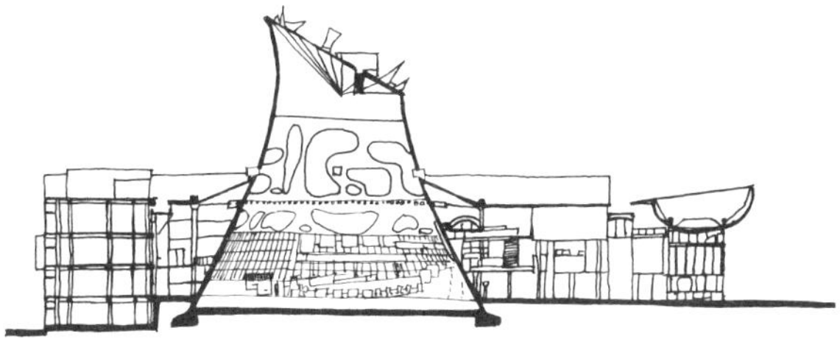

Roof as encoder of signs and symbols on its internal surfaces, brings human scale to the entire volume

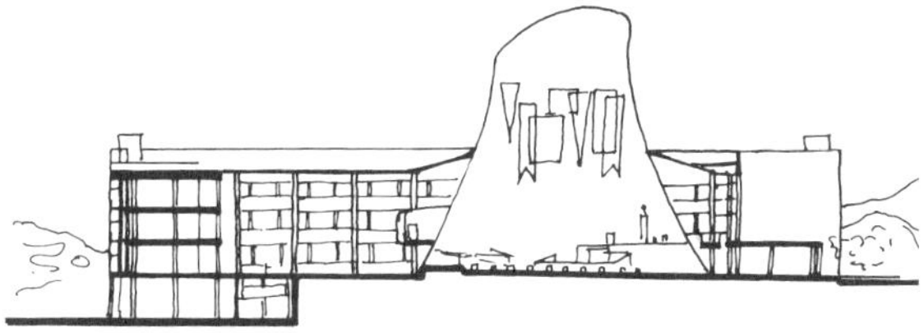

The symbolization on the roof reflects the sensitivity towards elements of environment and the immediate context

SHODHAN HOUSE, AHMEDABAD

The Shodhan House was built in 1951, by architect Le Corbusier in Ahmedabad. The plan reveals a structural simplicity under a floating roof parasol. This roof, along with the various terraces, forms a cascade and resembles a hollowed out cube. It raises above and shelters the whole raw-concrete structure beneath. Thus, the roof characterises the built-form and becomes an imagemaker.

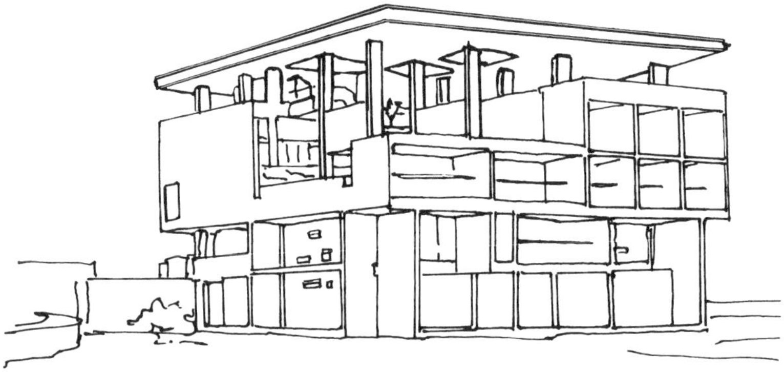

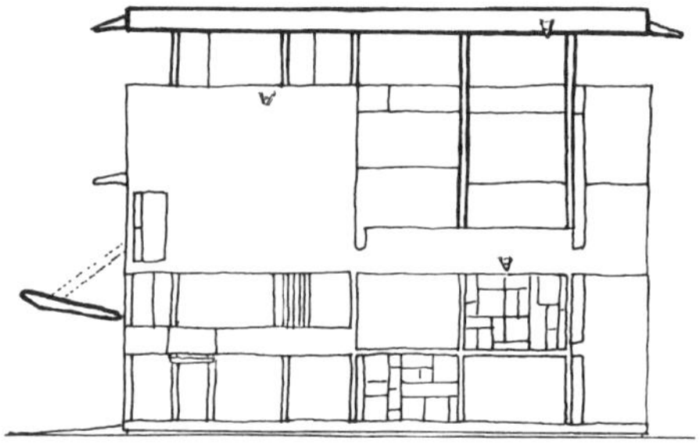

Elevation

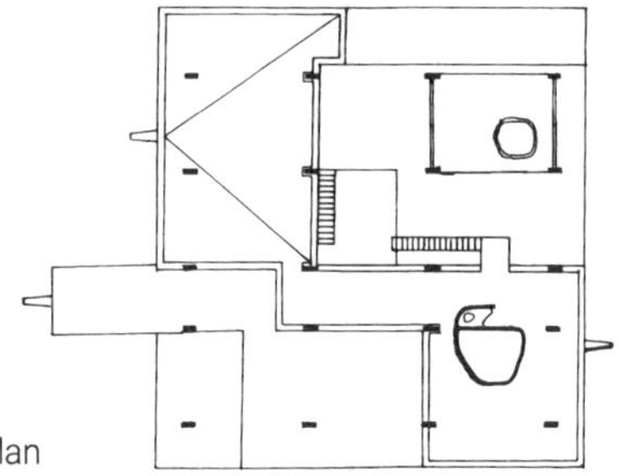

Plan

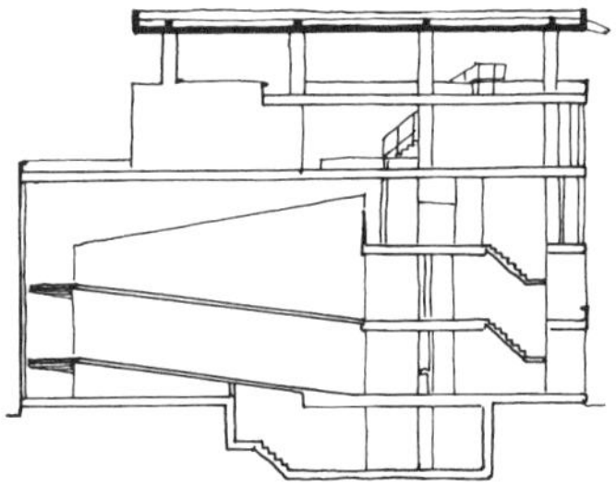

Section

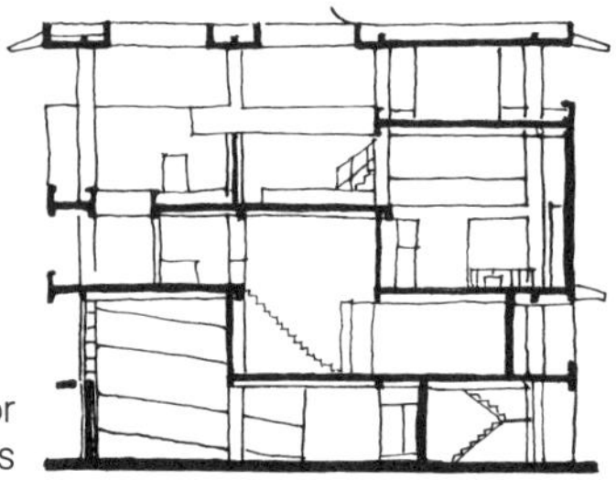

Section defining interior spaces/subspaces

Roof as a modulator of volume

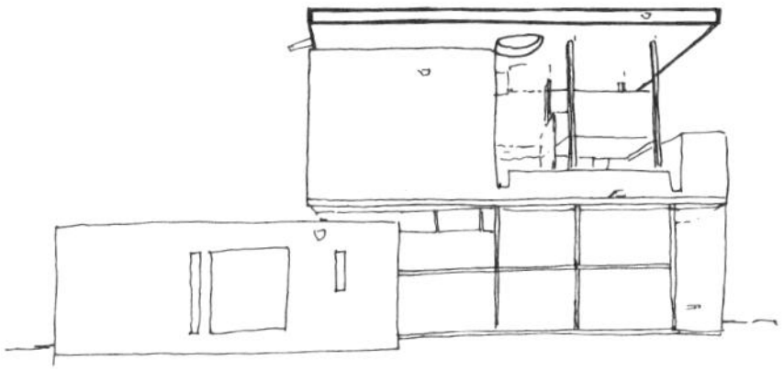

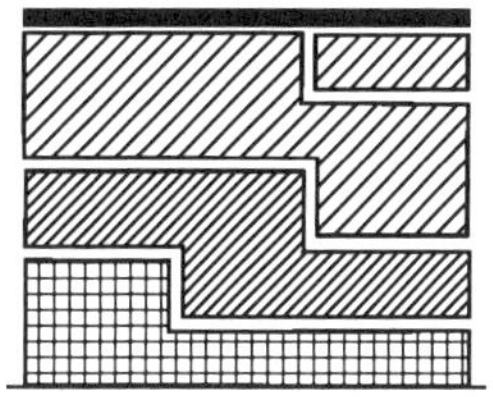

Roof modulating the inner volume

Roof as an overhead plan

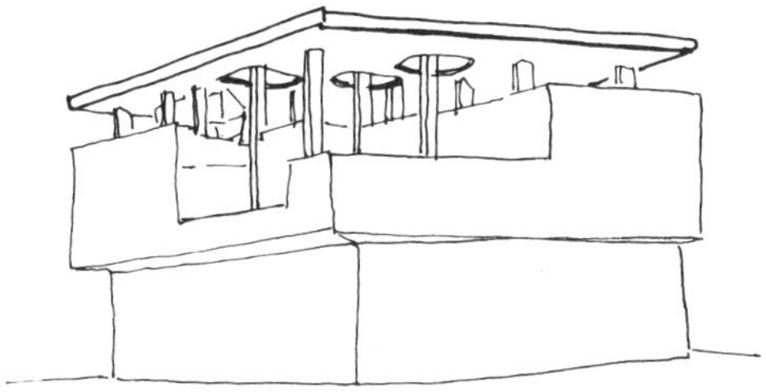

Roof as a shelter

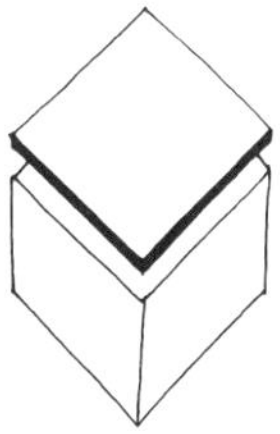

Roof with its planarity creates a unique spatial language

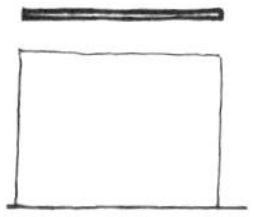

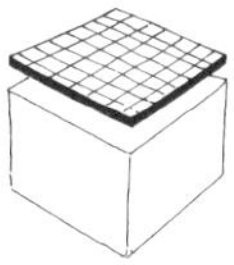

Roof as image maker

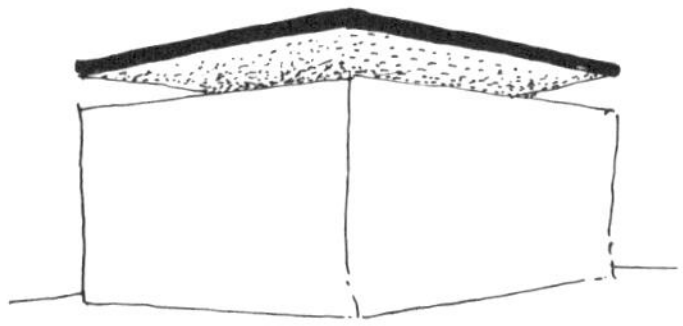

Ceiling streching over the enclosed space

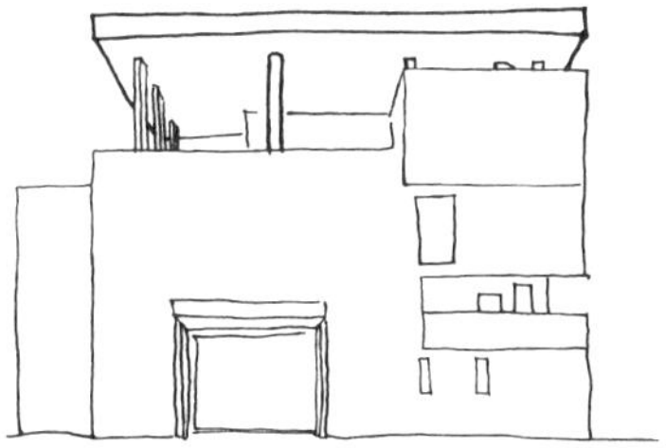

Roof as a spatial encloser

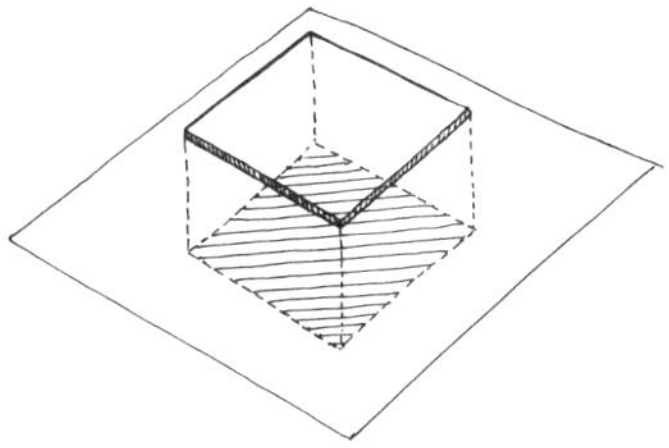

Roof as an enclosure defining space

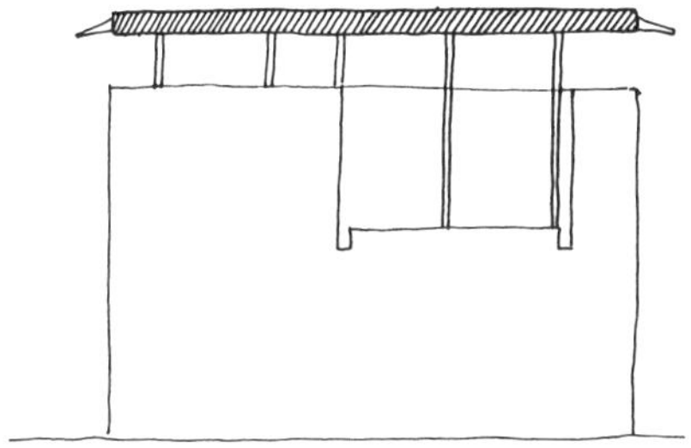

Detached roof plane perceived distinctly

BRIHADESHWAR TEMPLE, THANJAVUR

This temple, built in 11th century, is some 15 storeys (66 metres) and based on a square plan. The *garbha griha*, with the Linga shrine at its centre, has only one exit but surrounding pavilions adorn the floor levels externally and niches surround the slightly stilted ribbed dome at the peak of the pyramid.

The *shikhara* over the *garbha griha* presents itself as a distant landmark amongst the axially composed structure. The *shikhara* symbolizes the axis mundi, provides a vertical dimension to the temple and simultaneously becomes the predominant entity here.

The roof as the symbol of transcendence

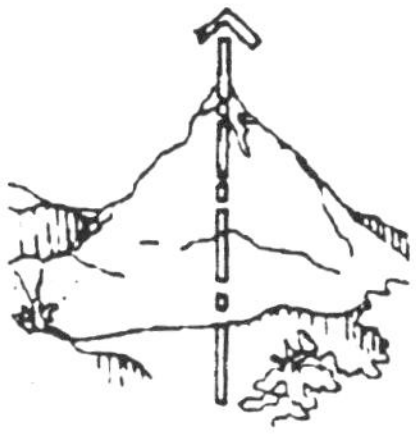

The axis mundi

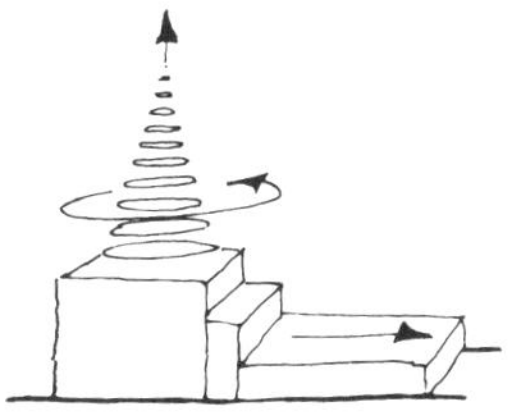

The visual reference created by volumetric diversity

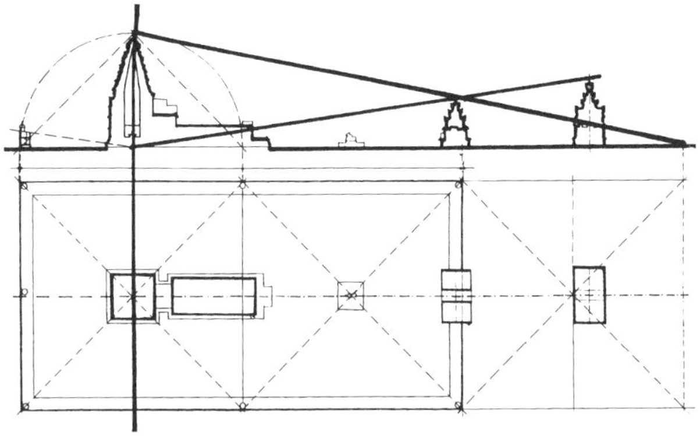

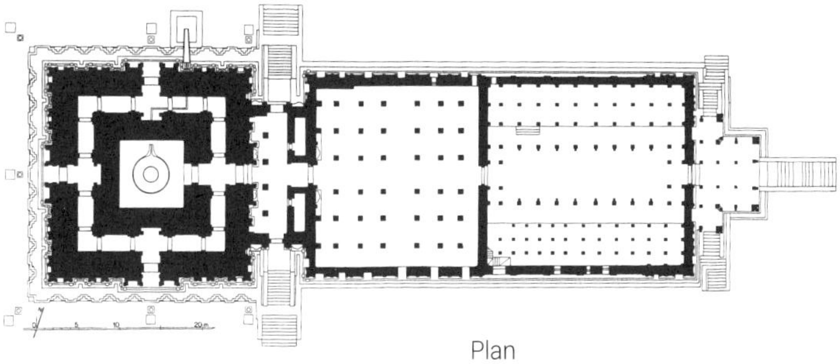

Plan

The plan conforming to the hierachy from profane to sacred, as the spaces become more enclosed, with vertical increase in volume

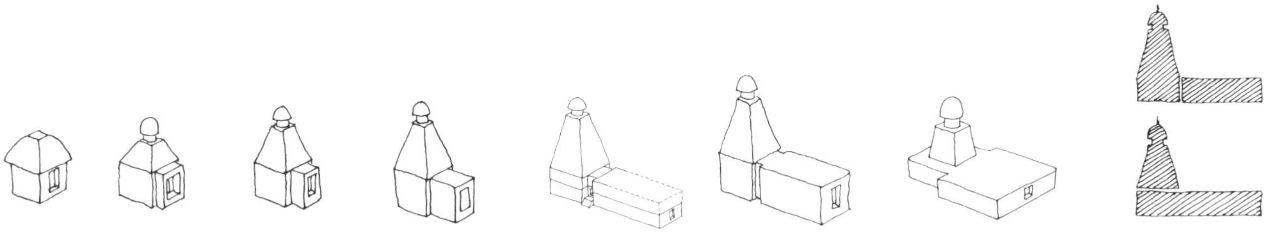

Evolution of roof in terms of spanning capabilities and spatial formation

Roof as an encoder of symbol

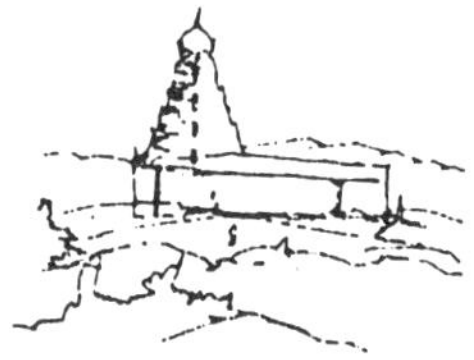

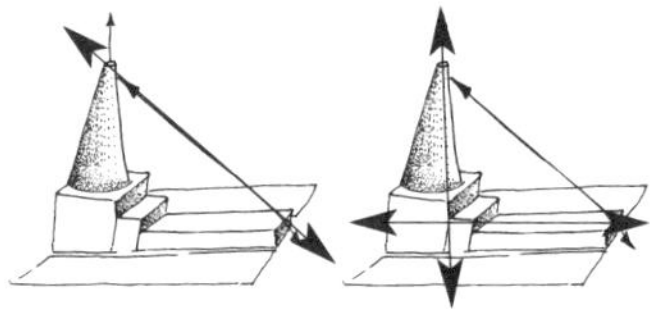

Roof with surface modulations with religious motifs of deities and mythological stories

Roof as modulator of volume

Section profile exposing the ceilling modulation and roof structure

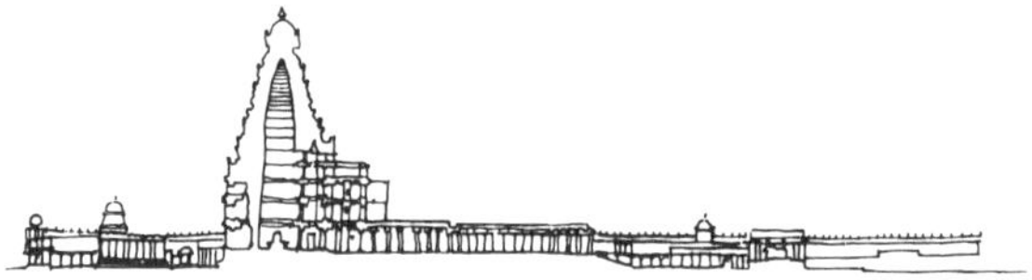

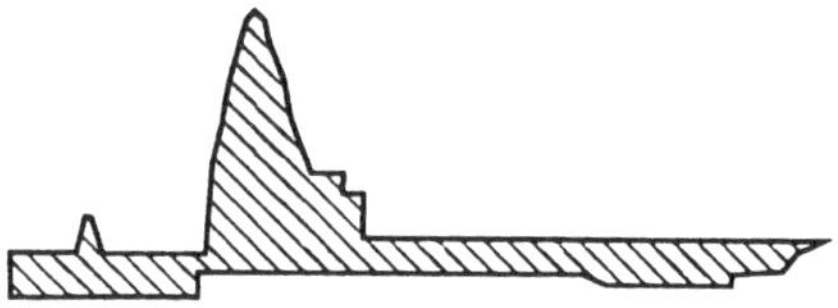

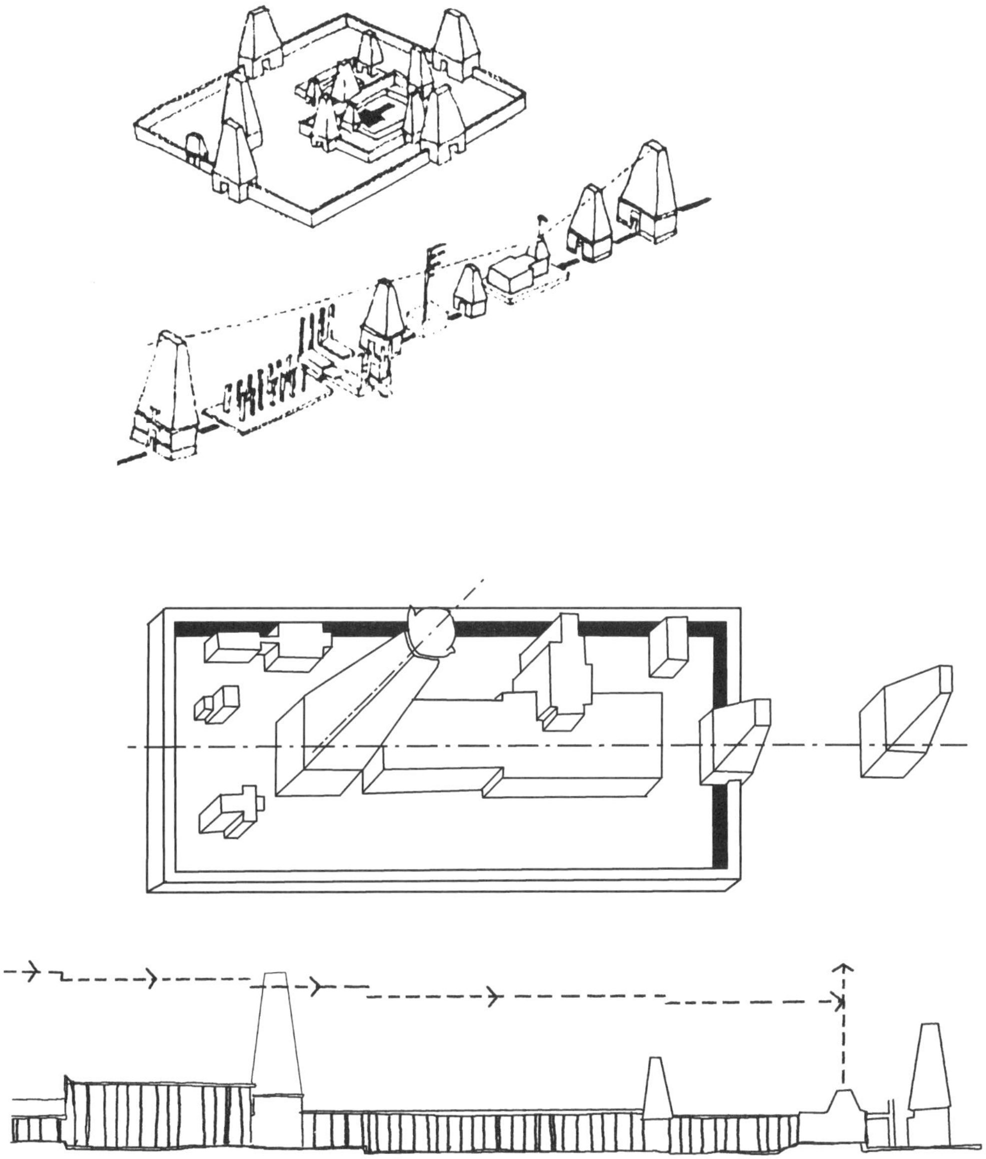

Roof becoming landmark of guiding movement with conspicuous presence

- The roof (outer skin) and the ceiling (inner face) are two potentially different aspects of an overhead plane and they could be understood and manipulated accordingly. The ceiling determines the perceptible volume and scale within and therefore should become a space modulator, while the roof imparts first visual clue and image/identity externally and should be explored such.

- Ceiling is less pragmatic and can afford to take metaphysical overtones to conjure notions.

- The roof (outer skin) gives the identity and image to the building/externally, where being the most visible element from distance, its form, profile and, scale become critical in its comprehension.

- The roof must be visible and contiguous over space. The feeling of shelter comes from the fact that the roof surrounds people at the same time that it covers them.

- Vary the ceiling height in order to create sub-spaces and to feel the relative intimacy of different spaces. The ceiling height in rooms is largely related to the number of people using the spaces. Although little complex for stacked units, the variation in height is desirable and possible as by providing storage space overhead, by having stacked alcoves, by raising the floor level with steps and platforms. The average ceiling height could reduce with successive space of the same living unit where the most public rooms for the large gathering are typically on the ground, while the intimate one above, as it progresses further away from the ground.

- Slopes of the roof or a vault of entire surface should be made visible by bringing the eaves of the roof down where people pause, for example, spaces such as, entrance, court, passage etc. This helps and offers desired transition from outside to indoors.

- The profile and expanse of the roof/ceiling profile offers directionality and pull/push correspondingly.

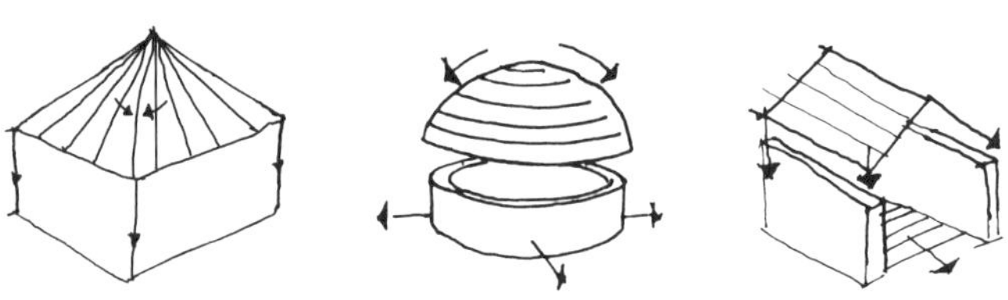

Roof with its outer skin

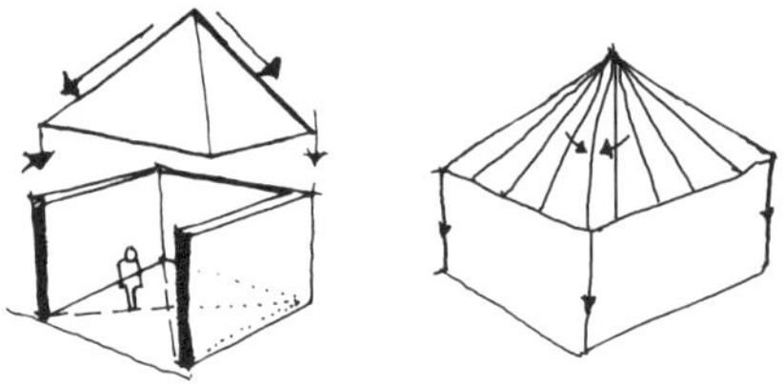

Roof with its outer face forms an image unique to itself

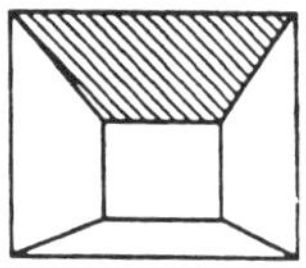

Ceiling as an inner face of the roof

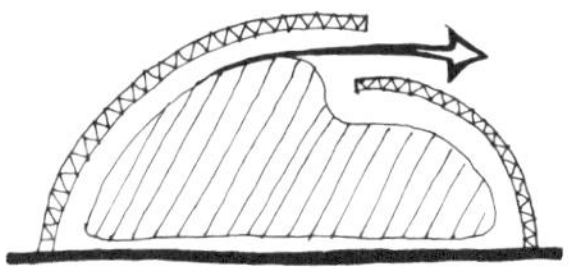

Varying height to form public to private spaces

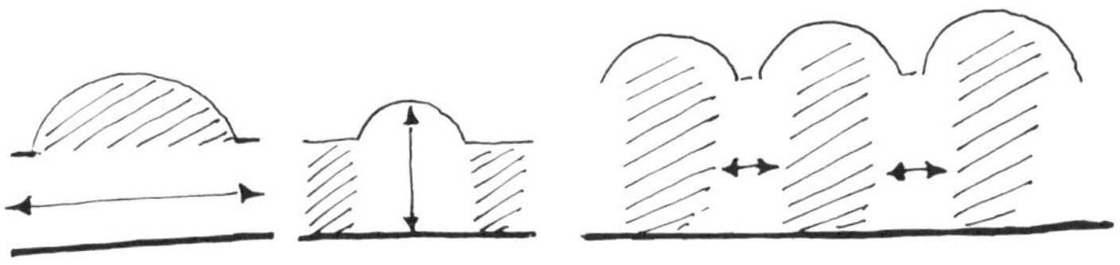

Spaces defined by internal form of the roof structure

Roof/ceiling defining spaces within

Alternatives to achieve variations in height

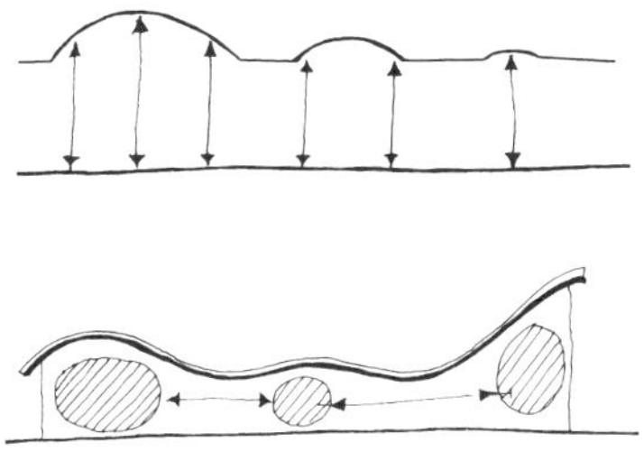

Roof percepting the volume and scale within

3 to 4 mts public gathering

2.1 to 2.7 mts semi-private

1.8 to 2.1 mts intimate spaces

Change in celling height with respect to different functions from public to private

Roof/ceiling providing shelter—its primary notion

Identity and character emphasized due to roof

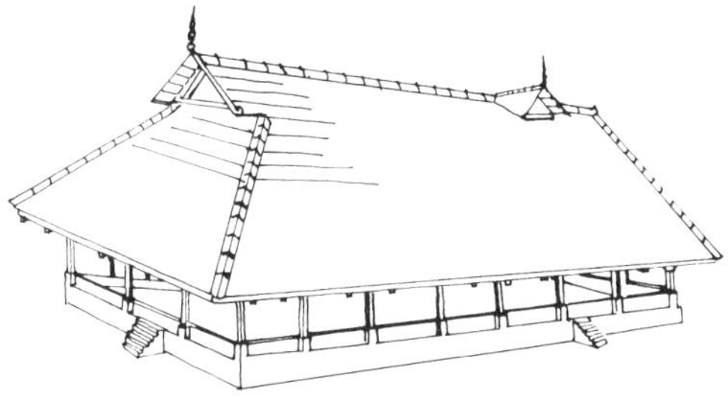

Roof as an image maker

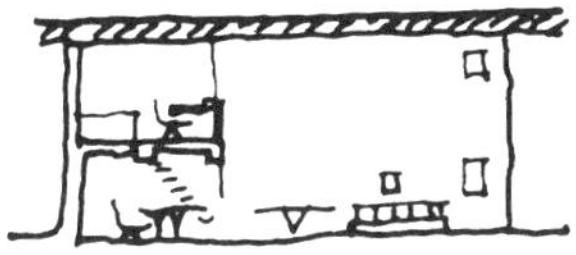

Provision of storage space

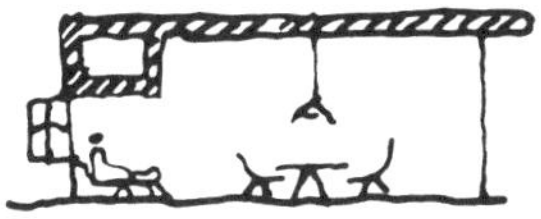

A stacked alcove/mezzanine level

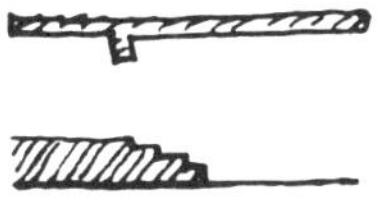

Raised floor level

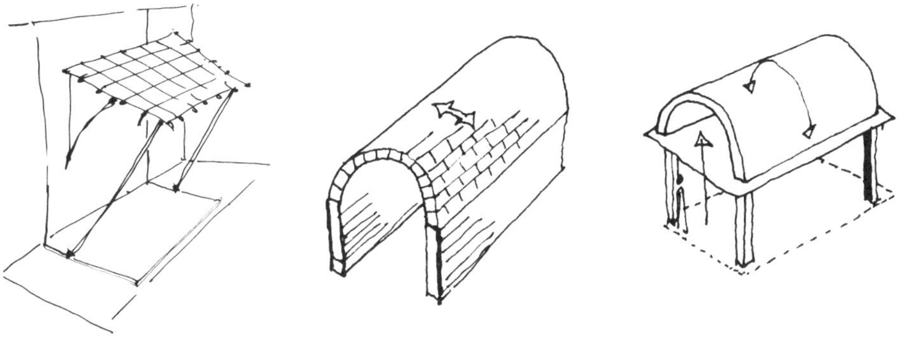

Entry node defined by modulating the roof profile

References

Acharya, Prasanna kumar. *Architecture of Mansara*. New Delhi: Munshiram Manoharlal Publishers Pvt. Ltd, 1980

Alex, William. *Japanese Architecture*. New York: George Braziller Inc., New York & England: Prentice Hall International Inc.,1963

Alexander, Christopher & Co. *A Pattern Language*. London: Oxford University Press, 1977

Ando, Tadao. *Architectural Monograph 14*. London: Academy Editions & New York, St. Marin's Press, 1990

——*Architecture, Visual Encyclopedia*. Amstredam: The Pepin Press, 2001

Bhagwat Sinh. *Bhagavadromandala* (Gujarati Dictionary), Vol. 1 to 9. Rajkot: Pravin Prakashan, 1986

Brown, Percy. *Indian Architecture* (Buddhist and Hindu). Bombay: Taraporevala Sons and Co. Pvt. Ltd., 1995

——*Indian Architecture,* (Islamic period). Bombay: Taraporevala Sons and Co. Pvt. Ltd., 1995

Chauhan, Shuchi. *Countinuty and Space in Indian Architecture*. Unpublished Thesis, Ahmedabad: CEPT University,1987

Ching, Francis D.K. *Architecture: Form, Space and Order*. New York: Van Nostrand Reinhold Co., 1979

Cooper, Ilay and Barry Dawson. *Traditional Buildings of India*. London: Thames and Hudson, 1998

Curtis, William. *Balkrishna Doshi: An Architecture for India*. Ahmedabad: Mapin Publishing Pvt. Ltd., 1988

Darasuram. *Epigraphical Study, De L'e cole Franca'ise D'Extreme*. Paris: Orient Memories Archeologiques, 1987

Encyclopedia Britannica Vol. 7 to 13. United Kingdom: Academy Edition, n.d.

Fletcher, Banister. *A History of Architecture–19th edition*. New York: The Butterworth Group, 1987

Glaeser, Ludwig. *The Work of Frei Otto*. New York: The Museum of Modern Art,1972

Goghari, Rathin. *The Role of Unbuilt space in Clustered Organization*. Unpublished Thesis, Ahmedabad: CEPT University,1991

Jain, Kulbhusan and Meenakshi. *Architecuture of the Indian Desert*. Ahmedabad: AADI centre, 2000

Jellicole, Geoffrey and Susan. *The Landscape of Man*. London: Thames & Hudson Ltd., 1996

Kagal, Carmen. *Vistara: The Architecture of India, Festival of India*. Mumbai: Tata Press Ltd., 1986

Khan, Hasan Uddin. *Charles Correa*. Singapore: Concept Media Pvt. Ltd., 1987

Krier, Rob. *Elements of Architecture*. London: Academy Editions, 1992

Lethoby, W.R. *Architecture: Mysticism and Myth*. London: The Architectural Press Ltd., 1974

Mookerjee, Ajit. *Ritual Art of India*. London: Thames and Hudson, 1985

Parikh, Smruti. *Historic Public Urban Spaces*. Unpublished Thesis, Ahmedabad: CEPT University,1984

Parmar, V.S. *Haveli Wooden Houses & Mansions of Gujarat*. Ahmedabad: Mapin Publishing Pvt. Ltd., 1989

Pfeiffer, Bruce Brooks & Yuki. *Futagawa F.L. Wright's Selected House* (Vol. 4), Falling Waters. Japan: A.D.A. Edita Tokyo Co. Ltd., 1990

Punjani, Shilpa. *Staircase: A Spatial Phenomenon*. Unpublished Thesis, Ahmedabad: CEPT University,1998

Schoenauer, Norbert. *6000 Years of Housing*. New York: W.W. Norton and Co., 1981

Sukla, D.N. *Vastu Sastra–Hindu Science of Architecture*, Vol I. New Delhi: Munshiram Manoharlal Publishers Pvt. Ltd., 1993

Tadgell, Christopher. The History of Architecture in India. U.K.: Longman Group Ltd., 1990

Vastu Shilpa Foundation, *Earthern Architecture of Kutchchh*. Ahmedabad: Vastu Shilp Foundation, 2002

Vastu Shilpa Foundation, *Living Environments: Housing Designs by Balkrishna Doshi*. Ahmedabad: Vastu Shilp Foundation, 1995

Yarwood, Doreen. *Encyclopaedia of Architecture*. London: B.T. Batsford Ltd., 1994

Francis D.K. Ching, Architecture, Visual Encyclopaedia The Pepin Press, Amsterdam, 2001

Zamos, Alexander. *Form and Structure in Architecture*. New York: Van Nostrand Reinhold Company, 1987

Periodicals

Architecture + Urbanism (A+U). January, 1971; August, 1972; October, 1976; August, 1984; November, 1986; August, 1987; September, 1987; November, 1987; April, 1988; May, 1988; July, 1988; June, 1989; August, 1989; November, 1989; July, 1990.

Architecture + Design. September-October, 1988.

Architecture. November, 1986.

GA Document, Special Issue 2 (1951-1991), Kenneth Frampton.

Marg. Vol. 39, No. 2; Vol. 32, No. 1; Vol. 33, No. 2; Vol. 34, No. 3; Vol. 36, No.4

Mimar. April-June, 1982; April-June, 1985; April-June, 1986; July-September, 1986; March, 1988.

Space Design (SD), February, 1980; April, 1986; July, 1986; September, 1986; October, 1986; September, 1988; December, 1988; July, 1989; November, 1989; January 1990; December, 1991.